T0246263

Praise for *Trouble with Gender*

'Everyone with opinions, or questions, about matters of sex and gender should read this book. It carefully and incisively unravels the tangled mass of ideas that cluster under the umbrella of gender. It does not engage in politics, or question the extent of human variability, or deny the reality of anyone's experience, but it does claim that there is no escape from the concept of sex as binary, and that the prevailing orthodoxy, which treats sex as socially constructed and an infinitely malleable continuum, is "tragically wrong". I challenge anyone who accepts that orthodoxy to explain in detail where the arguments presented here go wrong.'
Janet Radcliffe Richards, author of *The Sceptical Feminist* and *Human Nature after Darwin*

'Current academic discussions of sex and gender are dominated by advocates, dogmatists, poseurs, and obscurantists. *Trouble with Gender* offers a lucid, rigorous and judicious guide to the perplexed. It's an antidote to irrationality and also a pleasure to read.'
Christina Hoff Sommers, author of *Who Stole Feminism?* and *The War against Boys*

'Alex Byrne masterfully does what philosophers are supposed to do: clarify words and concepts, identify which ideas follow from which other ones, and distinguish what is from what ought to be. And despite the now incendiary subject matter, he accomplishes all this with a light touch and an appealing voice.'
Steven Pinker, Johnstone Professor of Psychology, Harvard University, and author of *Rationality*

'A refreshingly clarifying and forthright take on the philosophy of gender activism, cutting through the noise with incisiveness and wit. Anyone interested in the gender wars needs to read it.'
Kathleen Stock, author of *Material Girls*

'Alex Byrne's *Trouble with Gender* is an admirably clear and rigorous book that outlines the major parameters of what is often an off-kilter discussion. Combining philosophy and science with an eye for how issues of sex and gender are discussed in the media, Byrne gives the reader a lesson not only in how to think about these specific issues but also in how to think at all.'
Nina Power, author of *One Dimensional Woman* and *What Do Men Want?*

Trouble with Gender

Trouble with Gender

Sex Facts, Gender Fictions

Alex Byrne

Copyright © Alex Byrne, 2024

The right of Alex Byrne to be identified as Author of this Work has been asserted in accordance with the UK Copyright, Designs and Patents Act 1988

First published by Polity Press in 2024

Polity Press
65 Bridge Street
Cambridge CB2 1UR, UK

Polity Press
111 River Street
Hoboken, NJ 07030, USA

All rights reserved. Except for the quotation of short passages for the purpose of criticism and review, no part of this publication may be reproduced, stored in a retrieval system or transmitted, in any form or by any means, electronic, mechanical, photocopying, recording or otherwise, without the prior permission of the publisher.

ISBN-13: 978-1-5095-6001-1

A catalogue record for this book is available from the British Library.

Library of Congress Control Number: 2023934525

Typeset in 11.5 on 14 Adobe Garamond
by Fakenham Prepress Solutions, Fakenham, Norfolk NR21 8NL
Printed and bound in the USA by Sheridan, Chelsea, MI

The publisher has used its best endeavours to ensure that the URLs for external websites referred to in this book are correct and active at the time of going to press. However, the publisher has no responsibility for the websites and can make no guarantee that a site will remain live or that the content is or will remain appropriate.

Every effort has been made to trace all copyright holders, but if any have been overlooked the publisher will be pleased to include any necessary credits in any subsequent reprint or edition.

For further information on Polity, visit our website:
politybooks.com

Contents

Acknowledgements

Unsurprisingly, publishing this book was not a walk in the park.[1] For advice, thanks to Rob Tempio, Eric Henney, Max Brockman, and George Owers. Profuse thanks to Elise Heslinga and Ian Malcolm at Polity, whose support and suggestions have been invaluable. Thanks also to Caroline Richmond for expert copyediting and Maddie Tyler for shepherding the book through production.

Parts of this book draw on earlier work of mine.[2] Thanks to Berny Belvedere and Stew Cohen for having a backbone, and to the formidable team of Francesca Minerva, Jeff McMahan, and Peter Singer for starting the *Journal of Controversial Ideas* in 2021.

For a variety of assistance, including fact-checking, conversations, email exchanges, and feedback on drafts, gratitude is due (in random order) to: Sasha Ayed, Paul Vasey, Terry Goldie, Louise Antony, Peter Momtchiloff, Anca Gheaus, Mohan Matthen, Lisa Littman, Ed Schiappa, Abigail Shrier, Peggy Cadet, Ken Zucker, Maya Kaye, Sally Haslanger, Stella O'Malley, James Cantor, Daniel Kodsi, Corinna Cohn, Ari Koslow, Mary Leng, Katie Zhou, Sarah Pedersen, Jane Clare Jones, Rashad Rehman, Debbie Hayton, Callie Burt, Geoff Pullum, Jeremy Goodman, Abigail Shrier, Kieran Setiya, Rebecca Reilly-Cooper, Richard Wrangham, Nina Paley, Griffin Byrne, Rebecca Tuvel, Linda Rabieh, Anonymous Reviewers, Jesse Singal, Sam Berstler, Anne Lawrence, Joyce Benenson, Justin Lehmiller, and Nadine Strossen.

I am especially indebted to Ray Blanchard and Mike Bailey for much expert advice, and for modeling how to do sexology properly. I am even more indebted to three fearless philosophers and good friends, with whom I have discussed the issues in this book countless times and who have improved it immensely: Tomas Bogardus, Holly Lawford-Smith, and Kathleen Stock.

My greatest debt is to my wife Carole Hooven, sex enthusiast and endocrine specialist. Her influence pervades this book in almost every way, especially at points on which we disagree; to the extent that it is an enjoyable read, you have her to thank.

Preface

This book offers answers to fundamental questions about sex and gender. Although some of the chapters count as 'philosophy', and my day job is teaching and writing about that ancient discipline, I have presumed no knowledge of it. I wrote for a curious – and open-minded – general audience, not for specialists.

Many other philosophers have written about sex and gender. You might suppose that the philosophy in this book is a report from the cutting edge of research, like pop science books about behavioural genetics or cosmology. Surely all that philosophizing about sex and gender must have produced some gold, or at least shed some light? In my opinion, not very much. Despite their reputation in some quarters as unflinching logical thinkers, philosophers have done little to diminish the nonsense surrounding sex and gender and in some cases have even managed to increase it. I wrote this book partly to counteract these failings. Other parts of the academy have also fallen short. My aim is constructive, but sometimes construction requires preparatory demolition. The targets of my critiques are academics (and some in the medical profession) who ought to know better. I am sure they will not see it this way!

This book is not concerned with inflammatory social and political issues – sex categories in sport, transgender healthcare, etc. – that have recently consumed much oxygen in both the US and the UK. What's more, no one's pursuit of a dignifying and fulfilling human life is impeded by anything in the pages that follow – neither transgender people, nor women, nor gay people, nor any other relevant constituency. If there is any doubt about that at the start, I hope it will vanish by the end.

Introduction

> My great-aunt and the rest thought that by technically defeating male privilege they'd scored a great victory. What they didn't realize is that the greatest enemies of women aren't men at all, they are women …
>
> John Wyndham, *Trouble with Lichen*[1]

The transgender tipping point

In 2014, Russia annexed Crimea, the IPCC (Intergovernmental Panel on Climate Change) warned of the 'future risks and impacts caused by a changing climate', and an African-American man, Michael Brown, was killed by a police officer in Ferguson, Missouri. Among these momentous events was another – the May 29th issue of *Time Magazine* featured the transgender actress Laverne Cox on the cover, and announced 'The transgender tipping point … another civil rights movement … poised to challenge long-held cultural norms and beliefs'. The cultural change marked by the transgender tipping point is not quite as momentous as climate change but – as the intervening years showed – is proceeding far more rapidly.[2]

This challenge to 'long-held cultural norms' prompts important questions, debated endlessly in the press and on social media. What is gender? What is sex? What is a woman or a man? Are girls and boys born basically the same, apart from reproductive anatomy? What is gender identity, and do we all have one? The last question would not be asked were it not for the transgender tipping point; the first four are perennial favourites which bear on transgender issues but are much more general.

When gender is the topic, identity is not far behind. A recent book called *How to Understand Your Gender* is revealingly subtitled *A Practical Guide for Exploring Who You Are*. 'What am I?', asked the seventeenth-century French philosopher René Descartes. His first answer is 'a man'. On considering the matter more carefully he decides that is wrong: he is 'a thing that thinks', a ghostly mind. A thoroughly up-to-date René would give a different considered answer, a list of his most important 'identities': 'a white cisgender gay man', perhaps.[3]

A close companion to identity is the idea of the 'true' or 'authentic' self. When the former Olympic gold-medal winner Bruce Jenner came out as Caitlyn in a 2015 *Vanity Fair* cover story, Laverne Cox wrote, 'I am so moved by all the love and support Caitlyn is receiving. It feels like a new day, indeed, when a trans person can present her authentic self to the world for the first time and be celebrated for it so universally.' If Caitlyn Jenner has a true or authentic self, presumably the rest of us do too. Life is a journey to find and be our true selves, some say. What does that even mean?

This book is about these questions. The transgender tipping point gives them a useful focus, but they concern us all.

Trans rights

'Transgender equality is the civil rights issue of our time', tweeted Joe Biden during the race for the Democratic presidential nomination in 2020. Following Trump's ignominious exit, the Biden White House promptly added a field for pronouns to its website contact form, and on his first day in office Biden issued an executive order instructing federal agencies not to discriminate on the basis of gender identity in, among other areas, 'school sports'.[4] *#BidenErasedWomen* started trending on Twitter.

Will this 'civil rights issue of our time' turn out to be like the campaign for same-sex marriage? *Obergefell* v. *Hodges*, the Supreme Court decision that required all states to issue marriage licences irrespective of the partners' sexes, was announced in 2015, around the same time the Caitlyn Jenner *Vanity Fair* issue hit the newsstands. And in 2020 the Supreme Court ruled that 'an employer who fires an individual merely for being gay or transgender defies the law.'[5] (In this last respect, the US was twenty years behind the UK.) Perhaps in a few years progressive forces will have prevailed, and we'll wonder what the fuss was all about.

Things are not so simple. Gay rights infringe at best marginally on the rights of others. In 2012 a Christian baker in Colorado refused to design a wedding cake for Charlie and David – that this caused outrage and went to the US Supreme Court shows how far society has come.[6] Let's face it, gay rights are boring. Philosophers, who love introducing undergraduates to controversial claims, gave up years ago assigning academic articles arguing that homosexuality was immoral or that gay marriage should not be allowed. The arguments were unconvincing and, anyway, students weren't interested.

Although transgender-related conflicts can easily be exaggerated, they are more significant and wide-ranging. The New Zealand transgender woman weightlifter Laurel Hubbard, who competed as a man in 2014, competed as a woman at the 2019 Pacific Games and won two gold medals. The Samoans, who had to content themselves with silver, were not pleased. Hubbard went on to compete in the Olympic Summer Games in 2021. The following year, the US college swimmer Lia Thomas, a transgender woman who had previously competed on the University of Pennsylvania's men's team, won the NCAA 500-yard women's freestyle swimming championship. A furious debate ensued, with Caitlyn Jenner tweeting that the second place (female) finisher was the 'rightful winner'. Thomas was later nominated by UPenn for the 2022 NCAA Woman of the Year award. Dismissing these conflicts by denying the undeniable male athletic advantage is common: according to the storied American Civil Liberties Association (ACLU) – and with teenagers in mind – there is 'ample evidence that girls can compete and win against boys'.[7]

Efforts to promote women in the workplace are another flash point. The *Financial Times* 2018 list of top 100 'female executives' who are 'champions of women' included Pips Bunce from Credit Suisse at the admirable position of 32. Pips is also known as Philip and, in the latter guise, presents as a balding middle-aged man, married with two children. 'I split my time as Pippa and Philip about 50/50', Pips explained. Philip does not seem interested in fashion, but Pips has 'a massive wardrobe', with 'more high heels than my daughter and wife put together'. A feminist from some decades ago might well disapprove of this association between womanhood and stereotypical feminine clothing. Such views are now considered old-fashioned, at least in some circles – Pips received an LGBT+ inspirational leader award.[8]

Changes in the number and composition of people who medically transition from one sex to the other produce further controversies. In *AfterEllen*, an online magazine for lesbians, a woman wrote about the transgender men (people travelling in the opposite direction to Caitlyn Jenner, from female to male) behind the counter at her local Starbucks. 'They would have been young butch lesbians in any other era … The only difference between them and me is time – I was just one of the lucky ones to not be around at the time of the transcult.'[9] The number of children and adolescents seeking treatment at gender clinics has been rising rapidly, and it is foolish to pretend that the medical establishment or anyone else has got it all figured out.

The public debate, in both the US and the UK (and elsewhere), has become intense. Unlike the global average surface temperature, the transgender temperature will likely decline in the next decade, but there are no leading indicators. Some 2022 and 2023 headlines from UK and US newspapers signal that the trend is still upwards: 'University staff accused of colluding with trans activists to stop women's rights film', 'How the Tavistock gender clinic ran out of control', 'Transgender Americans feel under siege as political vitriol rises.'[10]

This book is *not* about these vitriolic political issues, although they will be touched on occasionally. Several recent books address them, from a variety of different perspectives. If you want arguments for the importance of single-sex spaces, why feminism should be for females, why feminism should be for everyone, why transitioning from one sex to the other should be left up to adults, why affirming medical interventions are vital for the health of trans youth, or why trans liberation requires the abolition of prisons and capitalism, I have some recommended reading.[11] One lesson of this book is that there is no straight line from (say) views about what women are, or about whether sex is binary and immutable, to policy.

Hyperbolic rhetoric can suggest that there is a male conspiracy to invade women's spaces, or a right-wing plan to perpetrate trans genocide, or something equally horrific. In fact, a strong humane thread of agreement – in which this book wholeheartedly joins – runs through all the disagreement. Trans people should be afforded dignity, have access to proper healthcare, and be allowed to live openly and safely without discrimination or stigma, like everyone else. Trans rights are human rights – as are women's rights, for that matter. Children struggling with gender issues should receive compassion and evidence-based treatment. Their families only want what is best for them and should be cut some slack as they try to weigh advice that is often conflicting and confusing. Nothing in this book undermines these obvious points. Relatedly, it is important to remember that trans activists and trans people are quite different groups. Many trans activists are not trans and – it can hardly be necessary to mention this – trans people themselves have a diversity of views. Doubtless the majority simply want to get on with life, attending to their careers, family, and relationships. Trans people are people, after all.[12]

Philosophy

More than seventy years ago, the French philosopher Simone de Beauvoir asked, 'What is a woman?' in *The Second Sex*, one of the canonical texts of modern feminism. 'Brilliant, imperious', the iconoclastic critic Camille Paglia called it – 'the only thing undergraduate sex studies needs'. That book is sometimes taken to have (implicitly) made a crucial distinction between *sex* and *gender*, now affirmed by many authorities. 'Gender interacts with but is different from sex', says the World Health Organization. Philosophers have devoted innumerable pages both to Beauvoir's question and to various ways of separating sex from gender. For historical reasons, these issues are the remit of *feminist philosophy*, a small but growing speciality within the discipline. (Gender studies is a closely related but separate field and is not part of philosophy.)[13]

Philosophers treat all sorts of touchy subjects, and unsurprisingly they tend to be keen on unfettered discussion and debate. One famous argument for freedom of speech was given by the Victorian philosopher John Stuart Mill in *On Liberty* (1859):

> The peculiar evil of silencing the expression of an opinion is, that it is robbing the human race; posterity as well as the existing generation; those who dissent from the opinion, still more than those who hold it. If the opinion is right, they are deprived of the opportunity of exchanging error for truth: if wrong,

> they lose, what is almost as great a benefit, the clearer perception and livelier impression of truth, produced by its collision with error.[14]

Regrettably, a small but loud faction within philosophy did not take these words to heart, attempting to silence the expression of certain opinions shortly after Caitlyn Jenner appeared on the cover of *Vanity Fair*, 'primped and pampered to look gorgeous'.[15]

'A modern-day witch hunt'[16]

Caitlyn Jenner's big reveal coincided with Rachel Dolezal's unplanned one – she was the tanned and curly-haired president of the NAACP (the National Association for the Advancement of Colored People) in Spokane, Washington, who identified as black. Dolezal had black adopted siblings, attended a historically black college, and had been married to a black man. She taught courses in Africana studies. All these qualifications were for naught – Dolezal, it turned out, was born of unmistakably white parents.[17]

Once this became public knowledge, hardly anyone thought Dolezal was black. The problem was palpable: why was Jenner's claim to womanhood so widely cheered? Jenner received a congratulatory tweet from President Obama, but Dolezal was mostly mocked and ridiculed. No *Vanity Fair* cover for her! The US political commentator Ben Shapiro was among many on the right gloating at the disparate treatment: 'Today, the entire left is struggling to explain how a white woman who identifies herself as black is not, in fact, black.'[18]

In the US, transgender and racial issues are like the two terminals of a powerful battery. Individually, they can give you a nasty shock. Connected together, the battery explodes. Rebecca Tuvel, then an assistant professor of philosophy at a small college in Tennessee, soon found that out. She sympathetically compared Jenner and Dolezal in an academic article published in *Hypatia*, the leading journal of feminist philosophy, in 2017.[19] Someone like Dolezal, Tuvel argued, was just as deserving of acceptance as Jenner: transracial people, like transgender people, should be treated with respect and understanding. Despite Tuvel's undeniably progressive credentials and junior status, this provoked an extraordinary reaction from her colleagues.

An open letter calling for the retraction of the article swiftly garnered more than 800 signatories, including many distinguished professors. One was Judith Butler, the acclaimed gender theorist, hailed as 'the most influential intellectual in the world'.[20] In an act of academic filicide, two others were senior philosophers who were on Tuvel's very own PhD dissertation committee.

The article was not retracted, and *Hypatia*'s editor – who subsequently resigned – firmly defended its publication. The journal's board of associate editors had the opposite reaction, posting an 'apology to our friends and colleagues in feminist philosophy, especially transfeminists, queer feminists, and feminists of color, for the harms that the publication of the article on transracialism has caused.' The least of Tuvel's many crimes was that she had 'deadnamed' Caitlyn Jenner, using 'Bruce' to refer to Jenner's previous Olympic-medal winning incarnation; the published article was subsequently amended and Tuvel apologized. (That Jenner herself was plainly unbothered by this sort of thing seemed not to matter at all.)[21]

Tuvel commented, 'the last place one expects to find such calls for censorship rather than discussion is amongst philosophers.' As I will recount in chapter 1, this was only the beginning. Similar outbursts of intolerance began regularly to blot philosophy. Philosophers had one job, to have an open discussion of transgender-related issues – of great public interest – under accepted academic rules where public shaming and no-platforming are not allowed. Exactly *why* they failed is an interesting question, important for the future of philosophy and public discourse more generally, although one which can be set aside here. *That* they failed is clear enough. Philosophy has had its crises, starting with Socrates's death sentence for worshipping false gods in 399 BC. That was not his fault, and he was found guilty by a jury of Athenian citizens, not fellow philosophers. In contrast, the current low point in the discipline is entirely self-inflicted. As one philosopher – writing under a pseudonym – put it in 2022, 'a vocal minority has labored successfully to make the topic radioactive. No one wants the Tuvel treatment.'[22]

Newspeak

Philosophy, which promises insight into the nature of reality, the meaning of life, and all that, is sometimes accused of false advertising

– even by philosophers themselves. Questions that initially seemed deep and non-linguistic supposedly turn out, after discussion deadlocks, to be shallow and linguistic. Do we have free will? Well, it all depends what you mean by 'free will'. If you mean *this*, then we clearly do; if you mean *that*, then we clearly don't. The impression that philosophical questions are 'just semantics' is almost always mistaken, but philosophers certainly do care a lot about words.

One reason for taking words to be important is that we use them to make distinctions. The words 'dog', 'perro', 'cat', and 'gato' allow speakers of English and Spanish to distinguish between dogs and cats, to say that dogs bark and cats don't, for instance. A concerning feature of debates around sex and gender is the attempt to *prevent* distinctions from being made, by prohibiting or redefining certain words.

Prime exhibits are the words 'female' and 'male'. The present day is characterized by a curious inversion of nineteenth-century attitudes towards sex. The Victorians were quite at ease with sex in the sense of female and male but publicly squeamish with sex in the sense of intercourse.[23] Now it is the other way around: the topic of sexual intercourse is almost impossible to avoid, but females and males are often spoken of in circumlocutions. 'Assigned female at birth' is the recommended phrase, suggesting the baby is arbitrarily picked for the pink rather than the blue team.

To take one of numerous examples, in a publication from the American Medical Association on 'advancing health equity', we read: 'Sex, *or more precisely*, "sex assigned at birth" is a label typically assigned by a doctor at birth based on the genitals you're born with.' Please note: this is the American Medical Association, whose mission is to 'promote the art and science of medicine and the betterment of public health'.[24]

You may have noticed some problems with this sentence, in particular that the phrase 'sex assigned at birth' is evidently *not* a 'more precise' replacement for the word 'sex'. Babies born with no doctor or medical authority in attendance will not have their sex 'assigned at birth'. They may not even have their sex recognized by anyone at birth, especially if abandoned by a distressed mother. And yet they will still have a sex: some human female babies have not been assigned female at birth. The point is even more obvious if we consider non-human females. Wild female rats are not assigned female at birth (and when they are bred by humans they are usually sexed later). The AMA's spurious claim of precision is a transparent attempt to prevent words such as 'female' from being used on their own when humans are the topic, allowing them to occur only within complex phrases such as 'assigned female at birth'.

George Orwell's *1984* has become something of a cliché in these contexts, but there's no beating it:

> It's a beautiful thing, the destruction of words ... Don't you see that the whole aim of Newspeak is to narrow the range of thought? In the end we shall make thoughtcrime literally impossible, because there will be no words in which to express it ... Orthodoxy means not thinking – not needing to think. Orthodoxy is unconsciousness.[25]

Astonishingly, some philosophers are on board with the Newspeak of today. They may have the best of intentions, thinking that blunt talk of female and male humans can cause unnecessary offence. However, as my undergraduate teacher, the philosopher Roger Scruton, once remarked, 'I was brought up to believe that you should never give offence if you can avoid it; the new culture tells us that you should always take offence if you can.'[26] The taking of offence is often used as a kind of emotional blackmail, cowing kind-hearted opponents into silence. I will try to avoid giving offence, but without compromising clarity of expression and the statement of relevant facts.

The plan of Trouble with Gender

The central questions of this book are examined beginning in the second chapter, which is about gender. What is gender, and how is it different from sex? (As that chapter explains, the chief problem is that the word 'gender' has been used to mean too many different things.) The third chapter is about sex. What is it to be female or male? Is sex binary, or on a spectrum, or (as influential academics say), 'socially constructed'?

Chapter 4 turns to Simone de Beauvoir's question, which has vexed feminist theorists for decades. What is a woman? 'Woman' was Dictionary.com's word of the year in 2022, an indication that Beauvoir's question has never been more popular.

Chapter 5 is about gender identity, whose rocket-like trajectory into mass media and the law began in the 1980s. Transgender people are supposed to have gender identities that are misaligned with their bodies, unlike the cisgender majority. Misalignment is taken to explain why some transition to live as the other sex. Is that familiar story true? Chapter 6 looks at a notoriously controversial theory of why some natal males transition to living as female.

One traditional axiom of feminism is that psychological and behavioural differences between the sexes are largely due to social or cultural forces, not to innate biology. That was always hard to square with the phenomenon of transsexualism, particular the male-to-female kind. Chapter 7 takes sex differences seriously. Men are generally the top dogs in societies, past and present. There never were matriarchies, but patriarchy is – or was – universal. Is biology a crucial part of the explanation?

The eighth and final chapter examines identities and true or authentic selves. When we claim an identity as our own, what are we doing? What – if anything – is the true or authentic self? And, if each of us has one, should we follow Caitlyn Jenner and aim to 'live our true selves'?[27]

I can sum up the argument of this book in one word: sex. That is the key to answering the main questions we'll be examining. There is a coda after chapter 8, in which the meaning of this cryptic remark will become clear.

Before beginning with gender in chapter 2, some more background to the current debates will be helpful.[28] After Rebecca Tuvel's transracialism ordeal came a series of spectacular cancellations, academic dustups, medical controversies, and inconsolable Harry Potter fans, all against the fervid backdrop of the Great Awokening, the latest iteration of the culture wars. Chapter 1 tells some of those stories.

ONE

Gender, Double Toil and Trouble

Trans women are women. Get over it!

Stonewall, UK LGBT rights organization[1]

Trans women are men. Get over it!

Debbie Hayton, trans woman[2]

#IStandWithMaya

J. K. Rowling, the creator of Harry Potter and one of the wealthiest people in the UK, closed out 2019 with an ultra-viral tweet:

> Dress however you please. Call yourself whatever you like.
> Sleep with any consenting adult who'll have you.
> Live your best life in peace and security.
> But force women out of their jobs for stating that sex is real?
> #IStandWithMaya #ThisIsNotADrill

This was in support of Maya Forstater, a British business researcher whose contract was not renewed because of her view that 'it is impossible to change sex or to lose your sex. Girls grow up to be women. Boys grow up to be men.' An employment tribunal had found that 'that belief is not worthy of respect in a democratic society.' Rowling's tweet garnered over 200,000 likes but also spawned many agonized opinion pieces. A *Vox* headline summed up the sentiment: 'J. K. Rowling's latest tweet seems like transphobic BS. Her fans are heartbroken.'[3]

Forstater had been active in opposing proposed reforms to the 2004 Gender Recognition Act that would make it considerably easier for a transgender person to legally self-identify as their chosen sex. Kathleen Stock, a philosophy professor at Sussex University, also had concerns. Stock was worried that the reform might allow 'badly motivated males' to gain access to hostels for homeless women, women's prisons, and so on. She noted that, while the reform was of great public interest, especially to women, 'nearly all academic philosophers – including, surprisingly, feminist philosophers – are ignoring it.'[4]

Although Stock took pains to distance herself from any kind of animus against transgender people, that didn't do her any good. 'Kathleen Stock is a TERF' and a 'transphobic bigot', declared a US philosophy professor on Twitter. 'TERF' was originally introduced as an acronym for 'Trans Exclusionary Radical Feminist' and – as acronyms often do – has gained a life of its own, becoming a pejorative term for people like Forstater, Rowling, and Stock.

(The non-pejorative term is 'gender-critical feminist' or, alternatively, 'sex-realist feminist'. The former will be used here, along with 'trans-rights activist' – 'trans activist' for short – for their opponents. The trans-rights activists may complain that they are critical of gender too, and that, anyway, the gender-critical feminists are not feminists. The gender-critical feminists may complain that they fully support trans rights, or that they intend to abolish gender, not just to criticize it. There is no terminology that pleases everyone.)

'TERF' appears at the swampy end of social media in phrases such as 'Punch a TERF', 'Kill all TERFs', 'Take out the TERF trash' – and these are some of the milder ones. Amazingly, 'TERF' has also been used as a descriptive label in philosophy and other academic disciplines.[5]

Holly Lawford-Smith, another heretic, is a political philosopher who teaches at the University of Melbourne. In March 2019 she was interviewed by the online *3AM Magazine*, one of hundreds of interviews of philosophers the publication had run over the years. 'My stance', she said, 'is that a person can't change sex (not even with sex reassignment surgery), that "gender identity" has no bearing on sex, and that with very few exceptions gender identity should have no bearing on a person's sex-based rights.'[6] *3AM* removed the interview following complaints, and the interviewer resigned from the magazine in protest.

Despite (or perhaps because of) its insulting flavour, 'TERF' was used freely in an opinion piece that appeared shortly afterwards in the *New York Times*. The author, another of Stock and Lawford-Smith's professional colleagues in the US, joined 'the critics of TERFs', arguing that 'the attempt to exclude trans women from the ranks of women reinforces the dangerous idea that there is a right way to be female.'[7] To judge by the almost 1,000 comments on the *NYT* website, many readers were unpersuaded. 'TERF is hate speech', one woman wrote. 'This essay is also completely disingenuous, as there is a difference between biological sex and gender.' Welcome to the TERF wars.

The social and political territory at stake in the TERF wars is not the subject of this book. Our focus will be on the ammunition lobbed by both sides – claims about sex, gender, gender identity, women, and men. A sub-plot is the failure of philosophy, partly traced in this chapter. As the British philosopher Bertrand Russell remarked in 1959 (when he was eighty-six), 'we have to learn to put up with the fact that some people say things that we don't like.'[8] More than sixty years later, some prominent philosophers had not heeded Russell's advice.

Twelve leading scholars

The treatment of gender-critical academics such as Stock and Lawford-Smith provoked a response from twelve philosophers (including the well-known psychologist and writer Cordelia Fine) in July of 2019. They published an opinion piece in the US higher education magazine *Inside Higher Ed*, writing that they 'reject calls for censuring or deplatforming any of our colleagues on the basis of their philosophical arguments about sex and gender identity, or their social and political advocacy for sex-based rights.' While expressing their support for 'transgender and gender-nonconforming individuals', the '12 leading scholars' (as the magazine called them) noted 'the too frequently cruel and abusive rhetoric, including accusations of hatred or transphobia, directed at these philosophers in response to their arguments and advocacy.'[9]

More than thirty philosophers, representing the feminist philosophy establishment, replied to the twelve scholars in a letter published on the blog of the American Philosophical Association. The letter said, correctly, that 'the nature of sex and gender and the relationship between them are not forbidden topics of philosophical discussion.' However, with academic freedom comes responsibility: 'There are many diverse, contentious views about gender and gender identity that can be – and are – engaged with in ways that do not call into question the integrity and sincerity of trans people nor the validity of their own understanding of who they are.'[10] The message was clear: certain topics *are* forbidden, after all.

Apart from being unprecedented in the discipline, this recommendation to limit enquiry had some noteworthy features. In past decades, feminist philosophers had not been shy about denying that trans women are women (to take the obvious example). Some of the letter writers themselves formerly held such views. Once respectable positions had been silently transmuted into heresies – indeed, they had been heresies all along.

Second, philosophers normally pride themselves on confronting disturbing hypotheses without blinking. Morality is a fiction, no one has any rights, having children is wrong, time is unreal, women and men do not exist, tables and chairs do not exist, it is impossible to be a woman without being oppressed, God is unsurpassably evil, other animals are not conscious – these may all be entertained or even endorsed without censure from colleagues. Why gender identity had to be fenced off from probing questions was unclear, to say the least.

After another letter calling for a similar prohibition, and protesting about a forthcoming talk by Kathleen Stock, one anonymous philosophical wit wrote:

> Junior members of the profession may be wondering what sorts of ideas may be discussed and debated by philosophers, and which may not. Which may be subject to skeptical inquiry and which may not .... Following is a helpful guide.
>
> You MAY question whether race exists and whether gender exists, you may question whether social kinds exist. For that matter, you may question whether any kinds at all exist, and for the measure, whether abstract objects or even whether the external world exists. You may NOT, however, question whether people can identify their own genders.
>
> You MAY question whether other minds exist, or whether anything at all exists except for yourself. You may even question whether time exists

> and space exists. You may ask whether all change is illusion. You may NOT, however, question whether people can identify their own genders.[11]

This list of permissions continued at some length.

Non-consensual co-platforming

The letter from the twelve leading scholars had little practical effect. The following month the Institute of Arts and Ideas, a UK organization promoting public philosophy, tweeted: 'How can philosophy help us understand transgender experiences? We asked thinkers on all sides of the debate.' The gender-critical side was represented by Lawford-Smith, Stock, and the redoubtable British feminist campaigner Julie Bindel; batting for the trans-rights team was the historian and gender studies academic Susan Stryker accompanied by two US philosophy professors. A paragraph or two from each of the six thinkers appeared on the institute's website. Stryker's prose bore the unmistakable imprint of gender studies ('the hegemonic biopolitical regime of which gender is a part', etc.), but apart from that it was all pretty tame stuff.[12]

Stryker and her philosophical comrades-in-arms did not take kindly to the discovery that their short pieces were part of (in the words of one of the philosophers) 'a symposium that platformed TERFs'. They persuaded the institute to remove their contributions and to publish their retraction statement. The trio complained that they were victims of 'a non-consensual co-platforming', a novel coinage for a non-existent offence.[13] (Academics are granted no veto over their fellow symposiasts.)

In her paragraph, Lawford-Smith expressed some scepticism about the claim that everyone has a gender identity; in hers, Stock suggested that a transgender identity is more than a matter of how one subjectively feels; and Bindel dusted off a familiar feminist trope: 'Being a woman is not an abstract, philosophical concept though. Under patriarchy, our position is rooted in material reality.' These unremarkable pronouncements were not well received. Stryker and the two philosophers claimed that their 'basic safety' was 'at risk', and that their gender-critical opponents were questioning 'transgender people's fundamental legitimacy as people who are entitled to the same respect as any other person':

> We refuse on principle to engage in any discussion that treats such positions as up for abstract intellectual debate, in the same way that we would refuse to participate in a conversation that debated whether the Holocaust actually happened, or whether corrective rape should be used to cure lesbianism, or whether or not the white race is superior to all others. There are limits to civil and intellectual discourse beyond which speech acts are simply acts of violence.[14]

As Lawford-Smith pointed out, the corrective rape analogy was a little insensitive, given that she, Stock and Bindel were all lesbians.

#Lettergate

In June of 2020, Rowling returned with a long form essay, 'J. K. Rowling writes about her reasons for speaking out on sex and gender issues'. She emphasized that she had nothing against trans people:

> I believe the majority of trans-identified people not only pose zero threat to others, but are vulnerable for all the reasons I've outlined. Trans people need and deserve protection. Like women, they're most likely to be killed by sexual partners. Trans women who work in the sex industry, particularly trans women of colour, are at particular risk. Like every other domestic abuse and sexual assault survivor I know, I feel nothing but empathy and solidarity with trans women who've been abused by men.

On the other hand, Rowling did not agree with the proposed move toward gender self-identification, and neither was she enamoured of its more aggressive supporters: 'Huge numbers of women are justifiably terrified by the trans activists; I know this because so many have got in touch with me to tell their stories.'[15]

Rowling was the recipient of a substantial amount of online abuse herself. As a journalist pungently put it, 'Inviting JK Rowling to "suck my trans dick" seems a mightily strange way in which to be "on the right side of history".' Rowling's essay probably did not change many minds. 'J. K. Rowling triples down on transphobia' was one typical headline.[16]

Shortly after Rowling published her essay, and when 'cancel culture' seemed to be reaching its zenith, a letter 'on justice and open debate' appeared in *Harper's Magazine* online. The more than 150 writers and artists who signed complained 'that the free exchange of information and ideas, the lifeblood of a liberal society, is daily becoming more constricted.' Noting that there are familiar culprits on the 'radical right', the real target of the letter was evidently the woke left, whom the letter charged with 'an intolerance of opposing views, a vogue for public shaming and ostracism, and the tendency to dissolve complex policy issues in a blinding moral certainty'. The letter ended with a call for 'good-faith disagreement without dire professional consequences'.[17]

Rowling was among the signatories, joining Noam Chomsky, Gloria Steinem, Margaret Atwood, Garry Kasparov, and Salman Rushdie. (In 2022, Rushdie's thirty-three-year streak of evading Ayatollah Khomeini's *fatwā* for writing *The Satanic Verses* came to a tragic end, when he was stabbed and seriously injured in upstate New York.) Perhaps it was a combination of 2020's Covid-19 lockdowns, the Black Lives Matter protests, the carnival of the Trump presidency, and the heat of summer – the mild call of the *Harper's* letter to restore some civility spurred frantic tweeting and hastily written online essays explaining why this was a terrible idea.

A handful of transgender people signed, but in a matter of hours one of them, the writer Jennifer Finney Boylan, tweeted an apology. Revealing a probably all-too-common motivation for signing such high-minded letters, Boylan confessed that she 'did not know who else had signed that letter'. She knew that 'Chomsky, Steinem and Atwood were in, and I thought, good company.' Finding herself non-consensually co-platformed with Rowling was clearly too much: 'The consequences', she wrote, 'are mine to bear.' Boylan later wrote an op-ed in the *New York Times* about abortion and trans rights, suggesting that 'TERFs' are 'people whose hearts – like the Grinch's – are two sizes too small.'[18]

The TERF industrial complex

Later in the summer of 2020, Grace Lavery, a professor in the English Department at the University of California, Berkeley, announced an online seminar on the 'TERF industrial complex', describing it on Twitter as 'an immensely influential set of anti-trans activists with one foot in Section 28 and another in Xtian purity culture', whose 'figureheads are a deranged sitcom writer and an analytic philosopher of literature'. Section 28 was a controversial 1988 UK law enacted under Prime Minister Margaret Thatcher, prohibiting the promotion of homosexuality in schools; it was repealed in 2000 in Scotland, and three years later in England and Wales.

The idea that Kathleen Stock (the 'philosopher of literature') was directing a sinister homophobic Christian movement was a little implausible. Admittedly the other alleged figurehead, the Irish comedy writer Graham Linehan, had sometimes let his unbridled enthusiasm for the gender-critical cause get out of hand. A serial tweeter with 600,000 followers, Linehan was banned from the platform for repeated violations of Twitter's rules against hateful conduct, the last problematic tweet being 'men aren't women tho' in reply to the Women's Institute wishing a happy Pride to their transgender members.[19] (The Canadian feminist Meghan Murphy had been banned earlier for similar sentiments; Holly Lawford-Smith was another casualty, for reasons that were never clear. The accounts of all three were restored after Elon Musk bought Twitter in 2022.)

Linehan had also intemperately suggested on Twitter that Grace Lavery's classes in queer and trans studies amounted to 'grooming'. But the anti-gay charge ('one foot in Section 28') had no legs, at least. And as for Christian purity culture, Linehan, along with some of the UK's most prominent atheists, is an honorary associate of the National Secular Society. He also co-created *Father Ted*, a sitcom which gently mocks Catholicism.

The TERF industrial complex – or, putting it more neutrally, the Rowling-aligned feminist campaign – was indeed effective. In September of 2020 the government announced that earlier plans to reform the Gender Recognition Act would no longer go ahead. 'A product', *The Spectator* reported, 'of remarkable grassroots political organization'. And, in 2021, Maya Forstater won her appeal. The belief that humans can't change sex, it turned out, was indeed worthy of respect in a democratic society.[20]

ROGD

Reforming the Gender Recognition Act was one battleground. Another was the medical treatment of young people with gender issues, raised by

Rowling in her long form letter. 'I'm concerned', she wrote, 'about the huge explosion in young women wishing to transition and also about the increasing numbers who seem to be detransitioning (returning to their original sex), because they regret taking steps that have, in some cases, altered their bodies irrevocably, and taken away their fertility.'

Gender dysphoria is persistent distress at one's sexed body and at the social expectations that are associated with having a body of that kind. As the American Psychiatric Association puts it, gender dysphoria is 'the aversion to some or all of those physical characteristics or social roles that connote one's own biological sex.'[21] Transitioning from one sex to the other is an attempt to make that aversion go away.

Gender dysphoria can be *early onset*, afflicting young children, or *late onset*, first occurring during puberty or much later in life. Natal males used to make up most early-onset cases and the vast majority of late-onset cases, but around 2010 the patient population noticeably started to change. Natal females were presenting with dysphoria that apparently began around puberty, and the sex ratio of dysphoric adolescents presenting to clinics switched, with females coming to outnumber males.[22]

This second front in the TERF wars opened up in 2017, when Lisa Littman, a US physician, published a half-page summary (a 'poster abstract') of a study on this new population of patients, coining the term 'rapid onset gender dysphoria' (ROGD). The summary reported that ROGD 'occurs in the context of peer group and online influences'. In her book *Everything You Ever Wanted to Know about Trans (but Were Afraid to Ask)* trans activist Brynn Tannehill discussed Littman's summary, taking up much more than half a page to do so. She accused Littman of 'deliberate academic malfeasance' and concluded that 'the abstract is an egregious example of biased junk science.' That was a shot across the bows.[23]

By 2018, Littman had moved to Brown University's School of Public Health, and a detailed account of her research was published in the biomedical journal *PLOS One*: 'Rapid-onset gender dysphoria in adolescents and young adults: a study of parental reports'.[24] Littman analysed lengthy questionnaires completed by 256 parents who had reported gender dysphoria in their children that commenced during or after puberty. She had posted recruitment information on three websites offering resources for parents sceptical of standard 'affirmative' treatment protocols for gender dysphoria, which allow the child to lead with the clinician following. More than 80 per cent of the adolescents were female, and the majority had other mental health issues.

According to many of the parents, their children's gender dysphoria was encouraged by the internet and especially videos about transitioning on YouTube. There was a tendency to rewrite history to accord with the new transgender identity:

> A 12-year-old natal female was bullied specifically for going through early puberty and the responding parent wrote 'as a result she said she felt fat and hated her breasts.' She learned online that hating your breasts is a sign of being transgender. She edited her diary (by crossing out existing text and writing in new text) to make it appear that she has always felt that she is transgender.[25]

Littman proposed two hypotheses for future research. First, that 'social and peer contagion' – a well-studied phenomenon which plays a significant role in the spread of eating disorders – was an important mechanism in propagating ROGD.[26] Second, that ROGD is a 'maladaptive coping mechanism' – a way of temporarily relieving stress that has negative consequences of its own, like heavy drinking. (When J. K. Rowling wrote in her long form essay about 'the huge explosion in young women wishing to transition', she cited Littman.)

Brown University issued a press release publicizing the article, which quoted Littman as prudently saying that 'more research needs to be done. Descriptive studies aren't randomized controlled trials – you can't tell cause and effect, and you can't tell prevalence.'[27]

The reaction from activists was vehement and immediate. A trans activist tweeted at *PLOS One* that the article 'was written using transphobic dogwhistles (sex observed at birth, for example)'. *PLOS One* meekly tweeted back, 'thank you for bringing this to our attention.' (In fact, 'sex observed at birth' occurs nowhere in Littman's article.) Five days later the journal commissioned a 'post-publication reassessment', and Brown removed the press release from its website. The dean of the School of Public Health wrote a letter to staff and students citing 'concerns' that Littman's study could be used to 'invalidate the perspectives of members of the transgender community'. The former dean of Harvard's medical school commented:

> In all my years in academia, I have never once seen a comparable reaction from a journal within days of publishing a paper that the journal already had subjected to peer review, accepted and published. One can only assume that the response was in large measure due to the intense lobbying the journal received, and the threat – whether stated or unstated – that more social-media backlash would rain down upon *PLOS One* if action were not taken.[28]

PLOS One published a revised version of Littman's article in March of the following year. The title had changed to 'Parent reports of adolescents and young adults perceived to show signs of a rapid onset of gender dysphoria', and the triggering phrase 'rapid onset gender dysphoria' – which, along with 'ROGD', had appeared many times in the original – now occurred only in the paragraph stating the conclusion. The revised version offered some clarifications and more information about the data collection and analysis, but the results were essentially unchanged. The republished article was accompanied by a 'Correction Notice', even though no 'corrections' (as these are usually understood in scientific publishing) had been made.[29]

The journal's editor-in-chief issued an apology 'to the trans and gender variant community for oversights that occurred during the original assessment of the study.'[30] Ironically, an important bit of context that had been buried in the original version was promoted to the revised abstract: 'Recently, clinicians have reported that post-puberty presentations of gender dysphoria in natal females that appear to be rapid in onset is a phenomenon that they are seeing more and more in their clinic.'

Activists were not the only ones riled up. Some clinicians who were proponents of the affirmative model also denigrated Littman's research. Diane Ehrensaft, director of mental health at the Child and Adolescent Gender Center at the University of California, San Francisco, was quoted as saying that Littman's sampling methods were like 'recruiting from Klan or alt-right sites to demonstrate that blacks really are an inferior race.' In other words, the parents were so bigoted that their claims of internet and peer influence on gender dysphoria were completely worthless. Ehrensaft later co-authored a letter to the *American Journal of Bioethics* which erroneously claimed that Littman's article was 'republished with significant corrections'.[31]

Irreversible Damage

Jennifer Finney Boylan (the apologetic signer of the *Harper's* letter) wrote in the *New York Times* that rapid onset gender dysphoria is a 'bogus new diagnosis'. Clearly, however, there was something to see here. 'I think a fair number of kids are getting into it because it's trendy', an experienced clinician (and trans woman) said in the *Washington Post*; 'Kids are all about being accepted by their peers. It's trendy for professionals, too.' And in any case the focus on allegedly prejudiced parents directed attention away from the girls who had begun to speak out. 'I lived with Rapid Onset Gender Dysphoria for three years', wrote one, 'believing wholeheartedly that I was not a girl, because the trans community told me that I didn't have to be.'[32]

Kenneth Zucker is a world authority on gender dysphoria and the editor of the leading sexology journal, the *Archives of Sexual Behavior*. (He has faced controversies of his own.)[33] In a 2019 article Zucker wrote:

> ... it is my view that [ROGD] is a new clinical phenomenon. I was seeing such adolescents in the mid-2000s in Toronto (I just didn't have a label for them) and, at present, they comprise the majority of my private practice adolescent patients. (Of course, I make no claim that my clients are representative of the adolescent population with gender dysphoria in general.)[34]

Irreversible Damage, Abigail Shrier's book about rapid onset gender dysphoria, appeared in 2020. Shrier, a journalist for the *Wall Street Journal*, had shopped her proposal around; one major publisher expressed great interest, only to say the next day that, if he accepted it, he would have a staff revolt on his hands. (He was very likely right.) In the end her only offer was from the conservative publisher Regnery.[35] (A sample from their list: Dinesh D'Souza's *The Big Lie: Exposing the Nazi Roots of the American Left*.)

Irreversible Damage had an alarmist subtitle – *The Transgender Craze Seducing Our Daughters* – and the US cover showed a small girl with a gaping hole in her abdomen, but Shrier had done her homework. She interviewed many parents, happily transitioned transgender adolescents and adults, activists, and researchers and clinicians, including Lisa Littman and Kenneth Zucker. She also spoke to young women who appeared to fit the ROGD profile and who had detransitioned (reverted to living as their natal sex). As the subtitle promised, the book came down firmly on the side of ROGD – the phenomenon is real and much as recounted by Littman's respondents. Still, Shrier was careful to express her support for transgender adults: 'Transgender people are living today with less shame or stigma and less fear of violence than at any point in living memory. That fact should gladden all decent people. Caitlyn Jenner should feel free to pursue a life of her choosing – that most American of wants.'[36] The book was blurbed by, among others, Zucker ('of great interest to parents, the general public, and health clinicians') and the psychologist J. Michael Bailey ('urgently needed'). (Bailey is also no stranger to controversy, as we'll see in chapter 6.)

Grace Lavery, the University of California English professor, tweeted: 'I do NOT advocate defacing library books. I DO encourage followers to steal Abigail Shrier's book and burn it on a pyre.' After the inevitable backlash, Lavery – who had apparently only 'read the cover' – clarified that she had not meant this seriously. The playful irony of the Berkeley English Department was likely lost on the average Twitter user.

Employees of the American Civil Liberties Association – which once defended the right of neo-Nazis to march through a Chicago suburb whose residents included Holocaust survivors – might be expected unanimously to disapprove of book burning. Not these days. Fault lines in the organization were exposed when Chase Strangio, a prominent ACLU attorney, tweeted 'Abigail Shrier's book is a dangerous polemic with a goal of making people not trans', and 'Stopping the circulation of this book and these ideas is 100% a hill I will die on.' The American Booksellers Association apologized for including the paperback of *Irreversible Damage* in a mailing of samples to members, calling it a 'serious, violent incident'. The Harvard Bookstore – a beloved fixture in Cambridge, Massachusetts, the home of Harvard and MIT – tweeted that the ABA was promoting 'dangerous, widely discredited anti-trans propaganda'.[37]

Reviews were no less divided. (The *New York Times*, unsurprisingly, did not review it.) *Irreversible Damage* was an *Economist* book of the year:

'Predictably controversial – yet there is not a drop of animosity in the book.' The reviewer for the *Los Angeles Review of Books*, it is fair to say, found more than a drop. 'The book's heartless dissection of delicate trans experiences' is written 'baselessly and brutishly', with 'grotesque misperceptions of trans identity'. The well-regarded Science-Based Medicine website published a complimentary review – 'well-researched … She brings up some alarming facts that desperately need to be looked into.' This was promptly retracted, and another review was substituted with a more balanced assessment: 'In brief, Shrier's book is a fear-filled screed, full of misinformation, biological and medical inaccuracies, logical fallacies, and propaganda.'[38]

The controversies around ROGD should have been low-hanging fruit for philosophers working in medical ethics, with perspectives on all sides represented. That is not what happened.

Ethicists AWOL

Psychological conditions such as depression and anxiety have sometimes been treated with surgery. In a particularly dark period in psychiatry ending in the 1950s, thousands were given lobotomies, neurosurgeries that severed connections in the front part of the brain. Most were women. Rose Kennedy, the sister of President Kennedy, was lobotomized when she was twenty-three, leaving her with the mental capacity of a child. The man who invented the procedure won the Nobel Prize.[39]

At least lobotomies (like drugs) were supposed to target the organic site of psychological disruptions. In contrast, the medical treatment of gender dysphoria attempts to fix the patient's distress, not by altering their brain, but by changing their sexed body. The surgical aspect puts this treatment in a class of its own. Surgery is currently not given for any other psychiatric condition. Cross-sex hormones alone can impair fertility, and surgery can eliminate it entirely. Lifelong medical care is required. As the Columbia University psychologist Heino F. Meyer-Bahlburg puts it, 'the long and difficult process of sex reassignment … includes hormonal and surgical procedures with substantial medical risks and complications.' This is *not* to say that medical transition is never advisable, and there are many satisfied customers. But it is a weighty decision.[40]

Gender dysphoric children raise particularly vexing issues. In the 1990s, Dutch physicians began to treat selected young patients with puberty blockers, drugs which suppress the hormones that kickstart puberty. These were thought to have a number of advantages, including 'buy[ing] time for all parties in the decision whether or not to start cross-sex hormones'. (The cautious Dutch were clear on the disadvantages, as well.) A natal female treated with puberty blockers when she was thirteen, and who went on to cross-sex hormones and surgery, was followed up twenty-two years later. The doctors saw 'a healthy and well virilized person' who is 'still is convinced that his choice to live as a man was the right one.' On the negative side of the ledger, the patient thought that the recent end of his relationship with his girlfriend had 'likely ... been related to his shame about his genital appearance and his feelings of inadequacy in sexual matters.'[41]

The Dutch approach caught on, and puberty blockers became a standard although controversial treatment in the US and the UK. Can a child on the cusp of puberty really give meaningful consent to blockers? But is it right to deprive highly distressed children of what arguably could be a cure? What if the child wants blockers but the parents disagree? Philosophers who specialize in ethics love these kinds of questions. They are also highly motivated to work on new and sexy ethical topics, such as racial bias in AI algorithms, rather than plough the same old furrows, such as the permissibility of abortion. One might have expected, then, a lively debate in the philosophical literature over puberty blockers.

One philosopher did publish an article in the *American Journal of Bioethics* in 2019, arguing that 'transgender adolescents should have the legal right to access puberty-blocking treatment ... *without parental approval*', assuming that this is recommended by medical professionals. The article was accompanied by twelve peer commentaries, mostly by clinicians and other healthcare professionals. Some of them sharply disagreed with the target article – exactly what is supposed to happen, with the hope that the truth will be more visible after the smoke of battle has cleared away. The two commentaries by philosophers, though, were supportive. One philosopher baselessly implied that without blockers there is a 'vastly increased risk of suicide'. The other philosophical commentary argued that the target article did not go far enough. No parental consent is needed before blockers can be given, but neither is an 'extensive mental health evaluation'. If any ethicists in philosophy were sceptical about trends in the treatment of gender dysphoric youth, they kept it to themselves.[42]

Bell *v.* Tavistock

Concerns over puberty blockers in the UK finally boiled over in December 2020 when a Divisional Court from the High Court of Justice ruled on the use of puberty blockers by the Tavistock and Portman NHS Trust's Gender Identity Development Service (GIDS). This was a judicial review of GIDS's practice, requested by Keira Bell, a former GIDS patient, and 'Mrs A', the mother of a patient on the waiting list. Bell was prescribed puberty blockers at sixteen, started testosterone a year later and had a double mastectomy at twenty. She later detransitioned, writing in her witness statement:

> ... It is only until recently that I have started to think about having children and if that is ever a possibility, I have to live with the fact that I will not be able to breastfeed my children. I still do not believe that I have fully processed the surgical procedure that I had to remove my breasts and how major it really was. I made a brash decision as a teenager, (as a lot of teenagers do) trying to find confidence and happiness, except now the rest of my life will be negatively affected. I cannot reverse any of the physical, mental or legal changes that I went through. Transition was a very temporary, superficial fix for a very complex identity issue.[43]

The Divisional Court heard from many expert witnesses. Annelou L. C. de Vries, an experienced clinician at the Amsterdam University Medical Center, expressed some characteristically Dutch caution: 'Ethical dilemmas continue to exist around ... the uncertainty of apparent long-term physical consequences of puberty blocking on bone density, fertility, brain development and surgical options.'[44] The evidence of Christopher Gillberg, a psychiatrist and an authority on autism, was quoted in the *Sunday Times*:

> Thousands of adolescents are being offered 'treatment' with puberty blockers, sex-contrary hormones, and then, finally for some, with a variety of surgical

> procedures. In the UK as in Sweden, this is in spite of the non-existent research evidence that these treatments are of any long-term benefit to the young people in question.[45]

One fact on which the court placed great weight was the almost inevitable progression from puberty blockers to cross-sex hormones, which have irreversible effects. Although blockers were initially envisaged as a pause button, allowing the patient and therapist to 'clarify gender confusion under less time pressure', it turned out that, in practice, almost everyone on blockers went on to cross-sex hormones. De Vries gave a figure of 98 per cent, and GIDS's own data (produced after the court hearing) were that forty-three out of forty-four patients progressed to hormones. One of the first papers on the Dutch experiment with blockers had warned that the blocker-button might turn out to be fast-forward rather than pause: 'Adolescents may consider this step a guarantee of sex reassignment, and it could make them therefore less rather than more inclined to engage in introspection.' The court thought that this hypothesis had something to be said for it. Informed consent, then, would require properly weighing the potential consequences of taking cross-sex hormones, including loss of fertility and negative effects on sexual function.[46]

The judgement concluded, 'It is doubtful that a child aged 14 or 15 could understand and weigh the long-term risks and consequences of the administration of puberty blockers', also suggesting that court approval is advisable 'in respect of young persons aged 16 and over'.[47] The Tavistock swiftly suspended referrals for under-sixteens.

It was hard not to feel sympathy for Keira Bell, especially when hearing her voice, permanently deepened by testosterone. Some managed to resist, though. A well-known trans activist tweeted, 'Keira Bell herself is a fucking evil person who overtly endorses conversion therapy for trans kids' – a nice example of *aggressive conformity*, demonstrating an extreme commitment to the values of one's in-group.[48]

Grace Lavery, the ever-quotable Berkeley professor, tweeted that the court's ruling was 'state-sponsored child abuse'. In an article on the decision, she wrote that a 'formerly highly marginal ideology, the so-called gender-critical position, has captured British institutions', and she urged feminists 'to take more seriously than we have the rise of this chimerical blend of biological essentialism and cultural conservatism.'[49]

In 2021 the judgement was overturned on appeal. The legal principle, the Court of Appeal ruled, was that clinicians, not courts, should be the ones to determine competence. The Divisional Court's conclusions about the ability of children to consent to treatment were therefore inappropriate. Despite the reversal, the momentum was in Bell's direction, and in 2022 the NHS announced plans to close GIDS – the world's largest clinic of its kind – following a critical interim report led by a senior paediatrician.[50]

Bell wrote: 'I do not believe in rigid gender expression. People should be comfortable and feel accepted if they explore different ways of presenting themselves. As I said in my statement after the ruling, this means stopping the homophobia, the misogyny, and the bullying of those who are different.'[51] One might have expected Bell's distressing story to have been sympathetically discussed in mainstream feminist philosophy, but it was not mentioned. Only the exiled gender-critical philosophers raised any concerns.

The empire strikes back

Despite being professionally shunned by many of her colleagues, vilified online, and periodically no-platformed, Stock persisted. 'It is quite a strange situation to work somewhere where people make it clear that they loathe you', she remarked in an interview in *Times Higher Education*, the UK's main news magazine for higher education. 'Increasingly', *THE* reported, 'the debate is less about whether Professor Stock's views are right but whether she should be allowed to voice them at all. To question the idea that a trans woman should be treated as a woman in all contexts is an act of "hate speech" that seeks to "erase" her identity, Professor Stock's critics contend.'[52]

In the 2021 New Year's Honours list, Stock was awarded an OBE (Officer of the Most Excellent Order of the British Empire) for 'services to higher education', specifically for her 'outstanding contribution to academia and the media, in defence of free speech'.[53] (The honours list had more than a thousand recipients, including a trans woman firefighter.) Stock's opponents were not pleased. Grace Lavery tweeted: 'A fitting recognition by the Tory vandals for a scholar working to discredit and undermine British higher education, her own students, and the British LGBT community.'

The Philosophy Department at the Open University (Britain's cherished institute of distance-learning) issued a congratulatory tweet, noting that 'Kathleen is a long-term friend of the department.' The OU's tweet contained no endorsement of Stock's views, explicit or implicit; nevertheless, it was promptly deleted by the department's head, on the unconvincing ground that 'we don't take sides from our departmental account.'

The inevitable open letter did not take long to arrive, with the alarming headline 'Open letter concerning transphobia in philosophy'.[54] Judith Butler did not sign, but some of those who had tormented Rebecca Tuvel over transracialism returned to denounce Stock and her 'transphobic fearmongering'. Some had gone for the trifecta, also signing the letter replying to the '12 leading scholars'. Eventually almost 800 signatures accumulated, many from graduate students and undergraduates. There were some big names in the profession. One well-known philosopher explained to his 65,000 Twitter followers how his conscience and high status left him no choice: 'Sadly, my tiny discipline of analytic philosophy has become the academic site of legitimation of a lot of toxic discourse against trans persons. As a senior member of my field, I have to sign.'

As the senior member's complaint about 'toxic discourse' indicated, the alleged problem in philosophy was not prejudice or discrimination against transgender people or those given to heterodox gender expression. One could hardly hope for a more tolerant atmosphere for breaking gender boundaries than in philosophy departments, where socially conservative views are almost non-existent. Rather, the problem was opinions.[55]

The open letter against Tuvel was full of specious accusations; the Stock letter was even more easily dismantled. The writers could not get the most elementary facts right, describing Stock as being opposed to the Gender Recognition Act. (She had opposed reforms to the GRA, not the GRA itself.) The letter perversely suggested that Stock had been honoured for her 'harmful rhetoric' instead of for – as was explicit – her support of academic freedom. As with Tuvel, various 'harms' were alleged with no supporting evidence. The letter implied that Stock's writings had impeded 'life-saving' medical treatments. There are no such treatments to be impeded. Perhaps the most forehead-slapping allegation was that the openly lesbian Stock was helping to 'reinforce the patriarchal status quo'.

Pointing out these absurdities had no discernible effect on the letter writers (apart from the addition of an 'erratum' correcting the mistake about the GRA): no signatures were retracted and no apologies tendered. This was not surprising. To object to the claims was to miss the point of the exercise.

The open letter concerning transphobia in philosophy was met shortly afterwards with yet another open letter, 'concerning academic freedom'. 'It cannot become our standard', the rival letter said, 'that where analysis and discussion of matters of public concern may cause offense, the social and institutional consequences of engagement are so costly that few will be willing to do the work.' That one ultimately received over 400 signatories from a diverse range of disciplines, including Alan Sokal (of 'Sokal Hoax' fame) and the philosopher Peter Singer (controversial for his views on euthanasia, among other things).[56] The new open letter coincided with a 7,000-word essay posted on the personal blog of a female philosophy graduate student whose chief hobby appeared to be the life and opinions of Kathleen Stock, purporting to unmask her as an ignorant anti-trans activist intolerant of dissent. According to one insider – in what was intended to be a compliment – the widely circulated post had been 'years in the making'.

'One of this wretched island's most prominent transphobes'[57]

Stock's troubles were far from over. Later in 2021, student activists at Sussex University put up posters around the campus demanding she be fired and posted a photo to Instagram of masked protestors setting off smoke flares over a large concrete plinth bearing the university's name, holding a pink and blue banner reading 'Stock Out'. Although the vice chancellor of Sussex came out with a strong statement supporting the 'untrammelled right' of members of the university 'to say and believe what they think', the local branch of the University and College Union, representing academics and staff, offered a decidedly backhanded defence. They did not 'endorse the call for any worker to be summarily sacked' but sought 'an urgent investigation into the ways in which institutional transphobia operates at our university'.[58] That could not have been anything but a thinly veiled reference to Sussex's (overall, lukewarm) support of the embattled philosopher.

Many leading figures in British philosophy, including some with a specialization in feminist philosophy, endorsed an open letter supporting Stock and 'the rights of colleagues to express unpopular opinions or raise difficult questions challenging popular orthodoxies'.[59] Grace Lavery chimed in from California, first taking an 'agnostic' position on whether Stock should be fired. That did not survive a close reading of Stock's tweets, and Lavery's position soon hardened. 'Kathleen Stock has lied twice in the last few days', she tweeted. 'One of those lies defamed a student. A threshold has been crossed, and Sussex University should fire her at once.' A naive observer would have strained to find any lying or defamation, but Lavery, a sophisticated professor of English, may have been using a style of literary interpretation that privileges the reader's reaction, rendering the plain meaning of the words irrelevant.

The hounding of Stock would at least have been understandable if her views were at the outer limits of acceptability, stretching the 'Overton window', but they were squarely in the British tradition of toleration and compromise. Her 2021 book *Material Girls: Why Reality Matters for Feminism* was very well reviewed in the major UK newspapers, while decried by more radical gender-critical feminists as being far too conciliatory towards transgenderism. One of them, with evident disapproval, quoted Stock as saying: 'Trans people are trans people. Get over it.'[60]

The reply by the feminist philosophy establishment to the twelve leading scholars, two years earlier, may or may not have been read by the 'Anti Terf Sussex' students, as they called themselves. In any event, the students effectively repeated its strictures against questioning the 'validity' of a transgender person's self-understanding. Stock could *think* certain things – perhaps! – but should certainly not broadcast the result of her cogitations. 'She has said publicly that she does not believe trans men are men or trans women are women', one student complained. 'It should not be acceptable for a professor to say things that might hurt someone but might also invalidate someone's identity and persona and who they are.'[61] The student (in 'media and communications') may have a shock if ever exposed to philosophy. For devoutly religious students, an introductory course in philosophy threatens to invalidate their identities from the start.

Other supporters of the students took a different tack. The problem was not invalidating identities but allowing the equivalent of a flat Earther or creationist to corrupt youthful minds. 'Stock's view of sex as immutable and binary is regressive and discriminatory – and at odds with science', wrote one Cambridge University academic in a letter to the *Sunday Times*. 'It shouldn't be controversial to argue against teaching outdated or harmful science at publicly funded universities.'[62]

The police advised Stock to install security cameras at her home and not to go to the campus unaccompanied. Shortly after the protests, she resigned from Sussex University, the culmination of more than three years of harassment.[63] 'Sussex is TERF free!', the student activists crowed on Instagram. Lavery tweeted that she was 'relieved that Prof. Stock won't be empowered to harm students further.'

Foxing Day

The depressing TERF wars were periodically lightened on the eastern side of the Atlantic by a motley crew of male British eccentrics, a group that can traditionally be relied upon for humour during dark times. Since the Irishman Graham Linehan lives in the UK, he gets an honourable mention, but there are plenty of others to choose from.

There is, for instance, Edward Lord (OBE, they/them), a neatly bearded non-binary Freemason. As chair of the City of London's Establishment Committee, Lord was an enthusiastic proponent of abolishing single-sex spaces. In 2018, the Freemasons – 'the world's oldest fraternity', complete with secret handshakes, Masonic aprons and arcane initiation rituals – allowed trans women as members of the United Grand Lodge of England, provided they initially joined as men. The journalist Helen Lewis drily remarked to Lord, 'I'm afraid I find it very hard to square your continued participation in the Masons with a genuine desire to smash patriarchy.'[64]

And then there is Eddie Izzard (she/her), an Emmy-winning comedian who once ran thirty-two marathons in thirty-one days for charity. A self-described 'lesbian trapped in a man's body', Izzard came out as gender fluid in 2020, oscillating between 'boy mode' and 'girl mode'. Her stated preference for feminine pronouns was greeted with both acclaim and ridicule, echoing across no-man's land. Some of the acclaimers and ridiculers swapped sides when Izzard defended J. K. Rowling against charges of transphobia.[65]

Perhaps the greatest contribution to comedy was made by the improbably named Jolyon Maugham (KC, he/him), a barrister specializing in tax law and relentless anti-Brexit campaigner. An interminable tweeter (at the time of writing, still tweeting), Maugham has a special talent for annoying gender-critical women on the platform. Responding to Maya Forstater's employment discrimination case, he tweeted: 'Deliberate misgendering of transmen and women will contribute to those deaths and self-harm. That is a very real wrong done by those who adopt extreme positions, including Maya.' In fact, Forstater had 'deliberately misgendered' no one. (In fairness to Maugham, he did once tweet that '"TERF" is widely heard and widely used as hate speech.')

On Boxing Day in 2019, Maugham, wearing his wife's kimono, clubbed to death a hapless fox which had become trapped in a henhouse in Maugham's garden. Any normal Englishman would have kept mum, but Maugham immediately recounted his victory on Twitter: 'Already this morning I have killed a fox with a baseball bat. How's your Boxing Day going?' The kimono, Maugham overshared, was green and 'too small'. After an investigation, the Royal Society for the Prevention of Cruelty to Animals declined to bring charges, since a post-mortem showed that Maugham had quickly shuffled off the fox's mortal coil with a mighty blow.[66]

It is tempting to search for some hidden meaning in the farce of the cross-dressing fox-in-the-henhouse-slaying barrister, a sign that the current trouble with gender ultimately makes sense, rather than being an inexplicable cultural spasm that will eventually recede into the historical mist, leaving some wondering whether it happened at all. If there are insightful explanations of the 'transgender moment', this book is not the one to unearth them. Instead, the following chapters will try to wriggle through the intellectual maze of sex, gender, and identity in search of the exit to reality.

Let's begin with gender.

TWO

'Gender' Trouble

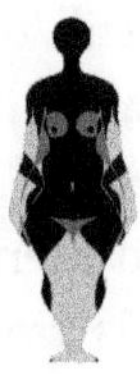

> Today, 'gender' slips uneasily between being merely another word for sex and being a contested political term.
>
> Ann Oakley, 'A brief history of gender'[1]

> There is no one concept of gender.
>
> Judith Butler, 'Why is the idea of "gender" provoking backlash the world over?'[2]

What is gender?

'Gender is a fact', the American comedian Dave Chappelle announced on a Netflix special in 2021. He was agreeing with what he took to be J. K. Rowling's view, declaring himself 'Team TERF', which prompted calls for his show to be cancelled.[3] Naturally Rowling's admirers were pleased, but some felt a correction was in order. 'I watched the latest Dave Chappelle special and it was hilarious', read one tweet, 'I think the only error he made was to confuse biologically allocated sex with socially constructed gender.' That is, Rowling's view was that *sex* was a fact. Did Chappelle really misspeak?

Words matter. 'Inflammable' sounds like it means the opposite of 'flammable', but the two words are synonyms. Putting 'inflammable' on a bottle of lighter fluid can be confusing, if not downright dangerous. The little word 'gender' may have been responsible for more confusion than any other.

'Sex' is a useful word; like many words, it has multiple meanings. One meaning of 'sex' is *sexual intercourse*; another meaning is *female or male*. 'Gender' is also useful, because it can be used to disambiguate 'sex': 'gender' never means *getting it on*. Marilyn Monroe said, 'Sex is a part of nature. I go along with nature' – she could not have made the same quip using the word 'gender'. When forms these days have a box labelled 'gender', usually what's wanted is your sex. The gender pay gap is simply the pay gap between females and males – 'sex pay gap' would do, although that might suggest a comparison of salaries in the porn industry.

Willard Van Orman Quine was a giant of twentieth-century philosophy, a fixture at Harvard until his death in 2000. The author of one of the most unreflective autobiographies ever written, Quine is unlikely to be encountered in a course on feminist philosophy or gender studies.[4] Still, he succinctly identified the social forces driving 'gender' as a label for the two sexes:

> The latter-day upheaval in sexual mores has increased the frequency of occasions for referring politely to copulation, and has thus created a demand for a short but equally polite word for the practice. The word *sex* has been pressed into that service, and thus rendered less convenient as a means of referring to the sexes. The resulting need has been met in turn by calling the sexes *genders*.[5]

For this reason, 'gender' earns its keep. Unfortunately, the word has accumulated other meanings or senses – to borrow a simile, like barnacles on a ship's hull. In these other senses of 'gender', gender is quite different from sex. The resulting *sex/gender distinction* is often held to be of great importance; as a textbook on feminist philosophy says, the 'distinction between sex and gender has been fundamental to the development of feminist thought, including feminist philosophy, since the late 1960s.'[6] And, outside the academy, it is common to hear the complaint that the authorities have written 'gender' when they should have written 'sex', or vice versa. Even comedians need to speak properly: Chappelle should have used 'sex', not 'gender'. *#SexNotGender* is a popular Twitter hashtag.

However, to use 'gender' with any of these *other* senses is worse than pointless, producing nothing but bamboozlement. *#Sex=Gender*. Or so this chapter will argue.

What are these alternative senses of 'gender'? There are four: gender as *femininity/masculinity*, gender as *sex-typed social roles*, gender as *identity*, and gender as *woman/man*. The first order of business is to explain why these should all be deprecated. When we're done with that, the havoc wreaked by 'gender' will be easier to see.[7]

Gender as femininity/masculinity

Our first alternative, gender as *femininity/masculinity*, is due to the US psychiatrist Robert Stoller. Unlike many drawn to the study of sexuality, Stoller appears to have had conventional tastes in sex. His tastes in wine may have been more adventurous. As Richard Green – another sexology pioneer – recounts, Stoller was 'very wealthy, living on a multi-acre secluded estate, with a stable, a pool, a wine cellar and live-in servants'. He was not without a sense of humour: the title of one of his papers about sex reassignment surgery is 'Near Miss'.[8]

Stoller's immensely influential 1968 book, *Sex and Gender*, distinguished its titular phenomena thus:

> *Gender* is a term that has psychological or cultural rather than biological connotations. If the proper terms for sex are 'male' and 'female,' the corresponding terms for gender are 'masculine' and 'feminine'; these latter may be quite independent of (biological) sex. *Gender is the amount of masculinity or femininity found in a person*, and, obviously, while there are mixtures of both in many humans, the normal male has a preponderance of masculinity and the normal female a preponderance of femininity.[9]

What does it take to have, say, a 'preponderance of femininity'? Stoller's young patient whose 'behavior, dress, social and sexual desires, and fantasies' are 'indistinguishable ... from other girls in Southern California' is an example. She is, he writes, 'quite unremarkably feminine'.[10]

Feminists in the 1970s seized on Stoller's distinction. His influence extended to the former US Supreme Court Justice Antonin Scalia, not a man known for his feminist sympathies: 'The word "gender" has acquired the new and useful connotation of cultural or attitudinal characteristics (as opposed to physical characteristics) distinctive to the sexes. That is to say, gender is to sex as feminine is to female and masculine is to male.'

Feminists tended to build in an anti-biological component to Stoller's conception of gender. They assumed that femininity and masculinity are not (even partly) the result of biological differences between the sexes but, instead, are imposed by society. As one feminist philosopher put it, gender 'pertains to the *socio-cultural constructs* of femininity and masculinity, comprising certain psychological traits, and certain modes of dress, grooming, language use, and bodily comportment, among other things.' This prejudges a complex empirical issue about the role of biology. (We'll touch on this later in this chapter, and in more detail in chapter 7.)[11]

Should we follow Stoller's recommendation to use 'gender' for 'the amount of masculinity or femininity found in a person'? There is certainly an important difference between sex (female and male) and feminine or masculine characteristics. Although feminine characteristics are more prevalent among females, and masculine characteristics are more prevalent among males, females can have masculine characteristics and males can have feminine ones. In fact, females can be pretty much as masculine as you like, and similarly for males and femininity. This is not a recent discovery. For example, the Roman writer Seneca the elder was not impressed with young men 'curling the hair, lightening the voice to the caressing sounds of a woman, competing with women in physical delicacy, and adorning themselves with filthy elegance'.[12] There has never been a general confusion or conflation of being female with being feminine or a failure to notice that the two do not always go together.

Why introduce a special piece of terminology, since we already have 'feminine' and 'masculine'? Admittedly there is no word that stands to 'feminine' and 'masculine' as 'sex' stands to 'female' and 'male', but there is no pressing need for one. More importantly, 'gender' is a positively misleading choice.

'Gender' derives from words meaning *type* or *kind* (e.g., the Latin 'genus'); hence the (ubiquitous) question 'What is your gender?' 'Gender' does not take degree modifiers such as 'more' and 'less'. One can, however, be more or less feminine (or masculine), as Stoller himself emphasizes. And, to complicate things further, a person can be masculine in some respects and feminine in others. Celebrities provide an endless supply of masculine–feminine blends of 'certain modes of dress, grooming, language use, and bodily comportment' – for instance the football (soccer) legend David Beckham, once dubbed 'the biggest metrosexual in Britain'.[13]

At one point, beguiled by his own neologism, Stoller writes of 'two resultant genders [corresponding to two sexes], masculine and feminine', but it is entirely unhelpful to think of people as being simply one or the other.[14] (Precisely because *grammatical* gender does not come in degrees, the word 'gender' is useful here.)

After introducing the unhappy terminology of 'gender' to stand for 'the amount of masculinity or femininity found in a person', Stoller scarcely uses it this way in the rest of *Sex and Gender*. Subsequent appearances of 'gender' in that book are mostly in the phrase 'gender identity'. As Stoller's own practice illustrates, if one wants to talk about mixtures of femininity and masculinity, the word 'gender' is best avoided.

Gender as social roles

Stoller's book left its mark on another: *Sex, Gender, and Society*, by Ann Oakley, published in 1972. Oakely was then a sociology PhD student at the University of London and dashed off her book in six weeks during the holidays. 'I still have my notes on Robert Stoller's remarkable *Sex and Gender*', Oakley said more than forty years later. Our second sense of 'gender' – gender as *sex-typed social roles* – can be traced to *Sex, Gender, and Society*.[15]

In the introduction, Oakley reproduces Stoller's account, pointing to:

> ... a crucial distinction it is necessary to make in our thinking about male and female roles – the distinction between 'sex' and 'gender'. 'Sex' is a word that refers to the biological differences between male and female: the visible difference in genitalia, the related difference in procreative function. 'Gender' however is a matter of culture: it refers to the social classification into 'masculine' and 'feminine'.[16]

Stoller's remark that masculinity and femininity are 'found in a person' shows he is thinking primarily of personality and attitudes (and consequent behaviour). But, as Oakley notes, occupations can also be masculine or feminine: 'One basic occupation in particular [the person in a household who is mainly responsible for the domestic duties] is exclusively feminine.' Oakley extends the 'gender' terminology to cover occupations or, more broadly, sex-typed social roles. To be responsible for the domestic duties is to occupy what she calls a *gender role*, a social role associated with a particular sex. The strength of the association may vary: male homemakers were rare birds in the 1970s, less so today. And, in addition to occupations (paid and unpaid), hobbies or pastimes are often sex-typed to some degree: for instance, scrapbooking and reading the *Fifty Shades* novels are feminine, while barbecuing and playing *Grand Theft Auto* are masculine. These can also be included as gender roles.[17]

Gender is sometimes explicitly equated with gender roles, as in this passage from a textbook on feminist philosophy, explaining the 'distinction between sex and *gender*': 'Traditionally, feminists have distinguished the *biological* categories of male and female sex from the *social* categories of men's and women's *gender roles* ... [i.e.,] the social roles of men and women ...' The chief example given of a gender role is 'primary caregiver'. The historian Gerda Lerner's 1986 feminist classic *The Creation of Patriarchy* has something similar: 'Gender is a set of cultural roles. It is a costume, a mask, a straitjacket in which men and women dance their unequal dance.' More frequently, gender is explained as a combination of femininity/masculinity and gender roles: 'Gender includes psychological qualities, intellectual traits, *social roles*, grooming styles, and other modes of self-presentation.'[18]

There is an important difference between sex and gender roles – social roles associated, in varying degrees, with females and males. As with gender in Stoller's sense, the distinction between sex and gender roles is not news. For instance, the Greek philosopher Plato (fourth century BC) asked in the *Republic* 'whether female human nature can share all the tasks of that of the male, or none of them, or some but not others.' His progressive answer was that females should perform these tasks, including the 'waging of war', although 'the lighter parts must be assigned to them because of the weakness of their sex.'[19]

'Gender role' is a handy piece of terminology, but the phrase does not involve a special sense of 'gender': here 'gender' simply means *sex*. Sociologists and anthropologists used to use 'sex roles' instead of 'gender roles'. The index entry for 'Gender role' in a work of sociology published in 1970 is: '*See* Sex role.'[20] Subsequently that switched

– gender roles are sex roles rebranded, just as the gender pay gap is the sex pay gap.

1975 saw the first issue of *Sex Roles*, a journal 'devoted to publishing both empirically based and theoretical articles that are relevant to sex-role socialization and change in both children and adults.' By the 1990s the journal required authors to use 'gender' and 'gender roles' instead of 'sex' and 'sex roles', but the publisher resisted attempts to change the title.[21] If you want to talk about sex-typed occupations, tasks and pastimes, 'gender role' is a good choice. It's even better than 'sex role', because that might suggest sexual positions – bottoms and tops and all that. But using the single word 'gender' to encompass gender roles is entirely unhelpful.

Gender as *femininity/masculinity* and gender as *social roles* are often given a 'normative' cast. That is, feminine attitudes and behaviours are understood as those that females *should* have, according to prevailing social values. Similarly with social roles: a female gender role, say *primary caregiver*, is not only a social role that females tend to occupy but one that they *should* occupy. We can call this twist on gender as *femininity/masculinity* and gender as *social roles*, gender as *norms*. Here's an example: 'As it is conceived ordinarily, sex is thought of as a set of fixed biological characteristics, whereas gender is construed as a set of variable *social norms* about the proper behavior of sexed individuals.'[22]

Since it's vital to distinguish between characteristics that females *typically have* and characteristics that societies deem females *should have*, mixing in norms or social rules to some definitions of 'gender' just multiplies misunderstandings. This can easily be avoided by reserving 'femininity/masculinity' and 'gender role' for neutral descriptive purposes. When societies' rules or expectations are the topic, the phrases 'norms of femininity/masculinity' and 'gender role norms' can be used.

Notice that gender as *norms* is primarily a feature of societies, not individual people. On the gender as *norms* conception, there is no obvious sense in asking 'What is your gender?' Here's an example from an article by five psychologists, to which we'll return at the end of this chapter: 'The term *gender* is used here to refer to sociocultural systems that include norms and expectations for males and females …'.

Two down, two to go. Next up: the use of 'gender' to mean *gender identity*.

Gender as identity

John Money became notorious for his role in the John/Joan case: a baby boy who had lost his penis in an overly enthusiastic circumcision in the late 1960s was raised as a girl on Money's advice. As sensationally recounted in John Colapinto's 2000 book, *As Nature Made Him: The Boy Who Was Raised as a Girl*, the experiment had an awful ending. (More on this in chapter 5.)

Born in 1921 in New Zealand, Money spent most of his career at John Hopkins University in Baltimore in the field of paediatric psychoendocrinology, the study of the relation between hormones and children's psychology and behaviour. The intimidating word 'psychoendocrinology' sounds like one of his inventions, although Money was not the first to use it. He was a prolific neologiser, coining 'acrotomophilia' (sexual attraction to amputees) and the sadly underused 'spookological' (occult, mystical), as well as a menagerie of others, such as 'troopbondance' (group allegiance), that deservedly did not catch on. The replacement in psychiatry of Freud's 'perversion' by the neutral 'paraphilia' (an unusual sexual interest) can be credited to Money. He once suggested that his research field be called 'fuckology', and happily that has been immortalized as the title of a book on his work. Money was a sexual libertarian and practised what he preached, organizing sex parties at conferences. (Philosophy conferences are more staid affairs.)[23]

Money introduced the phrase 'gender role' in a 1955 article published in the *Bulletin of the Johns Hopkins Hospital*. He was reporting research on 'hermaphroditic patients', who had 'an atypical mixture of male and female elements in the reproductive system'. By 'gender role', Money did not mean *sex-typed social role*, our second sense of 'gender'. Rather, he meant 'all those things that a person says or does to disclose himself or herself as having the status of a boy or man, girl or woman, respectively. It includes, but is not restricted to, sexuality in the sense of eroticism.' Later in the *Bulletin* article, 'gender' appears briefly detached from 'role': '… an hermaphroditic person's gender – his or her outlook, demeanor, and orientation.' Here Money basically identifies gender with what was sometimes called *psychological sex*, the sex of the mind as opposed to the sex of the body. Being psychologically female or psychologically male is very close to having – on some conceptions – a female or male gender identity. So, we can find in Money's 1955 article the use of 'gender' to mean *gender identity*.[24]

Despite his neologistic fecundity, Money is not responsible for the phrase 'gender identity'. That innovation is due to Robert Stoller and Ralph Greenson, his colleague at the University of California, Los Angeles (UCLA). (Greenson was Marilyn Monroe's psychiatrist; he discovered her body after the actress fatally overdosed in 1962.) 'Gender identity' first appears in papers Stoller and Greenson gave at the 23rd International Psycho-Analytic Congress in Stockholm in 1963.[25] During that period, psychoanalysis was still going strong in North American academic psychiatry; its terminal decline would begin in the 1970s.

Stoller's and Greenson's contributions were published in 1964, the year that President Lyndon B. Johnson signed the Civil Rights Act. Title VII of the CRA prohibited sex-based employment discrimination. The two psychiatrists could not have imagined that their psycho-analytical jargon would collide, more than fifty years later, with one of the greatest pieces of civil rights legislation in US history. The Equality Act proposes replacing all occurrences of 'sex' in the CRA with 'sex (including sexual orientation and gender identity)'.[26] The EA passed the House of Representatives in 2021 and at the time of writing is under consideration by the Senate.

Here's how Stoller defined 'gender identity': 'Gender identity is the sense of knowing to which sex one belongs, that is, the awareness "I am a male" or "I am a female".' Contemporary ideas about gender identity are much more obscure than this quotation suggests (extensive discussion will be postponed to chapter 5). Notice that Stoller could equally well have used the phrase 'sex identity' or 'sexual identity' (if the latter hadn't been taken for sexual orientation). In fact, 'sexual identity' *was* occasionally used instead of 'gender identity', as in the title of a 1974 book by the sexologist Richard Green: *Sexual Identity Conflict in Children and Adults*. And a well-known textbook says, 'it would be more appropriate to call it *sex identity*.'[27]

As we have seen, Stoller's preferred notion of gender was *femininity/masculinity*; he did not use 'gender' to refer to gender identity. But, if Stoller had taken a hint from Money's use of 'gender' in 1955, he could have.

As the gender studies academic Judith Butler remarked in 2004, 'gender now also means gender identity, a particularly salient issue in the politics and theory of transgenderism and transsexuality.' Gender as *identity* is apparent when the term 'cisgender' is defined as applying to people whose 'gender "matches" with the sex assigned at birth'. Here 'gender' means *gender identity.*[28]

Using 'gender' in this way is even less advisable than using it to mean *femininity/masculinity* or *sex-typed social roles*. Given that 'gender' has a common interpretation as *sex*, if someone says 'My gender is female' that could either mean *My sex is female* or *I have a female gender identity.* Unless the aim is to obfuscate, it is crucial to keep sex and gender identity apart. Greenson and Stoller have bequeathed to us a compact phrase for – as Greenson put it – 'one's sense of being a member of a particular sex'.[29] There is no reason at all to shorten it to 'gender'.

Gender as woman/man

Having dispatched gender as *femininity/masculinity*, gender as *social roles*, and gender as *identity*, there is one more to go. Like gender as *social roles*, this fourth sense of 'gender' can be traced to Ann Oakley's 1972 *Sex, Gender, and Society.*

Here is the opening of Oakley's sixth chapter, 'Sex and gender':

> 'Sex' is a biological term: 'gender' a psychological and cultural one. Common sense suggests that they are merely two ways of looking at the same division and that someone who belongs to, say, the female sex will automatically belong to the corresponding (feminine) gender. In reality this is not so. *To be a man or a woman, a boy or a girl, is as much a function of dress, gesture, occupation, social network and personality, as it is of possessing a particular set of genitals.*[30]

Why introduce the terminology of 'gender' to pick out the categories *woman* and *man* when 'sex' is already doing a fine job?[31] Simone de Beauvoir's 1949 book *The Second Sex* is all about women, and she didn't choose a misleading title. Surely there's not much of a distinction between being a woman and being a member of the 'second sex', namely female? Admittedly female babies aren't women, and neither are female lions, but any dictionary will tell you that the missing ingredients are *adult* and *human*. A woman is an adult female (that's why female babies aren't women) and a human female (that's why lionesses aren't women). If that is right, then Oakley is wrong: to be a woman is *not* 'a function of dress, gesture, occupation', and the rest. If an adult female human being is a plaid-shirt-wearing, manly, wood-chopping lumberjack, that doesn't make her a man – she's still a woman, albeit a woman who is masculine in many respects.

Be that as it may, the remarkable fact is that the view suggested by Oakley is orthodoxy among feminist theorists, both in philosophy and in gender studies. According to them, being a woman transcends biology: women are not (or are not only) the adult females of our species. More specifically, there is a social ingredient to being a woman, just as there is a social ingredient to being a princess, a widow, or an actress. Someone can be a princess only if she is a member of a royal family, which in turn requires complex social hierarchies. Someone can be a widow only if she once participated in the social institution of marriage. And someone can be an actress only if her society goes in for the dramatic arts. In contrast, adult females of our species can be found – at least in principle – living alone on desert islands with no social status of any sort, past or present; women, according to orthodoxy, cannot.[32]

On this view, the categories *woman* and *man* are *social* categories: being a woman or a man depends (in part) on social factors, just as being a princess depends on social factors.[33] Despite the title of her book, Simone de Beauvoir is often supposed to have been the first to recognize this profound truth. Judith Butler interprets her that way:

> If being a woman is one cultural interpretation of being female, and if that interpretation is in no way necessitated by being female, then it appears that the female body is the arbitrary locus of the gender 'woman', and there is no reason to preclude the possibility of that body becoming the locus of other constructions of gender. At its limit, then, the sex/gender distinction … [has] the consequence that 'being' female and 'being' a woman are two very different sorts of being. This last insight, I would suggest, is the distinguished contribution of Simone de Beauvoir's formulation, 'one is not born, but rather becomes, a woman'.[34]

And here's the historian and gender studies academic Susan Stryker, explaining what gender is in her book *Transgender History*:

> Gender is not the same as sex, although the two terms are often used interchangeably, even in technical or scholarly literature, creating a great deal of confusion. Gender is generally considered to be cultural, and sex, biological (although contemporary theories posit sex as a cultural category as well). The words 'man' and 'woman' refer to gender. No one is born a woman or man – rather, as the saying goes, 'one becomes one' through a complex process of socialization.[35]

Stryker, following many other authors, gives no hint that this position is at all controversial. Reading the literature, one gets the impression that Simone de Beauvoir discovered that 'a complex process of socialization' is required for becoming a woman, much as Nettie Stevens and others discovered sex chromosomes.[36] Relitigating established discoveries is usually a waste of time: we need to accept the facts and move on. Chapter 4 will examine whether Beauvoir discovered any such thing. But, whether she did, the view that *woman* and *man* are social categories has escaped the gender studies lab and spread into the wild.

Virginia Prince was a notable American heterosexual (natal male) cross-dresser and founder of *Transvestia* magazine, 'published by, for and about Transvestites'.[37] In 1997 Prince wrote:

> The sex words both for humans and for animals are 'male' and 'female', referring to the fact that the former make sperm cells and the latter make egg cells. The gender words are 'girl' and 'woman', 'boy' and 'man', referring to the social roles that egg makers and sperm makers generally play.[38]

For something more up to date, consider this passage from the 2015 bestseller *Sapiens: A Brief History of Humankind*, by the historian Yuval Noah Harari:

> Biologically, humans are divided into males and females. A male *Homo sapiens* is one who has one X chromosome and one Y chromosome; a female *Homo sapiens* has two Xs. But 'man' and 'woman' name social, not biological, categories. While in the great majority of cases in most human societies men

> are males and women are females, the social terms carry a lot of baggage that has only a tenuous, if any, relationship to the biological terms.[39]

Harari agrees that women and (adult human) females coincide in 'the great majority of cases'; nevertheless – as Butler says – the female body may be 'the locus of other constructions of gender'. Another contemporary example is from the trans activist Shon Faye's book *The Transgender Issue*: 'a point that feminists have largely agreed upon: the idea that being a woman is defined by *political* experience, how you are treated by others, especially those with power over you.'

Once we have agreed that being a woman and being an adult female of our species can come apart, and we have decided to use 'gender' to label the categories *woman* and *man*, the next question is, why only two? Since *girl* and *boy* are presumably social categories if *woman* and *man* are (as Prince assumes), the total should be at least four. But, even restricting attention to adults, there should be more than two genders – Butler's 'other constructions'. It is implausible that 'complex processes of socialization', or 'social roles, positions, behavior, self-ascription', would cleave into exactly two kinds, one lining up with *woman* and the other with *man*.[40]

What would these other genders look like? Luckily, these days we are presented with actual examples. Although the never-ending list of genders on the blogging website Tumblr – 'Genderblank: a gender that can only be described as a blank space' – can be taken with a pinch of salt, feminist philosophers typically regard the more familiar examples – genderqueer, pangender, agender – with the utmost earnestness. Gender as *woman/man*, which is now the standard conception of gender in philosophy, should therefore be understood as leaving space for alternatives beyond the 'binary' of *woman/man*. More accurately, it's gender as *woman/man/genderqueer/pangender/...*, but let's stick with the simpler formulation.

Appropriating 'gender' to label *woman*, *man*, and perhaps other categories such as *genderqueer* runs into the problem noted earlier for gender as *identity*. Since 'gender' is often used to mean *sex*, the question 'What is your gender?' now becomes confusingly ambiguous. On one interpretation, it is asking for your sex; on another, it is asking for something quite different, concerning what 'complex processes of socialization' you have undergone, your 'social roles, positions, behavior, self-ascription', and the like.

There is another problem, this time fatal. With gender as *femininity/masculinity*, gender as *social roles*, and gender as *identity*, at least there is something that should be *distinguished* from sex. Neither being feminine, nor occupying female-typical social roles, nor having a female gender identity are *the same* as being female. Females don't have to be feminine, males can do the housework and have female gender identities, and so on. These are three versions of the so-called sex/gender distinction that are both genuine and important. With respect to the three versions, this chapter is simply making a *terminological* point: using the word 'gender' to label either *femininity/masculinity*, *sex-typed social roles*, or *gender identity* is a bad idea if we seek clarity and understanding.

However, in the case of pairs such as *woman* and *(adult human) female*, the problem is entirely different. Chapter 4 will argue that these categories *are* the same, and therefore there is no distinction in need of labelling.

Gender as sex

In common parlance 'gender' means *sex* (i.e., *female or male*), and adding other meanings only makes communication harder. What goes for ordinary talk goes for academic writing too. A *Scientific American* article, 'How is the gender of some reptiles determined by temperature?', is not about reptilian psychology or grooming styles. An article in the journal *Sexual Development* about 'bending genders' in fish is not about piscine masculinity or femininity but about how fish of many species change sex during the life cycle. The Harvard biologist David Haig has documented how 'gender' has supplanted 'sex' in academic writing since Money's use of it in 1955:

> The most important factor was the adoption of 'gender' in the 1970s by feminist scholars as a way of distinguishing 'socially constructed' aspects of male–female differences (gender) from 'biologically determined' aspects (sex). This distinction is now only fitfully respected, and 'gender' is often used as a simple synonym of 'sex'.[41]

Back in 1968, Stoller noted that '*sex* and *gender* seem to common sense to be practically synonymous.'[42] To insist that 'gender' bear some other meaning is either to fruitlessly attempt to turn back the linguistic tide or else to press on regardless of the ambiguity, kicking up dust and then complaining about the view.

This is not a trivial grammatical issue, such as 'which' versus 'that' or whether sentences can be ended with prepositions. 'Gender' is everywhere, from the law to medicine, and misunderstandings can have serious consequences. Muddleheaded ways of using the word can usually be traced to academics, who have managed to confuse themselves even more than they have confused the rest of us. You can avoid the weeds by skipping ahead to the next chapter, but for those who would like some examples, here are two particularly interesting ones.

Judith Butler on gender and performativity

Judith Butler's most famous book is *Gender Trouble: Feminism and the Subversion of Identity*, published in 1990. Its influence outside the academy has been immense. No doubt only some in the educated elite can recite chapter and verse, but they may be the ones running your schools and writing your laws.

What is *Gender Trouble*'s central topic? What is this 'gender' that produces so much trouble? We have already seen Butler saying that 'the female body is the arbitrary locus of the gender "woman"' – here the relevant notion is gender as *woman/man*. And that is what she has in mind on the second page of the Preface to *Gender Trouble*. Right after mentioning a 'very binary frame for thinking about gender', she writes:

> I asked, what configuration of power constructs the subject and the Other, that binary relation between 'men' and 'women,' and the internal stability of those terms? What restriction is here at work? Are those terms untroubling only to the extent that they conform to a heterosexual matrix for conceptualizing gender and desire? What happens to the subject and to the stability of gender categories when the epistemic regime of presumptive heterosexuality is unmasked as that which produces and reifies these ostensible categories of ontology?[43]

This gives a fuller taste of Butler's prose style than the previous short quotations. Without worrying about the precise content of this passage, clearly *man* and *woman* are what she calls 'gender categories'. However, in the later preface to the 1999 edition, Butler reflected:

> I sought to counter those views that made presumptions about the limits and propriety of gender and restricted the meaning of gender to received notions of masculinity and femininity. It was and remains my view that any feminist theory that restricts the meaning of gender in the presuppositions of its own practice sets up exclusionary gender norms within feminism, often with homophobic consequences.[44]

Here she has in mind gender as *femininity/masculinity*, quite different from gender as *woman/man*.[45]

Unclarity about the pertinent sense of 'gender' is not the only problem with Butler's work. A frequent complaint is that her prose is convoluted and clogged with unnecessary and obscure words, but this is a relatively minor issue. Bad writing, although not to be admired, is sometimes excusable. Some ideas are genuinely difficult, and their initial formulation may be suboptimal – the first glimpse of the truth may be, like Mount McKinley on most days, obscured by clouds. What's more, great thinking is no guarantee of great writing. For both these reasons, the great thinker's interpreters and commentators may put her insights much better than she did.

However, Butler's claims, to the extent they are intelligible, are not backed by any serious argument or evidence. Neither do they offer promising conjectures or hypotheses for future research, or even new ways of seeing or categorizing old truths. The best way of checking whether this is right is to read books and articles that attempt to explain Butler's ideas.[46]

Martha Nussbaum is one of the most eminent contemporary philosophers and a contributor to feminist philosophy, among many other areas. She once observed that Butler's way of writing belongs to the 'traditions of sophistry and rhetoric' rather than philosophy. Butler does have a PhD in philosophy (from Yale), but her background is in what is sometimes (rather confusingly) called the *continental* school. Philosophers in this school's canon tend to be unduly revered, which can produce sloppy standards. The rival *analytic* school, dominant in the leading Anglosphere philosophy departments, has a healthier disrespect for the major figures in the field. Still, even in analytic feminist philosophy, Butler is treated with arms-length admiration, as someone with deep insights, despite her often incomprehensible methodology – a kind of quantum field theorist of gender.[47]

Butler's best-known idea is that gender is 'performative', by which she means that:

> … gender is in no way a stable identity or locus of agency from which various acts proceed; rather, it is an identity tenuously constituted in time – an identity instituted through a *stylized repetition of acts* … the body becomes its gender through a series of acts which are renewed, revised, and consolidated through time.[48]

What does 'gender' mean in this quotation? Just before, Butler mentions the well-worn line from Beauvoir's *The Second Sex*, 'One is not born, but rather becomes, a woman', so presumably gender as *woman/man* is the pertinent kind. Butler is saying, then, that someone becomes a woman 'through a series of acts which are renewed, revised, and consolidated through time'. Being a woman or a man is '*a corporeal style*, an "act", as it were, which is both intentional and performative'.[49] This sounds incredible on its face. Even without looking at other cultures, there is plainly no 'corporeal style' common to all women, who can act however they please without ceasing to become women.

Incredible though Butler's view may be, she does give a reason for it, using the actor and drag queen Divine in the John Waters movie *Female Trouble*,

> … whose impersonation of women implicitly suggests that gender is a kind of persistent impersonation that passes as the real. Her/his performance destabilizes the very distinctions between the natural and the artificial, depth and surface, inner and outer through which discourse about genders almost always operates. Is drag the imitation of gender, or does it dramatize the signifying gestures through which gender itself is established? Does being female constitute a 'natural fact' or a cultural performance, or is 'naturalness' constituted through discursively constrained performative acts that produce the body through and within the categories of sex?[50]

(A series of unsettling questions rather than statements is another characteristic feature of Butler's prose.)[51] Since Divine (the actor Glenn Milstead) did not disguise the fact that he was male, we can be sure that Butler's 'her/his' was not an early attempt to respect someone's pronouns. Rather, the uncertainty-inducing slash reinforces the rhetorical impression that there is not much difference between impersonating a woman and actually being a woman or between impersonating a female and actually being female. Notice also that Butler seems to be using 'gender' in this quotation indifferently between gender as *woman/man* and gender as *sex*.

In any case, does Divine's impersonation 'implicitly suggest' that being a woman is a 'corporeal style', a matter of repetitively acting in certain ways? Of course not. The mime artist Marcel Marceau famously imitated the actions of a man trapped in a box, moving his hands along the imaginary sides. Marceau played the part more convincingly than a man trapped in a real box, who would probably curl up in a ball sobbing. That does not suggest that really being trapped in a box is 'a kind of persistent impersonation' or 'cultural performance', or anything of the sort.

A less hopeless idea is that gender as *femininity/masculinity* is 'instituted through a stylized repetition of acts'. This is implied by passages such as the following: 'That gender reality is created through sustained social performances means that the very notions of an essential sex and a true or abiding masculinity or femininity are also constituted as part of the strategy that conceals gender's performative character.' Ignore the bit about 'essential sex' (that's for the next chapter). Here Butler is saying that our 'sustained social performances' of femininity and masculinity give a misleading impression: they 'create the effect of the natural, the original, and the inevitable', but femininity and masculinity are thoroughly artificial, culture-bound, and avoidable. As she puts it in a later book, *Undoing Gender*: 'Terms such as "masculine" and "feminine" are notoriously changeable; there are social histories for each term; their meanings change radically depending upon geopolitical boundaries and cultural constraints on who is imagining whom, and for what purpose.' A tincture of travel or history shows that feminine and masculine behaviour, dress, attitudes, and so on, are not the same in every place and at every time. Wearing earrings, for instance, is a practice that goes back thousands of years; sometimes feminine, sometimes masculine, sometimes neither. Are femininity and masculinity in general as culturally contingent as wearing earrings?[52]

Butler appears to think so, and this comes out particularly clearly in another discussion of drag queens later in *Gender Trouble*: '*In imitating gender, drag implicitly reveals the imitative structure of gender itself – as well as its contingency*.'[53] In *Undoing Gender* she recalls evenings 'at the gay bar, which occasionally became a drag bar':

> I ... experienced in that moment a certain implicit theorization of gender: it quickly dawned on me that some of these so-called men could do femininity much better than I ever could, ever wanted to, ever would. And so I was confronted by what can only be called the transferability of the attribute.[54]

The example of drag is ironic, because it illustrates how femininity and masculinity *are* 'true and abiding', at least to an important extent. Indeed, in the above quotation, Butler herself recognizes that she just doesn't have femininity in her. Gay men the world over are similar on a range of characteristics. As children they tend to exhibit cross-gender behaviour, with female-typical play styles, a preference for female-typical toys and for playing with girls. As adults they are more likely than straight men to have careers in arts and entertainment. Cross-dressing in gay culture is not exclusively a Western phenomenon, and neither is it recent or a Western import. Earlier we saw the elder Seneca complaining about feminine men in ancient Rome. And the sociologist Fred Whitam observed:

> Male homosexual subcultures produce remarkably similar entertainment forms, such as female impersonation shows. While many social scientists assume that such behaviour results from cultural transmission, these behaviours seem to appear spontaneously, predictably, and indigenously in different societies. Philippine homosexual men, except perhaps for the very wealthy, do not know that drag shows exist in the United States. American homosexual men do not know that Thais are performing female impersonation shows in the nightclubs of the resort town of Pattaya.[55]

The drag queen is not merely imitating femininity, as Dustin Hoffman did in the movie *Tootsie*.[56] Rather, the drag queen is expressing his own femininity, which he may have despite his culture's attempt to beat it out of him.

Psychologists against the gender binary

The brain-melting protean powers of 'gender' are not confined to philosophy and gender studies. In 2018 an article appeared in the academic journal *American Psychologist*: 'The future of sex and gender in psychology: five challenges to the gender binary'. The lead author was the distinguished psychologist Janet Shibley Hyde, known for her defence of the *gender similarities hypothesis*, that 'males and females are similar on most, but not all, psychological variables.'[57] The word 'gender' in the phrase 'the gender similarities hypothesis' means *sex*. What does it mean in 'the gender binary', as it occurs in the title of the *American Psychologist* article?

The article's abstract is quite clear: the gender binary is the view that 'humans comprise only two types of beings, women and men.' Since the phrase 'females or males' is later substituted for 'women and men', the word 'gender' is being used to mean either *woman/man* or *sex*. Hyde and her four co-authors, then, are going to give five lines of evidence against the view that every (adult) human being comes in one of two types, *woman* and *man*, or *female* and *male*. That is certainly interesting. It also is rather odd, because if there are some adult humans who are neither women nor men, or neither female nor male, why would *psychologists* have been the ones to discover them? Wouldn't biologists or medical practitioners be better qualified?

However, it soon becomes apparent that the article is not going to deliver as advertised, when on the second page the authors explain what they mean by 'gender': 'The term *gender* is used here to refer to sociocultural systems that include norms and expectations for males and females, which vary as a function of intersections with other factors ... as well as psychological processes such as identity, femininity, masculinity, and gender-conformity and nonconformity.' The pertinent sense of 'gender' is not, after all, *woman/man* or *female/male* but a mishmash of *gender norms* (features of 'sociocultural systems'), *femininity/masculinity*, and *gender identity*, the latter two being features of persons, not societies. The authors also say: 'In this article, the term *gender/sex* is frequently used, to recognize that the biological and the sociocultural are typically inseparable.' That makes as little sense as using the term 'poverty/health' to recognize that the medical and the socioeconomic are interconnected in complex ways. Science is all about distinguishing various explanatory factors, not lumping them together. And what does 'gender/sex' *mean*? The authors never adequately explain it.[58]

The 'gender/sex' terminology is on display in the first of the 'five challenges to the gender binary'. Various brain regions are measurably different between (human) females and males – in volume and connectivity, for example. We can then take someone's brain and classify a particular region as female-typical if it has the form more common in females or male-typical if it has the form more common in males. The relevant finding is this: females usually don't have brain regions that are all female-typical and males usually don't have brain regions that are all male-typical. That is simply a discovery about sex differences in brain structure. Whether it has any larger significance is unclear; it has nothing to do with the promise in the abstract to show that there are some non-men and non-women. The authors sum up – sexily but unhelpfully by saying that 'most brains are gender/sex mosaics.'[59]

That was the 'challenge from neuroscience' to the gender binary. The second is the 'challenge from behavioral neuroendocrinology': 'Androgens and estrogens are not two distinct sets of sex hormones – one set for women and one set for men – but rather hormones that are found in all humans. That is, human bodies produce hormones like estradiol, testosterone, and progesterone regardless of gender/sex ....'[60] The assumption implicit in the last sentence is that particular people have a 'gender/sex'; however, the authors have not attached any sense to this way of speaking. What was meant could have been put much more straightforwardly: human bodies produce hormones such as estradiol *regardless of sex*.

The third challenge to the gender binary, from 'psychological research', is presented in an even more confounding fashion. Psychological research on 'gender/sex differences ... rests on an assumption that there are just two categories of people: females and males.'[61] Again, what was meant was *sex* differences, not 'gender/sex' differences, whatever those may be.

The implication is that the assumption of two categories is wrong. The third challenge is simply Hyde's gender similarities hypothesis, that the sexes are very similar psychologically. That hypothesis poses no threat at all to the idea that humans come in two types, *female* and *male*.

The fourth challenge is again from psychological research, this time on 'transgender and nonbinary individuals'. They are said to 'pose a direct challenge to the gender binary' because they demonstrate that 'sex assignment at birth does not invariably predict individuals' felt gender identity.'[62] Psychology, we are told at the beginning of the article, takes 'the gender binary' for granted. Since the existence of transgender people is said to be incompatible with the gender binary, past psychologists must have unthinkingly assumed that transgender people did not exist. They made no such assumption.

The fifth and final challenge is from 'developmental psychology'. The idea is that various social practices 'causally contribute to children's tendency to categorize the self and others into the categories of male and female, and develop gender/sex stereotypes and prejudices.'[63] How could that possibly show that some human beings aren't in fact either female or male?

This is not to say that the research reported in the article is unimportant – although lots of it is contested. What seems to have happened is that the unfashionable 'gender binary' was deemed a timely target, and the diverse research programmes of the five authors were artificially pressed into service to undermine it. At the end of the article the gender binary is retrofitted to make the five challenges relevant. The gender binary isn't, after all, the view stated in the abstract: 'humans comprise only two types of beings, women and men.' Rather, it's the view that there are two sets of 'brain features, hormones, psychological characteristics and gender identity' that cleanly distinguish the women from the men. That is: certain gross features of a person's brain, their levels of hormones, their psychological characteristics, or their gender identity will tell you infallibly whether they are a woman or a man, female or male. If the authors meant to be correcting current thinking on this matter, they were pushing at an open door.[64]

In a telling footnote, the authors report that, 'as is true of the field of gender/sex research, we – as a group – do not agree completely on the terminology used to refer to men and women (i.e. sex versus gender).'[65]

The article could have been an interesting report on a variety of sex differences instead of a convincing demonstration of how the word 'gender', unless used simply to mean *sex*, poisons everything it touches.

Dave Chappelle got it right: *#Sex=Gender*. We'll be following his lead for the rest of the book.

THREE

Clownfish and Chromosomes

I had reached the conclusion myself that sex was not a division but a continuum, that almost nobody was altogether of one sex or another, and that the infinite subtlety of the shading from one extreme to the other was one of the most beautiful of nature's phenomena.

Jan Morris, *Conundrum*[1]

Do we *truly* need a *true* sex?

Michel Foucault, *Herculine Barbin*[2]

Sex talk

Sex seems clear enough: there are two sexes, female and male, and – perhaps with some extremely rare exceptions – every human is either one or the other. Magnus Hirschfeld, a sexology pioneer whose Institute for Sexual Research in Berlin was ransacked by the Nazis in 1933, thought this naive. 'All human beings', Hirschfeld said, 'are intersexual variants.' Harry Benjamin (who had known Hirschfeld in Berlin) was another major figure in sexology and the author of *The Transsexual Phenomenon* (1966), the first book on sex reassignment. Benjamin reproved 'the simple man in the street', who thought 'there are only two sexes.' 'Modern researches', he wrote, have produced 'more obscurity, more complexity. Instead of the conventional two sexes with their anatomical differences, there may be up to ten or more separate concepts and manifestations of sex.' Wacky views about sex are not uncommon among sexologists.[3]

You may remember the furore caused by the psychologist Jordan Peterson, back in 2016. He had posted a video to YouTube criticizing Bill C-16, then being considered by the Canadian Parliament. This legislation would amend the Canadian Human Rights Act and the Criminal Code by adding 'gender identity or expression' to the list of characteristics protected against discrimination and 'hate propaganda'. (C-16 was passed the following year.)[4] Peterson was concerned that this would make refusing to use someone's preferred pronouns illegal, amounting to compelled speech. In October of 2016 the current affairs show *The Agenda* examined the issue; guests included Peterson and Nicholas Matte, a University of Toronto lecturer in transgender studies.

Matte threw down the gauntlet early on, saying that 'it's not correct that there is such a thing as biological sex ... that's a very popular misconception', with the air of an expert setting everyone straight on the causes of global warming. Peterson replied, 'Well, I don't understand what the claim that there's no such thing as biological sex means ... Let's call it an error to suggest that there's some sort of scientific consensus about that.' This episode of *The Agenda* has been viewed on YouTube over 10 million times.[5]

Matte probably meant, not that sex is a complete fiction, but that it is socially or culturally 'constructed'. That is one of the better-known claims of Judith Butler's *Gender Trouble*: 'If the immutable character of sex is contested, perhaps this construct called "sex" is as culturally constructed as gender; indeed, perhaps it was always already gender, with the consequence that the distinction between sex and gender turns out to be no distinction at all.' This is a Butlerian 'perhaps' – she evidently agrees that sex is culturally constructed. We'll leave this knotty topic for the end of the chapter. Two other frequent claims about sex are easier to interpret – that sex is a 'spectrum' and that there are more than two sexes. The biologist and gender studies academic Anne Fausto-Sterling once argued in the *New York Times* that the number of sexes is 'at least five'. A related claim is that sex is not 'binary'. Before trying to sort all this out, let's start where the sex-sceptics never do, with basic biology.[6]

Sex in biology

The Greek philosopher Aristotle (fourth century BC) is famous for numerous contributions to logic, ethics, metaphysics (the study of what exists and how it all hangs together), psychology and rhetoric. Academic disciplines were not separated then as now, and Aristotle also wrote a lot about biology, including the sexes. Observing the animal kingdom, one natural hypothesis is that animals come in two varieties, females and males. The females are the ones who give birth or else produce eggs from which the offspring hatch. The males play a crucial role in this process, in many species at least: unless they eject something onto the eggs or inject something into the female, no babies get produced. As Aristotle put it, 'by a male animal we mean that which generates in another, and by a female that which generates in itself.'[7]

This division is correlated with animals' appearance and behaviour. Aristotle knew that the females are usually the ones who care for their young, and that fancy weapons are found on males, such as the cock's spurs or a stag's antlers. In insects, he observed, the males are generally smaller than the females. In humans it's the other way round, and Aristotle did note that the brains of men were on average larger than those of women.[8]

Although Aristotle thought that men should rule, this was not because their bigger brains better equipped them for politics: according to him, the brain was an organ for cooling the blood. He made some other mistakes, calling the queen bee the king. He denied that worker bees are female because, he thought, no females have defensive weaponry, yet the worker has a barbed stinger. He connected the sexes with heat: males are warmer than females, which explains why the brains of men are bigger. And in the *Generation of Animals* he infamously says that 'the female is as it were a mutilated male', a line which is actually not as bad as it seems. He simply meant that women and eunuchs (castrated or mutilated males) have some interesting similarities.[9]

For Aristotle, the division between female and male was of fundamental importance to an understanding of nature. For all he knew, though, the division is relatively superficial, like that between animals that fly and those that don't. Bats, birds, insects and even some fish can fly, but the biologists see multiplicity where the ordinary person might see uniformity. For example, bat wings and bird wings are different in many ways and evolved independently.

Aristotle may have gone beyond the available evidence, but he did get it right: sex is fundamental. In the nineteenth century, Darwin formulated his theory of sexual selection, on which competition for mates is an important driver of evolution.[10] Sexual selection explains Aristotle's observation that males are more often the ones with weaponry. (More on this in chapter 7.) Understanding evolution is impossible without bringing sex into the picture.

What is the principle that divides the sexes? For an answer, we should turn to biologists, not gender studies professors or philosophers. (Likewise, if you want to know what the nature of gold is, you should ask a chemist, not a financial historian.) However, in one of many ironies that attend academic discussions of sex and gender, the answer is right there in Simone de Beauvoir's *The Second Sex*: the sexes 'are basically defined by the gametes they produce.' Gametes are sex cells – sperm and eggs. More specifically, as the biologist Richard Dawkins explains in his 1976 classic *The Selfish Gene*: 'One group of individuals has large sex cells, and it is convenient to use the word "female" for them. The other group, which it is convenient to call "male", has small sex cells.' Or, as the biologist Joan Roughgarden puts it: 'To a biologist, *"male" means making small gametes*, and *"female" means making large gametes.* Period!'[11]

The quotation from Dawkins might sound as if the biologists are using 'female' and 'male' as ('convenient') technical terms, and that they could equally well have used 'male' for the individuals with large sex cells and 'female' for the individuals with small sex cells. But that isn't what Dawkins means. Much earlier on in *The Selfish Gene* he tells us that the female praying mantis has the habit of biting her mate's head off, using 'female' with its ordinary English meaning.[12] As it turns out, female praying mantises are the ones with large gametes, so the biologists do not need to make any linguistic stipulations. The account in terms of gametes should be thought of as a *discovery* about the nature of the sexes. We are familiar with the female–male division in everyday life but imperfectly understand it; scientists can set us straight.

Aristotle wrote about the sexes more than two millennia ago without knowing anything about gametes, just as he wrote about water without knowing anything about hydrogen and oxygen. Subsequently, biologists and chemists made discoveries about the very phenomena Aristotle wrote about: they discovered that males have small sex cells and that water contains hydrogen and oxygen. Aristotle was ignorant of the nature of water and had some wrong opinions about it (he thought it was an element). Many contemporary scientific issues concern topics completely foreign to Aristotle, such as protein folding, lithium-ion batteries, and gene splicing. He had no opinions, right or wrong, about those. But humans have thought and talked about water, and females and males, since civilization began.[13]

Gamete size is a simplified story of sex. Roughgarden tells us that the sperm of some fruit flies are twenty times longer than the bodies of the sperm-producing males.[14] The usual pattern of large eggs and tiny sperm is an effect of something deeper. The male contribution is merely to inject some genetic material into the egg, delivered in the most competitive way possible. Typically, the best strategy for males is to go for small and numerous sperm rather than big and few. The female contribution includes the genetic material together with various complicated bits of apparatus needed to manufacture an organism from the blueprint supplied by DNA. Hence there are female-only species, which reproduce by parthenogenesis. They not only have the blueprint but the materials and machinery needed to turn the genetic vision into reality. A parthenogenetic male-only species would never get off the drawing board.

The sheer diversity of females and males shows why the textbook account of sex has no serious rivals. Consider, for instance, the idea that the female–male division can be explained in terms of primary or secondary sex characteristics, such as a vagina or breasts, or behaviour such as giving birth. Evolution has equipped the sexes in different species with different ways of reproducing and producing and nourishing their young. These features are (imperfectly) correlated with sex; they are not sex itself. Only female mammals have breasts, and female humans are unique in having prominent ones when not nursing. Male seahorses get pregnant, and there are cave-dwelling insects in which the female has a penis and the male has a vagina, with sperm flowing in the reverse direction.[15]

Sex chromosomes are no better. The equation *female=XX* is confused for a reason having nothing to do with the occasional human female with (for example) three X chromosomes instead of two. Females of numerous species have either different sex chromosomes (as in birds) or else no sex chromosomes at all (as in alligators and some other reptiles). The XX/XY system is one of many *sex determination* systems. It is the mechanism by which placental mammals such as humans typically become female and male; other animals and plants use different means to achieve the same result.[16] Whenever someone says that being female or male is a matter of having certain chromosomes, that is a sure sign that the discussion has gone off the rails.

We can also see why speaking of the 'opposite sex' can be misleading. Producing large gametes is not opposed to producing small ones – an organism could produce both. And some do, like almost all flowering plants and some animals such as slugs. These are *hermaphrodites*, both female and male.[17] Strictly speaking, males are not the *opposite* sex – they are the *other* sex.

And the textbook account of sex makes another possibility apparent. If an organism went from being a large-gamete producer to a small-gamete producer, or vice versa, it would have changed sex. And, in fact, that possibility is a reality: a male-to-female sex-changing clownfish goes from being a small-gamete producer to a large-gamete producer, with testicular tissue degenerating and ovarian tissue developing. This ability to transform from one sex to the other – sequential hermaphroditism – is found in many other fish, although not in mammals or any other vertebrate.[18]

Roughgarden's pithy definition in terms of 'making' gametes should not be taken too literally. Females and males might not make gametes for a variety of reasons. A baby boy is male, although sperm production is far in his future, and a post-menopausal woman does not cease to be female simply because she no longer produces viable eggs.

Consider worker honeybees. Contrary to what Aristotle thought, they are female, as the seventeenth-century English beekeeper Richard Remnant argued in *A Discourse or Historie of Bees*: 'That the lesser [worker] Bees are the females, I thus prove: It is the female that beares the seed in her body, but the lesser Bee beares the seed in her body and blowes [deposits] it, therefore they are the females.' Worker honeybees occasionally produce eggs – they are 'laying workers'. But this is rare because the workers' ovarian development is usually inhibited by chemicals secreted by the queen. In one species of bee, the female workers are all permanently sterile, even in queenless colonies. The female workers of this species were on their way to producing large gametes, but never made it to the end. That suggests an elaboration of

Roughgarden's definition: females are the ones who have advanced some distance down the developmental pathway that results in the production of large gametes. Similarly, males are the ones who have advanced some distance down the developmental pathway that results in the production of small gametes. That is better, if not completely right. It is accurate enough for our purposes.[19]

Understanding that the sexes 'are basically defined by the gametes they produce' prepares us for something that we'll confront shortly. In principle, some females could outwardly look and behave like males, or some males could outwardly look and behave like females. Real life examples are provided by *sexual mimicry*, which happens in a variety of species. For instance, in the giant cuttlefish, some males adopt the colouring of females so that they can hang around a male-guarded female in the hope of sneaking a mating. Female spotted hyenas are highly aggressive and dominant, and to complete the package they have a long clitoris that looks like a penis, complete with a fake scrotum. Imagine that, due to a rare mutation, there was a human being rather like this, male-looking, with a penis-like clitoris, an empty scrotum and ovaries. That person would no more be male than a female hyena.[20]

The crucial point to bear in mind is that the two sexes have no special connection to humans; females and males probably evolved more than a billion years ago, and they are widespread across the animal and plant kingdoms.[21] The methodology of studying sex in gender studies and feminist philosophy focuses almost exclusively on ourselves, and other organisms are rarely mentioned. That is like studying cars by focusing on Lamborghinis.

Two sexes, not a spectrum

If there are more than two sexes, some species will have a third intermediate gamete, with some of the cellular machinery required to turn DNA into an organism, but not all of it. No such gamete has been found, and there are theoretical reasons to suppose that it would never have evolved. There are therefore exactly two sexes: females, whose associated gamete contains DNA together with all the required cellular machinery, and males, whose associated gamete contains DNA and is equipped with the means of getting that DNA into the female gamete.

Sometimes the claim that sex is binary just means that there are two and only two sexes: in that sense, sex *is* binary. (We'll see another more interesting interpretation of the binary claim in a moment.)[22]

Height is a feature of humans that is a kind of 'spectrum'. People range from short to tall. We can line up women, say, in order of height, with the four-and-a-half footers at the left end and the six-footers at the right. Take Miranda, a tall woman at 5' 10", and over to the right. The closer in the line someone is to Miranda, the more similar in respect of height she is to Miranda. If Carrie and Charlotte are both short, but Charlotte is taller than Carrie, then Charlotte is more similar in respect of height to Miranda than Carrie is.

Now imagine trying to do the same for sex. Instead of the short people on the left and the tall people on the right, we have the females on the left and the males on the right. (Perhaps there are some people in the middle who are neither clearly female nor male – we don't need to worry about this.) If sex is a spectrum, there should be two females on the left – call them Anne and Betty – with one of them being closer to a male – call him Charles – on the right. Suppose the order is: Anne, Betty, Charles. Betty is closer to Charles, so she should be more similar in respect of sex to Charles than Anne is.

There are ways of making sense of this. For instance, Anne and Betty make large gametes, Charles makes small gametes, but Betty on very rare occasions makes some intermediate ones. However, given that, in fact, there's no intermediate gamete, Betty can't be more similar in respect of sex to Charles than Anne is. True, Betty might be more muscular than Anne, or hairier than Anne, or have a deeper voice than Anne, or in some other way better resemble Charles than Anne. But this is not similarity in respect of sex; it's similarity in *other* respects. Betty may be more muscular than Anne, or more masculine than Anne, but she is not 'more male' than Anne. In respect of *sex* – female and male – Anne and Betty are *exactly* similar.

To switch examples, consider three giant cuttlefish, a mate-guarding male, the guarded female, and (what biologists call) a sneaky fucker, a male cuttlefish with female markings. In respect of coloration, the sneaky cuttlefish resembles the female more than the mate-guarding male does. But, in respect of sex, the mate-guarding male and the sneaky male are entirely alike.[23]

There are only two sexes, and sex is not a spectrum. But it could still turn out that, in one clear sense, sex is not binary. Let's turn to that next.

The female/male binary

We saw that one interpretation of 'sex is binary' is that there are exactly two sexes. Another, perhaps more popular, interpretation is this: every person is either female or male, and no one is both. Let's give these two interpretations labels:

2-Sexes: There are exactly two sexes.
Binary-Sex: Every person is either female or male, and no one is both.

If there are three sexes, or fifty-seven sexes, or 20,000 sexes, *2-Sexes* is false. Even if there are only three, it would be misleading to say that *2-Sexes* is 'almost true', on the ground that three is not much different from two. It would be more honest to admit complete defeat: if there are three sexes then the two-sex thesis is false without qualification.

In contrast, it is not misleading to say that *Binary-Sex* is almost true if only a tiny fraction of the population falls outside the two categories *exclusively-female* and *exclusively-male*. Similarly, it is 'almost true' that everyone has ten fingers. When Richard Dawkins wrote (in 2022), 'sex is pretty damn binary', he had *Binary-Sex* in mind.[24]

Sometimes people say 'Sex is dimorphic', or 'Humans are a sexually dimorphic species', when they mean to endorse either *2-Sexes* or *Binary-Sex*. This can be confusing. When biologists say that a species is highly sexually dimorphic they mean that the females and males of that species are phenotypically very different. For instance, maybe the males are much larger than the females, as is the case with elephant seals. Or maybe the males but not the females are brightly coloured, as in many birds. Or maybe the males are essentially small parasitic scrotums stuck onto a host female, as in some deep-sea anglerfish.[25] Humans are moderately sexually dimorphic compared to other apes. (Adult male gorillas are about twice the size of the females.) Many bird species are not sexually dimorphic at all – they are sexually *monomorphic*. Sexual dimorphism, as usually understood, has nothing to do with whether sex is binary.

We have seen that *2-Sexes* is true; does that mean that *Binary-Sex* is true too? No. For instance, plenty of people could simply be sexless, neither female nor male nor any other sex. (And some organisms *are* sexless, such as the microscopic freshwater-dwelling Amoeba proteus.) Given that *2-Sexes* is true, it is still an option to deny *Binary-Sex*.[26]

How could we show that *Binary-Sex* is false? The simplest way would be to exhibit some people who are either both female and male or else neither female nor male. And that is indeed the most popular tactic – the relevant people are those with so-called 'intersex' conditions. But before examining whether any of these people really do fall outside the sex binary, let's address an argument that threatens to show that the question 'Is sex binary?' is ill-conceived.

Many kinds of sex

In 1955, John Money and two of his Johns Hopkins colleagues, Joan and John Hampson, distinguished between seven 'variables of sex'; as Money put it many years later, 'sex is not unitary, but multivariate.' For instance, there is *chromosomal sex*: someone is chromosomally female if they have XX chromosomes. Someone's *hormonal sex* is determined by their levels of active sex hormones: someone is hormonally male if, roughly, they have high active levels of testosterone. And then there is *genital morphologic sex*: a vagina versus a penis. Earlier we saw Harry Benjamin saying that 'there may be up to ten or more separate concepts and manifestations of sex' – he surely had Money's variables in mind.[27]

These distinctions are useful, especially for doctors. For example, some people are chromosomally female but hormonally male with a male genital morphology. However, they can have the effect of making the quest for sex itself look as misguided as the search for the Loch Ness monster. As an analogy, consider poisons. Is chocolate poison? It is for dogs but not for humans. Is cyanide poison? It is poison for humans but not for the Golden Bamboo Lemur, who thrives on a daily dose lethal to any other primate of its size.[28] Imagine someone saying, 'Forget about poison-for-dogs, poison-for-humans, poison-for-lemurs and the rest! I just want to know: are chocolate or cyanide *simply poisons*?' This person is confused: there are substances that are poisons-for-dogs, and substances that are poisons-for-humans, but nothing that's just plain poison, full stop.

Are the many-kinds-of-sex like the many-kinds-of-poison? If so, there's no sense asking whether someone is simply female. We can say that she's chromosomally female, hormonally female, morphologically female, and so on, but the closest we can come to plain female is that she is female on all these dimensions. And there are yet more dimensions – Money and the Hampsons had *reproductively* female, *assigned/reared* female and *gonadally* female. Benjamin added *legally* female, *psychologically* female and *socially* female; the list can be continued with *neurologically* female, *behaviourally* female, and so on. It looks rather unlikely that anyone would score female on every one of these. Further, many of these 'variables of sex' are spectrum-like. Levels of active sex hormones can be high, low, or in the middle; various brain regions can be more-or-less female- or male-typical.

If all we've got are these many dimensions, it's not really that sex *isn't* binary – the issue of whether sex is binary is misplaced from the start. Instead, we should say something like this:

> Science has not been able to categorically distinguish a male from a female. There's no one simple test to determine whether an individual is a woman or a man. It's not an either/or dichotomy, but a multidimensional spectrum on several axes, from the biological to the social to the psychological.[29]

Along similar lines, and citing Money's 'layers of sex', Anne Fausto-Sterling argued, in a 2018 article for the *New York Times* titled 'Why sex is not binary', that 'two sexes have never been enough to describe human variety.' Subsequently, she summarized the conclusion as: 'biological sex is multilayered and complex, rather than simply dichotomous', a better way of putting it than the *NYT* title. And much earlier, in an article called 'The five sexes', she dramatically claimed that 'sex is a vast, infinitely malleable continuum.'[30]

However, on closer examination these exciting and subversive conclusions quickly collapse. Sex and poison are not analogous – at least, not in the way suggested above! We can explain what it is to be poison-for-dogs without assuming that there is such a thing as plain poison. (Indeed, making that assumption would not help the explanation in the slightest.)

But the explanation of the different 'variables of sex' *relies on* the simple categories of *female* and *male*. To be chromosomally female is to have the sex chromosomes *typical of (human) females*; to be hormonally male is to have the hormonal profile *typical of (human) males*; to be genitally female is to have the genitalia *typical of (human) females*, and so on.

The categories of *female* and *male* are thus implicit in Money's taxonomy. There is a multidimensional spectrum, but it is not of *sex*: rather, the dimensions are *related* to sex, like hormones, or genital or brain morphology. Far from showing that the question of whether sex is binary is ill-posed, Money's taxonomy shows why it makes perfect sense.

Foucault and Barbin

Herculine Barbin was pronounced a girl when she was born in south-western France in 1838 and died by suicide as a man, Abel Barbin, when he was twenty-nine. The French philosopher and historian Michel Foucault came across Barbin's memoirs in the 1970s and published them as *Herculine Barbin: Being the Recently Discovered Memoirs of a Nineteenth-Century French Hermaphrodite*. Setting aside Barbin's fascinating but troubled life, what was her/his sex? Either female or male? Neither? Both female and male? In his introduction to Barbin's memoirs, Foucault says that the last double-sex option used to be favoured: 'For centuries, it was quite simply agreed that hermaphrodites had two.' However:

> Biological theories of sexuality, juridical conceptions of the individual, forms of administrative control in modern nations, led little by little to rejecting the idea of a mixture of the two sexes in a single body, and consequently to limiting the free choice of indeterminate individuals. Henceforth, everybody was to have one and only one sex … the doctor … had, as it were, to strip the body of its anatomical deceptions and discover the one true sex behind organs that might have put on the forms of the opposite sex. For someone who knew how to observe and to conduct an examination, these mixtures of sex were no more than disguises of nature: hermaphrodites were always 'pseudo-hermaphrodites'.[31]

If Foucault had stopped in his first sentence with 'biological theories of sexuality', not mentioning 'juridical conceptions' and 'administrative control', then the one true sex would have been on a firm footing. Biologists can correct common mistakes about sex – for instance, that only animals reproduce sexually, or that we all start life as female, or that to be female is to have XX chromosomes. Similarly, they could correct us on the sex of 'hermaphrodites'. But if some of the persuasion came from Foucauldian 'forms of administrative control', then the announcement that so-called hermaphrodites are pseudo-hermaphrodites looks like a political fiction rather than a scientific discovery.

As Foucault recounts, Barbin 'was finally recognized as being "truly" a young man.' Can we take the scare-quotes off the word 'truly', or was Barbin's reassignment solely the product of social forces rather than the result of 'deciphering the true sex that was hidden beneath ambiguous appearances'?[32]

In his edition of Barbin's memoirs, Foucault included a medical report of an examination conducted when she/he was twenty-two. 'Her chest is that of a man … without a trace of breasts. Menstruation has never occurred.' There was an 'imperfect penis'.

> The apparent labia majora … are only the two halves of a scrotum that remains divided … [with] bodies … [that] can be nothing other than testicles … above the anus lies a very narrow canal, a kind of adumbration of a vagina, at the bottom of which there is to be found no vestige of a cervix uteri.[33]

This does not look like a difficult case.

Barbin likely had 5-alpha reductase deficiency (5-ARD).[34] 5-alpha reductase is an enzyme that converts the steroid hormone testosterone into the more biologically active dihydrotestosterone, which masculinizes the genitals in the womb. People with 5-ARD have a mutation in the gene for this enzyme. Without (much) 5-alpha reductase, XY children are born with ambiguous genitalia and are sometimes sexed female and raised as girls. When puberty kicks in, the large amounts of testosterone produced by the testes masculinize the genitalia (to varying degrees), and at this point the 'girls' often switch over and start living as boys; they may go on to father children. The condition is sometimes called 'penis at 12'.

XY individuals with 5-ARD go down the male developmental pathway, albeit with a wobbly start. The female pathway is not traversed at all – no ovaries, fallopian tubes, womb, etc. XY newborns with 5-ARD can look female because the external genitalia develop as female in the absence of testosterone. The scientific literature classifies these people with 5-ARD as male.[35]

Herculine Barbin should not be the poster-child for the opponents of *Binary-Sex* – the thesis that everyone is either female or male, and no one is both. And when Fausto-Sterling argued against *Binary-Sex*, she did not rely on 5-ARD. Does her parade of cases do any better?

Herms, merms and ferms

In her 1993 article 'The five sexes', Fausto-Sterling describes some people who, she says, are 'clearly neither male nor female or ... perhaps both sexes at once'. The 'standard medical literature uses the term *intersex*' for these people, and Fausto-Sterling divides them into three groups, which she calls herms, merms and ferms. These groups were already recognized with (now outdated) medical terminology: true hermaphrodites, male pseudohermaphrodites, and female pseudohermaphrodites. The herms, or true hermaphrodites, Fausto-Sterling says, 'possess one testis and one ovary'; the merms 'have testes and some aspects of the female genitalia', and the ferms 'have ovaries and some aspects of the male genitalia'.[36] Herculine Barbin, then, was a merm or male pseudohermaphrodite.

Fausto-Sterling suggested that 'the three intersexes, herm, merm and ferm, deserve to be considered sexes each in its own right.' After controversy ensued, she clarified that she had 'written with tongue firmly in cheek', by which she seemed to mean that the proposal to *socially recognize* five sexes was not to be taken seriously. Fausto-Sterling did not walk back the claim that there are (at least) five sexes, and the many philosophers and others who cite her work take it at face value. (Recall the line from her later *NYT* article: 'Two sexes have never been enough to describe human variety.')[37]

Setting the herms to one side for the moment, the merms and ferms are doubtful counterexamples to *Binary-Sex*. As far as the ferms go, the main condition is congenital adrenal hyperplasia (CAH), a condition which exposes fetuses to excess androgens from their adrenal glands. CAH individuals with XX chromosomes have ovaries and female reproductive structures but genitalia that are masculinized to some degree: the clitoris can be enlarged, for instance. At least in industrial nations, they are routinely sexed female at birth, raised as females, and, although they can have fertility issues, many have children. The male pathway is not traversed at all – no testicles, vas deferens (through which sperm are transported), epididymis (which connects the testicle to the vas deferens), etc. The scientific literature classifies XX individuals with CAH as female.[38]

A representative condition that falls under Fausto-Sterling's 'merm' sub-group is androgen insensitivity syndrome (AIS). AIS occurs in XY individuals only; it is caused by a genetic mutation that partly or wholly disables the androgen receptor, through which testosterone acts on the body. Development starts down the male pathway, and the person's testes pump out male-levels of testosterone. In partial androgen insensitivity syndrome (PAIS) the hormone's effects are reduced, and in complete androgen insensitivity syndrome (CAIS) they are eliminated. In milder forms of PAIS, individuals are born as undermasculinized boys, often with a small penis, and are unproblematically male and raised as such.[39]

CAIS is another story: here the external phenotype is unambiguously female, with a vagina but no uterus and with undescended testes. Nothing seems abnormal at birth. If CAIS girls keep their testes, they will go through a feminizing puberty. (Estrogen is made in our bodies from testosterone; some of the inactive testosterone in a CAIS girl is converted to estrogen, inducing breast growth, female fat deposition patterns, etc.) CAIS girls develop like ordinary women but will not menstruate and are infertile. Because of the complete lack of androgen action, CAIS women are in a way *more* archetypally female than their ordinary XX sisters, with little body hair and unblemished skin; as the *New York Times* reports, 'Girls with the condition often grow into unusually beautiful women.' Still, they do not get on the large-gamete-producing pathway, and John Money called them 'simulant females'.[40]

This may be obvious, but it is worth emphasizing a point from Money's work on 'hermaphrodites' in the 1950s. Someone's true sex is one thing, but how they should be raised and treated is quite another. Consider this extreme case of CAH, reported about a decade ago: a '64-year-old Chinese man' presented to the urology clinic of a Hong Kong hospital. On examination, he had a 'small phallus'; a CT scan revealed ovaries and a uterus, resulting in a 'presumptive diagnosis of female with congenital adrenal hyperplasia'. 'As CAH was only better understood by the medical community in the later decades of the 20th century', the authors of this medical case report write, 'it was no surprise that our patient was not diagnosed at birth and was wrongly assigned male gender.' The doctors did not announce to the patient that the initial assignment should be corrected, that 'he' should take a female name, wear the traditional Chinese wrap-around skirt, and so forth. That would have been ridiculous. The patient had no issues with his life as a man; he was treated for his urinary symptoms and sent on his way.[41]

Merms and ferms may not refute *Binary-Sex*, but what about herms? Someone with 'one testis and one ovary' surely can't be female but not male, or male but not female, since the condition as described by Fausto-Sterling is symmetrical. An illustration in her book *Sexing the Body* (2000) reinforces the impression of sexual symmetry. True hermaphrodites are depicted either as female on one side and male on the other, a half-man half-woman familiar from circus freak shows a century ago, or else with two large breasts and an impressive penis, a figure featuring in contemporary pornography.[42] That leaves two options: these people are either both female and male (as suggested by the old terminology 'true hermaphrodite') or neither female nor male. Either way, *Binary-Sex* is false.

However, Fausto-Sterling's characterization of true hermaphroditism is misleading. The diagnostic for the condition is the presence of both testicular and ovarian tissue, which may not form a separate testis or ovary. She notes later in 'The five sexes' that some true hermaphrodites have an ovotestis, in which 'the testis and ovary … grow together within the same organ', which suggests that the two are stuck to each other like the halves of an Oreo cookie, but the ovarian and testicular tissues can be intermingled. True hermaphrodites typically have an ovotestis, not one testis and one ovary. Most are 46,XX, and some have given birth; 46,XY true hermaphrodites have become fathers. Some present to clinics later in life. Their phenotypes vary a great deal and are not accurately portrayed by Fausto-Sterling's illustrations.[43]

Whether any of Fausto-Sterling's herms is a counterexample to *Binary-Sex* is clearly a complicated matter. But true hermaphroditism is – and was – known to be exceptionally rare. (In 1982 the total worldwide number of cases reported in the medical literature was around 400.)

Fausto-Sterling's merms and ferms are not as rare, but still unusual. CAH is the most common intersex condition: a 1984 book about it put the incidence in 'a homogeneous Caucasian population' between 1 in 5,000 and 1 in 10,000. When Fausto-Sterling's 'The five sexes' essay appeared in 1993, it was clear that adding the herms, merms and ferms together could yield only a minuscule percentage. If Fausto-Sterling had simply managed to propagate the erroneous view that *all* these people fall outside the female–male boundary, perhaps not much damage would have been done (setting aside the feelings of some of the individuals concerned). And probably *Binary-Sex* needs a few minor qualifications anyway.[44]

Alas, that was only the beginning: the scale of the intellectual devastation turned out to be much greater.

The intersex minority caucus

In 'The five sexes', Fausto-Sterling speculated about the 'frequency of intersexuality'. We just saw that, according to sources available at the time, this is very low. Nonetheless, Fausto-Sterling wrote that 'intersexuals may constitute as many as 4 percent of births', attributing that estimate to John Money. On some estimates, that's more than the percentage of gay men and lesbians combined! As Fausto-Sterling remarked, that would mean that at her institution, Brown University, 'there may be as many as 240 intersexuals on campus – surely enough to form a minority caucus of some kind.'[45]

Wouldn't Brown's Health Services have noticed if many students had 'ovaries and some aspects of the male genitalia', and so on? Although childlessness is relatively high in the US, in some countries more than 97 per cent of women have children in their lifetimes.[46] Going by Fausto-Sterling's descriptions, one would have thought that herms and ferms would not generally be capable of giving birth. And many women are infertile for reasons having nothing to do with intersexuality. A small dose of common sense is enough to raise red flags on the 4 per cent figure.

Fausto-Sterling did address the obvious difficulty that the supposed intersexual 'minority caucus' on the Brown campus was invisible: 'Recent advances in physiology and surgical technology now enable physicians to catch most intersexuals at the moment of birth.' (Left unexplained was why this minority caucus remained undetected before these 'recent advances'.) Although she emphasized that the physicians' motives are 'in no way conspiratorial', they did conveniently align with the interest of 'the state … in maintaining a two-party sexual system'. (Why the state would have an interest in this matter, Fausto-Sterling did not say.) Foucault coined *biopower* for the state's use of medical technology to control the bodies of its citizens. The idea that biopower was surgically forcing intersexuals into the female/male straitjacket proved too tempting for Fausto-Sterling's readers in gender studies and philosophy to resist.[47]

In a 1993 letter to the journal *The Sciences*, in which 'The five sexes' appeared, Money denied having ever said that the frequency of intersexuality could be as high as 4 per cent, calling Fausto-Sterling's figure for intersexual Brown University students 'epidemiologically reckless'. Fausto-Sterling replied by supplying a quotation in which the 4 per cent claim was sourced (uncited) to Money. Although there 'are no accurate figures about the frequency (from all causes) of intersexuality', she said, 'intersexuals are not as rare as people may think.'[48]

The 1.7 per cent solution

Seven years later, Fausto-Sterling wrote an article with some of her undergraduate students at Brown, 'How sexually dimorphic are we? Review and synthesis'. That (confusingly titled) article explicitly set out to answer the question left hanging at the end of 'The five sexes':

> [T]he overall frequency of intersexuality is a matter of dispute. Fausto-Sterling … cited a figure attributed to John Money that the frequency of intersexuality might be as high as 4% of live births, but Money … responded that he never made such a claim. In fact, no well-documented overview of the frequency of intersex exists at present, and it is this lacuna that we address in the present article.[49]

'How sexually dimorphic are we?' trawled through numerous published studies, concluding that intersex conditions were present in 1.7 per cent of live births – not 4 per cent, but still eye-popping. How could almost one in fifty people have an ovary and a testis or the other two sexual combinations?

They couldn't. Despite the clearly stated intention to continue with the inquiry of 'The five sexes', intersexuality is given a completely different and much broader definition: 'We define the intersexual as an individual who deviates from the Platonic ideal of physical dimorphism at the chromosomal, genital, gonadal, or hormonal levels.' So, for example, if a boy is born with hypospadias, where the urethra does not open at the tip of the penis, his lack of 'an idealized penis' means he is intersex. People with XYY chromosomes, who grow taller than the average man but otherwise look like ordinary males, are also intersex. ('Intersex' is an ironic term here, given that XYY men were once called *supermales*, because they were supposedly more prone to violent crime.)[50]

The word 'intersex' suggests being *between sexes*. As we have seen, this is inappropriate for Fausto-Sterling's merms and ferms, with herms being a debatable case. It is certainly the worst possible label for people who do not fit the 'Platonic ideal' of female and male. A sparrow with a broken wing is not the Platonic ideal of a bird, the exploding 1971 Ford Pinto is not the Platonic ideal of a car, and (to my mind) Sex on the Beach is not the Platonic ideal of a cocktail. Yet the sparrow is a bird, the Ford Pinto is a car, and Sex on the Beach is a cocktail.

Even though one only had to read Fausto-Sterling's article to see the problem, the 1.7 per cent figure, repeated in her 2000 book *Sexing the Body*, went viral. The physician and writer Leonard Sax soon wrote a reply, pointing out that 'Fausto-Sterling herself has encouraged the belief that a significant fraction of the population is neither male nor female, but intersex.' Sax also noted that almost nine out of ten of Fausto-Sterling's 'intersex conditions' were accounted for by late-onset congenital adrenal hyperplasia (not the 'classical' form of CAH mentioned earlier), in which the genitalia are normal at birth; symptoms in women can include irregular periods and excess facial hair.[51]

The philosopher Carrie Hull also intervened, writing a letter to the journal in which Fausto-Sterling's article appeared, correcting 'numerous errors and omissions' in the latter's data collection and interpretation. That brought the figure for those falling short of the Platonic ideal to 0.37 per cent. Fausto-Sterling replied to Hull, not admitting any errors but not denying them either, leaving readers to 'judge for themselves'. Since

Hull had pointed out some incontrovertible mathematical mistakes, one would have hoped for more of a concession.[52]

Combining Hull's and Sax's criticisms, the estimate of the frequency of intersex conditions – as originally understood by Fausto-Sterling – becomes 0.015 per cent, more than 100 times lower than her initial figure. Since most people in this 0.015 per cent are clearly exactly one of the two sexes (like those with CAH), the dispute about *Binary-Sex* is left with a minute proportion of cases to haggle over, perhaps 1 in 20,000 births or even fewer. Academic – or sometimes intensely personal – interest aside, nothing of importance remains.

The efforts of Hull and Sax made little difference. The entirely bogus 1.7 per cent figure is frequently quoted. (A textbook in the sociology of gender uses it to conclude 'there's a chance that someone walking down your city sidewalk might in fact have both a penis and a vagina.') The figure is the source of the claim that intersex people are as common as redheads. Sax and especially Hull are typically ignored. The omission of Hull is particularly strange since she wrote a very good book entirely about sex, in which Fausto-Sterling's errors were clearly laid out.[53]

Disorders and differences

As we saw in the previous chapter, words matter. 'Intersex' is a highly misleading term and has clearly misled some philosophers. The old terminology of 'male/female pseudo hermaphrodite', 'true hermaphrodite', 'testicular feminization syndrome' (for AIS) and the like was unnecessarily stigmatizing. And 'true hermaphrodite', which implies both sexes at once, is dubiously accurate. In 2005, an international group reviewed current practice and proposed new terminology, set out in their 'Consensus statement on management of intersex disorders'. Fausto-Sterling's departures from the Platonic ideal, and her merms, ferms and herms, were now subsumed under *Disorders of Sex Development*, or DSDs. 'Male pseudohermaphrodite', 'female pseudohermaphrodite' and 'true hermaphrodite' were replaced by '46,XY DSD', 46,XX DSD' and 'ovotesticular DSD'. XX sex reversal, a very rare condition in which someone has a male phenotype but XX chromosomes, became 46,XX testicular DSD. (This condition, by the way, is another example illustrating why being female should not be equated with having XX chromosomes.) XY sex reversal, the female counterpart condition, became 46,XY complete gonadal dysgenesis.

People with DSDs are as heterogeneous as people in general, so it was no surprise that, when the international group issued an update in 2006, they noted that not everyone was happy with the new terms. Some pined for 'intersex', at least for some conditions. Others disliked 'disorders', preferring 'differences' or 'variations'. Even 'hermaphrodite' was not universally rejected. To yet others, 'disorder' is an appropriate clinical word for a range of conditions that usually require medical intervention. DSDs are not like differences in eye colour or skin tone: some are lethal if left untreated. And if one wants to understand what is going on, 'disorder' is appropriate. Something has gone wrong with the normal development into the female and male form; the amazing system of sex differentiation, as designed by evolution, is not working properly. Of course, the result is not a disordered *person*: indeed, he or she may be the most wonderful human being you could ever hope to meet.[54]

Many philosophers whose specialty is in sex and gender uncritically cite Fausto-Sterling on the frequency of intersex and/or the multiplicity of sexes, and there is little sign of the facts catching up. In a book about feminist philosophy published in 2020, we find:

> Pretending that there are only two options – male or female – is an oversimplification of a biological reality that is vastly more complex.
>
> As we become more aware of the oppressions experienced by nonbinary, trans, and intersex people, we can see how assigning a person's body a particular sex can be just as oppressive and reductionist as assigning them a gender. By Fausto-Sterling's estimate, people born with intersex conditions make up around 1.7 percent of the human population, which, philosopher Lori Watson points out, is roughly equivalent to the percentage of the US population who use a wheelchair.[55]

This passage repeats claims that are made again and again in the philosophical literature. Apart from the 1.7 per cent citation, it is an example of the ubiquitous but completely misguided attempt to connect intersex conditions with transgender people.[56]

What is the link between DSDs and transsexuality? Nothing much. Some DSDs are associated with a higher chance of gender dysphoria. But transgender or non-binary people usually develop physiologically along normal female and male pathways. (A few are 'intersex pretenders' on social media, falsely claiming a DSD diagnosis.)[57]

Wheeling in the mythical intersex minority caucus, and announcing that sex is 'a vast, infinitely malleable continuum', makes sex seem completely bewildering. That may sometimes be the point. One might have thought that the UK singer Sam Smith, who declared a non-binary identity in 2019 to great fanfare, was and remains a standard-issue male. If sex is a blooming buzzing confusion, even that apparently obvious fact needs to be reconsidered.

Sex and social construction

We have examined some claims about sex that are at least intelligible, although all are wrong: that there are more than two sexes, that sex is on a spectrum, and that some significant minority of people is neither exclusively female nor exclusively male. Another popular claim, endorsed – as we saw earlier – by Judith Butler, is that sex is socially (or culturally) constructed. What does that mean? Unfortunately, Butler herself is of little help.[58]

The sociologists Peter L. Berger and Thomas Luckman wrote *The Social Construction of Reality* in 1966, a classic of twentieth-century sociology. The book – which doesn't do much to clarify the title – seems to have been responsible for spreading the terminology into various academic disciplines, including gender studies. And the title serves to make an important point: whatever 'Sex is socially constructed' turns out to mean, the operative notion of social construction had better *not* apply to the whole of reality, to *everything*. The claim that sex is socially constructed is supposed to be a provocative and interesting claim about *sex specifically*. It should not be a corollary of the more general thesis that *everything* is socially constructed.[59]

Some things are literally socially constructed – made by groups of people working together. The pyramids, miniskirts and episodes of the HBO show *Sex and the City* were socially constructed in this sense. In the normal run of things, (human) females and males are produced by the mating of one female and one male. That's a kind of construction, loosely speaking. And the female and male parents are usually part of a society of some kind, often a wife and a husband. But clearly this is not what is meant by 'Sex is socially constructed'! That would not be interesting at all.

Sometimes sex is said to be socially constructed because surgeries are (or were) performed on some infants with DSDs to make their bodies more typical of one sex or the other. Fausto-Sterling describes 'the emergence of strict surgical enforcement of a two-party system of sex' as 'a most literal tale of social construction'. For instance, CAH females might have clitoral reduction surgery, a controversial practice that has not been entirely discontinued. But if the idea is that a variety of social forces tend to accentuate sexual dimorphism, making the bodies of human females and males slightly more different than they otherwise would be, there is no reason to single out people with DSDs. Body modification to accentuate one's sex is common, from breast implants in females to breast reduction in males. And why stop there? Bodybuilding for men and cosmetics and lip fillers for women also pull the sexes apart, as generally does fashion. All true, but unexciting. Fausto-Sterling sometimes suggests that those subject to 'surgical enforcement' have literally *changed* sex; this is certainly exciting, but it is not true.[60]

The psychologists Suzanne J. Kessler and Wendy McKenna wrote an interesting book called *Gender: An Ethnomethodological Approach* (1978). By 'gender', they mean *sex*, and, they say, 'the reality of gender is a social construction.' To their credit, they attempt to explain what this means. As Kessler puts it: 'By "social construction," we mean that beliefs about the world create the reality of that world, as opposed to the position that the world reveals what is really there.' Applied to sex (a.k.a. gender), the view would be that our beliefs about females and males *create* the reality of sexed organisms, as opposed to the position that sexual reproduction and the two sexes are a *discovery* – our beliefs about them reflect what is there anyway, independently of what we happen to think. That sounds considerably wilder than the idea of literal sex-changing surgeries. Philosophers are extremely interested in claims of this sort, and if Kessler and McKenna had a remotely plausible argument for it, they would have been fêted in the philosophical literature. They have not been.[61]

Philosophers sometimes use 'social construction' in a technical sense in which it applies to *categories*. If a category is socially constructed, then any object belonging to the category must exist (or have existed) within a society or social organization. The category *university professor* is socially constructed in this sense, because you can only be a university professor if you're part of a society with institutions of higher education. A *socially constructed* category is therefore the same as a *social* category, as explained in the previous chapter.[62] The category *lump of granite* is not socially constructed: although some granite lumps are statues in the town square, many are in nature, buried out of sight.

Clearly there are many female and male animals that do not live in a society of any kind. Indeed, there would have been females and males even if life on Earth had been destroyed by an asteroid half a billion years ago and humans had never evolved. In this sense of 'social construction', then, the categories *female* and *male* are not socially constructed; that is, sex is not socially constructed.

The social construction of sex is a blind alley – better, a dispiriting and bottomless rabbit hole. Enter at your peril. But, if sex is not socially constructed in any interesting sense, something else might be. Namely, gender, understood as the categories *woman/man*. So, what is a woman? That is the question of the next chapter.

FOUR

I am Woman

Within the terms of feminist theory, it has been quite important to refer to the category of 'women' and to know what it is we mean.

Judith Butler, 'Gender trouble, feminist theory, and psychoanalytic discourse'[1]

What *is* that?

Matt Walsh, *What Is a Woman?*[2]

Duelling definitions

Imagine a large billboard displaying, in striking white type on a black background, **woman** wʊmən *noun* **adult human female**. That was the work of a UK activist with the *nom de guerre* 'Posie Parker'. The poster went up in 2018, and Parker was adding her voice to the debate over proposed reforms to the 2004 Gender Recognition Act. If she had intended to cause a commotion, she succeeded. A doctor with the National Health Service, Adrian Harrop, complained and the poster was taken down. Parker (Kellie-Jay Keen-Minshull) and Harrop made a memorable appearance on Sky News to discuss the controversy, with Keen-Minshull wearing a black shirt that reproduced her poster. The first question went to Harrop: 'What is so offensive about the dictionary definition of women?'

'There is nothing inherently offensive with the dictionary definition of women', Harrop sensibly began, saying that the poster was part of a 'campaign against trans people, particularly against trans women', and that Keen-Minshull had 'sought to demonize trans women and to highlight them as dangerous sexual predators ... this poster ... is that campaign made flesh.' At the very least the billboard conveyed the message that trans women are not women; whatever the truth of the matter, one could understand how shouting it from the side of a building might be in poor taste.

Harrop could have wisely left it there, but a few minutes later he complained that 'you have explicitly excluded trans women from your definition of women ... that is not something that is appropriate in a modern and progressive society.' When asked by Keen-Minshull to explain his own view, the fresh-faced doctor declared that a woman 'is a person who identifies as a woman.' Intuitively, something seems wrong with that, even though it might not be obvious exactly what the problem is. Keen-Minshull saw the open goal, replying that 'what you and your misogynistic allies seek to do is erase what it means to be a woman in law and in life.'[3]

Forget about whether Keen-Minshull's poster was feminist activism at its finest, a gratuitous and bigoted provocation, or something in between. It dramatizes the main question of this chapter: what is a woman?

Given the amount of heat the question generates, one might think that the answer has far-reaching consequences, particularly for transgender women. Does it? We'll take that up at the end.

Dictionaries

Simone de Beauvoir famously asked 'What is a woman?' in *The Second Sex*. For our purposes (if not for Beauvoir's), we can interpret this as a request for *necessary* and *sufficient* conditions for being a woman. To illustrate, let's take a simple example. A *necessary* condition for being a rectangle is having four sides: it is impossible to be a rectangle without having four sides. A *sufficient* condition for being a rectangle is being a square (□): it is impossible to be a square without also being a rectangle. The necessary condition is not sufficient: a kite (◇) has four sides but is not a rectangle. The sufficient condition is not necessary: some rectangles (e.g., ▭) are not squares. A necessary *and* sufficient condition for being a rectangle is having four sides and equal interior angles. We can put it like this: to be a rectangle is to be a four-sided figure with equal interior angles. Or: a rectangle *just is* a four-sided figure with equal interior angles.[4]

What we want, then, is an informative and correct filling for the blank in 'To be a woman is to be a ___', or 'A woman just is a ___.' And, for many years, feminist philosophers have been hard at work on that project.[5]

But doesn't the dictionary settle the matter? If you look up 'rectangle' in any dictionary, you will find 'a plane figure with four straight sides and four right angles', or a slight variant saying the same thing. And the entry is right: that is exactly what a rectangle is. Now, if you look up 'woman', you will find 'adult human female', or a slight variant saying the same thing.[6]

You might think: game over! Dictionaries make the rules! To object to the dictionary is like saying that the Rules of Golf are wrong. You can object that some of the Rules of Golf are not conductive to an enjoyable game, and so should be changed, but that is not to say that the Rules are *incorrect*. Whatever the R&A – the official body in charge of the Rules of Golf – says, goes. The R&A is capable of stupidity but incapable of error. Likewise, you can object that some rules of English, as set out in the dictionary, are not conducive to clear communication, social justice, or whatever, and so should be changed, but that is not to say that the rules are incorrect.

This is a poor analogy, though. There is no official body in charge of the supposed rules of English. (Admittedly the French have the Académie Française, created by Cardinal Richelieu in the seventeenth century, which once vainly tried to purge the English loanword 'email'.) English dictionary compilers try to record, as best they can, the facts about what words mean. In that respect, a dictionary is no different from *The Sibley Guide to Birds*, which is a compilation of ornithological facts, not rules birds are supposed to obey. When words change their meaning or acquire an extra meaning (such as 'follow', one meaning of which is *subscribe to someone's social media*), the dictionary compilers do not protest or say this shouldn't be allowed but, instead, record the new meaning. When fresh words are coined and enter common usage (recent examples include 'folx' and 'sapiosexual'), the dictionary compilers add new entries. Words in natural languages, such as English, French, Swahili and the rest, have the meaning they do as the result of a coordinated and complicated group effort by speakers, which no one fully understands.

That is the first point: there are no rules of English (or rules of French, despite the Académie) analogous to the Rules of Golf. Dictionary definitions, like descriptions of North American birds, nutrition facts labels on food and the office phone directory, can get things wrong. Still, this doesn't show that the dictionary *is* wrong. We only have dictionaries because they are reliable. A compendium of politicians' private thoughts would no doubt be very useful, but in practice any attempt would be full of worthless speculation. *The Sibley Guide to Birds* might have a few minor mistakes, at worst. Nutrition labels are not as accurate but still useful. Since dictionaries provide facts about the meanings of numerous words, why think that they are all mistaken in the case of 'woman'?

This brings us to the second, more important, point. Words such as 'rectangle' are special cases. 'Rectangle' can be defined, at least in the sense that the dictionary entry gives necessary and sufficient conditions for being a rectangle. But this is an exception that proves the rule. The dictionary entry for 'chair', for instance, is something like this: a seat for one person, typically having four legs and a back. The word 'typically' is there to accommodate chairs that do not have four legs, or indeed any legs at all. Yet the definition isn't quite right, because a toilet is not a chair, despite being a seat for one person. Moreover, some stools have four legs and a back, but are not chairs. Although the entry is helpful, it does not supply necessary and sufficient conditions for being a chair.[7]

Since completely accurate definitions are a rarity, it is a distinct possibility that the entry for 'woman' is just as rough and ready as the entry for 'chair'. And, if it is, the dictionary still gives useful information. If you pick a woman at random, say Simone de Beauvoir, the chances are very good that she will be an adult human female; if you pick an adult human female at random – pretend you are an alien zoologist studying mature female Earthlings – the chances are very good that she will be a woman. But perhaps that's as far as we can go.

Social and biological categories

To a biologist or primatologist who studies chimpanzees, the species *Pan troglodytes*, the distinction between juvenile and adult chimps, and that between female and male chimps, is very important. So, we might fairly call *adult female chimpanzee* a *biological* category. By the same token, we can also call *adult human female* a biological category. Other biological categories include *juvenile male rat*, *mammal*, *gene* and *gamete*. According to the dictionary definition, women are the *Homo sapiens* counterparts of adult female chimps or adult female rats. (Similarly, girls, boys and men are the counterparts of juvenile female rats, juvenile male rats and adult male rats.)

Women and men, girls and boys, participate in all sorts of complicated social arrangements and have various social statuses (as do chimps, although to a less impressive extent). Women can be married; they can be widows; they can be particle physicists, prostitutes, proletarians and politicians. Until comparatively recently, in the US they were prohibited from voting or inheriting property. But if the category *woman* is the category *adult human female*, no social ingredient is part of what it is to be a woman. Space aliens could raise a solitary female human to adulthood in a cage, as a scientist might raise a rat. The result would be a woman – presumably a rather miserable one – who was not part of any human society.

Categories such as *widow* and *politician* are social categories: widows must belong to a society with the institution of marriage; politicians must belong to a society with some system of government. Our human female raised in the aliens' cage could not be a widow or a politician. If the dictionary is exactly right, *woman* is not a social category. And, as we saw in chapter 2, the orthodox view in feminist philosophy and gender studies is that dictionaries are not just wrong, but misleadingly so. Contrary to what they suggest, *woman* is a social category, as are *girl*, *boy* and *man*.

Although dictionary entries rarely specify the exact meanings of words, the entry for 'woman' can seem perfect as it is, incapable of improvement. Take this remark from Judith R. Shapiro, an anthropologist and a former president of Barnard College in New York City: 'The terms "man" and "woman," for example, serve to contrast male and female members of the larger class of human beings.' Shapiro takes herself to be drawing attention to a platitude. And, of course, it *would* be useful to have words to contrast (adult) male and female members of our species. What would those words be (in English), if not 'man' and 'woman'?[8]

One might have expected, then, that philosophers and gender studies academics would have *started* with the hypothesis that women are adult human females and then moved on to consider alternatives after they had refuted that one. That is the advisable methodology for detectives and inquirers in general: first investigate the most likely suspect to have committed the murder; if he proves to be innocent, consider alternatives next.

One might also have expected the same to go for sex. That is, those who think there are more than two sexes, or that sex is a multidimensional continuum, would have *started* with the hypothesis – clearly stated in many visible places by heavily credentialled biologists – that the sexes are defined by gamete size. The multi-sex or sex-is-a-spectrum or sex-is-a-social-construct hypotheses would have been seriously entertained only after the biological textbook view had been dispatched.

That is not what happened in either case. For sex, feminist philosophers and gender studies academics almost never mention the textbook view, no doubt because they are largely unaware of it. That is not surprising if your main introduction to the biology of sex is Anne Fausto-Sterling's *Sexing the Body*, which doesn't even contain the word 'gamete'. (As we saw in chapter 2, Beauvoir mentions the textbook view in the first chapter of *The Second Sex*, on biology, but that chapter is probably more often skimmed than carefully read.)[9]

Similarly, the idea that women are adult human females rarely makes an appearance in the philosophical literature. Instead, biological accounts of *woman* are described in ways that make them seem like contestable theoretical claims, not punchy platitudes fit for billboards or T-shirts. For instance: women are 'those possessing certain biological features such as vaginas, ovaries, XX-chromosomes, and the like'. If you put the view that *woman* is a biological category like that, there are obvious problems. What about women with triple X syndrome, who have XXX chromosomes? What about women who have had a bilateral oophorectomy, the removal of both ovaries? There are even women who lack vaginas, due to a birth defect called Mayer-Rokitansky-Küster-Hauser (MRKH) syndrome.[10]

Why do these academics typically ignore the simpler claim that women are adult human females? A plausible explanation is that they misunderstand the nature of sex. *Sexing the Body* and academic literature in the same genre give the impression that the category *female* could only be defined as a mishmash of characteristics such as genitalia, gonads, chromosomes and more. The biology textbook story of sex is thus not on the radar. Those who describe the biological view of *woman* in terms of vaginas, ovaries and XX chromosomes would deny they are *avoiding* talking about females – instead, they would say that they are just making the nature of femaleness more explicit.

What *is* supposed to be wrong with the idea that to be a woman is to be an adult female of our species? Before getting to objections, let's see why this biological view of the category *woman* is initially quite compelling.

'Female', 'Human', 'Adult'

We can argue for the biological view by examining the three components of 'adult human female' separately. Taking them in reverse order will be convenient.

First, 'female'. Being female is not a *sufficient* condition for being a woman, since there are female wallabies, worms and whales. Is being female a *necessary* condition for being a woman? In other words, must it be that, if someone is a woman, then she is female? Simone de Beauvoir thought so. Directly after the famous line 'One is not born, but rather becomes, a woman', she writes: 'No biological, psychic, or economic destiny defines the figure that the *human female* takes on in society.' In case there is any doubt, Beauvoir means to be talking about *biological* females – the phrase 'human female' indicates as much, and she mentions many non-human females in the first chapter of *The Second Sex*. Beauvoir does not argue that all women must be female – she takes it as obvious, needing no argument.[11]

She is hardly alone. Indeed, some quotations given in earlier chapters implicitly assume that belonging to the category *woman* guarantees that one also belongs to the category *female*. Examples are everywhere once you look for them. To randomly pick one, here's the last line of *The Woman That Never Evolved*, by the primatologist Sarah Blaffr Hrdy: 'Of all females, the potential for freedom and the chance to control their own destinies is greatest among women.'[12] No ordinary reader of Hrdy's book would think this sentence at all odd.

It is plausible that being female is a necessary condition for being a woman. What about 'human'? Is being human also a necessary condition? As the quotation from Beauvoir shows, she thought so. That is also plausible. In the 1968 movie *Planet of the Apes*, Dr Zira is a highly intelligent female primate, a psychologist and veterinarian with a soft feminine voice. A human version of Dr Zira would be a woman to admire. However, Dr Zira is a chimpanzee, and hence not a woman.

Finally, the 'adult' component. Not all human females are women, namely the young ones. But they just need to wait. Nothing social or psychological is required: there is no qualifying examination that must be passed or rite of passage that must be endured. The normal biological development of the human organism suffices. When discussing puberty, Beauvoir notes that the timing is different for females and males, with different consequences for when one becomes a woman or a man: 'the boy only reaches adolescence at about fifteen or sixteen; the girl changes into a woman at thirteen or fourteen.'[13] Here's a third plausible necessary condition for being a woman: being an adult.

Putting all this together, belonging to the category *woman* guarantees that one belongs to the category *adult human female*. What about the reverse? In other words: is being an adult human female *sufficient* for being a woman?

Are there any adult human females who are not women? Women are socially and psychologically a diverse bunch. There are women hunter-gatherers (and hunters), infertile women, lesbians, empresses, women warriors, unmarried women, polyandrous women; there are women with delusional disorders, extreme intellectual disability, dementia; and so on. Naturally there are patterns: human nature, and the social arrangements between women and men, are far from being infinitely plastic, but it is not credible that there is some social or psychological thread running through every single woman across the globe and into our ancient past.

Anthropology and sociology are needed to investigate the hierarchies and kinship structures of societies quite remote from ours. Identifying fellow humans as women or men is much easier. On April 22, 1770, Lieutenant James Cook caught his first glimpse of aboriginal Australians from HMS *Endeavour*. Sailing along the southeast coast, he saw 'several people upon the Sea beach. They appeared to be of a very dark or black Colour; but whether this was the real Colour of their skins or the Cloathes they might have on I know not.' Although the indigenous people had remained practically isolated from the rest of humanity for 50,000 years, and Cook knew next to nothing of their ways and customs, a closer sighting a week later revealed 'Men, Women, and Children on the S. Shore abreast of the Ship'.[14]

No extra qualification for womanhood appears to be required: being an adult human female will do nicely. So being an adult human female is a necessary *and* sufficient condition for being a woman. In other words, women just are adult human females.

Ewes, rams, and lexical universals

Hypotheses, whether they are about the cause of malfunctioning dishwashers, the structure of atoms, or necessary and sufficient conditions for being a woman, should ideally be supported by converging lines of evidence. Let's try to support the biological view from another direction.

Anyone in the business of hunting or farming needs to take a keen interest in the difference between male and female animals, and it is not surprising that long lists of gendered animal words are found in numerous languages. For instance, in English there are many expressions (often ambiguous) for adult females and males of various kinds of animals: doe/buck, sow/boar, hen/rooster, goose/gander, mare/stallion, peahen/peacock and ewe/ram, among others. It is not in dispute that 'ewe' refers to the category *adult female sheep*, that 'ram' refers to *adult male sheep*, and so on down the list. As we saw earlier, hardly any words can be precisely defined – these are among the exceptions that prove the rule.

It's hard to see why humans would be left out of this pattern. The adult sexed forms of our species are of great interest to everyone. We should expect, then, that English would have single words for the categories *adult human female* and *adult human male*. The only candidates are 'woman' and 'man'. And if 'woman' is the human equivalent of the ovine 'ewe' then, just as ewes are adult female sheep, women are adult human females.

Another examination of words provides more support for the biological view. This time, not gendered animal words but the equivalents of 'woman' in other languages: 'femme' in French, 'mwanamke' in Swahili, and so forth. There are approximately 7,000 languages spoken across the globe, from Aix-en-Provence to Zanzibar. Words in different languages can have the same meaning, such as 'woman' and 'femme', or 'cat' and 'chat/chatte'. Sometimes words in one language have no exact equivalent in another language: the French word 'terroir', useful to the country's cheese- and winemakers, has been imported into English for that reason.

Some words are *lexical universals* – they have equivalents (either a single word or a phrase) in all languages. Linguists have compiled lists of likely lexical universals. Perhaps surprisingly, there are hardly any of them. Here are some: 'man', 'woman', 'child', 'mother', 'head', 'eye', 'day', 'kill', 'make', 'good', bad', 'big', 'small', 'think', 'want', 'see', 'here', 'above', 'below'.[15] (A few more complete the list.) 'Woman' and 'man' are included, but nothing that is explicitly social – no 'chief', 'priest', 'midwife', 'village', 'celebration', 'feast', and so on. The psychology that is explicitly recognized is pretty basic: thought, perception and desire – there aren't even universals for emotions such as fear and anger. The idea that the lexical universal 'woman' denotes some kind of social position like *actress* or *housemaid* or *princess* is far-fetched: other universals have nothing cultural about them. The biological account, in contrast, fits very nicely with the cross-linguistic evidence. Whether you are a hunter-gatherer, a farmer, or a software engineer, adult human females and males are highly salient and relevant kinds of people, easily identified by sight.

It's a girl!

Our hypothesis, when spelled out fully, concerns a quartet: *woman*, *man*, *girl*, *boy*. In theory, one could have a mixed view: the category *girl* is the category *juvenile human female*, but the category *woman* is not simply the adult counterpart of *girl*; instead, it is some sort of social category. That is not credible on its face, and indeed no one has ever seriously proposed it. The view that *woman* is a biological category stands or falls with the corresponding view about the category *girl*. Is *girl* a biological category?

One notable feature of the philosophical literature discussing Beauvoir's question is the single-minded focus on women. Girls are barely mentioned (even though *The Second Sex* has a chapter called

'The girl'). This has the effect of making the idea that one becomes a woman 'through a complex process of socialization', in Susan Stryker's phrase (chapter 2), seem more plausible than it is. It is true that women undergo complex processes of socialization. Short of hypothetical and disputable examples of isolated human females being raised to womanhood by space aliens, any certifiable woman will have been subject to a long history of social influences. But what about girls? Of course, socialization starts early, but not *that* early: a newborn female has not yet undergone any process of socialization. And yet newborn females *are* girls. Moreover, they are girls even if abandoned at birth only to die shortly afterwards. If we move the focus to very young girls, the idea that being a girl has something to do with society or psychology looks quite unattractive.

If *girl* is not a social category, neither is *woman*. And if *girl* is the biological category *juvenile human female*, then the view that *woman* is its adult counterpart is all but irresistible.

Gender role reversals

We're not done with the case for the biological view yet. Theories can be tested by examining their predictions. If *woman* is the category *adult human female*, then we can't change who the women are by changing society, provided we keep the biological facts constant. Contrast the category *actress* – that has a biological component, because only females can be actresses. But it's not a biological category because we can change who the actresses are merely by changing who has roles on the stage and screen. Marilyn Monroe was an actress, but the female Monroe could have had a career in plumbing rather than acting. In that counterfactual situation, Monroe is not an actress, despite remaining female.

Imagine a society in which females and males have swapped social roles. In this society, the males push children in strollers and are sexually harassed and assaulted by the females, who jog brazenly through the streets shirtless. That is the plot of a French short film, *Majorité opprimée* (Oppressed majority).[16] The point was not that males would have been women, or non-men, if society had been completely different. The director was making the opposite point: the males are men, and the tables are turned, forcing them to be on the receiving end of sexist and boorish behaviour at the hands of women. This is exactly as predicted by the biological view: in the fictional world of the film, the sexually harassed people are adult human males and the harassers are adult human females.

Here's a real-life example. The writer Norah Vincent once resolved to try living as a man; she wrote a book – *Self-Made Man* – about her experiences.[17] This was not, she emphasized, a trial run for transitioning from female to male but an undercover investigation into the secret lives of men. Vincent's alter ego Ned joined an all-male bowling team, went to a strip club, and did other manly things. Her new mates thought she was a man and treated her like one of the boys.

As the subtitle of the reprint edition – *One Woman's Year Disguised as a Man* – implies, Vincent did not become a man. As it happens, she made some serious attempts to transform her body by weightlifting and eating lots of protein, but even if her preparations had included testosterone supplements she would have remained a woman.

We can put a further twist on the story. Imagine that Vincent read Judith Butler's *Gender Trouble* and became convinced for a few months during her fieldwork that her performance as a man made her one. If that had happened, she would have been wrong. Again, this is exactly as predicted by the view that the category *woman* is the category *adult human female.*

Putting all this evidence together, the view that women are adult human females looks solid. And yet, no one in the mainstream of feminist philosophy or gender studies believes it. Is that because they have discovered some decisive objections? In fact, there are hardly any serious engagements with the biological view, let alone a refutation.[18] For the most part, academics seem to have assumed that it must be false, because Simone de Beauvoir said so. What's even more amazing is that she didn't.

'One is not born …'

We have already seen that Beauvoir appears to think that being female is *necessary* for being a woman: no one can be a woman without being female. That doesn't mean that Beauvoir accepts the biological view, though. Granted that women must be female, *woman* could be like *actress*: no one can be an actress without being female, but *actress* is not a biological (and non-social) category. To be an actress, you need to be embedded in a society with certain theatrical practices. Perhaps Beauvoir thinks that, to be a woman, it's not enough to be a mature female of our species – one also needs to have undergone 'a complex process of socialization'.

It's quite doubtful that Beauvoir does think this. For example, in the introduction to *The Second Sex*, she contrasts the categories *woman* and *proletarian*: 'Proletarians have not always existed, but there always have been women. They are women in virtue of their anatomy and physiology.' Without society, there are no proletarians, aristocrats, kings and queens, or actors and actresses. 'Anatomy and physiology' are not enough to make someone a proletarian or an aristocrat, but they are enough to make someone a woman. Much later Beauvoir gave 'a positive definition of "woman"': 'a human being with a certain physiology'. That does not sound like someone who thought the category *woman* was a social category, such as *actress*.[19]

What was the point of her famous line, then? 'One is not born, but rather becomes, a woman' doesn't seem to fit with the view that someone is a woman 'in virtue of her anatomy and physiology'. The line suggests, rather, that female babies are not naturally destined to grow up as women, just as they are not destined to grow up as queens or actresses. Social influences of some kind are needed.

However, Beauvoir provides no argument that socialization is one of the qualifications for womanhood, and there is a much more appealing alternative interpretation ready to hand. What has been taken to be part of women's natural endowment – for example, being nurturing, empathetic, emotional, passive, accommodating – is rather the product of society. These presumed innate traits – what Beauvoir called the 'eternal feminine' – are trained into girls from the start. The lady that emerges after adolescence is not simply the result of normal human female development; instead, she is shaped and moulded by powerful social forces. We attribute the result mostly to nature; in reality, it's mostly nurture.

'Baby girls are manufactured to become women', Beauvoir said in an interview on French television in 1975. To support this, she mentioned and praised a book by an Italian educator, Elena Gianini Belotti, *What*

Are Little Girls Made Of?, subtitled *The Roots of Feminine Stereotypes*. 'The different behavior of the sexes', Belotti argued, is 'the result of the social and cultural conditioning to which children are subjected from their birth.' Beauvoir clearly meant that girls are manufactured to become *stereotypical* women, giving the illusion of the 'eternal feminine'. In a sense, a girl is not 'born a woman': she is not destined to be a *stereotypical* woman. To repeat the sentence after the famous one, 'No biological, psychic, or economic destiny defines the figure that the human female takes on in society.' Girls who were not socially and culturally conditioned to be stereotypical women would still literally grow up to be women – albeit women of an unusually liberated kind.[20]

In one of the numerous ironies that pervade this book, the woman who is supposed to have originated the idea that *woman* is a social category very likely disagreed with it.

One will search *The Second Sex* in vain for arguments against the view that women are adult human females. There are some interesting objections elsewhere, though, and we should not ignore them. Whether considering hypotheses about dishwashers, atoms or women, it is important to consider *all* the evidence, pro and con.

Counterexamples

The most straightforward way to object to the biological view is to produce a *counterexample*. In the case of the category *woman*, a counterexample would be a woman but who is not an adult human female or, conversely, an adult human female who is not a woman. And similarly for *man*. A counterexample to the view that men (just) are adult human males would be a man who is not an adult human male or, conversely, an adult human male who is not a man.

On the rare occasions when the view that women are adult human females is explicitly addressed in the philosophical literature, alleged counterexamples of the following sort are proposed. Imagine a person with a DSD (Disorder of Sex Development) who is not, say, male, but who looks like a man and lives as one – perhaps someone like the Chinese individual with congenital adrenal hyperplasia, described in the previous chapter. Let's give him a name – *Wei*. Wei is female but has male-appearing genitalia, was raised as a boy, and (let's suppose) thinks of himself as a man, is regarded by friends, family and co-workers as a man, and so on. Wei is happy with his life as a man. If this female individual *is* a man and *not* a woman, then we have a double counterexample to the biological view: specifically, someone who is a man but not an adult human male, and someone who is an adult human female but not a woman.

When we think about these sorts of cases, it's crucial to distinguish between the question of whether someone is a man and whether someone should be *treated as a man*, or *counted as a man*.[21] Imagine that Wei, passing through an airport terminal dressed as a Chinese businessman, accidentally goes into the women's bathroom rather than the men's. A woman protests: she is treating Wei *as a man*, and rightly so. Similarly, when reporting the gender composition of Wei's workplace, Human Resources properly includes Wei among the men. And when Wei plays basketball on the weekends, he plays on the men's team. It would be quite inappropriate for Wei to play on the women's team.

Except in rare medical situations, Wei should be treated or counted as a man and not treated or counted as a woman. By the same token, medical situations aside, Wei should be treated or counted as male and not treated or counted as female. But that is a quite different issue from whether Wei is a man or whether Wei is male. Indeed, he *isn't* male: that does not mean he should not be treated as one. If we confuse *being a man* with *being rightly counted as a man* we are liable to think that Wei is literally a man and not a woman, and therefore a counterexample to the biological view. Once these two are separated, clear counterexamples are not to be expected. Let's try something else.[22]

Social categories and socially significant categories

In his bestseller *Sapiens*, the historian Yuval Noah Harari gives some reasons why '"man" and "woman" name social, not biological, categories.' Harari's discussion has the virtue of clearly exhibiting a common conflation.

Being female, Harari says, is easy: 'A pair of X chromosomes will do it.' In contrast:

> ... becoming a man or a woman is a very complicated and demanding undertaking. Since most masculine and feminine qualities are cultural rather

> than biological, no society automatically crowns each male a man, or every female a woman. Nor are these titles laurels that can be rested on once they are acquired. Males must prove their masculinity constantly, throughout their lives, from cradle to grave, in an endless series of rites and performances. And a woman's work is never done – she must continually convince herself and others that she is feminine enough.[23]

He provides a table giving a concrete illustration of the point. In ancient Athens, females couldn't vote, couldn't be judges, were typically illiterate, and were legally owned by their father or husband. In modern Athens, females can vote, can be judges, are typically literate, and are legally independent. Females remain the same from ancient to modern, despite huge cultural upheavals: 'XX chromosomes', 'little testosterone', 'much oestrogen', and so on. In contrast, women are 'very different things' through the ages, changing as laws and customs change. *Woman* must therefore be a social category.

This kind of reasoning *does* work for some categories. For instance, criminals are very different things through the ages, changing as laws and customs change. Fagin, let's say, is a rogue and vagabond. That used to be a criminal offence in the UK, under the Vagrancy Act of 1824, which was repealed in 2013. Imagine Fagin in 2012, 'professing to tell fortunes', and so a 'rogue and vagabond' under the meaning of the Act.[24] He is a criminal. But when next year rolls around, by the stroke of a pen, he is no longer one. He does not need to stop his palmistry routine – the legal change by itself will move him from the criminal classes to the group of law-abiding citizens. Whether someone is a member of the category *criminal* at a particular time depends on the rules that societies impose on the populace at that time. A person will be ejected from the category *criminal* if societies make appropriate changes to their rules. *Criminal* is thus a social category.

Does this kind of argument go through in Harari's example of Athens? For vividness, imagine that the transition from ancient to modern all happened in one year. Xanthippe is an Athenian woman who can't vote, can't be a judge, can't read or write, and is legally owned by her father. A year later, Xanthippe can vote, is a judge (she quickly became literate and aced law school) and is owned by no one. Has Xanthippe ceased to be a woman, as Fagin has ceased to be a criminal? Of course not! Neither has she ceased to be a woman-in-one-sense and become a woman-in-another-sense. She was a woman in exactly the same sense throughout.

Harari's mistake is to conflate *social* categories with what we can call *socially significant* categories. Whether or not someone is a woman can have important social consequences, which vary from time to time and from place to place. Women may be allowed to vote or prohibited from voting; they may be expected to support their husbands or to have their own careers; they may be shunned for being lesbians or celebrated for marrying other women, and so on. That is, *woman* is a *socially significant* category.

Criminal is also a socially significant category. As is *female*: females may be allowed to vote as adults or prohibited from voting, and so on. *Lump of gold* is another example: if this large lump is made of gold, you're rich; if it's made of lead, you're not. However, as the examples of *female* and *lump of gold* show, socially *significant* categories need not be *social* categories. Females and lumps of gold can be found outside societies entirely, unlike criminals. There is no social ingredient to *being a lump of gold* – the structure of the component atoms suffices.

Harari correctly points out that *woman* and *man* are socially significant categories. But that comes nowhere near establishing his conclusion that *woman* and *man* are social categories.

Real men and women

Harari has another line of thought, suggested by his remark that males 'must prove their masculinity constantly, throughout their lives, from cradle to grave, in an endless series of rites and performances'. On this view, *man* is a category that has standards built into it, such as the categories *great writer* and *chess grandmaster*. To be a great writer or a chess grandmaster it's not enough to be a writer or a chess player; one also needs to meet certain exacting standards proprietary to writing and chess playing. A grandmaster might live in fear of losing his chess mojo and dropping out of the category *grandmaster*. Likewise for men:

'Males in particular live in constant dread of losing their claim to manhood. Throughout history, males have been willing to risk and even sacrifice their lives, just so that people will say "He's a real man!"'[25] This gives us another argument for the conclusion that *man* is a social category, one that does not rely on muddling up socially significant categories with social categories. If being a man is a matter of conforming to the exacting standards of manhood imposed by one's society, then *man* is a social category for the same reason *grandmaster* is.

The French radical feminist philosopher Monique Wittig thought something similar:

> Lesbians should always remember and acknowledge how 'unnatural,' compelling, totally oppressive, and destructive being 'woman' was for us in the old days before the women's liberation movement. It was a political constraint, and those who resisted it were accused of not being 'real' women. But then we were proud of it, since in the accusations there was already something like a shadow of victory: the avowal by the oppressor that 'woman' is not something that goes without saying, since to be one, one has to be a 'real' one.[26]

To be a man one must be a 'real' man; to be a woman one must be a 'real' woman. Therefore the category *woman* can't be the category *adult human female*, because someone can lose her claim to womanhood without changing her biology.

Wittig follows the argument where it leads. Only real women are women, lesbians are not real women, therefore lesbians are not women. Obviously, something has gone wrong. A tenuous grasp of reality is an occupational hazard of being a sophisticated French philosopher. (A line from George Orwell is relevant here and in many places throughout this book: 'One has to belong to the intelligentsia to believe things like that.')[27]

The problem is with the word 'real'. Imagine a bar of soap coloured and shaped to look exactly like a lemon. If someone is fooled and grabs the lemon-like soap to add juice to her lemon drop martini, I might say 'That's not a real lemon.' Here I am saying that the soap isn't a lemon, using 'real' to acknowledge that it nonetheless looks like one.

Contrast another use of 'real'. 'That's not a real cocktail', I say rudely, pointing at her lemon drop martini. I don't mean that it's not a cocktail; rather, I mean that it doesn't measure up to the proper standards for cocktails. A gin martini straight up with a twist – now that's a *real* cocktail. The sense in which lesbians are not 'real' women is this sense.

Lesbians don't measure up to society's standards for how women should behave – women should be feminine and heterosexual, not masculine and homosexual. (Of course, my own standards for cocktails, or a society's standards for women, might be quite deplorable.)[28]

A man who is afraid of not meeting expectations, and of losing his claim to manhood, is afraid that others will regard him as not behaving as men should behave. His concern is precisely *not* that he will cease to be a man – if he did, the expectations would vanish and the burden would be lifted. Rather, what agitates him is the prospect of continuing to be a man, shamed and belittled for his unmanly behaviour. If real men do not eat quiche, an adult human male cannot become an ex-man by tucking into the stuff.

Circularity and intangibility

This chapter cannot possibly catalogue every mistake and confusion on this topic; we'll close with a couple more. The first is Dr Harrop's suggestion, mentioned at the start of this chapter, that a woman is a person who identifies as a woman. As Judith Butler puts it (less clearly than Harrop), 'by "women" I mean all those who identify in that way.'[29] This is circular, in the sense that, if you don't understand the word 'woman' to begin with, you will not be able to understand the explanation, which uses the word 'woman'. It is thus not a definition as ordinarily understood. But that *doesn't* mean that it's not true. A square is a four-sided figure that can be cut by two lines into four squares – that is both circular *and* true.

However, the circular claim about women *is* clearly false. We'll turn to what 'identifying as so-and-so' might come to in chapter 8, but, whatever it means, presumably some sort of psychological competence is required to 'identify as a woman'. Some elderly females with dementia will fail the competence requirement, and thus will not be women, which is absurd.[30] And the parallel account for *girl* (which should also be true if the one for *woman* is) is even more clearly false. Newborn girls do not identify as anything.

The second is more a kind of smokescreen than a simple mistake. Although Butler confidently pronounces on who the women are when expedient – 'trans women are women ... of course they are'[31] – in *Gender*

Trouble and elsewhere she suggests that the word 'woman' is a sort of semantic shape-shifter, whose meaning is impossible to pin down, like the patterns in a rotating kaleidoscope. In this mood, any claim about women is obscure, contestable, unstable:

> On the contrary, if feminism presupposes that 'women' designates an undesignatable field of differences, one that cannot be totalized or summarized by a descriptive identity category, then the very term becomes a site of permanent openness and resignifiability. I would argue that the rifts between and among women over the content of the term ought to be safeguarded and prized, indeed, that this constant rifting ought to be affirmed as the ungrounded ground of feminist theory.[32]

Here is a somewhat plainer expression of the same idea, from the British journalist and self-described 'genderqueer woman' Laurie Penny: 'I consider "woman" to be a made-up category, an intangible, constantly changing idea with as many different definitions as there are cultures on Earth.'[33] Ordinary sentences containing 'woman' – say, 'The author of *Gender Trouble* is a woman' – are not usually met with blank stares or requests for clarification or disambiguation. We unproblematically and easily identify people as women every day, as did Aristotle more than two millennia ago. English speakers use the word 'woman' to label them, Spanish speakers use 'mujer' and Aristotle used 'γυνή' (*gyne*). If a linguist wanted an example of an unclear, arcane or hard to understand word, 'woman' would be the last on their list. Put another way, if 'woman' designates the undesignatable, so does every word, and language is meaningless.

Why this matters

If women are adult human females, or, more cautiously, if women must be female, then trans women are not women. Does this matter? Since gender-critical feminists frequently agree with this conclusion, and trans-rights activists proclaim the opposite, you might think it matters a lot. As an illustration, take the issue of whether trans women should be permitted to compete in women's sports. The following sentiment is quite common: 'Note that if you believe in full trans acceptance, the debate doesn't even arise. If trans women are women, then of course they should get to compete in women's sports.'[34] The link made in this quotation from 'full trans acceptance' to trans women being women is mystifying, since many trans women don't take themselves to be women. Setting that aside, the 'of course' is of course wrong. If the 50-foot woman wants to join the women's basketball team then she may reasonably be denied. Pleading that she is really a woman would be perversely to insist on the letter instead of the spirit, a kind of moralistic pedantry. Imagine that the chimpanzee Dr Zira from *Planet of the Apes* wants to play on the women's side, and that her relatively small size means that she is at a slight disadvantage. Why shouldn't she join in? To switch from the basketball court to more intimate spaces, Typhoid Mary should be kept away from women's locker rooms, despite being 100 per cent woman. And no one complains about a small boy accompanying his mother into a toilet with on the door.

The sports issue turns on the athletic advantages conferred by a male puberty balanced against the interests of natal males who move through life socially as women, not on whether trans women are women. And similarly for other areas of dispute, say about access to women's prisons or shelters, or self-ID laws. The gender-critical feminists maintain that females are an important political class, deserving of their own advocacy movement. They describe themselves as feminists, and, since feminism is naturally thought of as 'the advocacy of women's rights on the basis of the equality of the sexes', terminological awkwardness ensues if it turns out that natal males can be women. Gender-critical feminists are therefore motivated to think that they can't be.

On the trans-rights activist side, if one wants to ensure that trans women are treated as women in every circumstance, it is rhetorically extremely convenient if it turns out that trans women are women. No surprise, then, that, following the just quoted explanation of feminism from the US LGBTQ lobbying group Human Rights Campaign, we find: 'Trans women are women … There's [*sic*] no ifs, ands or buts about it.'[35] However, the substantial issues can (and should) be stated and debated without taking a stand on whether trans women are women. That settles nothing.

Does it matter at all, then, whether trans women are women, or whether trans boys are boys? Yes, it does.

A few years ago, the UK charity Stonewall devised this slogan: 'Trans Women are Women. Get Over It!' (See the epigraphs to chapter 1.) If standard English was intended, and assuming that the slogan is false, then the interests of trans people are not well served. If women are adult human females, this is not some esoteric truth that can be kept hidden by theoreticians in gender studies; to the contrary, it is a widely known fact. And it is a very short step from the premise that women are adult human females to the conclusion that Stonewall's slogan is false. It is obviously counterproductive to hang your activism on a slogan that is intended to be taken literally and that is widely known to be wrong. That would be like the Black Lives Matter movement adopting the slogan 'Only Black Lives Matter.'

That is one reason why the truth of these claims matters. And there is a much more fundamental point. Our fellow human beings deserve clear and non-deceptive communication, both from other people and from institutions. We all recognize that people should not be lied to, with carefully circumscribed exceptions. Suppose it is false that trans boys are boys, because boys are juvenile human males, and trans boys are not male. Then authority figures should not tell gender dysphoric natal female children or their parents that trans boys are boys. Perhaps they should not tell them explicitly that trans boys are girls – that is a trickier issue – but at the very least they should not be propagating falsehoods.

Whether trans women are women or trans boys are boys has little significance for public policy, sporting regulations, or the medical treatment of gender dysphoria. The importance of these questions lies elsewhere.

FIVE

The Rise of Gender Identity

With *gender* difficult to define and *identity* still a challenge to theoreticians, we need hardly insist on the holiness of the term 'gender identity.'

Robert Stoller, *Sex and Gender*[1]

Once we recognise that the number of gender identities is potentially infinite, we are forced to concede that nobody is deep down cisgender, because nobody is assigned the correct gender identity at birth.

Rebecca Reilly-Cooper, 'Gender is not a spectrum'[2]

What is gender identity?

Miley Cyrus, the singer and former star of the TV series Hannah Montana, 'often thinks about her gender identity', as reported by *Teen Vogue*. 'I think about being a girl all the time', she said. 'I'm always like, "It's weird that I'm a girl, because I just don't feel like a girl, and I don't feel like a boy".'[3] Miley Cyrus's puzzlement about her gender identity doesn't seem to have affected her much. She is in a relationship with a man; despite not feeling like a woman, she presents as a very feminine one.

For Jazz Jennings, her gender identity was a much more serious matter. Born in 2000 as Jaron, she 'started questioning her gender identity when she was two years old.' It turned out to be a female gender identity, not concordant with Jazz's natal sex. Jazz swiftly made a social transition to female, with a new name and girls' clothing, and appeared on *20/20* with Barbara Walters in 2007. She was given puberty blockers at age eleven, and her sex reassignment surgery in 2018 was covered in excruciating detail on the TV show *I am Jazz*.[4]

Are Miley Cyrus and Jazz Jennings unusual in having gender identities? Quite the opposite. An authoritative medical textbook on gender identity in children declares, 'Each of us has a gender identity, though many of us never give it much thought.'[5]

Gender identity would be of little interest if it always matched a person's natal sex. But it does not, or so we are told. In a small minority, sex and gender identity are misaligned: Jazz Jennings (if not Miley Cyrus) is an example. Accordingly, there are two kinds of people: *cisgender* people, whose gender identity matches their sex ('cis' means *on this side*), and the small minority of *transgender* people, whose gender identity doesn't ('trans' means *on the farther side*).[6]

A matching failure isn't necessarily a problem. Sometimes it's a good thing: if you want two magnets to stick together, you need them to have poles that *don't* match. However, in the case of gender identity, a misalignment between a person's gender identity and their natal sex is a problem – in Jennings's case, supposedly one requiring drastic medical intervention. WPATH (the World Professional Association for Transgender Health) says that *gender dysphoria* – distress at the sexed characteristics of one's body – 'is *caused by* a discrepancy between a person's gender identity and that person's sex assigned at birth.'[7] At least in this respect, cisgender people are the lucky ones.

Many leading clinicians and researchers agree with WPATH. Diane Ehrensaft is a psychologist and the mental health director of a large gender clinic associated with the University of California, San Francisco. She maintains in her book *Gender Born, Gender Made* that everyone has a 'true gender self' which 'begins as the kernel of gender identity that is there from birth.' Distress will result, she says, if one's true gender self is not 'in sync' with one's 'assigned gender'. Attempts to change one's true gender self or gender identity are futile: 'A person's gender identity is an innate, effectively immutable characteristic.' As the LGBTQ advocacy group GLAAD puts it, 'Like sexual orientation, gender identity is a fixed, innate trait that cannot be changed.'[8]

On the *orthodox view*, as we can fairly call it, everyone has a gender identity. Cisgender people are those whose gender identities are aligned with their natal sex, and transgender people are those whose gender identities are misaligned. This misalignment causes gender dysphoria. Gender identity is present early in life and is at least highly resistant to alteration. (Let's pass over the awkward fact that 'gender fluid' people think of themselves as having fluctuating gender identities.)

What is this apparently universal aspect of the human psyche, responsible for so much misery when it is out of sync with the body? Psychology does not have the best track record of discoveries of this importance. Sigmund Freud thought that all girls suffered from 'penis envy', which in normal development leads to sexual desire for people with penises. That tells us more about Freud than about girls. In the 1980s and 1990s, thousands of therapists embraced 'recovered memory syndrome', which led to a rash of spectacular allegations of child sex abuse; the syndrome was fictitious. Philosophers, accustomed to casting a sceptical eye on things others take for granted, might have been expected to give gender identity the same treatment, with mainstream feminist philosophers leading the investigation. That did not happen.[9]

Let's start where gender identity began, with the psychiatrists Robert Stoller and Ralph Greenson.

Core gender identity

Stoller and Greenson originally explained gender identity in 1964 as 'the sense of knowing to which sex one belongs'. In Stoller's later book *Sex and Gender* this became *core* gender identity:

> Almost everyone starts to develop from birth on a fundamental sense of belonging to one sex. The child's awareness – 'I am a male' or 'I am a female' – is visible to an observer in the first year or so of life. This aspect of one's over-all sense of identity can be conceptualized as a *core gender identity* ...[10]

During development, Stoller says, 'gender identity becomes much more complicated, so that, for example, one may sense himself as not only a male but a masculine man or an effeminate man or even a man who fantasies being a woman.' Exactly what this 'more complicated' kind of gender identity is, Stoller never made particularly clear.[11]

Stoller's explanation of core gender identity could be misinterpreted. If you *know* you are female, then you are female – you can't know what is false. Similarly, if you are *aware* that you are female, then you are female. One might think, then, that everyone with a female core gender identity is female: the idea of a *mistaken* core gender identity makes no sense. However, as Stoller points out, sometimes a person has a female core gender identity, despite actually being male. This sometimes happens when a male baby with a DSD (Disorder of Sex Development) is 'reared' as a female. Drawing on studies by John Money, Stoller notes that a male baby raised and socially treated as a girl can have a male core gender identity. Here the person does not know (and is not aware) that 'she' is male; instead, she is (wrongly) convinced that she is female. In other words, core gender identity is the *conviction* (right or wrong) of one's sex. Almost always one's conviction will amount to knowledge and one's 'fundamental sense of belonging to one sex' will reflect reality – but occasionally it won't.[12]

Core gender identity is important and well defined, and its development in children has been extensively studied. At around ages two to three children know that they are either girls or boys. (Stoller's estimate of a year was a little early.) Over the next two to four years they come to realize that their sex is not a temporary property and cannot be changed by altering clothing or behaviour. Wearing a dress or playing with dolls does not turn a boy into a girl.[13] There is no reason to suppose that core gender identity is innate, in the sense of not being learned. Children come to know what sex they are by observing themselves and others and realizing that they are one of two kinds of people – girls and women, boys and men.

Could gender identity, as it figures in the orthodox view, just be *core* gender identity? On the plus side, core gender identity arises early in life and is universal – everyone, or almost everyone, has a conviction either that they are female or that they are male. Changing someone's core gender identity is also very difficult, for the simple reason that it's hard to get people to deny the obvious.

However, transgender people, although they may have misaligned core gender identities, frequently do not: their core gender identity matches their sex. Take the trans man Buck Angel, who transitioned from female to male in his late twenties and subsequently enjoyed a long career in the porn industry as 'the Man with a Pussy'.[14] Testosterone has given Angel impressive muscles, a beard, and other physical trappings of maleness. He has found peace moving through the world as male and is happy to be identified and treated by others as a man. We can say that he has a *comfortable male identity*. But his core gender identity is not male – he is not shy about saying that he is female, despite all that testosterone. Buck Angel is no outlier: there are plenty of other examples like that. These people's experiences show that gender dysphoria is not caused by a misaligned core gender identity, at least not in general. Someone may have very severe gender dysphoria despite knowing what their sex is; indeed, knowing one's sex can make the dysphoria worse.

Orthodox explanations

Core gender identity is in good standing, but it is not gender identity as it features in the orthodox view. So, what is that kind of gender identity? There is no shortage of attempts at explanations; they are uniformly quite unsatisfactory.

The Yogyakarta Principles, emerging from an international human rights conference in Yogyakarta, Indonesia, in 2006, have had a worldwide influence on policy. According to Principle 1, 'Human beings of all ... *gender identities* are entitled to the full enjoyment of all human rights.' Gender identity is given this explanation: 'each person's deeply felt internal and individual experience of gender, which may or may not correspond with the sex assigned at birth ...' By now we have learned to be wary of 'gender'. Are the authors using 'gender' to mean *sex*? No, since they refer to individuals with 'more than one gender'.[15] What 'gender' is supposed to mean is anyone's guess.

Turning to a more authoritative source, WPATH gives a similar definition in their latest *Standards of Care* (SOC8): gender identity is: 'a person's deeply felt, internal, intrinsic sense of their own gender.' Again, in order to understand this definition we need to understand the word 'gender', and SOC8 does little to explain it, beyond saying that 'man and woman' are genders, and clearly implying that there are more. The previous *Standards of Care* (SOC7) is more forthcoming and includes this list: 'male (a boy or a man), female (a girl or woman) ... boygirl, girlboy, transgender, genderqueer, eunuch ...' SOC7 does a better job than the Yogyakarta Principles at explaining 'gender', trying to convey its meaning by giving many examples in the hope that the reader will catch on. The list itself needs explaining, though, because it uses special terms such as 'genderqueer'. What does 'genderqueer' mean? Here's the SOC7 definition: 'Identity label that may be used by individuals whose gender identity and/or role does not conform to a binary understanding of gender as limited to the categories of man or woman, male or female.' Being genderqueer seems very different from being a eunuch, another WPATH example of a gender. A eunuch is simply a castrated male. These days, ritual castration is a rarity, and the usual way of becoming a eunuch is through treatment for prostate cancer. (There is a more interesting road to eunuchhood – some men find the prospect sexually arousing.) WPATH's examples of genders have so little in common that it's hard to know how to continue the list.[16]

What's worse, we are now going round in a circle. 'Gender identity' is defined using 'genderqueer', and 'genderqueer' is defined using 'gender identity'. Note also that *transgender* is also one of WPATH's genders. This is another example of circularity, because SOC7 defines 'transgender' using 'gender identity': 'The gender identity of transgender people differs to varying degrees from the sex they were assigned at birth.' At no point do we get an explanation of gender identity that doesn't itself rely on the very notion to be explained.[17]

Switching sex

Let's try something else. Gender identity might be hard to define in words, and yet – famously like hard-core pornography – be a case of 'I know it when I see it.' Is there a way of bringing gender identity, allegedly submerged in most of us, to the surface?

In her book *Whipping Girl*, the writer and activist Julia Serano claims that everyone has a 'subconscious sex – a deep rooted understanding of what sex their bodies should be'. Transsexuals, Serano thinks, are people whose natal sex does not match their subconscious sex, for instance Serano herself, who was 'born male' but who has a 'female subconscious sex'. *Cissexuals* (Serano's term) are 'people who have only ever experienced their subconscious sex and physical sex as being aligned', the large majority of the population.[18]

Serano's terminology of 'subconscious sex' and 'cissexual' has not caught on. Putting her claims in the more standard way, *transgender* (or transsexual) women and men have *gender identities* that do not match their natal sex: a transgender woman is an adult natal male with a female gender identity, for example.

'Many cissexual people', Serano reports, 'seem to have a hard time accepting the idea that they too have a subconscious sex.' She has an imaginative exercise that is supposed to offer cissexuals a 'glimpse' of what usually goes unnoticed:

> When I do presentations on trans issues, I try to accomplish this by asking the audience a question: 'If I offered you ten million dollars under the condition that you live as the other sex for the rest of your life, would you take me up on the offer?' While there is often some wiseass in the audience who will say 'Yes,' the vast majority of people shake their heads to indicate 'No.'[19]

(Presumably 'living as the other sex' involves transforming one's body to match.) Serano's thought experiment reveals, she thinks, the deep attachment cissexuals or cisgender people have to their sexed bodies, in much the same way that an offer of ten million dollars to live in a different house might reveal the deep attachment one has to one's own home, shabby and modest though it may be.

Does it? The experiment has a confounding factor. Changing horses midstream might be undesirable even if one has no initial preference for one horse over the other. The same goes for changing houses and changing sex. The fact that one has already lived a good chunk of one's life as a man (say) makes uprooting it to live as a woman rather fraught, even if one would have been perfectly happy living as a girl and then a woman from the start.

Plato suggests how we can design a better experiment. He believed in metempsychosis, the transmigration of the soul after death into another body – man, woman, swan, lion, whatever. In the *Republic*, the soul of Epeius, the man who helped build the Trojan Horse, enters the body of a craftswoman.[20] Metempsychosis does not involve changing horses midstream, so the confound is removed. What if we asked people if they would like to be reincarnated as the opposite sex?

Some psychologists did just that. They took a fairly diverse sample of around 100 women and 100 men (none transgender) and gave them the following question: 'Suppose for a moment that reincarnation exists and that you had to select your sex in the next life. What would be your action?' Thirty per cent chose the other sex, with no significant difference between the women and men.

The psychologists also asked about temporary switches, removing the 'changing-horses-midstream' problem by asking questions such as: 'If you could become a woman for 1 day with nobody knowing, would you take that opportunity?' Almost seven out of ten men said they would, with similar numbers for women asked the corresponding question. Participants gave reasons for their answers, for instance (from a woman), 'It would be exciting to see how people react and treat you differently.' Three wrote 'Why not?' Some were attracted to the prospect of having different sexual experiences: 'Two men indicated that they wanted to play with their own breasts.'[21] As we'll see in the next chapter, this last motivation was predictable.

Fictional examples of gender swapping complement the psychologists' findings. In the 1991 Blake Edwards movie *Switch*, male chauvinist pig Steve is killed and reincarnated by the devil as the gorgeous Amanda. At first he is shocked by his transformation, but he soon recovers and starts to make the best of it. The transformation scene only works as comedy because Steve's reactions have some psychological plausibility to them. Becoming a woman seems to be something many men think they could get used to – the prospect does not strike them as a Kafkaesque nightmare, waking up as a giant beetle.

David and Brenda

Suppose we asked people about to go on a date, 'How would you feel if your date didn't turn up?' Those who said 'Crushed' probably would have been crushed, and those who said 'Secretly relieved' probably would have been secretly relieved. But mistakes can be made. Feelings of relief after being stood up might come as something of a surprise, with disappointment being the expected outcome. Asking people how they would feel in some hypothetical circumstance is not always a reliable guide to how they would feel if that circumstance came about. And if the hypothetical circumstance is of an unusual kind, error is more likely. Psychologists call predicting how one will (or would) feel *affective forecasting* and have documented various kinds of common affective forecasting errors.[22] So, although people typically seem comfortable with the idea of sex switching, perhaps their actual reactions would be very different.

Thought experiments, in other words, can only take us so far. But how could we perform an actual experiment? Here's one grisly idea: we castrate an ordinary baby boy and raise the child as a girl, making appropriate surgical alterations to the genitalia. On the orthodox view, gender identities are innate and close to immutable, and baby boys almost always have male gender identities. The child, then, will grow up as a girl, with something close to a girl's body, and is very likely to have a male gender identity.

What would we predict, if – to quote WPATH again – gender dysphoria 'is caused by a discrepancy between a person's gender identity and that person's sex assigned at birth'? 'Sex assigned at birth' has come to be a euphemism for 'sex at birth', which is unfortunate, since it is an impediment to understanding. In the usage common today, psychologists or doctors might write 'birth assigned males' where earlier they would have just written 'males' or 'natal males'. To put matters more plainly, WPATH is saying that gender dysphoria is due to a discrepancy between gender identity and sex at birth, and that is how the orthodox view was presented at the start of this chapter.[23]

If the orthodox view of gender identity really is as simple as that, then it predicts that the child in our grisly experiment would *not* suffer gender dysphoria. As we saw in chapter 2, while some animals do change sex, mammals do not. And the artificial means currently available – castration, the surgical creation of a neo-vagina and cross-sex hormones – won't do it either. The boy raised as a girl remains male. Like other ordinary males, he has a male gender identity. His gender identity therefore matches his sex, and no distress should ensue.

However, the earlier presentation of the orthodox view was too simple. First, note that, if gender dysphoria was produced by the discrepancy between sex and gender identity, then taking steps to transform one's appearance, with or without medical intervention, wouldn't help. But it does, at least for some. So, it's not exactly the discrepancy between *sex* and gender identity that is causing the problem. More accurately, it's the discrepancy between *sex characteristics* (having a female- or male-appearing body) and gender identity. Even more accurately, it's the discrepancy between (a) a person's gender identity and (b) the person's sex characteristics *and* the sex-typed ways in which the person is regarded by others (their *gender role*, for short). And WPATH explicitly recognizes this in a parenthetical remark in its explanation of gender dysphoria. Reproduced in full, the explanation is: '**Gender dysphoria**: Distress that is caused by a discrepancy between a person's gender identity and that person's sex assigned at birth (*and the associated gender role and/or primary and secondary sex characteristics*).'[24] The person's sex assigned at birth (i.e., their natal sex) is not irrelevant, but only because it (usually) results in the corresponding sex characteristics and gender role. In other words: natal males usually have male-appearing bodies and a male gender role. It would be clearer, then, to drop 'natal sex/sex assigned at birth' from WPATH's explanation of gender dysphoria and focus instead on sex characteristics and gender role. And since WPATH's 'primary and secondary sex characteristics' is too narrow – one might be distressed having a male-appearing face, for example – it would be better to say *bodily sex* characteristics. An improved statement of the orthodox view, then, would amend WPATH's explanation like this: '**Gender dysphoria**: Distress that is caused by a discrepancy between a person's gender identity and that person's gender role and/or bodily sex characteristics.'

Let's get back to our grisly experiment. We can now see that the prediction of the orthodox view is that our boy raised as a girl *would* (very likely) suffer gender dysphoria, because his male gender identity would conflict with his female gender role and/or female sex characteristics. Although an ethical review board is unlikely to approve the castration of normal newborns, the experiment has been performed a few times when baby boys have lost their penises in an accident.

The most famous is the John/Joan case, mentioned in chapter 2. David Reimer was one of a pair of identical twins born in 1965 in Winnipeg, Canada. Both brothers had a condition where the skin of the foreskin cannot be rolled back over the tip of the penis, and the treatment involved circumcision by applying a hot metal probe. David was operated on first, and his penis was severely damaged. (His twin Brian escaped the surgery.) When David was nineteen months old, his parents consulted with John Money at Johns Hopkins Hospital. From experience with more than 100 patients, Money and his co-investigators John and Joan Hampson had concluded that the 'sex of assignment and rearing is consistently and conspicuously a more reliable prognosticator of a hermaphrodite's gender role and orientation than is the chromosomal sex, the gonadal sex, the accessory internal reproductive morphology, or the ambiguous morphology of the external genitalia.' It's easier to construct a vagina than a penis; as one Johns Hopkins surgeon infamously put it, 'You can make a hole but you can't build a pole.' Money accordingly recommended that David be reassigned female and raised as a girl. When David was nearly two, his testicles were removed, a rudimentary vulva created, and he was relaunched as Brenda. (The names 'John'/'Joan' come from an anonymized account of David and Brenda's story; it is perhaps no coincidence that they are the names of Money's husband-and-wife collaborators.)[25]

As recounted in John Colapinto's bestseller *As Nature Made Him*, Brenda had a troubled childhood with behavioural and academic issues. From the start, Brenda did not take to her new role as a girl, and Colapinto writes of her 'subconscious conviction that she was a boy' when she was seven years old. Speculations about Brenda's subconscious aside, at age eleven a psychologist reported her as claiming that she was 'just a boy with long hair in girl's clothes'.[26] Money's grand plan, despite his claims of success in academic writings, evidently was not working.

To cut an agonizing story short, when Brenda was fourteen, her father told her the truth. A few years later, Brenda was transformed back into David, who endured a painful double mastectomy and a complication-riddled phalloplasty (the reconstruction of a penis); he went on to marry a woman. David took his own life in 2004, when he was twenty-eight years old.

A sample size of one is not a good basis for making sweeping generalizations. Still, the John/Joan case is suggestive. According to one physician with a specialty in transgender healthcare, it is a 'clear example of how one's gender identity is internal, supported by biology, and cannot be changed by external influences'.[27] In an episode of the podcast *Science Vs*, on 'the science of being transgender', the director of the Transgender Medicine Center at a New York hospital said:

> We cannot change people's gender identity despite the most intense program for doing so ... it's like the Truman Show ... We're raising somebody from infancy to believe something, having their parents part of the plan and

> surgically altering their body for the plan ... And still it fails. If that's not going to work, I don't think anything is going to work to change your gender identity.[28]

Apparently, raising otherwise normal boys to be girls cannot succeed. Have we now found some convincing evidence for the orthodox view of gender identity?

Clive and Clara

Not quite. Although the John/Joan case was a failure, another very similar case was by all accounts a success. A baby boy – let's call him Clive – was reassigned female because, like David Reimer, his penis had been burnt off during circumcision. David had been castrated at twenty-two months, but for Clive castration was much earlier, at seven months. Returned to childhood as Clara (to give her a name), she began cross-sex hormone therapy at age ten and had vaginoplasty at sixteen and again at twenty-six. By Clara's account, she never had gender dysphoria as a child, was happy living as a woman, and had no desire to cross over to the other side. Just as Buck Angel has a comfortable male identity, Clara had a comfortable female identity. This may be connected to her healthy pragmatic attitude:

> The patient's perception was that her mother was a 'matter-of-fact' individual who, when told that she needed to rear her child as a female, simply did so. The patient indicated that in this respect she is much like her mother and, despite numerous adversities, has decided that she simply has to get on with life and do whatever she can rather than worry or obsess about issues.[29]

Why did David Reimer suffer such torment? Was it just because he was reassigned later? After all, Money himself thought that sex reassignment should be carried out as soon as possible. 'Though gender imprinting begins by the first birthday', he and John and Joan Hampson wrote in 1955, 'the critical period is reached by about the age of eighteen months. By the age of two and one-half years, gender role is already well established.'[30]

David's delayed reassignment might have been a factor, but hardly the only one. His anguish as Brenda becomes understandable once more details are filled in. Brenda had stereotypically masculine interests and play preferences early on. As Brenda's twin Brian recalled, 'there was nothing feminine about Brenda ... We both wanted to play with guys, build forts and have snowball fights and play army.' They both enjoyed the 'rough and tumble' play characteristic of boys. Brenda's genitals looked unusual, with a penile stub remaining. Perhaps more importantly, she had her identical twin – an undisputed boy – to compare herself with. She was mocked by other children for her tomboyishness. The thought that she might belong with the boys seems quite natural. As Money and John and Joan Hampson put it: 'The salient variable in the establishment of a person's gender role and orientation is neither hereditary nor environmental, in any purist sense of those terms, but is his own decipherment and interpretation of a plurality of signs, some of which may be considered hereditary or constitutional, others environmental.' Children realize from a very early age that people come in two types, girls and women and boys and men. The child then needs to apply this classification to their own case – which type am I, girl or boy? If a female-assigned child is drawn to male playmates, shares interests with other males, and is generally made to feel unwelcome as a girl, then it would not be surprising if the child expressed unhappiness with being a girl, wanted to be a boy, or even said she was one. Brenda had plenty of signs indicating that the Boy Team was a more natural fit. No innate gender identity is needed to explain her distress.[31]

What about the contrastingly successful case? Like Brenda, Clara was a tomboy. She also had a penile stub. Unlike Brenda, she preferred to play with girls. As an adult, Clara had a stereotypically male blue-collar job. David (née Brenda) was exclusively heterosexual, but Clara had a bisexual identity and had sex with men and women. In sexual fantasy, she was more oriented towards women. Like Brenda, Clara had some signs that pointed to the Boy Team, although perhaps they did not point as strongly. There was no twin to compare herself to. In any case, as Money and the Hampsons say, different people may interpret the same signs differently. A child's temperament and personality, their familial and social relationships, and the presence or absence of psychopathology likely have an important role to play. Clara's experiment might have still been a success even if Clive had been reassigned later, and Brenda's might have remained a failure even if David had been reassigned earlier.[32]

We have doubled the sample size, but two isn't much better than one. Let's look at another kind of natural experiment, where the numbers are significantly larger.

Herculine Barbin revisited

Herculine Barbin was the subject of Foucault's musings on 'true sex' who probably had 5-alpha-reductase deficiency, or 5-ARD (chapter 3). People with 5-ARD are males who often appear female at birth. Later, the large increase in testosterone during puberty results in penile/clitoral growth, the descent (or partial descent) of the testicles, and the general masculinization of the body – more muscle and less fat than females and a deeper voice, among other things. 5-ARD is caused by a recessive genetic mutation and is a rare condition found mostly in isolated groups where inbreeding is common. In 1979 the medical researcher Julianne Imperato-McGinley famously discovered 5-ARD in thirteen families in a village in the Dominican Republic, and subsequently other clusters have been found in Papua New Guinea, Brazil, the Middle East, and elsewhere.[33]

Apart from the external genitalia, there is nothing female about a baby with 5-ARD. He has received the usual heavy prenatal testosterone exposure from his working testicles, and the effects on the brain are typical. Because of the appearance at birth, the baby will usually be raised as a girl. Unless the testicles are surgically removed, when puberty comes around the 'girl' is in for a big surprise.

The literature on these cases records little significant dysphoria before puberty, despite the generally masculine play style of the children. That is at odds with the orthodox view of gender identity, which predicts that males with 5-ARD raised as girls would soon vehemently reject their assignment, just like Brenda.

Puberty is a different story. With a sprouting penis, beard growth, and other signs of masculinization, one might expect that someone with 5-ARD would switch over to Team Man, even if their male equipment is stunted and facial hair is sparse. And indeed switching is not uncommon. One overview of many separate studies found that around 60 per cent who had female-appearing (as opposed to ambiguous) genitalia at birth changed to living as men after puberty.[34] Despite a presumably normal upbringing as a female, with no discordant signs from the genitals, a substantial proportion crossed over to the other side later in life. So much for the orthodox tenet that gender identity is an 'effectively immutable characteristic'.

The fascinating flip side of the above statistic is that switching is by no means universal. About four in ten stayed loyal to the home team. One hypothesis is that the switchers were motivated by the higher social status of males in their societies, but that is not supported by the evidence. There is no simple explanation for why some switch and some don't: sometimes both cases can be found in a single family. As might be expected, given the physical advantages conferred by male puberty, some people with 5-ARD who live as women are world-class athletes competing in the female category.[35]

Yet more natural experiments are furnished by other DSDs, and they are equally at odds with the orthodox view of gender identity. Let's look at one more example.[36]

Peggy

Peggy Cadet (not her real name) has partial androgen insensitivity syndrome, or PAIS. She has a defect in her androgen receptor gene that reduces her ability to respond to testosterone and other androgens. Despite the presence of internal testes pumping out male levels of testosterone when Cadet was in the womb, she was born in 1953 with only slightly masculinized female external genitalia and was baptized as a girl. Diagnosed later as a 'male pseudohermaphrodite', she was reassigned as male at two months, with the option of subsequent genital surgery. When she was eighteen months old, a urologist wrote: 'The prospect of creating an acceptable penis in this patient seems to me very remote. There is nothing there except a slightly enlarged clitoris …' Despite this, the reassignment was not reversed:

> My parents had a meeting with the doctors. The issue of my gender assignment was reopened but my parents had gone through a difficult time socially telling people that I was not a girl but a boy and the doctors did not want to actually say that their initial recommendation that I be a boy was a mistake – so a boy I remained.[37]

Cadet made, in her words, 'a somewhat girlish boy'. To her embarrassment, she developed breasts during puberty – this happens in androgen insensitivity syndrome because estrogen is made from testosterone. She had a double mastectomy when she was thirteen, unaware that living as a female was an option. She picks up the story:

> Through my teenage years, I gradually became aware that I had the same sexual feelings as most people my age, but I never revealed them to anyone. I just felt that area of life was closed to me. Also, my attractions were always for boys and took the form of obsessive infatuation for particular friends. These were typical teenage crushes, except that there was no place to go with these feelings. My future was an enormous question mark. How was I going to get along? How would I endure my unfulfilled sexual and romantic longings? How could I keep the secret of my physical difference, especially now that it seemed I would be smooth-cheeked, unmuscular, high-voiced, narrow shouldered and wide-hipped for the rest of my life? As a substitute for the social life I was missing, I retreated into fantasy and daydreaming.
>
> When I entered college at age 18, I discovered that the library had textbooks that actually covered AIS, and there I found an enormous revelation. Other people with the same condition as I were girls and women, and they were sexually active and even married! Things began to make more sense, especially the way the vague idea of eventual masculinization was being continually projected into the future. It was a mistake and I was supposed to be a girl! That thought was immediately followed by the realization that I had already had a choice in the matter, had had mastectomy, and that there could now be no turning back. It was three more years before my feelings of denied sexuality and social isolation built themselves into a crisis, and before I discovered that breast reconstruction was a possibility. Only then did I mention how I felt to another person, and at age 23 I moved to another state to begin my new life – nearly all my adult life – as a woman.[38]

Cadet changed her 'sex-of-living' (her phrase) for pragmatic reasons anyone can relate to. As she put it later:

> An underlying, unquestioned assumption in much writing on changes of sex-of-living is that 'gender identity' is an imperative, overriding psychological force. My own pediatric endocrinologist … told me when I was age 21

> that gender identity was 'an unshakable conviction.' However, he never asked me whether I experienced it that way.
>
> My actual inner experience was of gender identity as an ordinary, malleable conviction, vulnerable to changes in perception of facts. As a child, I had been told that medical authorities had concluded that I was male. However, later, as a young adult, I revised this to the belief that I was actually a person with AIS who should more appropriately be living as female. Perhaps those interested in the psychology of gender identity should pause to question the belief that 'gender identity' always exists as a profound, unalterable psychological force or drive. Some seem to be using as their model for gender identity the compulsion of transsexuals to live as their target gender, no matter what the impediments. If transsexuals did not have such a need, they would not be transsexuals, but it is a great leap to assume that all other persons' experience of gender identity is of the same nature.[39]

Peggy has been with her partner, an 'unremarkably heterosexual guy', for more than thirty years.[40]

The myth of gender identity

We can think of the orthodox view of gender identity as a kind of job description. Wanted: some psychological entity that has (at least) two settings, F and M. Everyone has one of these things; in natal females the setting is almost always F, and in natal males it is almost always M. The settings are innate and very hard to alter. In the unusual case where a natal male's setting is F, he will suffer gender dysphoria – distress at his sexed body – which may be alleviated by altering the body in the female direction; conversely for a natal female whose setting is M.

The lesson of our investigation is that nothing answers to that description. Robert Stoller's core gender identity, 'a fundamental sense of belonging to one sex', is partly qualified for the position: (almost) everyone has a core gender identity, and, although it is not innate, it is pretty much fixed. But a mismatch between core gender identity and one's sex characteristics and/or gender role is not responsible for gender dysphoria.

Other candidates, such as a sense of kinship with one sex, or being at ease with one's 'sex-of-living', or having a psychology more typical of one sex, are no better. Take, for example, the first candidate: to have a male gender identity is to have a sense of kinship with males; similarly, to have a female gender identity is to have a sense of kinship with females. This won't meet the first part of the job description (had by everyone): some people have no attachment to one sex over the other. It will not meet the second (difficult to change): a man might discover later in life that all his time spent in men's support groups was wasted and that friendships with women are much more fulfilling. And neither will it meet the third (results in distress when incongruent with sex characteristics): a feminine man might have a strong sense of kinship with women without any desire to alter his body or change his sex-of-living.[41]

The ideal job candidate for the gender identity position is not revealed by thought experiments, such as being reincarnated as the other sex. Neither is it revealed by real-life experiments where natal males have been assigned and reared as girls. As examples such as Clara, people with 5-ARD and Peggy Cadet show, the predictions of the orthodox view are not borne out.

Normally developing male fetuses receive a heavy dose of testosterone starting in the ninth week, secreted by their miniature testicles. Brenda, Clara and Peggy Cadet add to the very large pile of evidence that prenatal testosterone exposure masculinizes the brain, affecting sex-typed behaviour and interests. (Cadet had plenty of testosterone, but her brain could respond to it only weakly.) We'll revisit this issue in chapter 7; to summarize: the observable behavioural differences between girls and boys, and the differences in career choices between women and men, very likely have a significant prenatal component.[42]

Gender identity is a different matter. Probably many ordinary boys could have been successfully reared as girls, assuming that the parents were somehow on board with unnecessary surgery and deceptive childrearing. Limitations on fashioning working male genitalia make rearing girls as boys more difficult, but that complication seems to be the only one. On average, boys reared as girls would be more masculine than typical girls, and girls reared as boys would be more feminine than typical boys. Masculine girls and feminine boys can suffer greatly but usually cope with being different from their peers. Sometimes, having strongly masculine play styles and interests (like Brenda), perhaps coupled with a masculine appearance and other factors such as temperament and the social environment, does induce an unbearable feeling of being picked for the wrong side. From a very early age Brenda wanted to tear off her pink uniform and join the blue man group. If having a 'male gender identity' simply amounts to this sort of intense identification with boys and men, then Brenda's gender identity was part of the explanation. But the orthodox conception of gender identity does no explanatory work at all. As popularly conceived, gender identity is a myth.

Jaron and Jazz

Physically normal individuals can develop gender dysphoria – Jazz Jennings and Buck Angel are examples. But even without knowing that there are such cases, we might anticipate them. 'Prediction' is too strong a word, but the evidence from sex reassignment cases such as David Reimer's and people with DSDs such as 5-ARD suggest a hypothesis. Namely, that some very feminine boys, and some very masculine girls, will develop an extreme discomfort with their sexed bodies and strongly desire to change them to resemble the other sex.

The young Jaron Jennings was drawn to all things girly. Jaron's grandparents recalled an occasion when 'I marched down the stairs wearing a flouncy pink dress with a pink feather boa wrapped around my neck, along with my dress-up heels and loads of costume jewelry weighing down my wrists and fingers.'[43] Jaron's mother consulted the entry for Gender Identity Disorder in the *Diagnostic and Statistical Manual*:

> My mom read the DSM checklist to see if I fit the criteria for this so-called disorder and kept her own tally in her head.
> Does he insist that he is the other sex? *Yes.*
> Does he prefer to wear girls' attire? *Yes, oh yes.*
> Does he fantasize about being the other sex and cross-dress during make-believe? *All the time, YES.*
> Does he have an intense desire to participate in the stereotypical games and pastimes of the opposite sex? *Yep.*
> Does he have a strong preference for playmates of the other sex? *Only plays with girls, YES!*[44]

These criteria are from the fourth edition, the DSM-IV; in the DSM-5, the latest version (2013, revised 2022), Gender Identity Disorder becomes

'Gender Dysphoria', but the diagnostic criteria are very similar. This 'disorder' is more than gender nonconformity, since the first criterion in the DSM-IV is a 'repeatedly stated desire to be, or insistence that he or she is, the other sex'. And there are criteria additional to the ones listed by Jazz, including 'persistent discomfort with his or her sex or sense of inappropriateness in the gender role of that sex', and the requirement that 'the disturbance causes clinically significant distress or impairment.'[45]

Although 'Gender Identity Disorder of Childhood' was in the DSM twenty years before Jazz's birth, she was one of the first to be publicly identified as a 'transgender child'. For Jazz, that meant she had a 'girl brain and a boy body'. This sort of claim tends to rile up some people, who think it is sexist to talk about girl brains. But the problem is something else: if Jazz really had a girl brain in a boy body, she may well not have become dysphoric. One can raise boys (with their boy brains) in a facsimile of a girl's body with no untoward consequences; surgical complications aside, one could have as much success doing it the other way round. Jazz was uncomfortable in her boy body not because she had a girl brain but, rather, because she was highly feminine.[46]

The phenomenon of childhood-onset gender dysphoria provides another reason to think that the orthodox view of gender identity is wrong. Imagine a tree-climbing hockey-playing tomboy who unproblematically thinks of herself as a girl and who has no gender dysphoria. On the orthodox view, she has a female gender identity. A female gender identity, then, can happily coexist with masculine behaviour and interests. Therefore, on the orthodox view, there is nothing to stop a natal *male* child with masculine behaviour and interests from having a female gender identity; such a child would be liable to develop gender dysphoria. In other words, if the orthodox view is right we would expect to see some natal male children, stereotypically masculine in behaviour and otherwise psychologically normal, distressed at their sexed body. If there are such cases, they do not appear in the clinical literature.

Puberty dramatically increases sexual dimorphism, the bodily differences between females and males, and these changes make it impossible for a boy to ignore his sex. We might therefore expect that, in some boys with gender dysphoria, puberty will exacerbate the distress. As an (imperfect) analogy, consider fear of flying. That can be bad enough even if one has never been on a plane, and, once one is on a plane for the first time, aerophobia can intensify into a panic attack. However, sometimes getting on a plane will help: exposure to the feared stimulus can resolve the fearful feelings. So, we might also expect that, in other dysphoric boys, puberty will reconcile them to their sexed bodies and the dysphoria will abate.

It turns out that both expectations are correct. For example, a carefully conducted study of 139 boys who either met the DSM criteria for gender dysphoria or came close found that seventeen (12 per cent) were still dysphoric when followed up in adulthood. In clinical terminology, 12 per cent were 'persisters' and 88 per cent were 'desisters'. (Whether the boys met the criteria for a formal diagnosis or merely came close made no significant difference.) Of the seventeen persisters, only one was gynephilic – that is, heterosexual relative to natal sex. Around six out of ten desisters were classified as androphilic (homosexual relative to natal sex) or bisexual – vastly greater than the population base rate, which is around 2 to 4 per cent.[47]

The phenomenon of desistance gives us one last argument against the battered orthodox view of gender identity. Whatever explains the desisters' gender dysphoria, it cannot be a mismatch between their immutable gender identities and their sex characteristics and gender role. The desisters turn out to be 'cisgender' adults, and so their gender identities were in alignment all along. Their childhood gender dysphoria must have some other explanation. Could the orthodox mismatch explanation still apply to persisters? That is implausible: the fact that childhood gender dysphoria is similar in both persisters and desisters suggests that the *same* explanation holds for both groups. And, if it does, the orthodox mismatch explanation is redundant.

Cases of gender dysphoria like Jazz's – childhood onset accompanied by extreme gender atypicality – illustrate one classic pathway to a transsexual outcome for both sexes, with the resulting sexual orientation very likely being homosexual relative to natal sex. As we saw in the first chapter, a more recent (and not well-studied) route starts with 'rapid onset' gender dysphoria during adolescence, mostly affecting girls. All this is interesting enough. Fortunately for those who like marvelling at human complexity, transsexuality turns out to be even more fascinating. Another pathway to a transsexual outcome for males involves a curious self-directed kind of sexual attraction. The next chapter takes up that explosive topic.

SIX

Born in the Wrong Body

> Ever since I could form coherent thoughts, I knew I was a girl trapped inside a boy's body.
>
> Jazz Jennings, *Being Jazz*[1]

> I was three perhaps four years old when I realized that I had been born in the wrong body, and should really be a girl.
>
> Jan Morris, *Conundrum*[2]

James and Jan

James Morris was born in the West Country of England in 1926 and educated at Lancing College, a public (US: private) school whose alumni include the novelist Evelyn Waugh and Nana Akufo-Addo, the current president of Ghana. Morris studied English at Oxford University and became a renowned globe-trotting journalist, 'the Flaubert of the jet age'. Working for the London *Times*, he joined the ninth British expedition to Everest in 1953 and reported from 22,000 feet up the mountain on the first successful ascent, by the New Zealander Edmund Hillary and the Nepalese-Indian Tenzing Norgay. James married Elizabeth, whose father was a tea planter in (what is now) Sri Lanka, and the couple had five children.[3]

In 1972, James – now Jan – travelled to Casablanca for sex reassignment surgery. Two years later Jan published a best-selling memoir, *Conundrum*, about the most spectacular journey of her life. She described her transition in mystical terms: 'I never did think my own conundrum was a matter either of science or of social convention. I thought it was a matter of the spirit, a kind of divine allegory, and that explanations of it were not very important anyway.'[4] Morris contrasted herself with cross-dressers and gay men, who were more earthly beings:

> Both transvestites and homosexuals sometimes suppose they would be happier if they could change their sex, but they are generally mistaken. The transvestite gains his gratification specifically from wearing the clothes of the opposite sex, and would sacrifice his pleasures by joining that sex: the homosexual, by definition, prefers to make love with others of his own sort, and would only alienate himself and them by changing. Trans-sexualism is something different in kind. It is not a sexual mode or preference. It is not an act of sex at all. It is a passionate, lifelong, ineradicable conviction, and no true trans-sexual has ever been disabused of it.[5]

Transitioning is an ordeal, socially and professionally – to say nothing of the pain and expense. Morris took it all in stride, at one point taking advantage of his/her chameleonic condition in the London scene of private gentlemen and gentlewomen's clubs:

> At the Travellers' Club, for example, I was obviously known as a man of sorts – women were only allowed on the premises at all during a few hours of the day, and even then were hidden away as far as possible in lesser rooms or alcoves. But I had another club, only a few hundred yards away, where I was known only as a woman, and often I went directly from one to the other, imperceptibly changing roles on the way – 'Cheerio, sir,' the porter would say at one club, and 'Hullo, madam' the porter would greet me at the other.[6]

Dame Rebecca West was, like Jan Morris, a much-lauded journalist and travel writer. Her life was perhaps even more remarkable than Morris's: she was a suffragette, H. G. Wells's mistress, and the author of *Black Lamb and Grey Falcon*, a masterpiece about the former Yugoslavia.[7] Like Morris, West was awarded the CBE (Commander of the Most Excellent Order of the British Empire). She reviewed *Conundrum* for the *New York Times*, in effect noting that Jan Morris was no Jazz Jennings: 'He liked being a schoolboy; he liked being an undergraduate, a soldier, a writer, a husband and father; and he was that happy, happy man who does the things Walter Mitty wanted to do.' West was unconvinced by Jan's metamorphosis:

> She sounds not like a woman, but like a man's idea of a woman, and curiously enough, the idea of a man not nearly so intelligent as James Morris used to be ... when Miss Morris writes of the result of her hormonic treatment 'my small breasts blossomed like blushes' one feels sure she is not a woman. Almost any woman not feeble-minded would know that is a remark one must leave for other people to make.[8]

The spectacle of a member of the British establishment disputing, in the pages of the Gray Lady, whether one of her distinguished peers is in fact a woman, must be savoured and preserved for future generations. It will never happen again.

Ridgely and Nancy

Feminist philosophers write a lot about men's oppression of women. One might have expected them to take Rebecca West's side, or at the very least to wonder why a married father of five should want so desperately to become a woman. The question is less urgent applied to those travelling in the other direction: why wouldn't women want to move out of the oppressed class if they could? The transformation of ultra-feminine Jaron Jennings into Jazz is also comprehensible, especially since femininity in boys is disfavoured. But why would an exceptionally successful man such as Morris endure gruelling surgery, only to emerge lower in the social hierarchy, under the heel of the patriarchy? On questions like these, philosophers are remarkably incurious. In the contemporary mainstream literature, trans women are regarded as visitors from distant lands, bearers of great wisdom, and generally to be deferred to on matters of gender. Asking about their life stories is considered rude.[9]

Which, of course, it often is. However, academic disciplines are not supposed to trade understanding for decorum. In pursuit of understanding, then, let's turn to another example.

Ridgely Hunt was born one year later than James Morris, in New York. Like Morris, he attended a world-class university – Yale – and studied English. Like Morris, he served in the Second World War, Morris with the 9th Queen's Royal Lancers and Hunt with the US Army, where he rose to the rank of sergeant. Like Morris, Hunt was a globe-trotting journalist and a brilliant writer; he worked for the *Chicago Tribune* and travelled to Saigon in 1968 as the paper's combat correspondent, accompanying patrols and flying in helicopters with the First Air Cavalry, many times under fire from the North Vietnamese. Like Morris, Hunt was married with children – three, from his first marriage. He had an affair with a younger employee at the *Tribune*, divorced, and married his family's babysitter.

And, like Morris, Hunt met in the 1970s with the legendary sexologist Harry Benjamin in New York City, in pursuit of sex reassignment.

Hunt was greatly affected by Morris's *Conundrum* and was struck by their parallel lives.[10] As James became Jan with the help of hormones and surgery, Ridgely became Nancy, and her autobiography, *Mirror Image*, appeared in 1978. Unlike Jan, Nancy was more forthcoming about the forces that propelled her across the gender line. Describing her time as a boy at Pomfret, a Connecticut prep school for the New England elite, she wrote:

> Occasionally I even dated girls myself and always I was feverishly interested in them. I studied their hair, their clothes, their figures. And I brooded about the increasing differences between us. I seethed with envy while at the same time becoming sexually aroused – I wanted to possess them even as I wanted to become them. In my nighttime fantasies, as I masturbated or floated towards sleep, I combined the two compulsions, dreaming of sex but with myself as the girl, my partner blanked out because I so loathed the male body, even my own.[11]

Like Jan, Nancy was no Jazz.[12]

True transsexuals

Both Jan Morris and Nancy Hunt thought of themselves as 'true transsexuals', disparaging gay men and cross-dressers who also desired a change of sex. By the 1970s, clinicians largely agreed that transsexuality in natal males came in different varieties, although they disagreed both on what those varieties were and on issues of terminology. For example, the psychoanalysts Ethel Person and Lionel Ovesey distinguished 'primary' from 'secondary' transsexuals. In the first group, 'the transsexual impulse is insistent and progressive, and usually they cannot rest until they reach their objective.' They subdivided the second group into 'effeminate homosexuals and transvestites', who 'become transsexuals under stress'. Being psychoanalysts, they formulated an elaborate Freudian theory – now consigned to the dustbin of history – on which primary transsexuals develop a 'fantasy of symbiotic fusion with the mother to counter separation anxiety'.[13]

The psychiatrist Robert Stoller made a similar distinction, between 'true transsexuals', transvestites and homosexuals. 'True transsexuals', Stoller claimed, are never sexually aroused by cross-dressing (unlike transvestites) and are 'feminine, not effeminate'. 'They do not work in masculine professions' and are 'incapable of sexual relations with the opposite sex', so Jan Morris and Nancy Hunt would not qualify. Stoller drew the dividing line between true transsexuals and cross-dressing homosexuals at the penis: 'the transsexual has no interest in his own penis', unlike the homosexual.[14]

Later, Stoller borrowed Person and Ovesey's terminology, equating primary transsexuals with true transsexuals and conceiving secondary transsexuals as comprising 'a wastebasket category', a miscellany of 'men requesting "sex change"' who were not primary transsexuals. John Money dispensed with the primary transsexual category altogether and divided male transsexuals into two groups, 'effeminate-homosexual' and 'transvestitic'. Other researchers distinguished 'fetishistic' transsexuals, who had a history of sexual arousal from cross-dressing, from 'nuclear' transsexuals, who did not.[15]

The diagnosis of Transsexualism – 'persistent discomfort and sense of inappropriateness about one's assigned sex' – appeared in the third edition of the *Diagnostic and Statistical Manual* (1980). The DSM-III subdivided the diagnosis into three types, based on sexual orientation: asexual (corresponding to Person and Ovesey's primary transsexuals), homosexual and heterosexual. The pathway taken by Jazz Jennings was visible in the criteria for 'Gender Identity Disorder of Childhood' – in boys, 'a profound disturbance of the normal sense of maleness … preoccupied with female stereotypical activities' – but no explicit connection was made with later sexual orientation.[16]

Sissy boys

The connection with sexual orientation was shortly to become established, with the publication of Richard Green's *The 'Sissy Boy Syndrome' and the Development of Homosexuality* in 1987. Earlier studies had shown that homosexual men tended to report feminine childhoods, but memories are prone to distortion. Green recruited a group of feminine boys, matched them with a group of demographically similar boys, and followed both groups into early adulthood. Of the forty-four feminine boys Green managed to interview in adolescence, three-quarters said they were either gay or bisexual. All but one of the thirty-five boys in the comparison group reported being heterosexual, which is roughly what one would expect from a representative sample. Put another way: a very feminine boyhood increases one's chances of being gay by about twenty-five times. This strong link between childhood femininity in males and homosexuality has subsequently been confirmed over and over again; there is a similar link between childhood masculinity in females and subsequent lesbianism.[17]

Green had originally conceived his study as an investigation of the origins of cross-sex identity in transsexuals. In the 1960s he interviewed around a hundred people seeking sex-reassignment surgery, some patients of Harry Benjamin in New York, and others from Robert Stoller's UCLA clinic. Although 'extensive cross-gender behaviors' were invariably reported, Green noted the problem of 'the circular universe of transsexual autobiographies and clinical evaluations', where 'patients convince physicians of their transsexual nature by repeating the published developments of transsexuals who preceded them.' His investigation of 'pretransexuals' turned out to be really one of 'prehomosexuality'. More precisely, the study showed that feminine boys who ended up gay and those who ended up transitioning were cut from the same cloth, a phenomenon that can be observed in cultures all over the world. And, in the fifth edition of the DSM, the relationship between persisting childhood gender dysphoria and homosexuality is explicit: 'For both natal male and female children showing persistence, almost all are sexually attracted to individuals of their natal sex.'[18]

Male-to-female transsexuals who follow this pathway are sometimes called *homosexual* or *androphilic* transsexuals; understandably, the latter terminology is more acceptable than the former, since these individuals do not think of themselves as gay. Either way, this can be confusing. What is driving their childhood gender dysphoria is extreme femininity, not subsequent sexual orientation. When sexual orientation develops later, that may be part of the cost–benefit calculation that leads someone to transition – 'My life, including romance and sex, would be better lived as a woman' – but it is not the source of the initial cross-gender feelings. Moreover, extreme childhood femininity, even in those who go on to transition, is no absolute guarantee of an androphilic orientation. *Hyperfeminine* transsexuality is perhaps a better term.

Jan Morris and Nancy Hunt did not take the hyperfeminine pathway traversed by Jazz Jennings, although they both reported cross-gender feelings at an early age. 'For myself', Hunt wrote, 'I know that by the age of four I already had a girl's mind.' In the taxonomy of the psychoanalysts Person and Ovesey, Morris and Hunt were not secondary transsexuals of the homosexual type. They were not good candidates to be Person and Ovesey's primary transsexuals, who were 'essentially asexual'. Neither were they of the other secondary type, transvestitic transsexuals: sexual arousal by cross-dressing was absent from both Morris's *Conundrum* and Hunt's *Mirror Image*. Admittedly Morris's autobiography skated briskly over intimate details, but Hunt seemed commendably frank. And, to complicate the picture still further, Hunt had sex with many men after her reassignment surgery and ended up marrying a man. These early attempts at transsexual typologies were clearly unsatisfactory; a greatly improved one would shortly arrive.[19]

'The love that dare not speak its name'[20]

In the 1980s Ray Blanchard was working at the Gender Identity Clinic at the Clarke Institute of Psychiatry in Toronto, interviewing candidates for sex-reassignment surgery and conducting research into transsexualism, among other topics. (One of Blanchard's discoveries was the *fraternal birth order effect*, whereby boys with older brothers have higher odds of becoming gay.)[21] At the Clarke, he collaborated with Kurt Freund, a Czech sexologist who had sought exile in Canada when the Soviets invaded Czechoslovakia in 1968. Extending a recent hypothesis of Freund's, Blanchard proposed that the seeming diversity of natal male transsexuals outside the hyperfeminine (i.e., homosexual) type were different manifestations of a single underlying condition.

One candidate name for the condition was already in print – *automonosexualism*. The early sexologist Magnus Hirschfeld defined it as an attraction, felt by men, to 'the woman inside them'. 'Transvestism' (although not 'automonosexualism') is due to Hirschfeld, and perhaps that word took off because of its helpful descriptive content: *cross-dressing*. 'Automonosexualism' is nowhere near as good, so in a fateful step Blanchard coined 'autogynephilia', literally *love of oneself as a woman*. Autogynephilia, Blanchard wrote, is 'a male's propensity to be sexually aroused by the thought or image of himself as a female'. The previous emphasis on fetishistic transvestism, according to Blanchard, was misplaced. Using clothing as a prop is just one way of becoming aroused by the thought of oneself as a woman; putting on make-up or going to the hair salon might be another. And, indeed, no external fetish object or activity is necessary, as Blanchard's patient Philip was to demonstrate:[22]

> He began masturbating at puberty, which occurred at age 12 or 13. The earliest sexual fantasy he could recall was that of having a woman's body. When he masturbated, he would imagine that he was a nude woman lying alone in her bed. His mental imagery would focus on his breasts, his vagina, the softness of his skin, and so on – all the characteristic features of the female physique. This remained his favorite sexual fantasy throughout life. His other masturbatory fantasies were less frequent and much less powerful. One of these was the idea of dressing as a woman; another was the fantasy of himself, as a woman, being penetrated vaginally by a man. The latter thought began to occur to him in his thirties; by the time he presented to us, it was arising in one-third to one-half of masturbatory sessions. The imagined partner remained vague in outline, however: a nameless, faceless abstraction rather than a real acquaintance or remembered stranger.[23]

Philip felt no urge to cross-dress, despite having the opportunity to do so in the privacy of his own home.

The asexual transsexuals were not, on this view, really asexual. A better name for them would be 'analloerotics' (*not-other-erotics*) – people not sexually attracted to others, leaving open the possibility that their attraction is directed upon themselves. 'Analloerotic gender dysphorics', Blanchard suggested, 'represent those cases in which the autogynephilic disorder nullifies or overshadows any erotic attraction to women; those cases, in Hirschfeld's metaphor, in which "the woman within" completely supplants her fleshly rivals.'[24]

What about the fact that bisexuality is relatively common outside the homosexual group, as in Nancy Hunt's many dalliances with men? Here Hunt herself offers some clues: 'I had no sympathy for homosexuals and felt a positive revulsion for the coupling of two male bodies. Though I later slept with men, I remained a devout heterosexual.' And, during Hunt's second marriage: '… we made love, wildly and passionately, with me on the bottom in one of Ellen's nightgowns, imagining that I was the woman. Married male transsexuals usually have this fantasy, and I was to retain it for the five remaining years that I would live as an anatomic man.' Nancy Hunt was apparently turned on not by the male form (as gay men are) but by the idea of having sex as a woman. As Blanchard observed, a feature of much heterosexual pornography consumed by men is the presence of men in the action: somehow this adds power to the erotic stimulus. The presence – real or imagined – of men in autogynephilic sexual fantasies and activities is therefore to be expected. Blanchard called this *pseudobisexuality*.[25]

Blanchard distinguished four main types of autogynephilia, corresponding to different sexually arousing fantasies and kinds of behaviour: *physiologic*, *behavioural*, *anatomic* and *transvestic*. Examples of the first include fantasies of breast-feeding or menstruating. Examples of the second – behavioural autogynephilia – are having sex as a woman, either with a lesbian or with a straight man, or performing other 'womanly' activities such as 'using a feminine voice, a feminine name, a feminine walk, tossing my hair, and opening my legs'. Anatomic autogynephilic fantasies centre on having a female body, or one with female features, for instance: 'I was approximately 9 or 10 years old. I was overweight and I had begun to develop breasts, solely from my weight. I would soap my breasts in the shower and imagine I was really a woman with a real woman's breasts, and I would become extremely aroused.' (Recall from the previous chapter the men who wanted to play with their own breasts after reincarnation as women.) And transvestic autogynephilia is basically good old-fashioned transvestism or cross-dressing for the purpose of sexual excitement. These four types are often combined to varying degrees, as in Philip (anatomic and behavioural).[26]

One might suppose that anatomic autogynephilia would be more likely to lead to distress at one's male body and the desire for sex-reassignment. In one study, Blanchard confirmed that prediction, showing that men whose preferred fantasy was themselves as a nude woman as opposed to a clothed one generally had more intense gender dysphoria.[27] Autogynephilia, then, held out the promise of making the impulse to drastically transform one's body intelligible:

> Some men are most aroused sexually by the idea of wearing women's clothes, and they are primarily interested in wearing women's clothes. Some men are most aroused sexually by the idea of having a woman's body, and they are most interested in acquiring a woman's body. Viewed in this light, the desire for sex reassignment surgery of the latter group appears as logical as the desire of heterosexual men to marry wives [and] the desire of homosexual men to establish permanent relationships with male partners.[28]

As indicated by his comparison of autogynephilia with heterosexuality and homosexuality, Blanchard suggested that it can be conceived as an unusual kind of sexual orientation, inwardly directed.

Eonism

Magnus Hirschfeld was not the only one who had the basic idea of autogynephilia in the early twentieth century. Blanchard noted another, the English doctor, eugenist and sexologist Henry Havelock Ellis, author of the seven volume *Studies in the Psychology of Sex*, among other works. One might have hoped that a man who wrote so prolifically about sex must have enjoyed a lot of it, but Ellis was not like the priapic John Money, apparently being impotent. Ellis was also married to a lesbian.[29] One of his chief contributions to sexology was the dispassionate account of homosexuality in the first volume of the *Studies*, *Sexual Inversion*. That work first appeared in 1896, a year after the author Oscar Wilde had been imprisoned for 'gross indecency' with men.

Ellis was 'puzzled by people who took pleasure in behaving and dressing like the opposite sex and yet were not sexually inverted; that is, their sexual feelings were not directed towards persons of their own sex.'[30] He called this condition *Eonism*, after an eighteenth-century Frenchman, the Chevalier d'Eon, whose life story is almost impossible to believe.

D'Eon was a diplomat in Russia and England, a spy, and fought in the Seven Years' War for the French against the British alliance. From the age of forty-nine, the Chevalier lived as a woman for the rest of her life. In a prefiguring of today's controversies about transgender women in female sports, d'Eon competed in fencing tournaments (against men) and by reputation was the best female fencer in the world. Pulling off the most astounding feat of 'passing' ever achieved, those who had known d'Eon as a man believed that she had been an anatomically normal woman all along.[31]

In fact, d'Eon was doubtfully an Eonist, or a transsexual of any kind. Be that as it may, Eonism supposedly 'occurs in the kind of people who tend to be subject to fetichism', and 'also resembles, in some of its features, the kind of auto-erotism called Narcissism or erotic self-admiration.' 'In ordinary life', Ellis wrote, 'the subjects present no startlingly unusual traits and may seem quite ordinarily masculine, but sometimes sensitive and reserved, often devoted to their wives ... Though they do not often desire inverted sexual relationships, male Eonists sometimes feel an almost passionate loving for a woman's experiences, of pregnancy and motherhood.'[32]

And there is this memorable passage: 'On the psychic side, as I view it, the Eonist is embodying, in an extreme degree, the aesthetic attribute of imitation of, and identification with, the admired object. It is normal for a man to identify himself with the woman he loves. The Eonist carries that identification too far ...'.[33]

We'll touch on some criticisms of Blanchard's typology of male transsexuality later, but these historical antecedents are worth emphasizing in advance. Hostile accounts often give the impression that Blanchard is a crazed reactionary quack who invented autogynephilia out of thin air in the 1980s, much as L. Ron Hubbard devised the engram and other mythical postulates of scientology three decades earlier. That makes it much easier to dismiss the phenomenon entirely. Scientific advances usually build on earlier ones, and Blanchard's development of autogynephilia was no exception.

Identity inversions

A paraphilia is an unusual intense sexual interest. ('Para' means *abnormal.*) Examples are fetishism (sexual arousal by objects such as rubberwear or shoes, or body parts such as feet or hair), transvestic fetishism (where the fetish object is clothing of the other sex), voyeurism, exhibitionism, frotteurism (touching and rubbing strangers), masochism, sadism, paedophilia, and zoophilia (sexual attraction to animals). Some of these may not be so unusual.[34]

Obviously some paraphilias should not be acted upon – paedophilia being the most glaring example – although some are quite harmless. But even harmless paraphilias, such as fetishism, can impair normal functioning and cause distress. In such cases, the paraphilia is upgraded to a *paraphilic disorder*, a diagnosis in the DSM-5.

Are the paraphilias just a hodgepodge of those sexual inclinations strongly condemned by present sexual mores? No. First, although some paraphilias are viewed with revulsion – especially paedophilia – some are tolerated. 'My rubber fetish is fun, wonderful and an integral part of me … It has enriched my life', an anonymous fetishist wrote in a UK newspaper. National Fetish Day started in that country in 2008 – now International Fetish Day. More importantly, the paraphilias have a deeper unity. At least in their more extreme forms, they are found predominantly in men (with masochism being the main exception). They tend to occur together: for instance, exhibitionists are often also voyeurists. They sometimes develop in childhood and rarely go away, although they may decline with age. As the British rubber fetishist put it, 'I can't be "cured", and I don't want to be.'[35]

Interestingly, even if autogynephilia had never been observed, the study of paraphilias would predict – or at least strongly hint at – its existence. This is because of another fascinating fact about paraphilias, namely that they often have 'inverted' counterparts, where the external target of sexual attraction becomes internalized. Paedophilia, for example, sometimes occurs with *autopaedophilia*, where the sexually arousing stimulus is oneself as a child. Autopaedophilic activities include dressing as a child, or *pedovestism*. Another example is *acrotomophilia* (John Money's term for sexual attraction to amputees), which has an inverted counterpart, *apotemnophilia* (another Money coinage), where the sexually arousing stimulus is oneself as an amputee.[36]

You may never have heard of Midwest FurFest, held annually in metro Chicago. It is a convention for 'furries', people who have a keen interest in anthropomorphic furry animals, sometimes dressing up as Bugs Bunny and other cartoon characters. The furry community heavily skews male, and a significant number of furries are sexually attracted to anthropomorphic furry animals – *anthropomorphozoophilia*. And that paraphilia, too, has an inverted counterpart, named by the best word in this book, *autoanthropomorphozoophilia*.[37]

Heterosexuality in men should be distinguished from *gynephilia*, sexual attraction to adult females. Male paedophiles can be heterosexual too, and usually are. That is, they are attracted to female children. Gynephilia in men is the rule, not the exception, so is not a paraphilia. But it has enough in common with these examples to suggest that it should have an inverted form. And that would be autogynephilia.[38]

As expected, autogynephilia co-occurs with other paraphilias. *Autoerotic asphyxia* is the (dangerous) practice of cutting off oxygen to the brain to enhance sexual pleasure, for instance by strangulation. A study of 117 autoasphyxia fatalities found that more than four out of ten subjects (all male) were cross-dressed, wore make-up, or displayed some other sign of autogynephilia.[39]

By the same token, *androphilia* in men – sexual attraction to adult males – should also have an inverted form: *autoandrophilia*. But what would autoandrophilia in a male look like? After all, he already *is* a male, so the fantasy of having male anatomy would seem to be superfluous. The following may be an example, from the psychoanalyst George Zavitzianos, writing in 1972:

> He remembered that around puberty he saw two young athletes wearing jock-straps and got the impression that the jock-straps covered very large penises. After that, he tried to masturbate wearing a jock-strap himself and looking at himself in the mirror ... [T]he patient is using clothing of the same sex for his perverse behavior. When he looks at himself in the mirror wearing this apparel, he reacts with an erection. Looking at himself in the mirror is to him as stimulating as a homosexual relationship.[40]

Existence versus theory

'The study of autogynephilia', Blanchard once remarked, 'is, more than anything else, the study of what people *say* about their experiences.'[41] That is true of transsexuality in general: the very first investigators placed great value on first-person narratives, and Harry Benjamin included many of them in *The Transsexual Phenomenon*.

Especially in matters of sex, people are sometimes not completely forthcoming. They may leave details out. They may subtly distort their biographies, not intending to deceive, but as a means of maintaining an acceptable self-image. More straightforwardly, they might misinterpret their feelings and behaviour: we are far from transparent to ourselves. And on occasion they may simply lie. That first-person reports of sexuality are sometimes inaccurate is more than plausible – sometimes it is provable. For example, if you think about it for a moment, heterosexual men and women must have the same number of sexual partners, on average. Yet surveys consistently find that men report more opposite-sex partners than women.[42] Being judiciously sceptical of narratives by transgender people is merely to treat them as human beings.

Still, if the narrative is potentially shameful, embarrassing or humiliating, that is a reason for taking it at face value. 'How does a man's behavior sound more normal if he admits to pretending that his anus is a vagina while he inserts dildos into it than if he admits to a predilection for wearing panties?', Blanchard asked.[43] A rhetorical question, if ever there was one! And if further confirmation is needed, pornography supplies it. A sub-genre is 'sissy porn', in which men are coerced to dress and have sex as women.

As Blanchard emphasized, the existence of autogynephilia is one thing; its origin and role in transsexuality and gender dysphoria are quite another. Perhaps autogynephilia is merely correlated (in a sub-group of males) with a transsexual outcome and is not a cause of it. If that were true, autogynephilia would still be of considerable interest but would shed little light on the process of transitioning.

We have already seen some evidence that autogynephilia is connected with motivation to transition, namely Blanchard's finding that anatomic autogynephilia is associated with greater gender dysphoria. Further, sexual attraction is evidently one of the stronger male impulses, as attested by the many men who have ruined their careers and relationships over the reckless pursuit of sex. Only something that powerful can explain the extraordinary lengths some men go to in pursuit of the dream of becoming a woman, and autogynephilia fits the bill nicely.[44]

Anne Lawrence is a psychologist and former anaesthesiologist who transitioned in the 1990s and is a self-identified autogynephilic transsexual. She is the author of numerous papers in sexology and of the classic *Men Trapped in Men's Bodies: Narratives of Autogynephilic Transsexualism*. That book contains excerpts from hundreds of narratives from people who had experienced autogynephilia. Here's a sample of statements about whether autogynephilia is a motive for transition, one positive, one unsure, and one negative:

'I have always had highly charged erotic feelings associated with the development of female sex characteristics. It seems to me it's been the root cause of a greater commitment to transsexuality and it's what drives me from one step to the next.' 'I have been exploring transsexualism actively for maybe 6 months. Cross-dressing in the closet has been my outlet for 25 years. The thought of being a woman transports me. I don't seek only to be a woman in appearance, I want the full experience. Is it arousing? Sure. Is it the reason? I don't think so, but it is hard for me to differentiate.' 'My thoughts of being female almost always were accompanied by erotic feelings. But I don't believe it would be accurate to say that I transitioned because of erotic feelings, for I might well have done so anyway.'[45]

If a transgender woman says that her dysphoria is due in part to sexual feelings, she gains nothing other than the satisfaction of being honest. These sorts of reports are therefore credible. And, as the second quotation above shows, sometimes the reasons for one's actions are not easy to discern, a familiar phenomenon from everyday social interactions. Doubt even creeps into the third quotation. A reasonable working hypothesis is that, in autogynephilic males who transition, autogynephilia is part of the explanation.[46]

Another attractive – albeit more speculative – hypothesis is that gender dysphoria in natal males is always due (in part) either to hyperfemininity or to autogynephilia. As Blanchard put it: 'All gender dysphoric males who are not sexually oriented toward men are instead sexually oriented toward the thought or image of themselves as women' – clearly intending this to imply that there are two distinct causes of gender dysphoria. In a series of studies Blanchard provided a variety of evidence to support this hypothesis, but focusing on whether there are exceptions can be distracting. Even if there are, demystifying the occurrence of gender dysphoria in a large proportion of males is still a significant advance.[47]

Gay men sometimes deny – even sincerely – that they are homosexual. That is unsurprising and understandable. Remember the US evangelist Ted Haggard, fiery campaigner against gay marriage and – it turned out – faithful customer of a male prostitute? It would be naive in the extreme to think that autogynephilia will always be revealed if one asks hard enough.

'One of the most transphobic books in history'[48]

The Man Who Would be Queen (2003) is a book about feminine males and male-to-female transsexuals written by the psychologist J. Michael Bailey. A work of popular science, full of personal stories vividly told, it devoted one chapter to Blanchard's theory of autogynephilia, which Bailey presented with no reservations: 'Blanchard's observations transformed male-to-female transsexualism from a seemingly chaotic and bizarre collection of phenomena into two straightforwardly and clinically comprehensible patterns.'[49] The book was nominated for a Lambda Literary Foundation Award in the Transgender/GenderQueer category. That was the high point.

Some examples of contemporary cancel culture were related in chapter 1. Compared to Bailey's cancellation, these are like so many vicarage tea parties. A group of trans women, two of them highly accomplished academics, set out to ruin Bailey by any means necessary. There were allegations of scientific misconduct, and Bailey was investigated by his university, Northwestern. The Lambda nomination was withdrawn after a campaign. Bailey was accused of having sex with a transsexual research subject and of fabricating the ending of one of the book's stories. His family was targeted. One activist, Andrea James, put up on her website an 'Invective against J. Michael Bailey's "The Man Who Would Be Queen"' – one could hardly complain about the accuracy of the title. James displayed pictures of Bailey's children, asking whether his daughter was 'a cock-starved exhibitionist, or a paraphiliac who just gets off on the idea of it?' It was not just Bailey: Anne Lawrence also came under attack. Apart from being a self-identified autogynephilic trans woman, her blurb was on the back cover: 'a wonderful book on an important subject'. 'I used to be respected, even admired, within my community', she ruefully remarked later. 'Now many people see me as the anti-Christ.'[50]

The Mother of All Cancellations was met by the mother of all investigative journalism. The historian Alice Dreger wrote an article in 2008 totalling more than 50,000 words for the sexology journal *Archives of Sexual Behavior*, examining the controversy in exhaustive detail. She acquitted Bailey of all charges, while adding an admonition that he should have been 'more proactive in protecting the identity' of one of the book's subjects. Some parts of the book could have been phrased more sensitively, but it is doubtful that this would have made much difference. And Dreger revealed that Andrea James had corresponded with Anne Lawrence in 1998 over an article Lawrence had written for the magazine *Transgender Tapestry*, expounding Blanchard's ideas for a lay transgender audience. Lawrence's article was 'excellent', James wrote, and went on to praise Blanchard for his 'quite valid, even brilliant' observations, and 'readily admit[ting] to my own autogynephilia'.[51]

After Dreger's investigation, did the controversy about autogynephilia die away? Of course it didn't.

'A sex-fueled mental illness created by Ray Blanchard in 1989'[52]

The recent *Sage Encyclopedia of Trans Studies* – weighing in at nearly 1,000 pages – contains a terse entry for autogynephilia: '*See* Anti-Trans Theories'. Turning to 'Anti-Trans Theories', we find autogynephilia introduced under the sub-heading 'Autogynephilia: a debunked adult anti-trans theory'. The writer and trans activist Julia Serano is the only critic mentioned by name in the text, and indeed she is the invariable citation for the definitive refutation of Blanchard's various claims about autogynephilia. For example, a physician who reviewed Abigail Shrier's *Irreversible Damage: The Transgender Craze Seducing Our Daughters* mentions Blanchard's hypothesis, 'which suggests that transgender women are transgender because of a fetish. The hypothesis has been thoroughly rejected, and I will defer to Julia Serano for her breakdown of the many reasons why.' This is doubly wrong. First, Blanchard's hypothesis (or one of them) was not that *all* transgender women are autogynephilic, but only that the non-hyperfeminine ones are. Second – and ironically – Blanchard *overturned* the previous classification of some transsexuals as 'fetishistic'. One of Blanchard's chief contributions was the idea that, although transvestic fetishism was prevalent among a sub-group of males with gender dysphoria, it was merely a symptom of something deeper.[53]

Serano's main published criticisms are in her 2010 article 'The case against autogynephilia'. The title sounds as if Serano thinks that autogynephilia is a fictional condition, like demonic possession or the (US) playground diagnosis of cooties. That is not Serano's view, although her preferred terminology manages to give that impression.

Objections can be made to some of Blanchard's claims about autogynephilia and not others. For example, one might object to the two-type taxonomy by exhibiting examples of non-autogynephilic and non-androphilic male-to-female transsexuals. Or one might argue that autogynephilia is too unlike the classic paraphilias to count as one. We won't attempt here to assess all the objections from Serano and other critics; further references can be found in the notes.[54]

Instead, let's examine an instructive objection on which Serano places great weight, namely that autogynephilia cannot explain 'gender dysphoria and a desire to transition to female in nonandrophilic MtF transsexuals'. Although it initially seems plausible that autogynephilia is one of the causes, Serano argues that this is wrong, because autogynephilia develops in puberty, and cross-gender wishes in non-androphilic males appear earlier: 'The … perhaps most damaging finding for the presumption of causality is that many nonandrophilic MtF individuals report that they experienced an awareness of wanting to be female long before they ever experienced cross-gender arousal.' Nancy Hunt is an example: 'I know that by the age of four I already had a girl's mind.' Memories of one's feelings at the age of four should be treated with suspicion at the best of times, but Hunt also writes of cross-dressing during first grade. Serano points out that Blanchard's patient Philip is another example. To quote Blanchard: 'His first specific recollection of wanting to be a female dated back to age 6. Encountering a wishing well for the first time, he begged a penny from his father to throw in. His wish was that God would listen to his prayers and let him change into a girl.' Again, this might be convenient retconning, but there are plenty of other reports along similar lines.[55]

Proponents of the 'presumption of causality' can hardly have overlooked this phenomenon, and indeed they haven't. Anne Lawrence has discussed it in an illuminating article descriptively titled 'Becoming what we love: autogynephilic transsexualism conceptualized as an expression of romantic love', so let's turn to that next.

'An amatory propensity'

Blanchard's first characterization of autogynephilia was as an 'erotic (or amatory) propensity'. As we saw, he also conceptualized it as a kind of sexual orientation. The idea that autogynephilia was much more than self-directed horniness was there from the beginning. It is a mistake, Lawrence wrote, to think of autogynephilia 'as a purely erotic or lusty phenomenon, devoid of any of the other elements, such as admiration, affection, beneficence, and desire for closeness, that are usually associated with the word *love*, broadly construed, and that are considered to be expressive of a person's sexual orientation.'[56] The romantic-attachment component of sexual orientation, she suggested, may explain why some MtF transsexuals report that erotic feelings played only a minor role in their transitions, and why autogynephilic sexual arousal after transition frequently lessens or even vanishes. There is a parallel here with ordinary heterosexual and homosexual coupling, as Blanchard himself had pointed out: initial sexual infatuation evolves into a deeper emotional union.

With respect to childhood, Lawrence noted that sexual orientation in general manifests earlier than puberty, as non-erotic childhood crushes and the like. (Another relevant fact is that paraphilias can develop in childhood.) To this, Serano responds: 'By the same reasoning, men who love their own children, but who are not sexually aroused by them, could nevertheless be said to experience pedophilia.' Evidently this is not 'the same reasoning' at all. Lawrence is not conflating love – parental or otherwise – with sexual attraction. Rather, she is making the general observation that a person's sexual orientation can surface as non-sexual attachment before puberty. The hypothesis that autogynephilia is an unusual kind of sexual orientation fits rather nicely with – to quote Blanchard again – 'what people *say* about their experiences'.[57]

'The basic structure of all human sexuality'

Serano revisited the issue of autogynephilia in print ten years later with another article, 'Autogynephilia: a scientific review, feminist analysis, and alternative "embodiment fantasies" model'. This appeared in 2020 in a special issue of a sociology journal, with the title 'TERF wars: feminism and the fight for transgender futures'. Given the pejorative 'TERF', this was unlikely to be a balanced collection of diverse opinions, and it certainly wasn't. The editors' introduction to the special issue displayed the background ideology – 'gender and sex are discursively co-constituted', 'female and male are, themselves, socially constituted categories', and so on. Serano's article went beyond her earlier one principally by appealing to research supposedly showing autogynephilia in women: 'cisgender women frequently report FEFs' (FEFs are 'female/feminine embodiment fantasies').[58]

This hypothesis was always controversial, and the latest research strongly suggests that autogynephilia is either very rare or non-existent in females. However, for the sake of the argument, suppose the most extreme version of the hypothesis is true. *All* females are autogynephilic: at puberty, some become sexually aroused by wearing women's clothing; others are like Philip and masturbate to the image of 'their breasts, their vagina, the softness of their skin ...'; yet others have different autogynephilic fantasies, singly or in combination. Would that mean Blanchard is wrong? According to Serano: 'it seems both illogical and needlessly stigmatising to single out trans women as supposedly being "autogynephiles" for having similar erotic experiences (unless, of course, the label is primarily intended to pathologise trans women's sexualities even when they are female-typical).' The 'illogical' charge implies that it is unreasonable or unscientific to single out the minority of males who are autogynephilic if females experience autogynephilia too. It is not. Analogously, the fact that most women are androphilic does not mean that it is unreasonable to single out the minority of androphilic males. To the contrary: (exclusive) androphilia in males is extremely interesting, mostly because evolutionary considerations would lead us to expect that it would not occur. And likewise for the minority of males who are autogynephilic: it is entirely logical to single them out for special attention, because autogynephilia might explain why some of them go on to transition. Autogynephilia in females, if there is such a thing, is no threat to either the two-type taxonomy or the idea that autogynephilia can lead to gender dysphoria.[59]

The second charge, of stigmatization, is irrelevant to the truth of theoretical claims about autogynephilia. (Which is certainly *not* to say that the issue should be brushed aside.) But, in any case, if females are autogynephilic, that should make autogynephilia in some male-to-female transsexuals *affirming* rather than stigmatizing. The word 'autogynephilia' should be avoided, Serano thinks, partly because it is 'trans female/feminine-specific', but it isn't, at least if we focus on the root meaning, *love of oneself as a woman*. Granted that autogynephilia really is widespread, that is an argument for promoting the use of the word, if anything.

Serano's article has a glaring omission. Normally, in arguing against a scientific theory one cites the latest publications on the topic, particularly if they contain new data or arguments supporting the theory one opposes. Anne Lawrence's book – the one with numerous narratives of autogynephilia, as well as a huge amount of other relevant material – came out in 2013. In 2017 her review article 'Autogynephilia and the typology of male-to-female transsexualism: concepts and controversies' appeared in the journal *European Psychologist*. All the main criticisms are discussed, and all the main critics are cited, including Serano. Lawrence also mentions the issue of autogynephilia in women, a literature to which she contributed herself. No scholarly discussion of autogynephilia is complete without engaging these two works. In Serano's earlier 2010 article, Lawrence is cited. Yet, in the subsequent 2020 article, Lawrence is not cited at all. This is representative of the intellectual quality of the 'TERF wars' special issue.[60]

The writer and *enfant terrible* of trans studies, Andrea Long Chu, took the normalization of autogynephilia to the limit in her 2019 book *Females*. Blanchard – 'a truly loathsome man' – is apparently the new Freud, having (inadvertently) formulated a universal theory of the mind. 'Autogynephilia', Chu declares, 'describes not an obscure paraphilic affliction but rather *the basic structure of all human sexuality*.' Chu partly compensates for frivolity with uninhibited self-disclosures. She once gave a conference presentation called 'Did sissy porn make me trans?' – answering in *Females*, 'Sissy porn did … At very least it served as a neat allegory for my desire to be female.' An exasperated trans activist tweeted, 'all I want for Christmas this year is for Andrea Long Chu to get a better fucking therapist.'[61]

Autogynephilia is a captivating window into the extraordinary variety of male sexuality. One thing is for sure: attempts to draw the curtains will continue.

FtM

Henry Havelock Ellis thought there were female Eonists (people 'who took pleasure in behaving and dressing like the opposite sex' despite not being homosexual) and his *Studies in the Psychology of Sex* describes the nineteenth-century British Army surgeon James Barry, supposedly the male Eonist's 'feminine counterpart'. However, the transsexual label fits Barry – born Margaret Anne Bulkley – no better than it does the Chevalier d'Eon. Barry started living as a man at twenty, when he enrolled as a medical student at the University of Edinburgh in 1809, with his mother in on the scheme, and had a very successful career, serving in – among other places – South Africa, the Crimea and Canada. Barry's secret was revealed only after death, when the body of 'a perfect female' was discovered. As a woman, Barry was barred from medical school, and, as Ellis says himself, purported examples of female Eonists have either lived as men to make employment easier or else were 'sexually inverted' – i.e., homosexual. Barry seems to have been motivated by career prospects; there is no evidence of same-sex attraction or of cross-gender behaviour in childhood.[62]

Another of Ellis's examples of female Eonists clearly started down the hypermasculine pathway:

> Elsa B ... did not care for girls' playthings and would hide them away. She made no friends among other little girls but played with boys ... At the age of 14 or 15 she was much attracted to another girl and gratified her affection by kisses and embraces. Her erotic thoughts are exclusively directed towards women ...[63]

To sexologists in the later part of the twentieth century, this was the only route to transsexuality in females. 'Heterosexual cross-gender identity', wrote the sexologist Kurt Freund in 1985, 'virtually does not exist at all in women.' That is a little puzzling because, although extreme cross-gender behaviour in girls makes subsequent homosexuality much more likely, heterosexuality is also a possible outcome. One might expect, then, the hypermasculine pathway to produce some female-to-male transsexuals who are sexually attracted to males. And indeed subsequent investigators found androphilic FtM transsexuals. Research on this population is not extensive.[64]

Are there any female Eonists? That is, is there another pathway to a transsexual outcome in females, analogous to the autogynephilic pathway in males? Even if autoandrophilia exists in women, it might not spur transition – the condition might be less intense or differ in other ways. There are occasional reports of adolescent females developing gender dysphoria after fantasies of having sex as gay men, but this *autohomeroticism* appears to be quite rare, at least among the older cohorts of FtM transsexuals.[65] Although female-to-male transitioning is a more complex phenomenon than was once thought, it does not approach the variation found in males. Males are the more extreme sex in many respects, and transsexuality is no exception.

The Jazz Age

The present moment might be called the Jazz Age, defined as it is by the doctrine of girl brains in boy bodies.[66] Sometimes there is a mismatch between the sex of the brain and the sex of the body, and adjustments to the body are needed to restore psychic harmony. The mismatch might be manifest from the earliest years, or it might be largely suppressed until adulthood. Jan Morris and Jazz Jennings differ only in that Jan expressed her true self much later. Someone assigned male at birth and someone assigned female at birth can both suffer the same kind of mismatch. Swapping bodies would solve both their problems.

The Jazz Age coincides with the Age of Diversity, the celebration and elevation of human differences. It is thus ironic that the Jazz Age flattens the mountainous diversity in transsexuality, observed by many clinicians for at least a century, into a bland and featureless plain.

James Morris's transition to Jan was a great success, by any measure. Transitioning husbands often lose their wives, but Jan remained happily partnered with Elizabeth.[67] (The couple had to divorce after James morphed into Jan, but remarried in 2008.) Jan's career continued on its stellar trajectory, and she became a beloved and celebrated fixture in British culture – as the natives say, a 'national treasure'. Her transition to womanhood was successful in another way. Nancy Hunt made it just past three score years and ten, but Jan had a lifespan more befitting a woman, enjoying a vigorous old age until her death at ninety-four. In a scientific spirit, we may wonder which theory of her conundrum offers the best explanation. The Jazz Age, unfortunately, discourages such questions.

SEVEN

Is Biology Destiny?

> If evolutionary theory is correct, we cannot design twenty-first century woman from scratch.
>
> Anne Campbell, *A Mind of Her Own*[1]

> The biological differences between men and women make it inevitable that every society will be patriarchal.
>
> Steven Goldberg, *The Inevitability of Patriarchy*[2]

The subjection of women

Margaret Bulkley – a.k.a. the eminent surgeon Dr James Barry, whom we met at the end of the previous chapter – died in her mid-seventies after succumbing to dysentery, which was then raging through polluted Victorian London. She became the army's director of hospitals only thanks to her male alter ego. Dr Margaret Bulkley was never an option – women in Britain were admitted to medical school in 1869, four years after her death. That same year, the philosopher John Stuart Mill published *The Subjection of Women*, a classic essay on women's rights. At that point in the reign of Queen Victoria, women could not vote, could not become doctors or lawyers, and their husbands owned everything. Mill's book was an argument for change.[3]

Since the subjection of women is universal, Mill observed, it can appear part of the natural order of things. But it may be instead a widespread cultural tradition that is not mandated by nature or biology and which could easily be overturned. Mill gave the example of people in 'distant parts of the world', who learn that England is ruled by a woman – 'the thing seems to them so unnatural as to be almost incredible.' Would women flunk out of medical school, unable to master *Gray's Anatomy*, or fainting at the sight of blood? Probably not. Even if women fared on average worse than men, so what? They were, Mill said, just asking to be held to the same standards, and ignoring 'one-half of the whole quantity of talent' can hardly be to the betterment of humanity.[4]

Margaret Bulkley undoubtedly contributed more than her fair share to the betterment of humanity. When her sex was discovered, the editor of a medical journal churlishly questioned Dr Barry's talents in the operating theatre, but Barry's surgical prowess was well established.[5] If there was any question about whether women were constitutionally unfit to be surgeons, Margaret Bulkley answered it.

In democratic societies these days, women flourish as doctors, lawyers, pilots and politicians. In US colleges, they flourish more than men, who comprise a mere four out of ten students. Still, Victorian debates about the differences between the sexes, repackaged to reflect contemporary concerns, remain as heated as ever. Reviewing Gina Rippon's recent *The Gendered Brain* – subtitled *The New Neuroscience that Shatters the Myth of the Female Brain* – the neuroscientist Larry Cahill wrote that the book 'is so chock-full of bias that one keeps wondering why one is bothering with it.' At the other pole was the neuroscientist Lise Eliot: Rippon is 'a leading voice against the bad neuroscience of sex differences ... the book accomplishes its goal of debunking the concept of a gendered brain. The brain is no more gendered than the liver or kidneys or heart.'[6]

More than a century and a half ago, Mill took a cautious line, saying that no one is entitled 'to affirm even that there is any difference, much more what the difference is, between the two sexes considered as moral and rational beings.' The necessary scientific investigations, he said, had not yet been conducted. Who knows what would happen if women were given a proper education? That did not stop his contemporaries from opining on the matter – for instance, the Irish historian William Lecky: 'Physically, men have the indisputable superiority in strength, and women in beauty. Intellectually, a certain inferiority of the female sex can hardly be denied when we remember how almost exclusively the foremost places in every department of science, literature, and art have been occupied by men ...'. To be fair to Lecky, women had more than beauty on their side: women are 'usually superior to men in nimbleness and rapidity of thought', and, 'morally, the general superiority of women over men, is, I think, unquestionable.' Lecky was more conciliatory than another nineteenth-century intellectual, the German philosopher Friedrich Nietzsche, who said, 'When a woman has scholarly inclinations, there is usually something wrong with her sexuality.'[7]

As Rippon puts the view of some Victorians: 'Biology was destiny and the different "essences" of men and women determined their rightful (and different) places in society.'[8] You might think – with Rippon – that this is completely wrong, if not pernicious. This chapter will argue that there's actually some truth to it.

Rightful vs. different

First, we need to make a crucial distinction, indicated in the quotation from Rippon by the words 'rightful' and 'different'. Let's start with the *different* side of the distinction. Some men are taller than 8 feet. No woman is (maybe with one or two exceptions). Plausibly the explanation lies in human female and male biology, which makes these height outcomes *inevitable*. To put it in Rippon's way, the different 'essences' of men and women determine or guarantee their different places at the top of the height rankings. This is a neutral factual claim; it is not a claim about what we *should* do, for instance that we *should* give prizes to the tallest people, or to the shortest, or give no prizes at all.

Rippon, of course, is talking about different places *in society* – in politics, the workforce and domestic life – not places on the beanpole podium. The view that the different 'essences' of men and women make different social outcomes inevitable is called *biological determinism*. The biological determinist holds that human female and male biology determines or guarantees that the sexes occupy different places in politics, the workforce, or domestic life. This is a neutral factual claim; it is not a claim about what social policies we *should* enact, for instance that we *should* subsidize childcare, or marriage, or not subsidize anything.

Biological determinism seems to have a glaring problem. Biology makes it inevitable that all women are shorter than 8 feet. But biology does not likewise make it inevitable that all women are disenfranchised or absent from the legislature or medical schools – the proof is that they *do* have the vote and *are* politicians and surgeons. So why even bother discussing biological determinism? It is, you might think, plainly false.

We'll see why this dismissal is too hasty later, but, in any case – and this brings us to the *rightful* side of the distinction – biological determinism comes in another version. Namely, because of biology, the sexes *should* occupy different places in society – their 'rightful' places. As the feminist literary critic Toril Moi puts it, 'Biological determinism … considers that biology grounds and *justifies* social norms.'[9]

So biological determinists come in two different stripes, and it is important that we keep them separate. All biological determinists agree that there are biological differences between the sexes: they differ in what they make of them. Some biological determinists think that biology *makes it inevitable* that women and men occupy different places in society. Other biological determinists think that biology means that women and men *should* occupy different places in society.[10]

An example of the second kind of biological determinist is a contemporary of Mill, William Keith Brooks, an American zoologist and author of a seminal study of the oyster.[11] In his book *The Law of Heredity*, Brooks devoted a chapter to the intellectual differences between the sexes. While emphasizing that 'there can be no question as to relative superiority or inferiority', he argued that:

> The positions which women already occupy in society and the duties which they perform are, in the main, what they *should be* if our view is correct; and any attempt to improve the condition of women by ignoring or obliterating the intellectual differences between them and men must result in disaster to the race, and the obstruction of that progress and improvement which the history of the past shows to be in store for both men and women in the future.[12]

Brooks was not saying female biology *prevents* women from voting or from being senators. He was not saying that biological differences between females and males *make it inevitable* that the sexes occupy different places in politics, the workforce or domestic life. Instead, Brooks was saying that sexual biology *justifies* what he admitted was 'the conservative or old-fashioned view' – that the social and political divisions between the sexes in nineteenth-century America are more or less as they *should be*.

Brooks's brand of biological determinism does rely on the existence of relevant differences between the sexes: if, say, there are no significant 'intellectual differences' between women and men, then Brooks's conclusion about how society should be organized rests on a false premise. And feminist writers, in philosophy and elsewhere, have typically had an aversion to any sex differences, especially psychological ones, that cannot be laid at the feet of culture or social influences. That needs qualifying slightly, since the differences between female and male reproductive systems, and primary and secondary sex characteristics, are not denied by anyone. Still, even athletic differences have been chalked up to society's suppression of female talent.[13] The contemporary debate around transgender rights and single sex spaces has changed all that, making sex differences respectable again. Some feminists argue that sexual biology justifies various social policies, particularly in the case of sport.

Are these feminists right to think that biology is largely responsible for the sporting performance gaps between females and males? They are, as we'll see in a moment. Once this is accepted, the seemingly retrograde idea that the different 'essences' of men and women make different social or political outcomes *inevitable* will turn out to be not so bonkers, after all.[14]

Throwing like a girl

When the New Zealander and trans woman Laurel Hubbard qualified for the 2021 Olympic Games in weightlifting, that was just one of many such examples that focused attention on human sexual dimorphism, the bodily differences (e.g., in strength and height) between human females and males. Middle-aged feminists who had cut their teeth on Simone de Beauvoir's remark that 'no biological … destiny defines the figure that the human female takes on in society' were emphasizing that, in athletics, biology very much *was* destiny. Hubbard did not win a medal at the 2021 Olympic Summer Games in the women's superheavyweight division. However, she was competing, at the ripe old age of forty-three, against females twenty years her junior. Many felt Hubbard's participation was unfair.[15]

A few years earlier, the tennis legend Martina Navratilova had written: 'I am happy to address a transgender woman in whatever form she prefers, but I would not be happy to compete against her. It would not be fair.' (A US philosophy professor called her 'deeply transphobic'.) The journalist Helen Joyce's recent book *Trans* has a chapter subtitled 'How gender self-identification threatens to destroy women's sports', in which she points out the significant male athletic advantage. For instance, 'the fastest time ever run by Allyson Felix, the women's 400-metre Olympic champion, is beaten more than 15,000 times each year by men and boys.' An obscure man ranked 203 on the men's tennis tour handily beat Venus and Serena Williams after prepping with 'a leisurely round of golf and a few shandies'.[16]

How times change! Back in 1980, the feminist philosopher Iris Marion Young published an article called 'Throwing like a girl: a phenomenology of feminine body comportment motility and spatiality', which subsequently became a minor classic. Young noted that females and males move differently: 'not only is there a typical style of throwing like a girl, but there is a more or less typical style of running like a girl, climbing like a girl, ...' These differences, she suggested, have nothing to do with 'anatomy and physiology'. Instead, 'they have their source in the particular *situation* of women as conditioned by their sexist oppression in contemporary society.'[17]

Men can throw spears about a third further than women. The fastest baseball pitch by a woman is 69 mph. By a man it is 105 mph. Is this largely because – in Young's words – 'Women in sexist society are physically handicapped'? Young presented very little evidence that it is. And, in fact, there are anatomical sex differences, in particular in the 'pectoral girdle' (the shoulder blade and the collarbone), that give males a throwing advantage.[18]

At least Young conceded that 'there are indeed real physical differences between men and women in the kind and limit of their physical strength', and many other feminists had said the same. More grudgingly, in the same decade, the biologist and gender studies academic Anne Fausto-Sterling wrote in *Myths of Gender* that 'on average men are a bit taller and a bit stronger than women.' She thought that cultural nudges such as encouraging girls to be athletic might close sporting achievement gaps, if not eliminate them altogether. In the revised edition of her book in 1992, Fausto-Sterling claimed that 'there are very few absolute sex differences and ... without complete social equality we cannot know for sure what they are', citing a letter in the journal *Nature* in support. The letter, written by two doctors, charted the increase in running speed for female and male Olympic athletes over the twentieth century. Measured by world records, both sexes were running faster, but the rate of increase for females was greater. Fitting a straight line to the female data points, another one to the male points, and projecting them both into the future indicated that women would catch up to men in the marathon in 1998 and in the 1500 metres in 2029.[19]

This is a terrible method of prognostication. Followed to its logical conclusion, female athletes would eventually be breaking the sound barrier. And, anyway, a century of exclusion had left women at a considerable disadvantage, with plenty of easy ground to make up through proper training and increased participation. Even at the 1984 Summer Games in Los Angeles, female athletes were barely a fifth of the total. In fact, the sex gap in performance hasn't budged since the early 1980s, when *Myths of Gender* was published. The marathon world record in 1998 was 2 hours 6 minutes, with the fastest woman more than 14 minutes behind. The world record for the 1500 metres in that year has not been surpassed – 3 minutes 26 seconds, with the fastest woman of all time trailing by 24 seconds.[20]

Culture can affect the degree of sexual dimorphism – either by expanding or contracting it. If men but not women go in for body building, this will exaggerate differences in strength. If girls are intensively trained in baseball, this will reduce differences in throwing speed. The ancient Chinese practice of female foot binding made it difficult for women to walk, let alone run.[21] But culture is not the whole story. Men have physical advantages that are not explained by women's lack of exercise, socialization, cultural body modifications or poor diet.

There's nothing wrong in general with arguing – like the American oyster boffin William Keith Brooks – that society *should* be a certain way because of biological differences between females and males. We take the fact that women give birth and men don't to justify special protections for women against job discrimination, paid maternity leave, and so on. Or – less plausibly – one might argue that women should be banned from working as firefighters or miners because they are more vulnerable to physical injuries in these occupations. (The Soviet Union had a list of more than 400 jobs off limits to women, for similar reasons.)[22]

Or – more plausibly – one might argue that most sports should be sex-segregated, on the grounds that otherwise women would rarely win anything.

These sorts of arguments need assessing case by case. In other words, biological determinism, in its 'rightful' guise, cannot be dismissed across the board. And if someone wants to convince us that biological differences between the sexes justify a return to 1950s sex roles, Victorian marriage laws, evolution-based education for young men to prevent rape, or whatever, let's see the argument.[23]

The rest of this chapter is about the sexier kind of biological determinism, on which biology makes certain social outcomes *inevitable*. Our investigation starts with the fact that social or cultural factors at best partially explain human sexual dimorphism. So what else explains why women and men differ in strength and the like? The answer, in short, is sexual selection. That itself needs a brief explanation.

Sexual selection and psychological sex differences

In 1871, two years after Mill's *The Subjection of Women*, Charles Darwin published *The Descent of Man and Selection in Relation to Sex*. Natural selection, the topic of Darwin's earlier *On the Origin of Species*, is the process by which some organisms of a single species gain traits that allow them to leave more descendants than their fellows. For instance, a camouflaged moth will be more likely to survive and breed than one that is easily spotted by a hungry bird. Because many traits are heritable – passed from the parents to their offspring – natural selection will increase the frequency of some traits in the population and decrease others. Genetic mutations continually add tiny variations to traits, the raw material on which natural selection operates. As a result, organisms evolve: beaks change shape, coloration becomes camouflage, primitive light-sensitive cells become eyes, limbs turn into wings, human ancestors start walking on two legs, and so on. In *The Descent of Man*, Darwin examined *sexual* selection, the process by which males (or females) gain traits that lead to more or better-quality mates than their same-sex rivals.[24] (Since sexual selection works only because more or better mates lead to more descendants, it is best thought of as a kind of natural selection.)

In mammals especially, reproduction is a costly business for females: they have to gestate their young and feed them after birth, a large investment of time and resources. In contrast, male reproduction carries no such commitment – a one-night stand could do it. This asymmetry creates an incentive for males to compete with others of their sex for mating opportunities. The incentive is intensified by the fact that there are more males than females who are ready to mate, because pregnant females are out of the breeding pool. The stakes are high: females usually have no difficulty passing on their genes, but a male could either sire a huge family, at one extreme, or remain a frustrated bachelor, at the other. Males with traits that allow them to beat other males to the bedroom or the bower will pass these on to their sons. Thus males evolve enhanced weaponry such as large tusks, greater strength, intimidating roars, or plugs of glue deposited in the female's vagina after mating that block the sperm of other males. This is (a simplified sketch of) *sexual selection* – specifically, *intrasexual* (within-sex) selection by male–male competition.

Darwin postulated another kind of selection, *intersexual* (between-sex) selection, the result of females choosing among males. (That is the typical pattern, but it can occur the other way round, with the males being the choosers.) This was Darwin's explanation of functionally useless bodily adornments such as the colourful plumage of many male birds; these come with costs – for instance, making it harder to avoid predators.[25]

Sexual selection by (potentially) violent male–male competition is likely a significant part of the explanation of human sexual dimorphism. Men are much better equipped to fight – the average man is stronger in the upper body than 99.9 per cent of women, and the ability to throw projectiles accurately makes for an advantage in primitive combat. Deep voices in males may function as honest (hard to fake) signals of fighting ability.[26]

Staying in an evolutionary frame of mind, we see that there must be more to the story. What is the point of carrying a big stick if you're not prepared to use it? Threatening to chuck a rock isn't worth much if everyone knows you'll never follow through. Bluffing works only for so long. All else being equal, men with a propensity to use physical aggression at the right time in our ancestral past would have been reproductively more successful. If some physical differences between men and women are the result of sexual selection, we would expect some corresponding evolved psychological differences too.

Another, related, idea is that human females have more to gain than males, reproductively speaking, from being self-protective. A father may ultimately produce grandchildren even if he dies before his kids leave the nest; a mother cannot afford to be as cavalier about her own survival. As the psychologist Anne Campbell puts it, 'females should be more concerned with staying alive.' If a psychological trait helps with this concern, then we would expect it to be stronger in females. Fear is a self-protective emotion, and in fact females are, on average, more fearful than males.[27]

The point is that thinking of *physical* sexual dimorphism in humans from an evolutionary perspective leads very quickly to *psychological* sexual dimorphism. This is absolutely not to say that we should expect men to be from Mars and women from Venus, any more than we should expect the slowest male runner to beat the fastest female. Women and men have mostly the same problems to solve – they both need to find more or less the same kind of food and shelter and avoid the same predators, in the same environment – so psychologically they should be pretty similar. Also, unlike the vast majority of mammals, both human parents care for their offspring (although the male contribution is variable). It often pays a man to support his kids, since that improves their prospects of reproducing themselves. Still, human females remain the ones with an obligatory and substantial parental investment, and that should make for *some* evolved psychological differences.[28]

Feminism is needed because of our evolutionary history. One would not get that impression by reading philosophy or gender studies, however.[29]

We are building up to a qualified defence of the view that sexual biology makes certain social outcomes inevitable. One more piece of the foundation needs explaining: the role of boys' balls.

A natural experiment

If men differ from women in, say, being more prone to physical aggression, there must be some biochemical mechanism that brings this about. The prime candidate is the hormone testosterone, present in much greater quantities in males. When puberty comes around, rising levels of testosterone (T) secreted by the testes are responsible for the characteristic features of the human adult male – more muscle, longer and stronger bones, deeper voice, facial hair, and so on. Males are exposed to high T much earlier on, starting around nine weeks after conception, and this causes the fetus to grow male external genitalia.[30]

Does fetal testosterone do more in the womb than masculinize the body? Does it also masculinize the brain, inducing psychological and behavioural traits more distinctive of males than females? Decades of experimental work have shown that the hormone has these effects in a variety of non-human animals, including primates.[31] A reasonable initial hypothesis is that humans are no exception. And, if so, innate biology has a significant role in explaining sex differences in psychology and behaviour.

We've already seen some of the evidence for this hypothesis in chapter 5. Boys with 5-alpha reductase deficiency are exposed to normal T-levels in the womb, but because of undermasculinized genitalia at birth are often reared as girls; nonetheless, they are often reported as having a more masculine play style. The research here is sparse, largely because the condition tends to occur in isolated communities, making the collection of reliable behavioural data difficult. Congenital adrenal hyperplasia (CAH), a DSD (Disorder of Sex Development) mentioned in chapter 3, affords a much better natural experiment.

Overactive adrenal glands in CAH produce excess androgens, including testosterone, which in a female fetus can result in genital masculinization. The brains of girls with CAH are therefore exposed to more T in utero than unaffected girls, although much less than boys. The childhood play styles of CAH girls provide an important test for the hypothesis that fetal T masculinizes (some) psychology and behaviour.

Scientific claims should of course be critically scrutinized, particularly if they confirm one's prejudices or the pieties of the moment. But this coin has another side. If the research threatens to *disconfirm* one's prejudices, one must be careful not to dismiss it by overhyping the reservations and limitations that accompany every scientific study. Some feminist academics appear to have adopted the second approach to research on CAH. Reviewing the evidence in the mid-1980s, Fausto-Sterling concluded: 'The claim that clear-cut evidence exists to show that fetal hormones make boys more active, aggressive, or athletic than girls is little more than fancy, although harmless it is not.'[32]

There were alternatives to the hypothesis that prenatal T was responsible for the masculinized play of CAH girls. For instance, Fausto-Sterling conjectured that parents, 'knowing that their child had ambiguous genitalia', might have given her 'fewer dolls than her normal sister', with this kind of differential socialization producing the difference in behaviour.[33] But researchers found the early evidence to be more promising than Fausto-Sterling evidently did, and the scientific literature on this topic continued to grow. One of the most highly respected specialists in the study of prenatal hormonal influences on psychology and behaviour is Melissa Hines of Cambridge University. Summing up in a lengthy and comprehensive survey of the scientific literature, she wrote:

> It appears that gonadal hormones influence some aspects of human behavioral development in a manner similar to that documented in experimental studies of animals. This has been shown most clearly in regard to childhood play behavior, where information from clinical syndromes, from situations where hormones have been administered to pregnant women, and from studies of normal variability converge to indicate that T levels during early development promote more male-typical patterns of behavior.[34]

That was in 2009. Subsequently, the evidence has only become stronger, to the point of being overwhelming. Three years after Hines's article, Fausto-Sterling conceded that the hypothesis of prenatal hormonal influences was 'more than fancy'; however, she insisted it was still largely speculative: 'The question: does the early exposure to high levels of androgen affect the play behavior of these children, and can we attribute any differences to the effects of prenatal testosterone on the brain? … And the answer (drum roll please, wait while I open the envelope …) is – sort of, maybe, possibly?'[35]

Feminist scientists – that is, scientists who happen to be feminists – have made major contributions to every field. Moreover, bringing a feminist perspective to the lab or field site might sometimes correct blind spots, or suggest new hypotheses – intellectual diversity strengthens science. But viewing the data through ideological spectacles is always a bad idea, leading to a distortion of research findings and impeding the accumulation of knowledge.[36]

Patriarchy and testosterone

We are now ready to see the case for 'biology is destiny' – that is, the view that biological differences between women and men determine or guarantee that they will occupy different places in society. But does anyone really think that, even back in the nineteenth century? It is easy enough to find eminent Victorian men pronouncing on the lesser intellectual qualities of women, or their greater frailty or proneness to hysteria, and so on. (This was by no means invariably paired with the claim that women were the inferior sex – at the start of this chapter we saw the historian William Lecky extolling women's moral superiority.) These alleged differences, presumed to be rooted in biology, were sometimes held to *justify* certain distinctively Victorian sex-typed ways of organizing society. And sometimes not: John Stuart Mill conceded that there might be some significant biologically based psychological sex differences, but he denied that these would justify the traditional order. In any event, this is not biological determinism of the sexy kind we are interested in, on which biology makes social outcomes inevitable.

The *ne plus ultra* of this kind of biological determinism is the sociologist Steven Goldberg, who for many years was the chair of the Department of Sociology at City College, part of CUNY, the City University of New York. Some books have titles that pithily encapsulate the conclusion, and that includes Goldberg's *The Inevitability of Patriarchy*, published in 1973. For some time, the book had a place in the *Guinness Book of World Records* for the most rejections (sixty-nine) from publishers – here the patriarchy was doing Goldberg no favours.[37]

Goldberg's argument is straightforward and has three steps. First, every society, past and present, has been patriarchal, in the sense that 'males fill the vast majority of authority and leadership positions' in political, commercial and religious organizations. Second, the best explanation of this fact is biological: specifically, because males are exposed to much higher levels of testosterone than females. Third, this biological explanation means that every future society will be patriarchal: 'What is crucial here is that men and women differ in their hormonal systems and that every society demonstrates patriarchy, male dominance, and male attainment. *The thesis put forth here is that the hormonal renders the social inevitable.*'[38]

Goldberg was not arguing that biology *justifies* patriarchy: he was explicit that the conclusion was not that patriarchy was desirable. Neither, for that matter, was he saying that males are superior to females – he was explicit about that too.[39] Rather, his conclusion was simply that, like Benjamin Franklin's observation about death and taxes, patriarchy is certain. Notice that Goldberg does not hold the (absurd) view that female leaders are a biological impossibility; rather, his theory is that biology guarantees (or makes overwhelmingly likely) that male leaders will be in the 'vast majority'.

An updated version of the book, with a change of title to *Why Men Rule*, came out twenty years later. Goldberg noted that, while 'some critics have accused my theory of "biological determinism" … sometimes biological determinism is correct. A theory that predicted that because males are taller than females, the best basketball teams in every society will be comprised of males and that socialization will conform to this reality, and will increase the male-female difference in basketball ability, is "biological determinism": it is also correct.'[40]

'An obstinately turgid and pedantic anti-feminist tract'[41]

The reception of Goldberg's book was a little mixed. The reviewer for *Kirkus Reviews* (quoted above) characterized it as 'pathetically patriarchal'. The review by the Marxist-feminist anthropologist Eleanor Leacock began: 'It is a shame to have to take this book seriously.'[42] On the positive side, the psychologist Joseph Adelson wrote one of the blurbs on the back cover: 'a marvelous book, impeccably reasoned and vigorously argued'. One reviewer who liked it deserves special attention: the renowned anthropologist Margaret Mead, at the time one of the most famous women in America.

Mead's 1928 book *Coming of Age in Samoa*, with its description of sexually liberated Samoan girls free from adolescent turmoil, had an enormous cultural influence. In other work, Mead reported that, among the people living around Tchambuli Lake in Papua New Guinea, 'it is the women in Tchambuli who have the real position of power in the society … women dominate.' The Tchambuli (now known as the Chambri) were, Mead reported, a sex-role-reversed tribe, 'with the women the dominant, impersonal, managing partner, the man the less responsible and the emotionally dependent person'. 'We no longer have any basis', Mead concluded, 'for regarding such aspects of behaviour as sex-linked.'[43] Academics in gender and women's studies touted this as showing that patriarchy was far from inevitable.

For many years, Mead wrote a monthly column for the popular women's magazine *Redbook*. And in the October edition in 1973, her review of *The Inevitability of Patriarchy* appeared, nestled up to advertisements for Emko contraceptive foam, Tampax and Albolene – 'cleans make-up better than cold cream'. One might have expected Mead to say that Goldberg was refuted by the Chambri. But Goldberg had discussed the Chambri, arguing that a careful examination of Mead's ethnographic reports showed that her conclusions were unwarranted.[44] Mead did not mention the Chambri in her review and conceded that patriarchy *was* universal:

> It is true … that all the claims so glibly made about societies ruled by women are nonsense. We have no reason to believe that they ever existed … as far as we know, men everywhere *have* been in charge of running the show … men have been the leaders in public affairs and the final authorities at home – though women too have their spheres of independence and authority, acknowledged or unacknowledged.[45]

So Mead had no complaint about the first step of Goldberg's argument. She also did not dispute the second step, that the best explanation of patriarchy is the higher male exposure to testosterone. As Mead explained, Goldberg's primary source for his claims about hormones was none other than our old friend John Money: 'The data he cites on male-female hormonal differences are taken from reports of recent and very careful small studies by Dr. John Money, of Johns Hopkins University, and others on both human and animal subjects. The reporting of his sources cannot be faulted.'[46]

Instead, Mead objected to the third step, that the hormonal roots of patriarchy mean that it is inevitable, suggesting that, 'under very new conditions', the future might not resemble the past. That may be, but

Mead's point was abstract and undeveloped. (Perhaps the confines of *Redbook* were to blame.) One could similarly suggest that 'new conditions' would upend male dominance in basketball, but this is hardly plausible. Mead gave no reason to think that patriarchy is any different.[47]

If an expert such as Mead fails to rebut Goldberg's argument, that sounds ominous. If it had clear flaws, she would have pointed them out. Could it really be that Goldberg is right, and that biology *is* destiny? We need to look at the three steps in Goldberg's argument more closely.

The universality of patriarchy

The first step in the argument is that patriarchy is, in fact, universal. If this is true, then modern industrial societies are all patriarchal. But are the UK or the US really patriarchies? Gender discrimination is outlawed, and women are found at every level of leadership and decision making. The US almost elected a female president in 2016, and the UK has had three women prime ministers, Margaret Thatcher (elected in 1979, and the last century's longest-serving prime minister), Theresa May and – in 2022, the shortest-serving prime minister – Liz Truss.

We can usefully distinguish two kinds of patriarchy: *structural* patriarchy and *de facto* patriarchy. A structural patriarchy has laws or customs that explicitly ensure that the authority roles are entirely or largely occupied by men. For example, before the end of the First World War, women were unable to become Members of Parliament in the UK. Politically, the UK was then a structural patriarchy, and is now no longer. (Unlike Saudi Arabia, which, despite some recent loosening of restrictions on women, remains an absolute male monarchy.)

A *de facto* patriarchy has the same outcome – the dominance of men in public positions of authority – but not because of laws or customs that say that this is how things are done. Is the UK presently a de facto patriarchy? Goldberg officially requires a patriarchy to have males in the 'vast majority' of authority positions. Around a third of MPs are now women, and 'two-thirds' doesn't sound like a 'vast majority', so the UK is dubiously a de facto patriarchy under Goldberg's definition. But let's charitably understand a 'vast majority' to be a *supermajority* – say, at least three-fifths. Then the UK (at least with respect to politics) is a de facto patriarchy.

If Goldberg had claimed that *structural* patriarchy was universal, then his thesis would have been plainly false. His claim, rather, is that structural *or de facto* patriarchy is universal. Setting aside other modern societies for the moment, is that true about past societies?

Caution is needed here, because different writers understand patriarchy differently. For instance, in his book *Sapiens*, the historian Yuvel Noah Harari takes a patriarchal society to value 'men more highly than women', but this is not built in to Goldberg's conception of patriarchy. Neither is patriarchy supposed to imply that men control women's sexuality or are permitted to beat their wives. These social features are no doubt connected with patriarchy in Goldberg's sense, but they should be distinguished from it.[48]

Hunter gatherers or foragers – people who have not developed agriculture (some of whom are still around today) – are often regarded as having comparatively egalitarian relations between the sexes. 'In such societies', the historian Gerda Lerner wrote, 'the relative status of men and women is "separate but equal".'[49] If she is right, then patriarchy is not universal.

It is very difficult to investigate the structure of human societies millennia ago. Contemporary hunter gatherers can be studied directly and provide important evidence, but they may not be representative of prehistoric societies. With that caveat, gender egalitarianism among contemporary hunter gatherers appears to be limited. Although hunter-gatherer bands largely lack social hierarchies and women participate in decision making, the political advantage goes to men. One particularly egalitarian group is the Agta of the Philippines; nonetheless, men have significantly more influence than women in communal discussions. Another is the Aka, a group of forest foragers in Central Africa; the men devote significant time to childcare and have been called 'the best dads in the world'. Despite the Aka's flexible approach to gender roles, the men get the top jobs.[50]

A reasonable – albeit speculative – hypothesis is that authority was disproportionately male in pre-agricultural times. The record is much clearer after that. In the nineteenth century there was a burst of enthusiasm for the idea that some societies have been matriarchies – an idea periodically revived in the twentieth, but (as Mead remarked) which never caught on. 'Patriarchy', Harari writes, 'has been the norm in almost all agricultural and industrial societies.' And, if we understand patriarchy in Goldberg's way, the previous ten thousand years contain no clear exceptions.[51]

The best explanation of patriarchy

Assuming that patriarchy has been universal, or close to it, this is something that requires explanation. It is not credible that the universality of patriarchy is just a fluke, like meeting someone at a party who shares your birthday. Neither is it remotely plausible that patriarchy was culturally transmitted around the globe as English became the *lingua franca* of science and soccer the most popular sport. Columbus may have brought measles to the New World, but he did not bring patriarchy – it was already there. The obvious explanation is that there is *something* about the biological make-up of men and women – 'some universal biological reason', in Harari's phrase – that made male overrepresentation in authority positions, at least in the past, difficult to avoid.[52]

In chapter 5 we saw how John Money's attempt to raise David Reimer as Brenda ultimately proved a tragic failure. When the experiment seemed to be progressing nicely, Money presented his preliminary findings at a meeting of the American Association for the Advancement of Science in 1973. *Time* magazine reported:

> This dramatic case ... provides strong support for a major contention of women's liberationists: that conventional patterns of masculine and feminine behavior can be altered. It also casts doubt on the theory that major sexual differences, psychological as well as anatomical, are immutably set by the genes at conception. In fact, says Money, there are only four imperative differences: women menstruate, gestate and lactate; men impregnate. Many scientists believe that crucial psychological imperatives follow from these biological facts, limiting the flexibility of sexual roles. Money, however, is convinced that almost all differences are culturally determined and therefore optional.[53]

It is thus supremely ironic that Goldberg, in the very same year, appealed to Money's work to show that 'crucial psychological imperatives' *do* follow from the biological facts, specifically 'male hormonalization'.[54] And, on the question of what Money's work *did* show (or at least supported), Goldberg was completely right. He correctly decoupled two issues: first, whether boys could be raised as girls; second, whether behavioural and psychological sex differences are 'culturally determined':

> Most importantly, it would not even matter, to this theory, if a *normal* male could be *socialized* to a *female* gender identity (or vice versa). All questions of gender identity are irrelevant to this theory. All that is relevant here is one aspect [dominance tendency] of the differentiated behavior which is associated with the differentiated hormonalization of normal males and normal females.[55]

Money was well aware of the evidence implicating sex hormones in the different behavioural and psychological outcomes for females and males. He at times downplayed this when describing Brenda, but he always conceded that she had 'many tomboyish traits'.[56]

In another irony, Goldberg's case that male hormonalization explained the universality of patriarchy was much weaker than it could have been. Men everywhere tend to be the top dogs, he claimed, because they 'are more strongly "motivated" to exhibit whatever behavior is necessary to achieve position, status, or dominance'.[57] And it is this 'dominance tendency' that is supposed to be produced by greater exposure to testosterone, particularly prenatally and at puberty.

Goldberg's claims about male psychology might sound plausible, but he didn't offer much by way of evidence. Even granted the universality of patriarchy, men might be better at achieving high status not because they are more strongly motivated, but because they have more time to devote to its pursuit, not being encumbered by pregnancy and the feeding and care of children. Here Goldberg could have helped himself to some evolutionary thinking. Cross-culturally, women prefer men with resources, which makes evolutionary sense because mates with more resources means more reproductive success, given human biparental care. There is thus evolutionary pressure for men to acquire resources, which is closely connected with acquiring social status. And, as the sex with little obligatory investment in parenting, men should be more inclined to risky but potentially reproductively profitable behaviour. One would therefore expect men, on average, to be better motivated to scramble up the status hierarchy and more prepared to sacrifice for a chance to reach the top. That expectation is supported by psychological experiments. Goldberg's alleged male 'dominance tendency' stands on a decent theoretical foundation.[58]

Further, Goldberg didn't really present much evidence about the role of testosterone in explaining this psychological sex difference in humans – the work he cited was more suggestive than definitive, and he even got some details wrong. With the passage of half a century, it is fair to say that the case for the male hormonalization of psychology and behaviour is now much stronger. We have already seen one piece of evidence for it, namely the influence of testosterone on children's play styles.[59]

There is one big gap in Goldberg's argument, though. *De facto* male overrepresentation in leadership is one thing; rigging laws, customs and political systems in favour of men – *structural* patriarchy – is quite another. The male dominance tendency might explain why men tend to come out on top in politics if both sexes have equal opportunities, but it is unclear how it could explain institutionalized or structural patriarchy, where women are impeded from participating in the first place. What's more, in societies with structural patriarchy, the patriarchal laws and customs *by themselves* will explain male overrepresentation, with no apparent need to invoke the male dominance tendency.

Goldberg may yet be on to something, because the next question is: what is the explanation for the universality (until very recent times) of *structural* patriarchy? As with Goldberg's broader kind of patriarchy (structural or de facto), plausibly the answer will involve 'some universal biological reason', although to investigate this properly is beyond the scope of this book. Instead, let's turn to the last part of Goldberg's argument.[60]

The inevitability of patriarchy?

The final step takes us from the biological explanation of previous patriarchy to its future inevitability. This is a good place at which to clear up some misconceptions about 'inevitability' and 'determinism'.

First, by saying that patriarchy is inevitable or determined by human biology, Goldberg did *not* mean that no conceivable turn of events consistent with human biology could erase patriarchy. In John

Wyndham's novella *Consider Her Ways*, men have been wiped out by a virus, leaving women to reproduce by artificial means. If we imagine that the men left an amply supplied sperm bank, and that male babies are culled at birth, then that would be the end of patriarchy. Or maybe human evolution will close the sex gap in 'dominance tendency', and patriarchy will be gone. (One reviewer of *The Inevitability of Patriarchy* actually suggested this possibility.)[61] None of this threatens Goldberg's thesis, properly understood.

Keeping present human biology and an equal sex ratio fixed, and varying the social environment – the upbringing of children, the distribution of wealth, marriage and childcare arrangements, the political system, and so on – the authority wielded by women in the workforce and in politics will also vary. Goldberg is investigating the character of this dependency of female authority on the social environment. A quota system ensuring that women are most politicians and decision makers, and enforced by a totalitarian state, would spell the end of patriarchy. Even if this came about, it wouldn't mean that Goldberg was fundamentally misguided.

Here is something very much in the spirit of Goldberg's thesis that patriarchy is inevitable. Let the social environment vary within the boundaries of a modern prosperous well-populated liberal democracy. In one kind of social environment, there is a robust social safety net including generous childcare benefits and parental leave, girls are frequently exposed to powerful female role-models, education is excellent, and a modest amount of affirmative action is practised. Other kinds are obtained by adjusting these and other parameters. Then the Goldbergian thesis is this: the resulting outcomes are all patriarchal.

The problem for the third step of Goldberg's argument is that *these* sorts of 'gender equal' social environments are radically *unlike* the social environments that have prevailed throughout human history, even those in most of the last century. Modern social environments can make dramatic breaks with the past, with unpredictable effects. When Margaret Mead, in her 1973 review, speculated that 'new conditions' might overcome the patriarchal tendency, that was an insight.

And, in fact, in 2019 the heads of the ruling coalition government in Finland were all female. Moreover, most cabinet members were women, and the sex ratio in parliament was close to parity. However you slice it, this is not patriarchy. Even if we grant the first two steps of Goldberg's argument, the Land of a Thousand Lakes shows that the third step fails.

Nineteenth-century scientists had some misbegotten theories about human differences, such as polygenism, the idea that human races had separate origins. Polygenism is long discarded. Should we discard biological determinism too? No – that would be to throw out the stock along with the chicken bones.

The inevitability of inequality

Although Goldberg's argument does not work as stated, it is just the beginning. There are all sorts of apparently universal sex differences in psychology and behaviour that plausibly have roots in biological differences between the sexes that are themselves not explained by socialization or culture. The most obvious one – so obvious that it is often overlooked – is sexual orientation, a whopping psychological sex difference. Another obvious one is crime, especially lethal violence: men have always been responsible for the lion's share of homicides, mostly against other men. Combined personality differences between women and men are significant, and they do not bear an equal burden of psychopathologies. There is evidence that men are more variable in cognitive ability (as they are on many other dimensions), with a greater proportion at the high and low ends. Occupational interests show a large cross-cultural sex difference, often conceptualized as 'people vs. things'. Women are more people-oriented than men and prefer to be social workers or teachers than car mechanics or carpenters.[62]

Some of these sex differences – in occupational interests, for example – tend to be greater in more gender-equal societies such as Finland and Sweden, which suggests that they are not the sole products of socialization. Although as many women as men now graduate from medical schools, a present-day Dr Margaret Bulkley would still be in a minority: surgeons are mostly male, while women dominate in obstetrics and gynaecology. And gender representation seems to be easier to equalize in politics than in the more freewheeling world of business. There is no shortage of female Finnish politicians, but women make up fewer than 10 per cent of CEOs of Finland's publicly traded companies.[63]

Patriarchy may be explained by the human biological endowment without being guaranteed by it. Yet biological determinism, properly understood, is not wholly mistaken. The nature of the sexes very likely ensures a variety of different outcomes in any liberal democracy. In particular, men will commit more crime than women, and women and men will distribute themselves differently in the workforce. This is no cause for despair: there is nothing inherently troubling about women outnumbering men in psychology or vice versa in coding. To be sure, homicide will remain a problem for any society, but it doesn't much matter whether the perpetrators are mostly vengeful younger males, mostly vicious grandmothers, or a fifty–fifty mix of both genders. And, in any case, wishful thinking helps no one. Patriarchy is not inevitable, but sexual inequality is.

EIGHT

True Selves and Identity Crises

For every trans-sexual who grasps that prize, Identity, ten, perhaps a hundred discover it to be only a mirage in the end.

Jan Morris, *Conundrum*[1]

The transsexual journey is, in this case, less about finding our 'true selves' than our best selves.

Anne Lawrence, *Men Trapped in Men's Bodies*[2]

The Age of Identity

The endless variety of gender identities – woman, man, genderqueer, asexual, genderfluid, agender, ... – provoked the mocking internet meme 'I sexually identify as an attack helicopter.' That became the title of a 2020 short story, written by a transgender woman and published in a science fiction and fantasy magazine. The inevitable outrage descended like hail on the author, and the story was quickly unpublished, at her request. The magazine's editor posted a lengthy handwringing statement. 'We should', he confessed, 'have employed a broader range of sensitivity readers.'[3]

Gender identities are the tip of an identity iceberg. We live in the Age of Identity, which sees individual people as a nexus of identities – of gender, race, nationality, ethnicity, sexual orientation, and many more. Identity concept creep is everywhere. A person may be disabled, or middle-aged, or gay, or a woman, or a transgender man, without taking these features to define 'who they really are'. A gay disabled middle-aged artist may think of himself first and foremost as an artist, putting his Parkinson's disease and homosexuality on a par with his height and blood type. If asked 'Who are you?', our gay disabled artist will answer 'I'm an artist', not 'I'm a person with Parkinson's.' If he protests that his disability is not part of his identity, the new ways of speaking make that sound self-contradictory: disability, sexual orientation and the rest have been subsumed under 'identity characteristics'.

The manifestation of the Age of Identity is identity politics, albeit of a distinctive kind. If identity politics is the organization of political action around groups with identifying characteristics – class, ethnicity, sex, nationality, and so forth – then identity politics is as old as politics. When the gladiator Spartacus led a slave rebellion against the Roman Republic, he was practising identity politics, as were Gandhi, campaigning for Indian independence, and the British suffragette Emmeline Pankhurst, agitating for a woman's right to vote. But identity politics comes in a contemporary version, which stresses *identity*. The political scientist Francis Fukuyama puts it this way:

> Individuals throughout human history have found themselves at odds with their societies. But only in modern times has the view taken hold that the authentic inner self is intrinsically valuable, and the outer society systematically wrong and unfair in its valuation of the former. It is not the inner self that has to be made to conform to society's rules, but society itself that needs to change.[4]

The old ideals of freed slaves, countries in charge of their own destinies, and women being equal citizens with men have been replaced by a potpourri of different marginalized groups, each with a proprietary kind of lived experience and a striving for self-actualization. The album cover of Pink Floyd's *The Dark Side of the Moon* (1973) symbolizes the Age of Identity: a prism fractionating uniform white light into a rainbow.[5] No longer 'Out of Many, One' – these days it's 'Out of One, Many.'

The rainbow is no longer enough. The lengthening of LGB to LGBTQIA+ or LGBTQQIP2SAA+ has been paralleled by the addition of a five-striped chevron to the old pride flag, adding pink, light blue and white (the trans colours) and brown and black (for 'queer people of colour').[6] And that's not all: the chevrons enclose a yellow triangle with an embedded purple circle, symbolizing the 'intersex community'; yet further ornaments have been proposed. (As an aesthetic object, the new flag leaves something to be desired.) The groups in this wildly diverse mélange have very real concerns; whether they are sensibly lumped together is another matter.

As Fukuyama says, 'the focus on lived experience by identity groups valorizes inner selves experienced emotionally rather than examined rationally … That an argument is offensive to someone's sense of self-worth is often seen as sufficient to delegitimize it.'[7] Recall the letter from the feminist philosophy establishment (chapter 1) urging philosophers not to 'call into question the integrity and sincerity of trans people nor the validity of their own understanding of who they are.' This is quintessential identity politics.

This chapter is not about the origins of the Age of Identity, or when (or if) we may expect it to end. Instead, identity itself – the core of each of us – will be under the microscope. What is an identity, and what is it to have one? What – in Fukuyama's phrase – is 'the authentic inner self', and how is it connected with identity? And, finally: should we strive to *be* our authentic selves?

Identifying with *and* as

First, what *is* an identity? It's easy to give clear examples. Some people would put 'Canadian' on a list of their identities; others would put 'man'. In other words, identities include categories such as *Canadian* and *man*. But how far does the catalogue of identities extend? Could *attack helicopter* be an identity too?

Some people have *Canadian* and *man* among their identities; others don't. That observation leads to a second question: under what conditions does a person *have* an identity? Specifically, when is *Canadian* someone's identity? The simplest answer is that a Canadian identity belongs to all and only Canadians – citizens of Canada – but that doesn't seem right. Imagine someone who has been living in Mexico City for most of his life, and is a dual citizen of both Canada and Mexico. Despite being Canadian, he is known by everyone as Mexican and has no attachment to the Great White North. *Mexican* may be one of his identities, but not *Canadian*.

To take a real-life case, in some sense *man* was among Margaret Bulkley's identities, since she successfully played a respected Victorian medical man, Dr James Barry, for most of her life. But she was not a member of that category – she was not a man. Some non-men have *man* among their identities, and some men do not have *man* among their identities. Belonging to a category is neither necessary nor sufficient for having that category as an identity.

Let's look more closely at when a person has a particular identity. By considering some examples, we can see that there are two main ways in which someone could have an identity such as *Canadian* or *man*.

Someone – Gordon, to give him a name – might have a strong sense of kinship with Canadians. 'I *feel* Canadian, these are *my* people', Gordon says. He loves Canadian friendliness and humility, not to mention the Canadian Rockies and poutine. Among Canadians is where Gordon belongs, they are his in-group – at least according to Gordon. That is one way in which Gordon can claim a Canadian identity. Regimenting language slightly, we can put this by saying that Gordon identifies *with* Canadians.

In social contexts, Gordon might encourage others to classify him as Canadian. Perhaps he pronounces 'about' *aboot*, celebrates Canada Day, drinks Moosehead beer, and so on. Perhaps he affects a Canadian style of dress – a parka and woollen hat in the winter. An observer would take Gordon to be Canadian, or at least to be making the effort. This is the other route to a Canadian identity. Again regimenting language slightly, we can put this by saying that Gordon identifies *as* Canadian.

There are two other relevant facts that might be true of Gordon: he could *be* Canadian, and he could *believe* he is Canadian. That gives us four possibilities, which can be mixed and matched however we like. Suppose, for example, that Gordon is Canadian. That doesn't mean that he believes that he is – perhaps Gordon's parents deceived him into thinking that the family is American. And even if he believes (and knows) he is Canadian, Gordon might keep his status hidden – perhaps for some perverse reason he pretends to be English. So knowing that you are Canadian does not mean that you identify *as* Canadian. Neither does it mean that you identify *with* Canadians: Gordon might feel entirely alienated from his fellow Canucks.

Imagine now that Gordon does identify *with* Canadians: the Canucks are his tribe. He need not identify *as* Canadian: perhaps he doesn't do that because Canadians are the butt of many jokes, which Gordon does not like. He keeps his collection of Canadian hockey jerseys hidden in his basement. Further, Gordon need not believe that he is Canadian. Indeed, he need not *be* Canadian. One can identify *with* a group without being a member.

A gender-critical feminist might remark, '*Woman* is not an identity: I do not identify as a woman, I *am* one!' She does not (let's suppose) put in any effort to present as a stereotypical woman, either in dress or in behaviour. The visibility of sex being what it is, she is normally taken to be a woman, and she is happy to affirm it. She goes to a women's gym and has an F on her driver's licence. So she's wrong, strictly speaking: she does identify as a woman, at least in a minimal way, and *woman* is an identity. Her main point, though, is that identifying *as* a woman and *being* a woman are quite different: someone can identify as a woman without being a woman, or be a woman without identifying as one. And, on that, she is correct. Perhaps she identifies *with* women, but that is also a very different matter from actually being a woman.

Identities

Our first question was, what *is* an identity? An identity is a category such that people can identify *with* its members or *as* one of its members. Can we say more? Focusing on examples such as *Canadian* and *man*, identities appear to have three features. (We'll question whether this holds across the board shortly.) First, identities are categories of *people* – Canadians and men are people. Second, identities have associated *stereotypes* – Canadians are nice and fond of ice hockey, men don't like talking about their feelings. Third, identities have (loosely) associated socially imposed *norms* or *rules* – Canadians should be modest and law-abiding, men should be strong and assertive, or something along these lines.[8]

Here's another example that fits that template: the category *postman* (US: *mailman*). Postmen are people, the stereotypical postman is not fond of dogs, and there are rules governing the conduct of postmen – they should deliver to the correct address. Postmen typically identify *as* postmen; they don't operate undercover like spies. And while for many postmen delivering mail is just a way of earning a living, Postman Pat might identify *with* postmen. He collects Royal Mail memorabilia and thinks of himself as a member of the mail-delivering family. He is working on his autobiography, *In the Company of Postmen*.

So far, so good. However, expanding the diet of examples shows that norms or rules are not required. It makes sense to say that *gardener* is one of Pat's identities: his life revolves around gardening, and he is the president of the local gardening club. There are stereotypes about gardeners – they are middle-aged, middle-class, peaceful solitary types, fond of hearth and home. However, are there really norms or rules about how gardeners should behave? True, there's a right way to prune rose bushes, and gardeners can be praised for growing gigantic marrows or blamed for shirking weeding, but these don't amount to rules governing gardeners as such. Postmen have to deliver the mail to the correct address, and a man should (in some traditional circles) tip his hat to a lady. But a gardener who lets her weeds run riot may just be one who prefers native species and encourages wildlife. That is one of the many different and permissible ways to be a gardener. And if we imagine a society in which there are no special norms of behaviour applying to men that don't also apply to women, that need not prevent Pat identifying either *as* a man or *with* men.

Stereotypes are hard to avoid, but even they aren't essential to identities. Stereotypes are widely accepted generalizations about categories: Canadians are polite, men are emotionally challenged, postmen dislike dogs. These generalizations may be accurate or inaccurate.[9] If the category is unusual or esoteric, then it may have no associated stereotype. There's no stereotype associated with *pet food taster*, simply because most people have never heard of pet food tasters and can only speculate about the kind of person drawn to that career. Yet Gordon could identify *with* pet food tasters or *as* a pet food taster.

Gardeners and pet food tasters are people. Are identities at least categories of *people*? No. We met furries in chapter 6 – they are fond of *fursuiting*, wearing Bugs Bunny costumes and the like. Furries may identify *with* anthropomorphic furry animals which are fictional creatures. Since there are no anthropomorphic furry animals, no person is one. A furry in costume identifies *as* an anthropomorphic furry animal: he is encouraging others to classify him as a furry animal, or at least to play along with the pretence. (No one will literally take him to *be* a furry animal, but that doesn't mean he can't identify as one.)

All we can say about identities in general is that they are numerous and diverse. Certain kinds of identities – national identities, say – have some interesting features in common, but these do not hold of all identities. The real action is in our relationships to identities – *identifying with* and *identifying as*. That is how we claim them as our own. Presumably no one really has *attack helicopter* as one of their identities. But if it is possible to identify *as* Bugs Bunny it ought to be possible to identify *as* a Boeing AH-70 Apache. And identifying *with* attack helicopters is probably not beyond the reach of human psychology, peculiar and exotic as it may be.

Gender identity again

Robert Stoller defined *core gender identity* as the 'fundamental sense of belonging to one sex', the conviction that one is female or that one is male (chapter 5). Normally one's conviction that one is, say, male, is correct: one *is* male. But on rare occasions it isn't, and, moreover, newborn boys have no opinion as to their sex – they are males with no core male gender identity. We need to separate, then, *believing* that one is male and *being* male. Grayson, say, might *believe* that he (or she) is male. Grayson's sex is another matter. In addition, Grayson may encourage others to socially classify him/her as male; that is, Grayson might identify *as* male. And Grayson may feel part of the male tribe; that is, Grayson might identify *with* males.

Just as we saw for the corresponding four possibilities about Gordon, these can be freely mixed and matched. For instance, Grayson could be a female who knows she is, and who does not present as male: she isn't male, doesn't believe she's male, and doesn't identify *as* male. Nonetheless, Grayson could identify *with* men (males). Grayson is drawn to the comradeship of men and feels at home around them – they are her in-group. Or Grayson could be male and a transgender woman who identifies neither *as* male nor *with* males. She may (or may not) believe she is male.

Transitioning from one sex to the other involves identifying *as* the target sex. It also – at least in many cases – involves identifying *with* the target sex, a kind of tribal identity, akin to the identity of a patriotic Canadian. Indeed, sometimes the comparison with national identity is explicitly made, as in the following passage by the distinguished economist Deirdre McCloskey, who transitioned from (the slightly less distinguished) Donald at the age of fifty-three: 'Being Dutch is being homesick for Holland, inside your head … Does Deirdre treat *herself* as a member of the woman's tribe? *Am I a woman? Yes*.'[10] Here McCloskey blurs the difference between *being* a woman and identifying *with* women. Being Dutch is not being homesick for Holland: one can be Dutch and not give a fig about Holland. Conversely, one can yearn for the dikes, tolerance and penny-pinching of the Netherlands without being Dutch oneself. Others have also reached for the comparison with national identity. Here's an older example, from Harry Benjamin's *The Transsexual Phenomenon*:

> What is certain is that from babyhood I have known – call it intuition, call it recognition – known beyond all doubt that I belonged among the women, and have longed to take my place there. Englishmen born and raised in India go home to England. So with me, always: to become a woman would be to come home. A dull home, perhaps, that of a thirty-four-year-old spinster, but still and always home.[11]

On the orthodox conception of gender identity, it is a universal internal compass needle that may or may not align with one's sexed body, and that causes distress when misaligned. Chapter 5 argued that the orthodox conception is a myth. Talk of 'identity' in the transgender context is still helpful, though. If there is a kind of identity common to transgender women, in addition to identifying *as* a woman, it is identifying *with* women.[12]

Enbies

We can also clear some of the fog surrounding non-binary (or genderqueer) identities, unheard of a decade or so ago, and now claimed by many celebrities. Take the British singer Sam Smith, who recently declared a non-binary identity on Instagram and Twitter, with a consequent change of pronouns to *they/them* and much fawning press coverage. Smith identified *as* non-binary, encouraging people to classify Smith as non-binary. What is it to *be* non-binary, though? The newly revealed non-binary or 'enby' singer admitted to being 'at no stage just yet to eloquently speak at length about what it means to be non-binary'.[13]

The usual explanation – in the words of a 'non-binary sex educator' consulted by *Teen Vogue* – is that a non-binary person is 'someone who does not identify as a man or a woman, or solely as one of those two genders.'[14] What does 'identifying as a man' come to? The (somewhat stipulative) definition we earlier gave to 'identifying *as*' doesn't fit this case. In our sense, to identify as a man is to facilitate one's social classification as a man. That is, it is to encourage others – successfully or not – to classify one as a man in social contexts. This comes in degrees. One might put in a lot of effort, in dress, deportment, and so on. Or one might do the absolute minimum, such as choosing the Gents over the Ladies and ticking the M box on forms. Smith has not gone in for body modification and presents as a bearded adult male, so in our sense Smith identifies *as* a man, albeit rather half-heartedly.

The in-group kind of identification, identifying *with*, is of more help. Let's go back to Gordon, who identifies *with* Canadians. Canadians are a diverse bunch. They are not all friendly humble poutine-eaters and Moosehead-drinkers. Gordon, although he feels he belongs among Canadians, has no kinship at all with members of the White Boy Posse, a neo-Nazi criminal gang active in Western Canada. To be more specific, Gordon has a sense of kinship with *stereotypical* Canadians, not the totality of Canadians or any old sub-group of Canadians.

The same point goes for identifying *with* men or identifying *with* women. A sense of kinship with men is more precisely put as a sense of kinship with men who are stereotypical, or meet some presumed ideals of manhood, or are otherwise representative. For example, one might feel that the *masculine* men are one's tribe, where one belongs. Sam Smith clearly does not feel this way.

Although Smith was reticent 'about what it means to be non-binary', numerous self-declared non-binary people have offered explanations. A consistent theme is that being non-binary, or 'outside the gender binary', is being feminine in some respects and masculine in others: 'I don't like to classify myself as simply "masculine" or "feminine". I tend to be most comfortable in masculine clothes, while some of the personality traits I'm most proud of are that I'm compassionate, thoughtful, and emotionally expressive – traits that are often linked with femininity.' It would be misleading to classify most people 'as simply "masculine" or "feminine"'. But surely it isn't true that most people are non-binary! The notion of identifying *with* suggests a better alternative. One may identify with people who present as masculine men or feminine women; one may also identify with people who present as neither. That is a large (and very vaguely delineated) group. We can call them the *gender-stereotype defiers*, or the *gender atypicals*, bearing in mind that it doesn't take much to fall outside gender stereotypes. Butch lesbians are definitely gender atypicals, Laverne Cox and Marilyn Monroe are definitely not, while metrosexuals and emotionally expressive plumbers are to be found at the margins. To be non-binary is to identify *with* these gender atypicals.[15]

Admittedly, 'non-binary' does have a whatever-you-want-it-to-mean flavour – 'being non-binary means different things to different people'[16] – an ominous sign that the term is at present too vague and ambiguous to be worth bothering with. Perhaps it would be better to say that 'identifying *with* gender atypicals' is *one* way of making the word 'non-binary' useful and reasonably well defined, and the proposal should be taken in that spirit. Let's run through some of its desirable features.

First, although self-declared non-binary people often say that they are neither women nor men, this strikes even some trans-rights activists as a bit of a stretch. The blank in the mantra 'Trans women are women, trans men are men, and non-binary people are ___' is not filled in with 'neither women nor men'. Instead, the filling is either 'valid' or 'non-binary'. 'Non-binary woman' is no oxymoron. The proposal explains why: being a woman or a man is entirely compatible with identifying with gender atypicals.[17]

Second, one may identify with a group without being a member – Gordon does not have to be one of the Canadians to identify with them. Thus it is possible to be non-binary without being gender atypical oneself. That might seem like the wrong result, but some self-declared non-binary people are quite conformist. These people's self-declarations will be correct, provided that they identify with gender atypicals.

Third, on the orthodox view of gender identity as the direction of an internal compass needle, it is natural to think of non-binary people as trans. A cisgender man's compass needle points to M and so is aligned with his sexed body; a transgender woman's compass needle points to F, this time diametrically opposite her sexed body. The metaphor suggests that there should be people whose compass needles quiver between M and F – and these would be enbies.

This is hard to swallow, even for the most committed ideologue. There are people with a history of gender dysphoria and medical interventions who have found a non-binary identity to be a comfortable landing pad. But can Sam Smith seriously be compared to Jazz Jennings? What about comparing the American non-binary singer Demi Lovato (who presents as a conventional woman) to the bearded and ripped trans man Buck Angel? In an implicit but awkward recognition of the problem, it is common to speak of 'trans and non-binary people'.

With the demise of the orthodox view of gender identity we want to clearly separate the non-binary phenomenon from transsexualism; equating *being non-binary* and *identifying with gender atypicals* does that nicely. Merely identifying with a group does not lead to any distress, especially if one is in fact a member of that group. Since non-binary people are as a rule gender atypicals themselves, non-binary status has no interesting connection with gender dysphoria. That is quite unlike transsexualism, where dysphoria is diagnostic.

Finally, we can see why it's a mistake to subsume 'third genders', such as the *fa'afafine* in Independent Samoa or the *muxe* in Mexico, under the non-binary umbrella. Third genders (or 'third sexes') are cultural roles set aside for feminine gay men and (sometimes) masculine women. The *fa'afafine*, for example, are males selected in childhood on the basis of their feminine interests and who occupy a distinct cultural niche in Samoan society, with varying but mostly feminine gender presentations. One does not 'come out' as a *fa'afafine* as Sam Smith came out as non-binary. *Fa'afafine* have sex neither with women nor with each other, but instead with heterosexual Samoan men. They do not think of themselves as gay, however: 'the majority of *fa'afafine* are quite resolute in their assertion that Samoan "gays" and "homosexuals" do not exist.'[18] If there is a common thread of *identification with* running though the *fa'afafine*, it is identification with *fa'afafine*, not identification with gay men or with gender atypicals in general. And the *fa'afafine* social role has no non-binary counterpart – at any rate, not yet.

It doesn't make sense to suppose that there have always been third-gender individuals hiding among us, like Russian moles or closeted gay men. Third genders are identities with associated norms of behaviour.

Such norms would never arise if the third gender was invisible to others. Non-binary people, in contrast, do not have to reveal themselves as such. One can identify *with* gender atypicals and keep quiet about it. But an *identification with* naturally tends to make itself public if it is strong enough and widespread enough, and there is no social penalty attached to doing so. Gordon no longer has to express his identification with Canadians in the privacy of his basement – he can unashamedly sing 'O Canada' when he goes to watch the Toronto Maple Leafs.

What is the public expression of a non-binary identity? We are frequently reminded that there's no such thing as looking non-binary, and there's no non-binary accent or non-binary occupation. But there is the yellow, white, purple and black striped non-binary flag and – much more important – the use of *they/them* pronouns. Is this progress? That question deserves a digression.

Pronounmania

The current obsession with pronouns is a singular result of the confluence of the Jazz Age – girl brains in boy bodies, and vice versa – and the Age of Identity. This marks a complete break with the informal practice, as exhibited in Harry Benjamin's *The Transsexual Phenomenon* and the writings of other traditional sexologists, of using pronouns for transsexuals that match their sex-of-living. Benjamin and others referred to Christine Jorgensen, the first famous transgender woman in the US, with feminine pronouns out of simple courtesy, not for any theoretical reason. It was, perhaps, the best possible motivation for doing so.[19]

Whether someone should be referred to by 'she' or 'he' used to be obvious, even if sometimes it was not obvious whether the person was in reality a woman or a man. There was thus no need to make any announcements, or to wear pronoun badges, or to have pronouns in one's email (or snail mail) signature. Politeness and decency brought about the desired result by themselves. And, no doubt, that is exactly how many transgender women and men wanted it.

However, the explosion of non-binary identities in the last decade has swept the old order away. A non-binary person may look exactly like a cisgendered normie, an ordinary woman or man, with a gendered name to match. Judith Butler, referred to with feminine pronouns in thousands of pages over many years, and as patently female as she always was, is now legally non-binary. 'I am enjoying the world of "they"', she remarked recently.[20] ('They' was Merriam-Webster's word of the year in 2019.) Although Butler herself does not mind 'she' and 'her', 'they' and 'them' are her pronouns in the more progressive reaches of journalism and academia.

They/them are only the beginning. Neopronouns – e.g. *xe/xir*, *fae/faer*, *kitten/kittenself* – can be multiplied beyond limit.[21] Public announcements are therefore essential, and anxiety over 'misgendering' becomes omnipresent.

Neopronouns are nothing new. In the nineteenth century, many (unsuccessful) proposals were made to add sex-neutral third-person singular pronouns to English, for instance 'e' (*he/she*), 'es' (*his/her*), 'em' (*them*). Fortunately *kitten/kittenself* and the like remain mostly a youthful online fad, but in 2015 Harvard University allowed students to declare their pronouns of choice, including 'ze, hir, and hirs'. The director of an LGBTQ resource centre approved of this innovation, commenting that 'misidentifying an individual's gender is a "microaggression" … These acts can work to erode a person's feelings of value.' Exactly what gender is identified by 'ze' was left unclear.[22]

Normies and old-school transsexuals need no pronoun badges. Still, those who do will stand out even more if they are the only ones. Hence the trend in universities and elsewhere – as yet only partially completed – for everyone to state their pronouns, non-binary or not. Not everyone is on board: the former gender-bending Culture Club singer Boy George described pronounmania as a 'modern form of attention seeking'. You can guess how that went down.[23]

Since nothing screams *he/him* more than a jacket and tie and male pattern baldness, these declarations sometimes come off as a little ludicrous. To be sure, there are poseurs and virtue-signallers among the normie pronoun advertisers, but many are kind and compassionate people who would like to show some solidarity. Nevertheless, it is doubtful they have thought the matter through.

There is nothing wrong with *being* non-binary – feeling a sense of kinship with gender atypicals. But non-binary people are not outside the gender (sex) binary: Sam Smith is as male as Daniel Craig. There is no tension at all between identifying with gender atypicals and being referred to by 'he', and indeed some self-declared non-binary people are happy with the old pronouns. Some aren't, though, and you might think that respecting their pronoun preferences is a harmless indulgence, like calling Elaine's boyfriend (in the famous Seinfeld episode) 'Maestro'. If using 'they' makes some people feel better, why not go for it?

The problem with pronounmania isn't some pedantic concern about the ungrammaticality of 'Sam Smith has recorded their new album' – language is flexible and changes to meet our needs. Nor is it that keeping track of people's pronouns requires effort to override the reflex that connects perceived sex to 'she' and 'he'. That is certainly something to consider – Sam Smith's mother, apparently, 'struggles to remember to use their pronouns' – but, if the goal is worthwhile, we'll find ways to make reaching it easier.[24]

To see the chief downside, imagine what it would be like if 'they' was consistently used for those (usually gender-atypical) people with a non-binary identity, reinforced by the normie majority's preference for 'she' and 'he'. 'She' and 'he' would be more strongly associated than they are now with gender stereotypes. Since non-binary people tend to avoid calling themselves 'women/girls' or 'men/boys', these words would also strengthen their stereotypical associations. 'Masculine woman' and 'masculine girl' might start to sound jarring, surely an unhealthy result. Enbies frequently proclaim their desire to overturn gender stereotypes, but the widespread use of 'they' risks producing exactly the opposite result. Needless to say, such an outcome could hardly be *less* feminist. Simone de Beauvoir would not have approved.

One might have expected feminist philosophers, then, to try to halt the pronoun bandwagon. Instead, pronounmania turned out to be as polarizing as everything else. While the gender-critical philosophers resisted, the establishment went all in, with the American Philosophical Association handing out pronoun stickers at conferences.

The true self

The Age of Identity is not just about the proliferation and veneration of identities. The 'authentic inner self' (Fukuyama's phrase) or the true self is a central figure too. Whether we should bring our authentic selves to work is debated by human resources managers – if that doesn't convince you that authentic or true selves are important, nothing will.

Presumably identity and the true self are in some way connected, but how? That is not immediately clear. Take Postman Pat, who identifies *as* a postman and *with* postmen. His identity is unqualifiedly *postman*, yet it sounds odd to say that this is part of his true self. What if Pat changes career and becomes a train driver, in the process transferring his group allegiance from postmen to train drivers? He may still be the same old Pat we know and love. You can't shrug off your true self as easily as that.

Let's leave the connection between identity and the true self for later. First, we need to get clearer on what the true self is supposed to be. 'Self' is a slippery word. It has an innocuous sense in which Pat's 'self' is simply Pat, Pat himself. But Pat's true self is not Pat. Pat might be on a quest to discover his true self, but that is not a quest to discover Pat. Pat weighs 170 pounds, but surely his true self doesn't weigh 170 pounds – it may not be the kind of thing that weighs anything at all. The true self sounds like an entity that is somehow 'in' Pat, something ordinarily hidden but which can be discerned through special mental exercises, an 'inner homunculus, a unique little thing composed of parts tinted by race, sex, and gender'.[25]

The true self is looking very mysterious. But there is a more promising way of explaining this way of talking: Pat's true self is simply *who Pat really is*. The true self is not an inner homunculus; the phrase is just a grammatically misleading way of talking about Pat's characteristics – specifically, those characteristics that answer the question 'Who is Pat, really?'

This needs some elaboration. Isn't *every* characteristic of Pat's something that partially answers the question 'Who is Pat, really?' If Pat is a postman, then that is 'really' a characteristic of Pat's – he 'really is' a postman. Similarly, if Pat feels cold, not hot, then he really does feel cold, and really doesn't feel hot. But Pat's true self is not so compendious – it does not include being a postman and feeling cold even if Pat is out delivering the mail in a snow storm.

'Really' in the question 'Who is Pat, really?' isn't simply a rhetorical device of emphasis. To make it a little clearer, we could swap out 'really' with 'fundamentally', 'deep down' or 'essentially'. And the characteristics of interest should be *psychological*: perhaps Pat is fundamentally composed of atoms, but this is not part of his true self. The question could be rephrased as 'What is Pat's psychological nature?' The basic idea should be coming into view. Pat's 'true self' is a compendium of his permanent and stable psychological traits that (at least sometimes) explain his temporary and contingent behaviour.

Personality traits are good candidates. Pat is agreeable and conscientious. It is natural to think these personality traits have little to do with Pat's upbringing or cultural milieu – if he had been raised in Giza, Egypt, instead of the English village of Greendale he would still have been agreeable and conscientious, although not a postman. Also Pat is not going to lose these traits, unless something drastic befalls him, such as Alzheimer's. In this way, Pat's agreeableness and conscientiousness are stable and permanent. They are part of the explanation of why he became a postman, a job which requires discipline, reliability and a friendly disposition.

Pat is also gay, another good candidate for a permanent and stable trait. Sexual orientation takes some time to develop, but when it does it is pretty much fixed (especially in males). Pat's homosexuality is also not the result of his upbringing – an absent father, an over-protective mother, and so forth. Those theories were jettisoned years ago. If he had been raised in Giza he would still have been gay, although not the out gay man he actually is, married to another man. When Pat accepted his sexual orientation and came out in his twenties, it would have been appropriate for him to say, 'Now I can now live authentically, as my true self.' Being gay is not under Pat's or anyone else's control, and in his society there's no need to repress this fundamental aspect of himself.

Having sketched the true self, let's turn now to the connection with identity.

Identities and essentializing

Identities can be dangerous things. As the philosopher Kwame Anthony Appiah points out, we are inclined to *essentialize* certain identities, to think that there is 'some inner essence that explains why people of a certain social identity are the way they are'.[26] This is the bridge between identities and true selves. Canadians aren't just ordinary people who happen to live in a society that prizes modesty and the rule of law.

They are naturally modest and law-abiding, unlike Americans, who are naturally boastful and disrespectful of authority. Canadian Gordon isn't modest and law-abiding because he was raised in Canada; rather, those characteristics are part of his true self.

When we claim an identity as our own, by identifying *as* or (especially) *with* the relevant group, this leads to what psychologists call *out-group bias* and *in-group favouritism*. Gordon may disdain non-Canadians, for instance Americans (after all, they are braggarts and law-breakers), and give preferential treatment to members of his own tribe. Americans, in their turn, may mock the white bread people to the North, and war breaks out before you can say 'eh'. Out-group bias and in-group favouritism can be induced simply by dividing people up randomly into two groups. Dr Seuss realized this long before the psychologists did their experiments: in *The Sneetches*, the difference between the star-bellied sneetches and the others is a superficial green star which can be stuck on or removed, but that does not prevent those with stars from thinking themselves superior.[27]

Essentializing sounds bad, but it's a vital cognitive habit. If we fall sick after eating ivory funnel mushrooms, the best explanation might be that mushrooms of this kind have – in Appiah's phrase – 'some inner something' that poisons us. Perhaps we fell sick for some other reason, or perhaps by a fluke ate some of the very rare ivory funnel mushrooms that are poisonous, but these hypotheses may well be implausible. We should sensibly avoid ivory funnel mushrooms in the future, or experiment to see if the 'inner something' can be destroyed by cooking. Similarly, after encountering a few fierce wolves we might reasonably think ferocity is part of a wolf's nature, not a malleable characteristic that could easily be erased completely. Wolf pups will likely grow up to be fierce, no matter how we raise them. Essentializing is crucial to knowing about the non-living world too. Water has some distinctive properties – it's transparent, it freezes in the winter, boils over a fire, and so on. The chemistry of water begins by essentializing it – making hypotheses about the invisible structure of water that would explain its distinctive observable features.

Essentializing kinds of people is sometimes reasonable. There are no special Canadian brainworms or Canadian genes that explain why Canadians are polite, or speak English and French, or like ice hockey.

But the measles virus explains why this group of people have spots, and an extra (partial) copy of chromosome 21 explains why that group of people have the characteristic Down syndrome appearance. Attributing the historical prevalence of patriarchy and male overrepresentation in lethal violence to higher testosterone exposure is a form of essentializing. There is a danger of overdoing it, concluding that every man has a patriarchal and homicidal disposition which may be suppressed by society but never eradicated altogether. However, unless women and men are like Canadians and Americans, some psychological and behavioural sex differences are going to be explained by 'inner somethings'.

Essentialist claims can also plausibly be made of humans as a whole. For instance, we evolved to be social creatures who form coalitions and group allegiances; this seems to be very firmly embedded in the human psychological design plan. That is why we will continue to have identities, with consequent in-group favouritism and outgroup-bias. The scientific investigation of human nature can explain why we sometimes over-actively essentialize ourselves, attributing visible behavioural differences between ethnic or national groups to the presence of something abiding and internal rather than to external environmental or cultural influences. Essentializing can correct its own excesses.

A paradigm case of essentializing is the orthodox view of gender identity. Everyone has an 'inner something', a gender identity, that may be congruent or incongruent with their sexed body. This results in two fundamentally different kinds of people, the cisgendered and the transgendered.[28] If someone has always been content with their sex-of-living, the explanation is the match between their sexed body and gender identity. Distress with one's sex-of-living is explained by a mismatch.

In the case of a mismatch, why not try to resolve the issue by altering the person's gender identity rather than by altering the person's body? The reason is that someone's gender identity is supposed to be part of their nature, their very essence, their true self. The body, in contrast, is a mere container or a vehicle, no more part of a person's nature than their clothing or hairstyle. To change someone's gender identity would be to alter them so radically that they are 'not the same person'; to change the body would not.

If that is right, then the distinction between transgender and cisgender people applies across the board, even for children. There are trans kids and cis kids, even though it may take time for the children themselves to realize which group they are in. But, with the demise of the orthodox view of gender identity, does this make sense?

Trans kids

The treatment of gender dysphoria in children is controversial, to put it mildly. Painting with a very broad brush, there are two opposed protocols. One, currently dominant in the US, and mentioned in chapter 1, is affirmative care, where a clinician facilitates a child 'exploring' their gender identity, not leading but following. As the psychologist Diane Ehrensaft puts it, 'the underlying principle is that gender in all its variations is a sign of health, not illness; the clinical goals are not to "fix" gender but to provide the space for children to explore and establish their authentic gender self', and: 'When it comes to knowing a child's gender, it is not for us to tell, but for the children to say.' Social transition, including a change of name, pronouns and clothing is encouraged, if that is what the child wants. Puberty blockers, which may be prescribed to eight-year-olds, are viewed as a vital treatment option, preventing a child from going through the 'wrong' puberty.[29]

The other protocol is 'watchful waiting'. Gender variant behaviour is allowed, but social transition isn't; children are encouraged to socialize with others of their natal sex and to broaden their conceptions of what life as a woman or a man can be like. Puberty blockers are used – if at all – more cautiously than in the affirmative approach, and the risks are taken very seriously. (A point worth emphasizing is that gender dysphoric children often have other psychiatric conditions, such as anxiety, depression, or autism spectrum disorder.)[30]

Advocates of the affirmative approach frequently speak of trans kids as one might speak of gay kids. Interestingly, some proponents of watchful waiting do too. Gay kids are not made, they are discovered, although discerning sexual orientation at an early age is a highly fallible science. With trans kids, discovery may be easier, at least to the trained professional. 'Can we actually tell if a very young child, prepubertal, is transgender?', Ehrensaft asks, answering 'Yes, we can.' The treatment of dysphoric children is thus conceived as the project of separating the trans kids from the cis ones, trying to avoid medical interventions with the latter. 'My own clinical experience', Ehrensaft reports, 'told me that you could discern one group of children from the other prior to adolescence, not with 100% accuracy, but not far from it.'[31] Gender dysphoria usually resolves around puberty; on Ehrensaft's view, when it does, that only shows that the child was not really trans to begin with. The child was cisgender all along, and their misery was not due to a misaligned gender identity. But if the child is truly trans, their dysphoria will not resolve normally, and (given the opportunity) they will transition sooner or later.

Despite the way some clinicians talk, being trans is not a medical diagnosis. Children and adults may be diagnosed with gender dysphoria, but this is neither necessary or sufficient for being trans. It is not sufficient because – as just noted – many children with gender dysphoria grow out of it, and these children are supposed to be cis. If a child's cross-sex identification is 'insistent, persistent and consistent', this increases the chances that dysphoria will remain after puberty but by no means guarantees it.

Having gender dysphoria is not necessary for being trans because transgender men and women who are finally at ease with their sexed bodies do not thereby cease to be trans. A further point is that gender dysphoria can be more or less intense, but someone cannot be 'more trans' than another. Mild gender dysphoria is probably a feature of many ordinary adolescent girls' lives. Similarly, some people learn to live with stronger forms without taking themselves to be transgender.

Understood in a minimal way, the categories of *trans woman* and *trans man* are unproblematic. A trans woman is simply an adult natal male who has transitioned (or who is in the process of transitioning) because of gender dysphoria. (Transitioning involves at least changing one's sex-of-living; hormones and surgery are optional.) *Trans girl* and *trans boy* are also unproblematic, if these categories are given a parallel account. A trans girl is simply a juvenile natal male who has transitioned (or who is in the process of transitioning) because of gender dysphoria. (Again, medical treatment, like puberty blockers, is not required.) But, on this conception of being trans, it is a transitory trait. A former trans boy (or even a former trans man) can be a later cis woman, for instance. By the same token, being cis is a transitory trait too. No one is born trans. This is not what the promoters of 'trans kids' have in mind.

Alternatively, one could retrospectively classify children as trans if they become transgender adults. But a transgender child, on this conception, might easily not have been transgender. One can't transition without the opportunity, which may be absent or else socially discouraged. A deeper point is that gender dysphoria itself is highly dependent on social factors – an unsurprising result, since that holds for psychiatric conditions in general. Prevalence rates, and the sex ratio of those suffering from gender dysphoria, change over time and from place to place. For feminine androphilic males specifically, the availability of a gender role designed for them may be one way to reduce dysphoria. At any rate, little distress was reported by two psychologists who interviewed more than fifty members of the Samoan third gender, the *fa'afafine*. Both gender dysphoria and the phenomenon of transitioning from one gender (sex) to the other (or to a metaphorical third gender) are, unlike sexual orientation, thoroughly culture-bound.[32]

'One of the stately homos of England'[33]

The life of the great British eccentric and raconteur Quentin Crisp illustrates how Ehrensaft's 'authentic gender self' is a will o' the wisp, a phantom not worth pursuing. Born in 1908 with the unpromising name of Denis Pratt, Crisp was a flamboyant feminine gay man during a time in which sex between men was illegal, and thousands were sent to prison. His most famous book, *The Naked Civil Servant*, was published in 1968, a year after male homosexual acts were decriminalized – provided that the parties were at least twenty-one. (It took more than thirty years before the ages of consent for homosexuals and heterosexuals were equalized.) Crisp had a taste for provocative remarks, once saying that, if there were a genetic test for homosexuality, aborting gay fetuses should be allowed. Nonetheless, he was a big inspiration to many gay men, including the Culture Club singer Boy George. 'Oi, Quentin Crisp' was a playground taunt when Boy George (George O'Dowd) was a young teenager.[34]

Crisp's last book was completed shortly before he died, in 1999. 'At the age of ninety', he revealed, 'it has finally been explained to me that I am not really homosexual, I'm transgender.' His convincing lifelong performance as a gay man notwithstanding, Crisp's 'actual fate' was 'that of a woman trapped in a man's body'. He approvingly quoted 'Ms. Morris, the man who had the operation': 'It was never a question of sex. It was a question of gender.'[35] That was Jan Morris (chapter 6); Crisp and Ms Morris doubtfully had much in common.

By Crisp's own account, transitioning would not have worked: 'I think my body is too like a man's body to have lived as a woman with any kind of success.' Had he been born in Samoa, Crisp would have lived as a *fa'afafine*, 'in the manner of a woman'. Had he been born in England a century later, in 2008, he might have been identified as a trans kid and started on puberty blockers, sending him down a medical pathway to cross-sex hormones and surgery, and finally to living as a woman. Sterility would not have bothered him, since he never cared much for children; the risk of sexual dysfunction might have done. Still, his actual achievements during a time of widespread and extreme prejudice are not to be sniffed at, and he did die with a million dollars in the bank. Living openly as a feminine gay man in an inhospitable age, he managed through sheer force of will to make the best of it. Each of these three options has its pros and cons, but none expresses Crisp's true self more than any other.[36]

Received opinion in genderology leads inexorably to the conclusion that Quentin Crisp was not a gay man. He was not gay; he was not even a man. In fact, Crisp was a straight woman. This is a form of argument called *reductio ad absurdum*, where one's assumptions are shown to lead to an absurdity, to the detriment of the assumptions. We can only hope that Crisp would have seen the funny side of it all.

An absurdity would be a fitting ending for the final chapter, but there is one more item on the agenda. To use one of John Money's neologisms, our true selves are not so spookological, properly understood. Should we aspire to be them?

The best self

In one sense we cannot help but be our true selves. Being sexually attracted to men was part of Quentin Crisp's true self, and there was nothing he could realistically do about it. On the usual understanding, though, a closeted Crisp would *not* have been his true self, despite being just as androphilic. *Being* one's true self means not disguising or burying one's stable and permanent psychological traits. (Crisp may have gone a little overboard in this respect.)

The problem with being one's true self in this sense can be obscured by our tendency to see true selves as good. And it's not just that people have high opinions of *their* true selves, holding others' true selves in lower esteem. They tend to think *everyone's* true self is good, or at least better than indicated by the person's actions. This is the reverse of the usual pattern, where we judge others more harshly than we judge ourselves. It is easy to find fault with someone else's ill-considered tweet, but if it's our tweet we are more likely to excuse it as a minor slip. We take others' true selves to be surrounded by a halo: the tweeter is fundamentally a decent person, despite their reprehensible behaviour. Interestingly, there is some evidence that this is a cross-cultural phenomenon.[37]

This tendency to sanctify the true self plainly has limits. To take a case of infamy from Crisp's time, no one said that the 1960s child murderers Ian Brady and Myra Hindley were good people, deep down. Hindley was known as 'the most evil woman in Britain'.[38] And once it's clear that true selves are not always good, the way is open to realize that the permanent and stable traits of ordinary people are usually a mixed bag. If you are inclined towards anger or selfishness, please don't be your true self. Avoiding certain situations and learning to recognize warning signs can help.

As the psychologist Anne Lawrence puts it at the end of *Men Trapped in Men's Bodies*:

> We create our feminine personas by trying to express and embody the feminine virtues, whatever we think these are. For me, they include gentleness, nurturance, empathy, agreeableness, cooperation, friendliness, and grace. These qualities do not describe how I am naturally, but they describe the way I want to be and try to be … The transsexual journey is, in this case, less about finding our 'true selves' than our best selves.[39]

Lawrence is describing one specific kind of transsexual transition, but the point isn't confined to transsexuality and is quite general. Sometimes we aren't naturally the way we should be; complete transformation is not possible, but that doesn't mean we can't be better. *Be your authentic true self!* is one of the worst pieces of advice.

Lawrence is not suggesting that life is solely a quest for self-improvement, a voyage that begins and ends at home. It's not all about me. There are friends, lovers, family and others in the expanding circle of moral concern, including non-human animals. Ruminating about myself takes attention away from what really matters. One of the many troubles with gender in the Age of Identity is this impulse towards narcissism.

In the introduction I wrote: 'I can sum up the argument of this book in one word: sex. That is the key to answering the main questions we'll be examining. There is a coda after chapter 8, in which the meaning of this cryptic remark will become clear.' Let us hope so.

Coda

Certain differences between man and woman will always exist.

Simone de Beauvoir, *The Second Sex*[1]

Sex glues this book together. Chapter 2: gender = sex. More carefully put: using 'gender' to mean anything other than *sex* is to obscure important issues for no good reason. Chapter 3: sex is binary. There are exactly two sexes, female and male, and everyone (or very nearly everyone) is either one or the other. Sex is not 'a vast, infinitely malleable continuum' or socially constructed in any interesting sense. Chapter 4: women are the mature females of our species, men the mature males. Orthodoxy in feminist philosophy and gender studies is tragically wrong. Chapter 5: core gender identity, 'the sense of knowing to which sex one belongs', is universal. It is not, however, gender identity as it figures in the received account of being 'trans' or 'cis': *that* kind of gender identity is a myth. Chapter 6: one type of male-to-female transsexuality vividly demonstrates how male sexuality is different from the female kind. Chapter 7: the historical universality of patriarchy highlights other – more significant – respects in which the sexes differ.

That leaves chapter 8. Is there much of a connection between identity and the true self and sex? Taking identity first, one typically has no option but to identify *as* female or male – a normie's sex is invariably apparent. Trans women and men also identify as female and male, their respective sexes-of-living. Only the few who have reached a state of genuine androgyny are exempt. Sex might seem more distant from the true self: if (as I suggested) one's 'true self' is a compendium of one's permanent and stable psychological traits, then one's sex is not included. But it is impossible to ignore. One may not know or care whether one is made of atoms, yet knowledge of one's sex is almost unavoidable. We are sexed beings, and that shapes both personal relationships and the structure of society. Our lives cannot be disentangled from our sex, whatever our sexual orientation or sex-of-living.

Some medieval Christian theologians held that sex is a superficial human characteristic. We are made in the image of God, who is sexless, so that is our nature too. The resurrected Christ appeared as a man only because the disciples would not have been convinced otherwise; in reality, the Son of God is non-binary. There are no females or males in heaven; according to the medieval theologian and philosopher John Scottus Eriugena, 'after the unification of man, that is, of his two sexes, into the original unity of nature in which there was neither male nor female but simply man there will immediately follow the unification of the inhabited globe with paradise.' Second-wave feminists of the 1970s had a secular version of this fantasy, in which the revolution would not abolish sex but render it as socially inconsequential as eye-colour.[2]

Setting the afterlife aside, the significance of sex will always be with us. Humans are exceptional animals in many ways, but not in this one. It's not simply that we come in two sexes, but that we come in two sexed forms – humans are sexually dimorphic. If human females and males were practically indistinguishable, there would be no trouble with gender and no need for this book. It is not all trouble, though: without sexual dimorphism, much of value in our society, art and culture would be absent. Underneath the – surely transient – contemporary social currents discussed in this book is the human condition.

Notes

Acknowledgements

1 Alex Byrne, 'Philosophy's no-go zone', *Quillette* April 17 (2023), https://quillette.com/2023/04/17/philosophys-no-go-zone/.

2 In addition to my publications listed in the references: Alex Byrne, 'Is sex binary?', *Arc Digital* Nov 1 (2018), https://medium.com/arc-digital/is-sex-binary-16bec97d161e; 'Is sex socially constructed?', *Arc Digital* November 30 (2018), https://arcdigital.media/is-sex-socially-constructed-81cf3ef79f07; 'What is gender identity?', *Arc Digital* Jan 9 (2019), https://medium.com/arc-digital/what-is-gender-identity-10ce0da71999; 'Pronoun problems', *Journal of Controversial Ideas* 3: 1-22 (2023), https://journalofcontroversialideas.org/article/3/1/229.

Introduction

1 Wyndham 1960/2022: 48. *Trouble with Lichen* is a 1960 novel by the British sci-fi writer John Wyndham, in which a strain of lichen is discovered that slows aging, extending the lifespan to centuries. Limited supply means availability only to 'Mayfair's feminine élite'. Relations between the sexes, transformative medical technology and its revolutionary social consequences are all prominent themes. The present book isn't linked to *Trouble with Lichen* only through the title.

2 '… changing climate': The Core Writing Team et al. 2014: 13; '… tipping point': Steinmetz 2014.

3 *How to …*: Iantaffi and Barker 2018; 'a man' and 'thing that thinks': Descartes 1642/1984: 17, 19. Descartes was a life-long bachelor, although he had an illegitimate daughter who died at age five.

4 Biden 2021.

5 Liptak 2020.

6 The Court decided in favour of the baker on religious freedom grounds, while noting, 'Our society has come to the recognition that gay persons and gay couples cannot be treated as social outcasts or as inferior in dignity and worth' (Kennedy 2018: 9).

7 Medley and Sherwin 2019.

8 'champions of women': Bannerman 2018; 'I split my time …': Bunce 2017.

9 Fox 2019.
10 *The Telegraph* December 16 (2022); *The Times* February 11 (2023); *New York Times* December 10 (2022).
11 Noteworthy books on the trans debate as it has played out in the UK: Stock 2021, Joyce 2021, Faye 2021 (the first two 'gender-critical', the third on the 'trans-rights' side – see chapter 1).
12 Humane thread: Joyce 2021: 3–4; Stock 2021: 240; Lawford-Smith 2022a: 94–5.
13 'Brilliant …': Paglia 1991a: 243; an instructive (and uncomplimentary) assessment of *The Second Sex* is Sommers 2010. 'Gender interacts …': World Health Organization 2021. Crediting Beauvoir for a distinction between sex and gender is misleading: 'gender' is not in her book, and whatever kind of sex/gender distinction that can be read back into it was made long before by others (see Kirkpatrick 2019: 262). A good introduction to feminist philosophy is Stone 2007.
14 Mill 1869/2006: 23.
15 Bissinger 2015.
16 Singal 2017.
17 Doležal and Reback 2017; 'People often said that I was a Black girl in a white body' (109).
18 Moyer 2015. See also Brubaker 2016: ch. 1.
19 Tuvel 2017a. The transracial analogy had been mentioned much earlier in the introduction to the 1994 edition of Janice Raymond's *The Transsexual Empire* (1979/1994: xv–xvi); for more on that book, see note 9 to chapter 6.
20 Telò 2022.
21 'apology …': Jaschik 2017. Jenner unbothered: 'Bruce existed for sixty-five years, and Caitlyn is just going on her second birthday. That's the reality' (Jenner 2017: vii); 'Bruce' was used freely in the *Vanity Fair* cover story.
22 'the last place …': Tuvel 2017b. Academic philosophy is predominantly male, but specialists in feminist philosophy are overwhelmingly women. The social dynamics in this sub-field appear to fit the generally observed pattern of female intrasexual competition: enforced equality, overt competition only among high-status females, and the use of social exclusion (ostracism) to dispatch rivals. (Male-dominated sub-disciplines have another set of issues.) See Benenson 2013; Benenson 2014: ch. 6; Campbell 2013: 98–100, ch. 4; for feminist infighting specifically, see Lawford-Smith 2022a: 117–29, 2022b. '… the Tuvel treatment': Whittaker 2022: 21.
23 Unsurprisingly, the clichés about Victorian attitudes towards sex are oversimplifications. For instance, orgasm in women was widely held to be important, partly because conception was supposedly very difficult without it (Mason 1994: ch. 4).

24 'Sex . . .': AMA & AAMC 2021: 14, emphasis added; 'promote the art . . .': AMA 2022.
25 Orwell 1949/1961: 51–3.
26 Scruton 2018.
27 In 2015 Jenner tweeted that she was 'so happy ... to be living my true self'. These sorts of sentiments are common among transgender people; see Mason-Schrock 1996 for a study of how the 'true self' figures in transsexual self-narratives.
28 See also Murray 2019: ch. 4, and the books cited in note 11 above.

Chapter 1 Gender, Double Toil and Trouble

1 Duffy 2018.
2 Hellen 2019.
3 'Girls grow up . . .' and '. . . not worthy of respect . . .': Tayler 2019: paras 39.7, 85; '. . . fans are heartbroken': Romano 2019.
4 Stock 2018.
5 Some examples of the use of 'TERF'. Philosophy: McKinnon 2018; Stanley 2018; Ásta 2018: 90; Hay 2020: 120–9. The first two were the subject of a letter of complaint on one of the two main philosophy blogs: Allen et al. 2018. Trans studies: Sadjadi 2020: 509; Lavery (2020a) declines to use 'TERF' on the grounds that it is *too* 'value neutral', preferring 'gender-critical', a phrase she thinks 'conspicuously stupid' (397–8, n. 2). Psychology: Schudson et al. 2019. Sociology: Williams 2020; Worthen 2022. Feminist/gender studies: Schuller 2021: ch. 6; Thomsen and Essig 2022; Breslow 2022. The *grande dame* of gender studies, Judith Butler (see the following chapter), mind-bogglingly said in 2020, 'I am not aware that terf is used as a slur' (Ferber 2020).

Slurs and other pejoratives sometimes get 'reclaimed' by their targets ('queer', for instance). 'TERF Island' originated as a pejorative for the UK; probably because the phrase was amusing, it now appears on gender-critical accessories such as mugs and T-shirts. 'Terves' was a gender-critical adaptation of 'TERFs'; a trans-rights activist coined 'terven' as a collective noun, and gender-critical feminists promptly adopted it (the similarity to 'coven' was part of the appeal).
6 Lawford-Smith 2019b.
7 Hay 2019.
8 Russell and Freeman 1959: 28:55.
9 Bermúdez et al. 2019.
10 Alcoff et al. 2019.
11 Anonymous 2019.
12 Leiter 2019.
13 Lawford-Smith 2019a.
14 Dembroff et al. 2019.

15 Rowling 2020.
16 'Inviting JK Rowling …': Massie 2021; 'JK Rowling triples down …': Lampen 2020.
17 Schuessler and Harris 2020.
18 'The consequences …': Singal 2020b. From Boylan's perspective, other problematic signatories may have included the journalists Jesse Singal and Katie Herzog, both of whom had expressed vaguely Rowling-adjacent views. 'people whose hearts …': Boylan 2021.
19 Blackall 2020.
20 '… remarkable grassroots …': Kirkup 2020. One factor in the policy change was the wildly popular parenting website Mumsnet, which became a forum for women sceptical of the proposed GRA reforms. 'A toxic hotbed of transphobia', according to one critic; users had a different perspective: 'I came for the babies, stayed for the feminism' (Pedersen 2020: 13, 121). GRA reforms were passed by the Scottish Parliament at the end of 2022, only to be blocked by the UK government in January 2023. On women's opposition to the reforms, see Pedersen 2022. Forstater's appeal: Choudhury et al. 2021.
21 Quoted in Schneider et al. 2009: 28.
22 Early onset: Ristori and Steensma 2016; late onset: Zucker et al. 2016. See also Zucker and Bradley 1995. Altered sex ratio: Aitken et al. 2015; Zucker and Aitken 2019. See also Zucker 2019: 1983–4 and van der Loos et al. 2023.
23 '… online influences': Littman 2017; '… junk science': Tannehill 2019: 129, 131.
24 Littman 2018a.
25 Ibid.: 16.
26 Anorexia becomes more acute if patients socialize together:

> 'Anorexia' had agency and power in these patient groups as both an individual and a collective identity. The patient community developed clear boundaries (defined by the *Diagnostic and Statistical Manual of Mental Disorders* (DSM) clinical categories), ties of relatedness, values and a status hierarchy. Peers worked hard to become 'better anorexics' and share tips and tricks as part of their joint allegiance and the strength of connectedness to 'the anorexic club'. (Allison et al. 2014: 119)

27 Brown University 2018.
28 Flier 2018. For more background see Verite 2018.
29 Republished paper: Littman 2018b. The Correction Notice, written by Littman (2019), did not even hint that anything was incorrect in the original. Neither were there any material omissions. Littman had earlier made the limitations completely clear: '… it is a descriptive study … not a prevalence study … Another limitation of this study is that it included only parental perspective. Ideally, data would be obtained from both the parent and the child and the

absence of either perspective paints an incomplete account of events' (Littman 2018a: 35–6). A subsequent much larger study (1,655 surveys completed by parents who contacted ParentsofROGDKids.com) found that 75 per cent of the children were female, with the mean age of reported gender dysphoria onset being fourteen years (Diaz and Bailey 2023: 4). Like Littman, the authors took pains to state the limitations (11–12).

30 Heber 2019.

31 '… inferior race': The Economist 2018; '… significant corrections': Clark et al. 2019: W2. The editor-in-chief of *PLOS One* had mentioned 'significant corrections' in his apology (Heber 2019).

32 '… new diagnosis': Boylan 2019. '… it's trendy …': Solovitch 2018. That clinician (Erica Anderson) subsequently co-authored an article in the *Washington Post* with another clinician, Laura Edwards-Leeper, in which they mentioned 'how other factors (e.g., autism, trauma, eating disorders/body image concerns, self-esteem, depression, anxiety) may help drive dysphoria' and that 'the messages that teens get from TikTok and other sources may not be very productive for understanding this constellation of issues' (Edwards-Leeper and Anderson 2021). Edwards-Leeper was then the chair of the child and adolescent committee of the World Professional Association of Transgender Health (WPATH), and Anderson was a recent former president of the US branch (USPATH). Anderson resigned from the USPATH board of directors in 2021, saying, 'I cannot abide the tactics of muzzling leaders in the USPATH/WPATH' (Davis 2022).

'… not a girl …': GuessImAfab 2019. Many other examples are easy to find. Those sceptical of ROGD sometimes imply that there are no such first-person testimonies: 'The voices of trans teenagers alleged to have ROGD are conveniently absent from writings promoting the theory' (Ashley 2020: 780).

33 Singal 2016; Rizza 2018.

34 Zucker 2019: 1987. See also Zucker 2017: 407; Kaltiala-Heino et al. 2018: 38.

35 Shrier, personal communication.

36 Shrier 2020b: 145.

37 ACLU and neo-Nazis: Strum 1999; '… I will die on': Shrier 2020a; '… violent incident': WSJ Editorial Board 2021.

38 'Predictably controversial …': *The Economist* 2020; '… heartless dissection …': Fonseca 2021. One particularly unmoored criticism in Fonseca's review was that Shrier's sources 'originate, not from the peer-reviewed realms of medicine, science, and law, but from the partisan op-ed sections of Fox News and The Washington Post.' One only has to leaf through *Irreversible Damage* to see that Shrier's citations include many peer-reviewed papers, no Fox op-ed, and only one from the *Washington Post*, about laws requiring the use of 'preferred pronouns'.

'well-researched ...': Hall 2021a; '... fear-filled screed ...': Lovell 2021. Hall, the author of the retracted review, subsequently published a revised version on her own website: Hall 2021b.

ROGD is almost never mentioned by mainstream feminist philosophers. An exception is George and Goguen 2021, but that paper characterizes Shrier's book as 'a representative piece of propaganda' (3) and concedes nothing to Littman. 'We do not have the space in this paper to discuss all the flaws in the ROGD hypothesis', the authors write (4, fn. 5), referring readers to citations that 'have already refuted the various claims of trans youth panics' (15). These are mostly to 'activist community and popular press responses' (15, fn. 10); the citations to the academic literature include: Costa 2019, which does not attempt to refute anything ('Data such as those collected by Dr. Littman about parents' views and experiences with youth who show sudden signs of gender dysphoria should be further investigated and documented' (2)); Temple Newhook et al. 2018 (the reply by Zucker (2018) is not cited); Ashley 2019 (the reply by Zucker et al. (2019) is not cited); Restar 2020 (Littman's reply (2020) is not cited); and a paper in (of all places) the *European Journal of English Studies*, which fails to add anything beyond citing Costa, Temple Newhook et al., Ashley and Restar (Slothouber 2020).

39 Caruso and Sheehan 2017; Terrier et al. 2019.

40 The desire to become an amputee has sometimes (controversially) been treated with surgery. For a discussion of the ethical considerations, see Dua 2010. For a comparison with surgery for gender dysphoria, see Elliott 2000. See also chapter 6. '... risks and complications': quoted in Zucker 2018: 238.

41 '... start cross-sex hormones': Gooren and Delemarre-van de Waal 1996: 72 (see also Cohen-Kettenis and van Goozen 1998: 248); '... well virilized ...' and '... inadequacy in sexual matters': Cohen-Kettenis et al. 2011: 845, 846. A helpful historical overview of the Dutch protocol is Biggs 2022a; for criticism of the Dutch studies that formed the basis for 'gender-affirming' care in the US and the UK, see Abbruzzese et al. 2023.

42 '... *parental approval*': Priest 2019: 45, emphasis added; '... risk of suicide': Dembroff 2019: 60. There is as yet no evidence that puberty blockers reduce suicidality, let alone suicide (Biggs 2020). Transgender adults are significantly more likely to commit suicide than adults in the general population; the suicide risk is three to four times higher according to one study (Wiepjes et al. 2020), nearly twenty times higher according to another (Dhejne et al. 2011). All-cause mortality is also significantly increased. Adolescents referred to the UK's Gender Identity Service over the period 2009–17 were at a 5.5-fold increased risk of suicide. This is from a very low base rate and amounts to an annual suicide rate of 13 per 100,000. Probably a substantial proportion of the increase is accounted for by comorbid conditions known to be associated with

suicide, for instance autism. See Biggs 2022b. '… health evaluation': George and Wenner 2019: 82.

The sole exception to the absence of robust philosophical debate over transgender social/ethical issues was in the niche area of the philosophy of sport. See Pike 2020 and the references therein.

43 EWHC 2020: para 83.

44 Ibid.: para 62.

45 Griffiths 2021a.

46 'clarify gender …' and 'Adolescents may …': Cohen-Kettenis and van Goozen 1998: 248. A later article on the 882 children and adolescents who were started on puberty blockers at the Amsterdam clinic during the period 1997–2018 reported that 93 per cent of the 707 eligible patients proceeded to cross-sex hormones (van der Loos et al. 2023). The authors could not 'exclude the possibility' that blockers 'make adolescents more likely to continue medical transition' (407).

47 EWHC 2020: paras 151, 152.

48 Aggressive conformity: Joshi 2021: 80–1.

49 Lavery 2020b. Lavery's article contained many mistakes (Singal 2020c).

50 For a summary of the interim report, see Barnes 2023: 334–9. That book is an excellent in-depth account of events leading to the closing of the Gender Identity Development Service.

51 Bell 2021.

52 Grove 2020.

53 Stock, personal communication.

54 Bettcher et al. 2021.

55 Accurate figures are not available, but anecdotally gender-nonconforming people are not underrepresented in philosophy. And in the US gay men and lesbians have significantly higher levels of educational attainment than bisexuals and heterosexuals. For instance, gay men are about 50 per cent more likely to have a JD, MD or PhD than straight men. (The picture for lesbians is more complicated.) One possible explanation is that this is a way for feminine males to compensate for social stigma (Mittleman 2022).

56 Jacobson et al. 2021. Full disclosure: I signed this one. Sokal Hoax: in 1996 the New York University physicist Alan Sokal managed to publish a deliberately incomprehensible paper, 'Transgressing the boundaries: towards a transformative hermeneutics of quantum gravity', in *Social Text*, a well-known academic journal of cultural studies. For the paper and the aftermath, see Editors of Lingua Franca 2000.

57 Turner 2021.

58 Lawrie 2021; McKie 2021.

59 Abell et al. 2021.

60 Brunskell-Evans 2021. This is a slight misquotation from *Material Girls*, which actually reads: 'Trans people are trans people. We should get over it' (Stock 2021: 240).

61 Griffiths 2021b.

62 Blaxter 2021.

63 Adams 2021.

64 Lord and single-sex spaces: Turner 2019; '… smash patriarchy': Ward 2018.

65 Telegraph Reporters 2021. The comedian may have other uses: according to one study, exposure to Izzard 'could reduce prejudice toward transvestites' (Schiappa 2022: 40).

66 BBC 2019.

Chapter 2 'Gender' Trouble

1 Oakley 1997: 30. Oakley is discussed later in this chapter; her observation that 'gender' is a 'contested political term' is even more true today than it was a quarter of a century ago.

2 Butler 2021. Another way of putting Butler's point that there is 'no one concept of gender' is to say that the word 'gender' has multiple related meanings – see the start of this chapter.

3 Yang 2021.

4 Not impossible, though. See Nelson and Nelson 2003.

5 Quine 1987: 78. See also Haig 2020: 388–9.

6 Stone 2007: 30.

7 A similar taxonomy is in Stock 2021: 37–40, although the first two alternatives are compressed together. See also Haslanger 2012: 227–8; Lawford-Smith 2022a: x–xi.

8 '… live-in servants': Green 2009: 613; 'Near Miss': Stoller 1982.

9 Stoller 1968: 9–10, second emphasis added.

10 Ibid.: 17.

11 '… new and useful connotation …': Scalia 1994: 157, n. 1. Diamond 2002: 321 quotes the Scalia passage and notes that Scalia's Supreme Court colleague Ruth Bader Ginsburg used 'gender' to mean *sex*. See also Moi 2001: 86–7. '… *socio-cultural constructs* …': Friedman 1991: 200, emphasis added.

12 Quoted in Olson 2017: 145. Olson points out that Roman male effeminacy was not always associated with homosexuality. See also David Beckham in the main text below.

13 Simpson 2002.

14 Stoller 1968: 29. For a helpful discussion of how masculinity and femininity have been conceptualized by psychologists, see Lippa 2005: ch. 2.

15 Six weeks: Oakley 1984: 125; 'I still have …': Oakley 1972/2016: 5.

16 Oakley 1972/2016: 21–2. This passage can be read as defining the sex/gender

distinction so that the gender side is trivially 'a matter of culture', but this is clearly not Oakley's intent. See also note 14 to chapter 7.

17 'One basic occupation …': Oakley 1972/2016: 110; see also 132–3. Oakley likely borrowed 'gender role' from the sexologist John Money. For Oakley, gender roles (more exactly, 'aspects of gender role') include sex-typed ways of urinating (ibid.: 127), which are not paradigmatic social roles. But if there is a distinction between Oakley's gender roles and sex-typed social roles, she doesn't make much of it. See also Kessler and McKenna 1978: 11–12; Jeffreys 2014: 4–5.

18 'Traditionally, …': Saul 2003: 19, third emphasis added. Another example: 'The term "gender," as it has been developed in contemporary feminist theory, refers to the sexually specific roles that are occupied by men and women in various societies' (Dupré 1986: 449). '… a costume, a mask …': Lerner 1986: 238. See also note 22 below. 'Gender includes …': Friedman 1996: 78, emphasis added.

19 Plato 2004: V 453a, 457a.

20 Holter 1970: 293.

21 Katz 1975: 1; Frieze and Chrisler 2011.

22 Jaggar 1983: 112, emphasis added. Other examples: gender 'is the cultural definition of behavior defined as appropriate to the sexes in a given society at a given time' (Lerner 1986: 238); '*gender* commonly refers to the social roles expected for males and females within a given culture' (Vasey and Bartlett 2007: 482).

23 Paraphilia: Goldie 2014: 75–6; fuckology: Downing et al. 2015; sex parties: Goldie 2014: 37.

24 '… atypical mixture …', 'All those things …', and '… person's gender …': Money 1955: 253, 254, 258; psychological sex: Meyerowitz 2004: 6, 99. A person's 'gender role and orientation', Money explained in a subsequent paper, is his or her 'psychologic sex' (Money et al. 1957: 334). In a book published forty years later, Money's retrospective definition of 'gender' in the 1955 paper is practically the same as Stoller's: '… ['gender'] signified the overall degree of masculinity and/or femininity that is privately experienced and publicly manifested in infancy, childhood, and adulthood, and that usually though not invariably correlates with the anatomy of the organs of reproduction' (Money 1995: 19).

25 Money (1985: 282) attributes 'gender identity' to another UCLA academic, the psychologist Evelyn Hooker, and Colapinto 2006: 25 wrongly attributes it to Money.

26 Congress.gov 2021.

27 'Gender identity is …': Stoller 1964a: 220. See also Stoller 1968: 29–30. '… more appropriate …': Archer and Lloyd 2002: 67, fn. 1, emphasis added. See also Diamond 2002 and Hines 2004: 235. On Green's conception of gender

identity (a.k.a. sexual identity), it included sexual orientation (Green 1974: xv). When Green was a medical student at Johns Hopkins, Money was his advisor (xvii).

28 'gender now ...': Butler 2004: 6. An example from psychology: 'one's gender (one's sense of identity as a boy or girl) ... one's sex (determined by one's anatomy and chromosomes at birth)' (Fast and Olson 2018: 620; see also 624, table 1, 'child's gender'). Philosophy: Barnes 2016: 33, fn. 42. However, this usage is relatively rare in the philosophical, sociological, and psychological literature. More often, gender identity is included only as one component of gender: '... people who study the differences and similarities between women and men have sometimes made a distinction between sex and gender ... gender itself is multidimensional. One dimension is *gender identity*: thinking of oneself as male or female' (Lips 2013: 2–3). See also Maitra 2016: 690.

'gender "matches" ...': M. Richardson 2013: 374, n. 3. Another example: 'Following current recommended practice, we use the term "cisgender" to refer to individuals whose gender corresponds to their sex assigned at birth' (Warrier et al. 2020: 2).

29 Greenson 1964: 217.

30 Oakley 1972/2016: 115, emphasis added. In a book published two years later, the radical feminist Andrea Dworkin wrote: '"man" and "woman" are fictions, caricatures, cultural constructs' (1974: 174).

31 Here and elsewhere in this book the jargon of *categories* will be useful. A prolix way of saying that Lola is a cat is to say Lola has the property (or feature, or attribute) of *being a cat*. And, instead of saying that she has this property, we can say that she belongs to, or is a member of, the category *cat*. (Words for categories will be italicized: the category *cat*, the category *dog*.) Saying that Lola is a cat, and saying that Lola belongs to the category *cat*, are equivalent; that is, they are ways of saying the same thing. A note chiefly for philosophers: we'll assume for convenience that necessarily equivalent categories are identical (Byrne 2020: 3784, fn. 2).

32 A clear statement of the orthodox position from the feminist philosopher Mari Mikkola:

> Speakers ordinarily seem to think that 'gender' and 'sex' are coextensive: women and men are human females and males, respectively, and the former is just the politically correct way to talk about the latter. Feminists typically disagree and many have historically endorsed a sex/gender distinction. Its standard formulation holds that 'sex' denotes human females and males, and depends on *biological* features (chromosomes, sex organs, hormones, other physical features). Then again, 'gender' denotes women and men and depends on *social* factors (social roles, positions, behavior, self-ascription). (Mikkola 2016: 21)

33 The term 'social category' is not unambiguous. The psychologist Judith Rich Harris uses it to mean *category of people* (Harris 2009: 126, 132, 159). When she says that *girl* is a 'social category' (xviii), she does not mean that *being* a girl depends on social factors, simply that the category is a way of grouping people.

34 Butler 1986: 35.

35 Stryker 2008: 11.

36 Sometimes Beauvoir is creatively invoked against the claim that people cannot change *sex*: 'Contrary to the famous de Beauvoir phrase that one is not born a woman, but becomes one, TERFs claim that one's birth-assigned sex is forever one's sex' (McKinnon 2018: 484).

37 Prince 1960.

38 Prince 1997: 470, quotation marks added. In fact, Prince was ahead of Oakley: in her 1971 how-to guide for transvestites (cross-dressers), *How To Be a Woman Though Male*, Prince wrote, 'it is possible to be a woman (gender) without being a female (sex)' (1971: 171). 'A bio-chemist and successful businessman, Charles Prince (a pseudonym) had long cross-dressed and ventured into public' (Bullough 1991: 64). In the 1960s, Prince argued 'that a person could transition permanently – live all the time as a woman, maybe even using hormones to develop breasts and curves – and yet do so without resort to genital reassignment surgery' (Burns 2018: 29; see also Prince 1971: 166–70). Prince was less than progressive: 'In spite of her open disdain for gay people, her frequently expressed negative opinion of transsexual surgeries, and her conservative stereotypes regarding masculinity and femininity, Prince (who began living full-time as a woman in 1968) has to be considered a central figure in the early history of the contemporary transgender political movement' (Stryker 2008: 46).

39 Harari 2015: 148.

40 '... defined by *political* ...'; Faye 2021: 237. For an example (well known in philosophy) of the sort of view Faye has in mind, see Haslanger 2012: 230 (roughly: to be a woman is to be oppressed because one is perceived as an adult female).

Many genders: 'Beauvoir's theory implied seemingly radical consequences ... that sexed bodies can be the occasion for a number of different genders, and further, that gender itself need not be restricted to the usual two' (Butler 1990b: 152; see also 9).

41 Haig 2004: 87, extra quotation marks added.

42 Stoller 1968: ix. Here's the sexologist Harry Benjamin (see the following chapter), a few years earlier: 'According to the dictionary, sex is synonymous with gender. But, in actuality, this is not true' (Benjamin 1966: 3). John Money, looking back in 1996: 'the meaning of the term *gender* underwent two changes. One change is simple: gender has become a synonym for sex as either male or female' (Money and Ehrhardt 1973/1996: xii). And Virginia Prince: 'our culture

makes no distinction between sex and gender, considering the two words as just saying the same thing' (Prince 1971: 167).

43 Butler 1990b: xxx.

44 Ibid.: viii.

45 Here's an example where Butler uses 'gender' for *both* gender as *femininity/masculinity* and gender as *woman/man*: '*gender itself* becomes a free-floating artifice, with the consequence that *man* and *masculine* might just as easily signify a female body as a male one, and *woman* and *feminine* a male body as easily as a female one' (ibid.: 9, first two emphases added).

At one point in her later book *Undoing Gender*, gender becomes (something like) gender as *norms*: 'Gender is the apparatus by which the production and normalization of masculine and feminine take place along with the interstitial forms of hormonal, chromosomal, psychic, and performative that gender assumes' (Butler 2004: 42). Notice that this explanation of gender uses the word 'gender', making the explanation circular. Butler goes on to explicitly distance 'gender' from gender as *femininity/masculinity*, as *woman/man* and as *female/male*: 'The conflation of gender with masculine/feminine, man/woman, male/female, thus performs the very naturalization that the notion of gender is meant to forestall' (43).

46 Helpful (albeit not very critical) books on Butler are Salih 2002 and Lloyd 2007. Kirby 2006 is less accessible. I should emphasize that these authors would not agree with the negative assessment in the text! Lloyd takes gender to be femininity/masculinity (Lloyd 2007: 30, 34, 43), or some extension thereof (32), but Salih and Kirby perhaps prudently leave gender unexplained. One of the best (also sympathetic) short essays on Butler's *Gender Trouble* is Chambers 2015.

47 'traditions of sophistry …': Nussbaum 1999. 'Continental philosophy' was originally a label for mostly French and German philosophy that came after the exceptionally influential German philosopher Immanuel Kant (1724–1804). So-called analytic philosophy has its roots in mathematical logic, as exhibited in the work of the German philosopher Gottlob Frege (1848–1925) and the British philosopher Bertrand Russell (1872–1970). The labels are now quite unhelpful (see Leiter 2004).

48 Butler 1988: 519, 523. See also Butler 1990b: 191. Subsequently Butler tied performativity more closely to language: 'what I'm trying to do is think about performativity as *that aspect of discourse that has the capacity to produce what it names*. Then I take a further step, through the Derridean rewriting of Austin, and suggest that this production actually always happens through a certain kind of repetition and recitation' (Butler et al. 1994: 33). 'Derridean': concerning the French philosopher Jacques Derrida. 'Austin': the British philosopher J. L. Austin, who produced an influential analysis of the kinds of actions – stating,

ordering, questioning, promising, etc. – that can be performed by speaking (Austin 1975), and who coined the term 'performative utterance'.

49 Butler 1988: 521–2.

50 Butler 1990b: xxxi.

51 As pointed out in Nussbaum 1999.

52 'That gender reality …': Butler 1990b: 192; 'create the effect …': ibid.: xxxi; 'Terms such as …': Butler 2004: 10.

53 Butler 1990b: 187. Butler draws inspiration from *Mother Camp*, anthropologist Esther Newton's study of drag queens and female impersonators in 1960s America. Butler contrives to conjure a paradox out of nothing, quoting this passage from Newton's book:

> Drag says 'my "outside" appearance is feminine, but my essence "inside" [the body] is masculine.' At the same time it symbolizes the opposite inversion; 'my appearance "outside" [my body, my gender] is masculine but my essence "inside" [myself] is feminine.' (Butler 1990b: 186; see Newton 1972: 103, square brackets in original)

Butler comments: 'Both claims to truth contradict one another and so displace the entire enactment of gender significations from the discourse of truth and falsity' (186–7). This is a misreading and there is no contradiction. The first inversion is female appearance/male body, while the second inversion is male body/feminine self. These are compatible: a male can have a female appearance and a feminine self.

54 Butler 2004: 213.

55 Whitam 1987: 178; see also Norton 1997: ch. 1. Femininity and occupational interests in gay men: Bailey 2003: pt. II; LeVay 2017: 59–62.

56 Cf. Butler 1993: 85.

57 Hyde 2005: 581.

58 'The term *gender* …' and '… the term *gender/sex* …': Hyde et al. 2019: 172. One of the authors earlier explained gender/sex as follows: 'Gender/sex refers to a mix of gender (socialization) and sex (biology), when neither are meant to be solely evoked' (van Anders 2013: 202, fn. 4). It is unclear what a 'mix' of socialization and biology is supposed to be, so this does not help; see also Del Giudice 2023.

59 Hyde et al. 2019: 174.

60 Ibid.: 176. The quotation continues: 'and levels of estradiol and progesterone are similar in men and women.' However, women's average levels of both hormones are significantly higher (Bell 2018).

61 Hyde et al. 2019: 176–7.

62 Ibid.: 179–80.

63 Ibid.: 183.

64 An example of contested research: the research reported in the 'challenge from neuroscience' has some serious methodological problems (Del Giudice et al. 2016; see also Anderson et al. 2019). For a reply to Del Giudice et al. by one of the authors of Hyde et al. 2019, see Joel et al. 2016. 'brain features, hormones, …': Hyde et al. 2019: 183.

65 Ibid.: 172, fn. 1.

Chapter 3 Clownfish and Chromosomes

1 Morris 1974/2002: 42.

2 Foucault 2010: vii. As we'll see later, Foucault's answer to this rhetorical question is clearly 'No'.

3 '… intersexual variants': quoted in Bauer 2004: 46; 'the simple man …': Benjamin 1966: 4–5 (see also Benjamin 1963). Benjamin lent his name to the Harry Benjamin International Gender Dysphoria Association, which later became WPATH, the World Professional Association for Transgender Health. For Hirschfeld and the Nazis, see Kennedy 2007: 30–2. For more on Hirschfeld, Benjamin and others, see Meyerowitz 2004: ch. 1. See also Joyce 2021: 12–21.

4 Statutes of Canada 2017.

5 CBC 2016. Matte: 11:20; Peterson: 24:10.

6 '… immutable character …': Butler 1990b: 9–10; 'at least five': Fausto-Sterling 1993b.

7 Aristotle 1995: I.2.716a13–14. See also Mayhew 2010: 22, fn. 7, 30, fn. 5.

8 Mayhew 2010: 62, 70.

9 The brain, the king, weaponry: ibid.: 71–2, 19, 24. Despite calling the queen the king, Aristotle thought not that king bees were exclusively male but that they (and worker bees) contain 'in themselves both sexes as plants do' (Aristotle 1995: III.10.759b30). See Mayhew 2010: 22. '… mutilated male': Aristotle 1995: II.3.737a27–8. Mayhew (2010: ch. 4) makes a persuasive case that Aristotle 'observed what he did about eunuchs and castrated animals and concluded that eunuchs are similar to women – females are like mutilated males – in a number of interesting ways' (66).

10 Darwin 1871/2004: pt. II.

11 '… basically defined …': Beauvoir 1949/2011: 26. Beauvoir does, however, think that 'it is very difficult to give a generally valid description of the notion of female' (31). See also note 9 to chapter 4.

'One group …': Dawkins 1976/2016: 183, quotation marks added; 'To a biologist …': Roughgarden 2004: 23. Roughgarden is an outlier in not accepting Darwin's sexual selection theory (see Clutton-Brock 2007: 1882; for a good review of her book, see Coyne 2004).

12 Dawkins 1976/2016: 6.

13 Philosophers will recognize that the points in this paragraph derive principally from Kripke 1980: 116–44.

14 Roughgarden 2004: 25; see also Lüpold et al. 2016.

15 Pregnant males: Stölting and Wilson 2007. Female penises: Yoshizawa et al. 2018.

16 Beukeboom and Perrin 2014; Bachtrog et al. 2014. A few rodents have XY sex-reversed females in addition to ordinary XX females and XY males. The variant X chromosome in these XY females prevents the Y from having its normal effect (Graves 2002).

17 In flowering plants, sperm and eggs are contained in *pollen* and *ovules*. Their sexual systems are complicated: some have flowers that are both male (pollen-producing) and female (ovule-producing), some have separate male and female flowers, some have male and hermaphroditic flowers, and some have female and hermaphroditic flowers. In about 6 per cent of species the sexes are separated, so there is no hermaphroditism: individual plants produce either pollen or ovules but not both. See Barrett 2002.

18 Vega-Frutis et al. 2014.

19 '… lesser Bee …': Remnant 1637: 3–4. For historical controversies in Britain about the 'gender roles' of bees, see Prete 1991. Sterile workers: Boleli et al. 1999.

20 Cuttlefish: Ebert 2005. Hyenas: Muller and Wrangham 2002.

21 Evolution of sex: Lehtonen and Parker 2014.

22 Gamete evolution: Parker 2011; Lehtonen and Parker 2014. 'Sex is binary' as *There are exactly two sexes*: Soh 2020: 17; Wright and Hilton 2020. Since humans are the animals of interest, the relevant claim is really that *humans* come in exactly two sexes. Some biologists think of so-called *mating types* (found in organisms which produce equal-sized gametes) as sexes, as in the title of a *Discover Magazine* article, 'Why this fungus has over 20,000 sexes' (Scharping 2017). And a biologist once proposed that a species of ant has four sexes. This was not the discovery of an intermediate gamete, though. Rather, the male and female ants each come in two types (Parker 2004).

23 'Sneaky fucker' actually occurs in the scientific literature; 'kleptogyny' is a more anodyne term for the phenomenon.

24 Dawkins 2022.

25 Vollrath 1998: 161–2.

26 What about the other way around? Suppose that *Binary-Sex* is true: every person is either female or male, and no one is both. That doesn't mean that *2-Sexes* is true, because in theory some females or some males could *also* be a third sex. If some females, say, are also *xmale* (the third sex), and every person is either female or male, and no one is both, then *Binary-Sex* is true and *2-Sexes* is false. But if we make the natural assumption that, *if* there is a third sex, then

some people are xmale without also being female or male, then *2-Sexes* must be true given that *Binary-Sex* is.

27 'variables of sex': Money et al. 1955: 302; '... but multivariate': Money 2002: 35. Money 1968: 11 lists ten 'developmental variables of sex'.

28 Glander et al. 1989.

29 Hall 2013. Hall wrote the complimentary review of Shrier's *Irreversible Damage* mentioned in chapter 1. A similar example: 'The notion of "true sex," however, is problematic. When there is discordance among the biological variables of sex in an individual, there is no reason that one variable should hold precedence over the others as the indicator of that person's sex' (Byne 2010: 102). Contrastingly, the psychologist Diane Ehrensaft thinks some variables are more important than others:

> current medical understanding recognizes that a person's sex is comprised of a number of components including: chromosomal sex, gonadal sex, ... pubertal hormonal sex, neurological sex, and gender identity and role. When there is a divergence between these factors, neurological sex and related gender identity are the most important and determinative factors. (Ehrensaft 2017a: para 20).

On this view, the other factors drop out as irrelevant: all that matters to someone's sex is their 'neurological sex, and gender identity and role'.

30 'two sexes have never ...': Fausto-Sterling 2018; '... sex is multilayered ...': Fausto-Sterling 2020a; '... malleable continuum': Fausto-Sterling 1993a: 21. Fausto-Sterling was not the first to suggest that sex is a 'continuum', although perhaps the most influential (Stock 2021: 18–20). The first epigraph to this chapter ('... sex was not a division but a continuum ...') is one earlier example; in 1974, Andrea Dworkin, citing Money on variables of sex, wrote: '*We are, clearly, a multisexed species which has its sexuality spread along a vast continuum where the elements called male and female are not discrete*' (Dworkin 1974: 183). She also cites a passage from Ann Oakley to support the claim that 'There are cultures in which there are no great differences in somatotype of men and women' (179); see note 19 to chapter 7.

31 Foucault 2010: viii. Foucault's claim that earlier, more enlightened times had allowed the 'free choice of indeterminate individuals' is quite doubtful (DeVun 2021: 156).

32 Foucault 2010: xi, viii.

33 Ibid.: 125–6. Judith Butler's paraphrase of the medical report makes Barbin out to be more ambiguous (Butler 1990b: 132).

34 Wilson 1999: 732.

35 See, e.g., Imperato-McGinley et al. 1974; Maimoun et al. 2011; Robitaille and Langlois 2020. (Females can have 5-ARD, but with no dramatic effects.) In

the special case of 5-ARD XY individuals living and athletically competing as women, they may be described as females, perhaps because to do otherwise would invite potentially serious blowback (for an example, see Fénichel et al. 2013).

36 Fausto-Sterling 1993a: 20.

37 '... firmly in cheek': Fausto-Sterling 2000a: 19. Some examples from feminist philosophy of taking Fausto-Sterling at her word: 'Anne Fausto-Sterling has proposed that, in addition to males and females, there are three major groups of "intersexual" bodies' (Stoljar 1995: 269); 'as feminist historians of biology and medicine have pointed out, we find that there are more than two sexes' (Witt 2011: 35); 'Some authors have argued that we should acknowledge the continuum of anatomical differences and recognize at least five sexes' (Haslanger 2012: 243); 'the claim from feminist biologist, Anne Fausto-Sterling, that there are five sexes, not just two' (Cudd 2012: 21); 'Fausto-Sterling (2000) has argued that there are at least five sexes' (Richardson 2022: 6).

38 At one point in *Sexing the Body*, Fausto-Sterling says that 'CAH kids have the potential to become fertile females in adulthood' (Fausto-Sterling 2000b: 59; she means *XX* CAH children). And in a subsequent book she writes that XX individuals with CAH 'can be *mistaken* for boys at birth' (Fausto-Sterling 2012: 39, emphasis added).

39 Deeb et al. 2005. The androgen receptor gene is on the X chromosome, so an XX individual with CAIS would have to have defective genes on both Xs. It is impossible to inherit an X with a defective androgen receptor gene from the father (an XY CAIS individual is infertile), which is why CAIS occurs only in XY individuals. (It is theoretically possible for an XX individual to have CAIS if the maternal X had the defective gene and the paternal X suffered a de novo mutation.)

40 Estrogen made from testosterone: Hooven 2021: 67-9; '... beautiful women': Angier 1998; 'simulant females': Money 1955: 255 (see also Hamerton 1971: 160–2).

41 Fang et al. 2013: 21-2. Clinical communication with DSD patients can be delicate: see, e.g., Byne 2010: 102, note †.

42 On the circus hermaphrodites, see Padva 2018; mythical races of hermaphrodites are mentioned in antiquity. Very rarely, some animals (usually insects) actually are male-bodied on one side and female-bodied on the other, a condition called *bilateral gynandromorphism*. 'She-males' are (male) pornographic actors with breasts and a penis, usually transgender women who have had hormone therapy but not genital surgery. An erotic attraction to she-males (more politely, *gynandromorphs*) is called *gynandromorphophilia* (Hsu et al. 2016; see also Blanchard 1993b; Lehmiller 2018: 94–5). Gynandromorphophiles seem to be exclusively or largely male; for a first-person account, see Nicholson 2020.

43 '... in the same organ': Fausto-Sterling 1993a: 22; true hermaphrodite phenotypes: Shannon and Nicolaides 1973; Krob et al. 1994. For particular cases that have some resemblance to Fausto-Sterling's second illustration, see Overzier 1963: 211; Money 1968: 121. 46,XX, 46,XY: normal humans have 23 pairs of chromosomes, hence 46 in total. Two of the 46 are sex chromosomes; the others are *autosomes*.

44 The presence of an ovotestis does not mean that the animal in question is neither solely female nor solely male. In some species of moles, the female has an ovotestis (Carmona et al. 2008). Around 400: Berkovitz et al. 1982: 290; '... Caucasian population': New and Levine 1984: 62.

45 Percentage of gays and lesbians: Bailey et al. 2016: 52–3; '... 240 intersexuals ...': Fausto-Sterling 1993a: 21. In the same year, Fausto-Sterling repeated the 4 per cent figure in the *New York Times*: 'John Money of Johns Hopkins University, a specialist in the study of congenital sexual-organ defects, suggests that intersexuals may constitute as many as four percent of births' (Fausto-Sterling 1993b).

46 UN 2013: 17.

47 'Recent advances ...' and '... two-party sexual system': Fausto-Sterling 1993a: 22, 21; biopower: Foucault 1978/1990: 140. Fausto-Sterling mentions biopower in 'The five sexes' (1993a: 24). A recent illustration of the popularity of the idea that surgery is used to maintain the two-party sexual system: 'At birth, bodies are sorted as "male" or "female", though many bodies must be mutilated to fit one category or the other' (Srinivasan 2021: xi). An earlier example: 'The belief that gender consists of two exclusive types [female and male] is maintained and perpetuated by the medical community in the face of incontrovertible physical evidence that this is not mandated by biology' (Kessler 1990: 25).

48 '... reckless': Money 1993; '... not as rare ...': Fausto-Sterling 1993c. 'The five sexes' supplied no citation for the attribution of the 4 per cent figure to Money. On the quotation that Fausto-Sterling gave in her reply, see note 53 below.

49 Blackless et al. 2000: 151. Despite the title of Blackless et al. ('How sexually dimorphic are we?'), sexual dimorphism has nothing in particular to do with the development of the reproductive system.

50 Hypospadias: Blackless et al. 2000 did not count hypospadias separately in reaching the 1.7 per cent figure, since hypospadias can be present in other conditions that they did count – for instance Partial Androgen Insensitivity Syndrome. Supermales: there is scant evidence of their supposed violent tendencies (S. S. Richardson 2013: 84–102).

51 '... but intersex': Sax 2002: 174. CAH: Merke and Bornstein 2005. The cultural anthropologist Katrina Karkazis interprets Sax's conclusion that 'human sexuality is a dichotomy, not a continuum' (Sax 2002: 177) as 'a quick and troublesome leap from biology to behavior: he [Sax] extends ideas about sexual

dimorphism to sexual behavior by assuming that individuals with gender-atypical anatomies will naturally express opposite-sex attraction' (Karkazis 2008: 294). This is incorrect, as Sax's sentence after the one quoted makes clear. Sax is using the phrase 'human sexuality' to mean *sex (female, male) in humans*.

52 Hull 2003: 114, 116; in retrospect (see Speiser et al. 2018), Hull's revised estimate of the incidence of non-classic CAH was too low but still more accurate than Fausto-Sterling's. In the second edition (2020) of *Sexing the Body*, Fausto-Sterling mentions Hull's letter, but again without confirming or denying that Hull had identified any errors (Fausto-Sterling 2020b: 324–5).

53 '... both a penis and a vagina': Ryle 2021: 10; that textbook says that the 1.7 per cent are neither female nor male (498). Redheads: Yaeger 2017; UN 2017; Quinn 2019: 4:56. Commendable exceptions to the philosophical practice of overlooking both Sax and Hull are Stone 2007: 39 (citing Hull but not Sax) and Dea 2016: 87–6 (citing Sax but not Hull).

Hull recounts the Fausto-Sterling saga in her book (Hull 2006: 66–8). She writes that she is 'disturbed that Fausto-Sterling and her co-authors permit their numbers to stand uncorrected ... in response to my corrections, Fausto-Sterling implies that our differing conclusions are simply part of the intellectual conversation raising awareness of intersexuality' (68). Fausto-Sterling's source for the 4 per cent figure she attributes to Money is Epstein 1990, from which she quotes the following passage: 'Robert Edgerton cites a statistic of 2 to 3 percent in ... *American Anthropologist* 66 (1964): 1289. Dr. Iraj Rezvani of St. Christopher's Hospital for Children in Philadelphia believes this estimate to be too high, while John Money asserts that the incidence of gender disorders approaches 4 percent' (Epstein 1990: 131, n. 6; Fausto-Sterling 1993c). Dr Rezvani's reservations should have given Fausto-Sterling pause.

Epstein's citation, Edgerton 1964, reads: 'The incidence of marked intersexuality in man is estimated to be 2–3 per cent (Overzier 1963)' (Edgerton 1964: 1289). Overzier 1963 is the authoritative edited collection *Intersexuality*, an English translation of the German original (1961). However, the figures in Overzier were evidently mistranscribed by Epstein and are actually an order of magnitude lower. Overzier, the editor, writes in a 'Conclusion' at the end of the book: 'It is estimated that the incidence of the types of intersex described in this book is 0.2–0.3% of the total population' (Overzier 1963: 534). It is not clear how Overzier's 0.2–0.3 per cent was calculated, but the types of conditions described in *Intersexuality* match those in Blackless 2000 reasonably well. Amusingly, Overzier's estimate is close to Hull's 0.37 per cent, forty years later.

In a follow-up article seven years after 'The five sexes', Fausto-Sterling wrote: 'I reported an estimate by a psychologist expert in the treatment of intersexuals, suggesting that some 4 percent of all live births are intersexual' (Fausto-Sterling 2000a: 20), not mentioning that Money had earlier denied ever saying such a thing. Corrections are often overlooked. The fictitious 4 per cent figure is cited in Dreger 1998: 211, n. 79; Greenberg 1999: 267, fn. 7; and Rothblatt 2011: 5; it is the source of the feminist philosopher María Lugones' claim that '1 to 4% of the world's population is intersexed' (Lugones 2007: 194).

Other even wilder percentages appear in gender studies and philosophy. Judith Butler, discussing the work of the geneticist David Page, writes:

> Although the pool that Page and his researchers used to come up with this finding was limited, the speculation on which they base their research, in part, is that *a good ten percent of the population has chromosomal variations that do not fit neatly into the XX-female and XY-male set of categories.* (Butler 1990b: 145–6, emphasis added)

Butler offers no citation for this completely incorrect figure – sex chromosome abnormalities appear in around 1 in 400 live births (Berglund et al. 2020); see also Hull 2006: 66. And according to the feminist philosopher Linda Martín Alcoff:

> Up to *an estimated 10 percent of all babies born have ambiguous, indeterminate, or multiple primary and secondary sexual characteristics*, and it has recently become more widely known that U.S. physicians routinely perform surgery on these 'naturally' transgendered children in order to force them into our culture's ideal of anatomical polarity. (Alcoff 2006: 159, emphasis added)

This short passage combines (1) an impressive exaggeration of the incidence of DSDs, (2) a misunderstanding of secondary sex characteristics (they appear at puberty), (3) the conflation of intersexuality and transsexuality, and (4) the trope of biopower (see note 47 above).

54 On terminological preferences among people with DSDs, see Davis 2015: ch. 4; Lundberg et al. 2018; Reis 2021: ch. 7. Human DSDs occur in other mammals; for DSDs in cats and dogs, see Meyers-Wallen 2012.

55 Hay 2020: 118. Other recent examples from philosophy that mention the 1.7 per cent figure: Ásta 2018: 71; Mikkola 2022: sect. 3.2 ('Recognition of intersex people suggests that feminists (and society at large) are wrong to think that humans are either female or male'). The last citation is the entry 'Feminist perspectives on sex and gender', in the *Stanford Encyclopedia of Philosophy*, the gold standard for online academic encyclopaedias.

A recent book, *Gender: What Everyone Needs to Know*, puts estimates 'as to the number of people who are intersex … from about two in every thousand to two in every hundred people', with the authors (who specialize in transgender health) clearly implying that the higher 2 per cent estimate is more accurate (Erickson-Schroth and Davis 2021: 18). The source for that estimate is Blackless et al. 2000; Hull and Sax are not cited. The 1.7 per cent figure (also citing Blackless) appears in the latest version of the World Professional Association for Transgender Health's *Standards of Care* (Coleman et al. 2022: S93).

56 A typical passage: 'The experiences of trans and intersex people show us that not all humans fit perfectly into two clear-cut categories of biological sex; indeed, the belief there are two separate sex categories is itself an erasure of sex variations that occur either naturally or through medical modification' (Faye 2021: 242). See also Hausman 1995: 149–53.

57 DSDs and gender dysphoria: Zucker 1999; Callens et al. 2016. Intersex pretenders: Cadet and Feldman 2012; Cadet 2023. A notable intersex pretender was 'Agnes', a transgender woman who succeeded in fooling Robert Stoller (Hausman 1995: 1–2).

58 An exception is this passage from an article by Butler in the UK magazine the *New Statesman*: 'A stronger "institutional" variation of social construction emerged in the 1990s, and it focused on the fact that sex itself is *assigned*. This means that medical, familial, and legal authorities play a crucial role *in deciding what sex an infant will be*' (Butler 2019, second emphasis added). The claim that sex is socially constructed is then the claim that a person's sex depends partly on the decisions of medical and other authorities. Here Butler is conflating *sex* with *assigned sex*: assigned sex depends on decisions, not sex – see the introduction.

59 *The Social Construction of Reality*: Berger and Luckmann 1966. Social construction about sex specifically: cf. Stock 2021: 63–4.

60 '… literal tale …' and 'sex is, literally, constructed': Fausto-Sterling 2000b: 32, 27; clitoral reduction surgery: Liao et al. 2019.

61 'the reality of gender …': Kessler and McKenna 1978: 6; '… create the reality …': Kessler 1998: 133, n. 1.

62 The 'social category' terminology is better, because 'constructed category' is misleading: the only things that get constructed are (at best) members of the category, not the category itself. Social construction in philosophy: Haslanger 2012: chs. 2, 6; Mallon 2016; Ásta 2018. Social construction in the hands of non-philosophers tends to mix sensible points ('Prior to 1973 homosexuality was a disease and was classified in the Diagnostic and Statistical Manual of Mental Disorders … diseases are not simply objectively defined medical entities but social ones' [Burr 2015: 46]) with profound-sounding obscurity ('reality … becomes unstable and multiple, dependent on the historically and culturally situated perspective of the perceiver' [ibid.: 92]).

Chapter 4 I am Woman

1 Butler 1990a: 324. Butler herself does not think it is 'important to refer to the category "woman" and to know what it is we mean': see the quotation from Butler at the end of this chapter.

2 Folk 2022: 42:45. To 'If you're not here for women, we ask you to leave!', shouted at him at the 2021 Women's March in Washington, DC, the conservative provocateur Matt Walsh replied 'What *is* that?' Walsh's documentary *What Is a Woman?* brought Keen-Minshull's slogan (see the start of this chapter) to the US four years after its appearance on a poster. In the last scene of the documentary, Walsh's wife gives Keen-Minshull's answer to the title question.

3 Harrop and Keen-Minshull 2018. In November 2021, a tribunal of the General Medical Council determined that Harrop had engaged in 'deplorable behaviour' on Twitter, sending 'inappropriate, insulting and at times intimidatory communications' to women with whom he disagreed on transgender issues. He was suspended from practising medicine for one month (Flanagan et al. 2021). Keen-Minshull (later just Keen) is also a controversial figure, a 'Poundshop Marine Le Pen' according to her detractors (Perry 2022b); the US Poundshop equivalent is Dollar Tree.

4 For philosophical discussion, see Dorr 2016 (aficionados only).

5 Mikkola 2022: sect. 4. It should not be assumed at the start that the project can be completed. Louise Antony is one prominent feminist philosopher who thinks it can't (2020).

6 For example, the first entries for 'woman' in the *Oxford Dictionary of English* (Stevenson 2010), the *Merriam-Webster Dictionary* (Merriam-Webster 2022), the *Oxford English Dictionary* (OED 2022), and the early nineteenth-century *An American Dictionary of the English Language* (Webster 1828) are, respectively: *adult human female*, *an adult female person*, *an adult female human being*, and *the female of the human race, grown to adult years*. Note that Merriam-Webster's definition has *person* instead of *human being*, but in that same dictionary the first entry for 'person' is *human*.

7 On the absence of definitions, see Fodor 1998: chs 3, 4.

8 Shapiro 1981: 446. As the philosopher Talia Mae Bettcher puts it, 'On the face of it, the definition "female, adult, human being" *really does seem right*. Indeed, it seems as perfect a definition as one might have ever wanted' (2009: 105). In line with orthodoxy in feminist philosophy, Bettcher thinks the definition is incorrect.

9 The biological textbook view of sex is not entirely ignored in feminist philosophy; one (rare) exception is McKitrick 2015: 2576. Interestingly, McKitrick immediately qualifies her endorsement of the textbook view in a footnote, saying that it is 'not uncontroversial', citing among others Judith Butler and Anne Fausto-Sterling.

In the second edition of *Sexing the Body*, published twenty years after the first, Fausto-Sterling does mention gametes (once, in an endnote): 'humans have binary gametes – there are eggs and there are sperm … But the moment we move from sex cells to whole human beings … we lose the certainty of binary classification' (Fausto-Sterling 2020b: 476, n. 131). She does not mention the biological textbook view of sex.

10 '... vaginas, ovaries, ...': Saul 2012: 199. That paper overlooks the 'adult' component of 'woman', an omission which is surprisingly frequent in the feminist philosophy literature. MKRH syndrome: Herlin et al. 2020.

11 The most recent translation of *The Second Sex* omits the indefinite article from 'One is not born ...' (Beauvoir 1949/2011: 283). At one point Beauvoir suggests that some women are *not* female: 'It is sometimes said that older women form "a third sex"'; it is true they are not males, but they are no longer female either' (ibid.: 43), but this is contradicted by many other passages, e.g.: 'And the fact is that she [woman] is a female' (ibid.: 21).

12 Hrdy 1999: 188.

13 Beauvoir 1949/2011: 329. One might dispute Beauvoir's claims about when juvenile males and females become adults, but that would not be to object to the biological view.

14 Cook 1893: 239, 242.

15 von Fintel and Matthewson 2008: 151. See also Goddard and Wierzbicka 2013: 50–3.

16 Rubin 2014.

17 Vincent 2006.

18 The main (now dated) exception is Stoljar 1995, which takes the biological view seriously and argues against it. See Byrne 2020 for an examination of Stoljar's arguments. Other relevant material from the philosophical literature includes Bettcher 2009; Bogardus 2020; Dembroff 2021; Byrne 2021; Heartsilver 2021; Stock 2021: ch. 5; Byrne 2022a; Mason 2022; Arvan forthcoming. Jarvis 2022 reports the results of a survey asking questions about a fictional 'gender reversal' scenario; not surprisingly, respondents' answers were generally consistent with the biological view.

Whatever 'woman' means, we can ask whether we should continue to use it with that meaning. Perhaps the word should be retired, or perhaps we should try to change its meaning. This question has been extensively discussed in philosophy: see, e.g., Jenkins 2016; Haslanger 2020; Stock 2022; Bogardus 2022.

19 'Proletarians ...': Beauvoir 1949/1989: xxiv. The translation in Beauvoir 1949/2011 is more literal: 'there have always been women; they are women by their physiological structure' (8). '... certain physiology': Brison 2003: 192. In a 1972 interview Beauvoir said, 'In *The Second Sex,* I said that women are an inferior *caste*. In principle, one can leave one class to move into another, but caste is the group into which one is born and which one cannot leave. If you are a woman, you can never become a man' (Beauvoir 1980: 146).

20 'Baby girls ...': Beauvoir and Servan-Schreiber 1975: 3:00; 'The different

behavior ...': Belotti 1976: 14–15. The US edition of Belotti's book had an introduction by the anthropologist Margaret Mead (see chapter 7). Belotti's book was first published in Italian as *Dalla parte delle bambine* (On the side of the girls) in 1973 and then translated into French as *Du côté des petites filles* in 1974.

21 For an extensive treatment of when certain kinds of people are 'counted as' women or men by laws and regulations, see Schiappa 2022.

22 'Third sexes/genders' found in many traditional societies (see chapter 8), for instance the *hijra* on the Indian subcontinent, might be thought to provide another kind of counterexample to the biological view. If (adult male) *hijras* are not men, then the biological view is wrong. But it is hardly clear that they are not men: the sociologist Stephen O. Murray reports a native of Pakistan as insisting 'that *hijras* ... are a kind of man (not a third sex or third gender), socially regarded as inadequate men because of their failure – or refusal – to procreate' (Murray 2000: 310). See also Byrne 2020: 3792, fn. 16.

23 Harari 2015: 152.

24 Vagrancy Act 1824.

25 Harari 2015: 152.

26 Wittig 1993: 104.

27 Orwell 2000: 316.

28 On the word 'real', see Stock 2021: 164–5.

29 Ferber 2020.

30 Cf. Barnes 2022.

31 'Trans women are women, of course they are, because "women" is a social and historical category that gets expanded with time' (Butler and Jones 2021: 28:58). There are two instructive mistakes here. The first is that the category *woman* has changed. Consider this example: the word 'meat' used to mean *solid food*. Subsequently the word changed its meaning, becoming more exclusive: it now applies only to the flesh of animals (but not fish). The category *meat* did not change; rather, the word 'meat' once picked out the category *solid food* and now it picks out another category, *animal flesh*. When we speak of the category *meat* in contemporary English, we are speaking of this second category.

What Butler should have said, then, is that the word 'woman' has changed its meaning, like the word 'meat'. Unlike the word 'meat', 'woman' has become more *inclusive*, applying to more people than it did before. In particular, although it used *not* to apply to trans women, now it does. Surely Butler thinks the same is true of 'man'. That has also become more inclusive, now applying to more people than it did before. (If trans women are women, then trans men are men.)

Butler's second mistake is to think that this alleged change makes the 'right' sentences come out true, for instance 'Trans women are women', and 'Trans women are not men.' If the alleged change is a real change, the first sentence is true, but the second sentence is *false*. If 'woman' and 'man' have become more inclusive, they still apply to the people they used to apply to. Presumably, back in the regressive past, 'man' applied to trans women (perhaps because it once meant *adult human male*). But then 'man' in the new sense *also* applies to trans women. (For discussion of a related analogy between 'trans woman' and 'adoptive mother', see Byrne 2022b: 6–7.)

32 Butler 1995: 50. ('Resignifiability': the capacity to change the meaning of something.) Butler took the idea that 'woman' is not a 'stable signifier' from the poet and philosopher Denise Riley (Butler 1990b: 4). Riley succeeds in illustrating how people's ideas about women have changed over time and place but confuses this with 'semantic shakiness inherent in "women"' (Riley 1988: 5). Recently some philosophers have suggested, for unconvincing reasons, that 'woman' has multiple closely related meanings (going beyond those found in dictionaries); this has a similar vertigo-inducing effect to Butler's claim that the 'term becomes a site of permanent openness and resignifiability'. See Byrne 2021: sect. 3.

33 Penny 2015.

34 Robinson 2021.

35 Human Rights Campaign 2021.

Chapter 5 The Rise of Gender Identity

1 Stoller 1968: viii. On the same page, Stoller says, 'While the work of our research team has been associated with the term *gender identity*, we are not militantly fixed either on copyrighting the term or on defending the concept as one of the splendors of the scientific world.' As we will see later, Stoller's caution was prescient.

2 Reilly-Cooper 2016.

3 McNamara 2017. The phrase 'gender identity' first got a toehold on the public consciousness when the diagnosis of Gender Identity Disorder appeared in the 1980 edition of the psychiatric bible *The Diagnostic and Statistical Manual of Mental Disorders* (DSM).

4 'Jaron' is Jazz's name in Jennings 2016, but is a pseudonym, as is 'Jazz Jennings'; 'started questioning …': Bever 2015.

5 Forcier et al. 2020: 2.

6 'Transgender' has a more inclusive sense in which it applies to 'anyone whose *gender … presentation* does not align stereotypically with the gender assigned to them at birth' (Burns 2018: xvii, emphasis added; see also Stryker 1994: 254–5, n. 2). In this (unhelpfully) inclusive sense, heterosexual cross-dressing men, butch lesbians and drag queens are all transgender.

7 WPATH 2012: 96, emphasis added; a less clear statement is in the subsequent

Standards of Care (Coleman et al. 2022: S252). Other examples: gender dysphoria is 'a state of emotional distress *caused by* how someone's body or the gender they were assigned at birth conflicts with their gender identity' (Lopez 2017, emphasis added); it 'refers to psychological distress *that results from* an incongruence between one's sex assigned at birth and one's gender identity' (Wamsley 2021, emphasis added, reproducing an explanation from the American Psychiatric Association).

8 '… the kernel …' and 'in sync': Ehrensaft 2011: 78, 80; '… effectively immutable …': Ehrensaft 2017a: para 39. Admittedly, in *The Gender Creative Child*, Ehrensaft says that gender identity is partly influenced by 'nurture' (Ehrensaft 2016: 33) and denies that it is 'innate' (34, 248). But she also says that 'a small minority of people receive messages from their brain telling them that the gender they are is not in congruence with the *F* or *M* marked in their birth records … It is those brain signals that are *not malleable*' (248, emphasis added). To add to the apparent inconsistency, see Hidalgo et al. 2013, in which Ehrensaft was a co-author: it is a 'myth' that gender identity is 'fixed at or before birth' (288).

'… cannot be changed': GLAAD 2020. Other examples: 'If gender identity is, as seems increasingly certain, *hardwired into the brain at birth* …' (Rudacille 2004: 292, emphasis added); 'trans people are essentially assigned genders at birth that don't match their inherent, *biologically set* identity' (Lopez 2017, emphasis added).

9 Penis envy: the psychiatrist Robert Stoller took it seriously (1968: 30), as did Simone de Beauvoir (1949/2011: 287–94, 753–4, 761–2). On feminist interpretations of penis envy, see Lawford-Smith 2022a: 95–6. Recovered memory: Ofshe and Watters 1996. It wasn't just therapists: one prominent proponent of recovered memory was a Harvard psychiatrist (ibid.: 4). Gender identity: the scepticism came from gender-critical philosophers (Stock 2021: ch. 4; Lawford-Smith 2022a) and Anca Gheaus (2023), a political philosopher with some GC sympathies. For representative examples of the treatment of gender identity by mainstream feminist philosophy, see McKitrick 2015 and Jenkins 2018 (see also Lawford-Smith 2022a: 53). Plausibly, the general lack of scepticism from feminist philosophers is partly due to the history of charges of 'exclusion' within feminism (ibid.: 125–9).

10 Stoller 1968: 29; see also Stoller 1964a: 223.

11 Stoller 1968: 10. In a paper published (in French) just before he died in 1991, Stoller wrote that gender identity 'refers to a complex system of beliefs about oneself: a sense of one's masculinity and femininity' (Stoller 1992: 78).

12 See Stoller 1968: 30. There is another complication, also related to DSDs. A person with a DSD might think they are neither female nor male. In this case, the person, as Stoller puts it, 'does not have a clear-cut [core] gender identity as either male or female' (1964b: 456).

13 Berenbaum et al. 2008.

14 Coldwell 2015.

15 Alston et al. 2006: 10, emphasis added; 6, n. 2; 6, n. 1, 8. The second quotation confusingly continues, '… including the personal sense of the body (which may involve, if freely chosen, modification of bodily appearance or function by medical, surgical or other means) and other expressions of gender, including dress, speech and mannerisms.'

16 'a person's deeply felt …': Coleman et al. 2022: S252; '… eunuch …' and '… male or female': WPATH 2012: 96. 'Male or female' appears to refer to the two biological sexes (see the entry 'Sex' on the same page). WPATH anachronistically cites Stoller 1964a (Stoller said nothing about 'alternative genders'). Eunuchs and sexual arousal: Johnson et al. 2007.

17 'WPATH 2012: 97; a slightly different definition of 'transgender' is in SOC8 (Coleman et al. 2022: S252). The sociologist Sally Hines gives a definition of 'gender identity' that is not circular. It refers, she writes, 'to each person's internal sense of being male, female, a combination of the two, or neither. It is a core part of who people know themselves to be' (Hines 2018: 10). Apart from the obscurity of 'internal sense', what is meant by a 'combination' of being female and being male? In the case of some DSDs, one can make some sense of this peculiar way of talking. It is clear, though, that Hines did not have DSDs in mind.

Here are two more explanations of gender identity, this time in terms of 'inner sense' instead of Hines's 'internal sense': 'Gender identity is a person's inner sense of belonging to a particular gender, such as male or female' (Ehrensaft 2017a: para 21); '*Gender identity* is a person's inner sense of their gender as male, female, or something else' (Erickson-Schroth and Davis 2021: xii). Notice that both explanations use the word 'gender'. A few pages later the authors of the second quotation give another explanation of gender identity, 'our self-conception of who we are – our innermost sense of being a man, a woman, or something else entirely' (2; see also 27). This is confusing, because the authors sharply distinguish *sex* ('usually assigned at birth as either male or female' (1)) from *gender* ('Just as we are assigned a sex at birth, we are also assigned a gender' (2), by which they mean *boy* or *girl*). Given that *male* and *female* are not (apparently) supposed to be genders, it is not clear how to interpret the first explanation.

18 Serano 2007: 87, 250, 78, 33.

19 Ibid.: 87. Stock (2021: 111) briefly discusses a similar thought experiment as described in an article in *Vox* (Lopez 2017) and attributed there to 'Lily Carollo, a trans woman in North Carolina'.

20 Plato 2004: 620b.

21 Byers et al. 2016: 150, 151, 152. Using an internet (and non-representative) sample, Lehmiller found 'that 11 percent of the women I surveyed reported

sexual fantasies about becoming men and that 20 percent had fantasized about dressing up as men' (Lehmiller 2018: 97–8), which suggests that sex-switching fantasies are not uncommon in the non-transgender population.

22 Wilson and Gilbert 2005.

23 Sometimes 'sex assigned at birth' is not a euphemism but a way of dodging any commitment to a person's sex. For example, Bouman et al. (2017) recommend that 'authors … use terms such as *birth assigned sex*, or (if appropriate) *legal sex*, instead of *natal male* or *natal female*. Authors should not use the term *biological sex* or *natal sex* … The term *actual sex* … should be avoided' (3). 'Assigned sex' dates back to the 1950s, when John Money was investigating treatments for 'hermaphroditism' (see chapter 3). In the early usage, 'assigned sex' was not a euphemism either, but here the entire point was to *distinguish* between sex and assigned sex: sometimes a male child, say, would be assigned and raised as a female.

24 WPATH 2012: 96, emphasis added.

25 'sex of assignment …': Money et al. 1957: 333; '… make a hole …': Hendricks 1993: 15; 'John'/'Joan': Colapinto 2006: 209.

26 Ibid.: 82, 114.

27 Eckert 2021.

28 Science Vs 2018: 11:08.

29 Bradley et al. 1998: 3.

30 Money et al. 1955: 310, quoted in Goldie 2014: 181.

31 '… nothing feminine …': Colapinto 2006: 57. Tomboys: 'The term, when it was coined in 1556, meant an extra-boisterous boy … By 1656, it had begun to describe a girl who acted more like a rambunctious boy' (Davis 2020: 17). 'The salient variable …': Money et al. 1957: 335.

32 The psychologist Kenneth Zucker was one of the co-authors of the paper about Clara, Bradley et al. 1998. Colapinto is sceptical of the conclusions and recounts interviewing Zucker about the paper in 1998 (Colapinto 2006: 251). Colapinto suggests that Clara may have been 'telling the researchers what they wanted to hear when she stated that she never harbored any doubts about her gender' (251). Since Clara was forthcoming about her behavioural masculinity and bisexual orientation, there is no reason to think she was hiding anything else. She was also interviewed three times (not twice, as Colapinto has it) by Susan Bradley, a highly experienced child psychiatrist and an expert in Gender Identity Disorder (as it was then called: see chapter 5). After the paper appeared, Zucker spoke with Chernick, another of the co-authors (and Clara's gynaecologist), who reported that she was still, as reported in the paper's abstract, 'living with … a woman, in a lesbian relationship' (Bradley et al. 1998: 1, Zucker, personal communication).

Colapinto (2006: 251) writes that 'Zucker admitted that the case could not be deemed an unalloyed example of the efficacy of sex reassignment' because of Clara's masculinity and sexual attraction to women, but this is a projection on Colapinto's part. He thinks that 'Zucker has for years attempted to modify homosexuality … in boy and girl children' (249), which is simply untrue: 'In *none* of our publications have we ever endorsed prevention of homosexuality as a therapeutic goal in the treatment of children with GID, although we note that this might have been a goal of some therapists and also of some parents' (Bradley and Zucker 2003: 267; see also Zucker et al. 2012: 391).

33 See note 35 to chapter 3.

34 Cohen-Kettenis 2005. See also Khorashad et al. 2016.

35 Bennett et al. 2019.

36 See also Mazur 2005: 'The literature to date documents that a female gender identity apparently without gender dysphoria develops in XY individuals born with a micropenis and assigned female' (419).

37 Harper 2007: 116.

38 Ibid.: 117–18.

39 Cadet 2011: 1101.

40 Cadet, personal communication.

41 For a helpful elaboration of gender identity understood as 'identification with' females (e.g.), see Stock 2021: 127–41; see also chapter 8. Stock recognizes that her 'identification model' of gender identity does not meet the job description in the text.

42 The relationship between testosterone and sexual orientation is much murkier. How people end up heterosexual, homosexual or bisexual is not well understood. But – as suggested by Brian's and Clara's attraction to women and Peggy Cadet's attraction to men – the evidence shows that there are strong pre-natal influences of some sort. See Bailey et al. 2016; LeVay 2017; Hooven 2021: 201–7.

43 Jennings 2016: 8.

44 Ibid.: 9–10.

45 APA 1994: 537–8. For discussion of the diagnostic criteria in the DSM-III (1980), the DSM-III-R (1987) and the DSM-IV (1994), see Zucker et al. 1998; Zucker 2010. The alternative to the DSM is the World Health Organization's ICD (International Classification of Diseases), but for diagnoses related to gender identity the two are very close (de Vries et al. 2021). Bowing to the inevitable, in the 2022 text revision of the DSM-5 (DSM-5-TR), 'natal male/female' is replaced by 'individual assigned male/female at birth' (APA 2022: 513–14).

46 Jazz was featured in a 2006 *Village Voice* article under the pseudonym 'Nicole' (Reischel 2006). The psychologist Kenneth Zucker and another important figure in the field, Heino F. L. Meyer-Bahlburg from Columbia University, were both quoted as expressing some reservations about Nicole's early social transition. See also Tuerk 2011: 772. 'girl brain …': Jennings 2016: 136. See also the epigraphs ('… girl trapped inside a boy's body …', '… born in the

wrong body ...') to the following chapter. Another example from the UK trans activist Christine Burns: 'The more science is inclined to look, the more it finds to substantiate the discovery that children like the little "boy" in the picture above really did already have the brain of a little girl' (Burns 1997). Not every transgender person finds the 'born in the wrong body' narrative helpful (see, e.g., Bettcher 2014; Missé 2022). Another example of extreme femininity, from a mother describing her son Jack, who 'transitioned into my daughter' at age ten: 'Jack was more "girly" than any biological girl I had ever known' (Pepper 2012: 129, 130).

47 The study: Singh et al. 2021; information on sexual orientation was available for 108 of the 122 desisters. See also Ristori and Steensma 2016. Prevalence of homosexuality: note 45 to chapter 3.

Chapter 6 Born in the Wrong Body

1 Jennings 2016: 1.
2 Morris 1974/2002: 1.
3 'the Flaubert ...': attributed to the journalist Alistair Cooke (blurb to Morris 1974/2002); Everest: Holden 1974.
4 Morris 1974/2002: x.
5 Ibid.: 5–6.
6 Ibid.: 104.
7 Gibb 2014.
8 West 1974. Subsequently the *NYT* printed some letters from readers critical of West's review.
9 The philosophers may be encouraged in their reticence by stern passages such as the following, from Julia Serano's *Whipping Girl*: 'The unceasing search to uncover the cause of transsexuality is designed to keep transsexual gender identities in a perpetually questionable state, thereby ensuring that cissexual gender identities continue to be unquestionable' (Serano 2007: 188). Serano recommends 'simply accepting transsexual accounts – which almost invariably describe some sort of intrinsic self-knowledge or subconscious sex' (188–9).

Morris was discussed by the feminist writer and women's studies academic Janice Raymond in her 1979 book *The Transsexual Empire* (which contains the notorious line 'All transsexuals rape women's bodies by reducing the real female form to an artifact, appropriating this body for themselves' [1979/1994: 104]). Raymond conjectured, rather implausibly, that Morris transitioned because of 'the decline of his male vigor', thus getting the 'best of both worlds' because 'women are often more vigorous when they are older and the cultural pressures have subsided' (89).

Although contemporary feminist philosophers typically draw a veil over the science of transsexuality (and especially the topic of this chapter), there are exceptions, namely – no surprise by now – the gender-critical apostates (see Stock 2021: 235–9; Lawford-Smith 2022a: 105–10); see also the journalist Helen Joyce's *Trans* (Joyce 2021: ch. 2). The philosophers' neglect is especially striking, because the theory of transsexualism explained in this chapter periodically appears in books aimed at a general readership: Bering 2013: 162–4; Bloom 2002: 69–80; Dreger 2015: ch. 2; Lehmiller 2018: 94–9; Murray 2019: 195–9; Soh 2020: 126–36.

10 Hunt 1978: 137.

11 Ibid.: 60. The majority of this passage is quoted in Lawrence 2007: 510; Lawrence 2013: 32; and Bering 2013: 163.

12 Hunt's *Tribune* obituary: Colarossi 1999; a reminiscence by a *Tribune* colleague: Moore 2016. Another (distinctively British) example is Roberta Cowell (born 1918). As Robert, Cowell was a Spitfire pilot in the Second World War, a prisoner in Stalag Luft I, a racing car driver and a father of two. She was the UK's first male-to-female transsexual. See Kennedy 2007, and also Burns 2018: 17–19, 23–5.

13 Ovesey and Person 1974a: 112, 110, 111. Stoller had a similar Freudian view (1975: 55).

14 Stoller 1975: 147. Here's Hunt on 'screaming transsexuals', 'many of whom aren't true transsexuals at all but gay or effeminate men': 'they mince on six-inch platforms from one gay bar to another, from one homosexual assignment to the next. As women they are parodies.' 'The real transsexual', Hunt wrote, 'harbors an abiding distaste for his own male genitalia … the homosexual wouldn't want to lose his penis for anything in the world' (1978: 24–5). In 1965, Ira B. Pauly, who would later become president of the Harry Benjamin International Gender Dysphoria Association, wrote that for the 'small percentage who appear to seek the operation [sex reassignment] as a means of rationalizing their homosexuality … the term pseudotranssexual might be considered' (1965: 175).

15 'a wastebasket …': Stoller 1982: 270; effeminate-homosexual/transvestitic: Money and Gaskin 1970: 255; fetishistic/nuclear: Buhrich and McConaghy 1978: 73. Other examples: MacKenzie (1978: 254) distinguished 'classic transsexualism, effeminate homosexuality in the male and hypermasculine homosexuality in the female, and transvestism'; the sociologist Deborah Heller Feinbloom (1976: 17–18) wrote that 'male cross-dressers' can be divided into homosexual ('dresses for vanity or to be sexually attractive to other men') and heterosexual ('in the beginning his cross-dressing is for erotic needs'). For more on these early classification schemes, see Blanchard 1989a: 317–20.

16 APA 1980: 264.

17 Childhood gender-nonconformity and sexual orientation: Steensma et al. 2013; Li et al. 2017.

18 'extensive cross-gender …', 'the circular universe …', and 'prehomosexuality':

Green 1987: 7, 8, 12; 'For both natal male …': APA 2013: 455. The 2022 text revision of the DSM dials sexual orientation down somewhat and adds some obfuscating language about 'self-identification': 'Studies have shown a high incidence of sexual attraction to those of the individual's birth-assigned gender, regardless of the trajectory of the prepubescent child's gender dysphoria. For individuals whose gender dysphoria continues into adolescence and beyond, most self-identify as heterosexual' (APA 2022: 515). The connection with homosexuality was noted much earlier by Money and Gaskin: 'In the idealized case of effeminate-homosexual transsexualism, the patient recalls a boyhood of having been a sissy, afraid of competitive rivalries and dominance among boys. He was interested in pretty and artistic things, usually stereotyped as feminine, and especially in feminine domestic activities and clothing' (1970: 255).

19 '… a girl's mind': Hunt 1978: 40; '… asexual': Ovesey and Person 1974b: 127; cross-dressing: Hunt did report it, without mentioning sexual arousal (1978: 68, 109).

20 Witticism borrowed from Dreger 2015: 66 ('a love that would really rather we didn't speak its name'), but changed back to the original quotation, from Lord Alfred Douglas's poem 'Two loves'.

21 Blanchard 2018; Ablaza et al. 2022 found an effect for girls with older brothers (see also Kabátek et al. 2021).

22 'the woman …': quoted in Blanchard 1989a: 318. As Blanchard notes, 'automonosexualism' is due to the German sexologist Hermann Rohleder, who used it for another condition, not autogynephilia. 'a male's propensity …': Blanchard 1991: 235.

23 Ibid.: 239.

24 Blanchard 1989a: 324.

25 Hunt 1978: 262, 110; pseudobisexuality: Blanchard 1989b: 622, Blanchard 1991: 247.

26 '… opening my legs': Lawrence 2013: 106-7; '… soap my breasts …': Blanchard 2005: 440. The DSM-5 distinguishes between *transvestic disorder* 'with fetishism' (arousal by clothing) and 'with autogynephilia' (arousal by thought of being female); see Fedoroff 2020: ch. 8.

Virginia Prince (see chapter 2) wrote *The Transvestite and His Wife* in 1967, with the cover advertising 'All the problems and pleasures of transvestism discussed in detail – especially as they affect the marital relationship.' She included a letter from Gene, a 'transvestic husband', to his wife, which includes this passage – in retrospect a clear expression of autogynephilia:

> All of us, and I can make that wide sweeping statement with no fear of contradiction because I live in this transvestic world every day of my life, adore you real women,

> love you and revere you, cherish and idolize you, respect and envy you, just because you are what you are; women, – beautiful, gentle, soft, delicate, lady-like, weak women. And we are so intensely attracted to you as lovers and objects of adoration that we desire above all else to *literally share* every facet of your treasured existence. (Prince 1967: 86–7)

Richard Novic is a Harvard-educated psychiatrist and cross-dresser (transvestite), who held nothing back in his 2008 memoir *Alice in Genderland.* Trying his hand at masturbation at seventeen: 'I ran again and again into the same disturbing fact: I could either struggle for satisfaction, or I could relax, imagine I was a woman, and whammo' (Novic 2008: 10).

Monica Helms, who designed the pink, white and blue transgender flag, is a transgender woman and former US Navy submariner with two sons. In her memoir *More Than Just A Flag* she writes: 'Sexual excitement topped the list of what came over me when wearing women's clothes. However, as time went on that feeling became less and less important, while the need to express my feminine side would grow exponentially' (Helms 2019: 62). On the waning of autogynephilic arousal, see the main text below.

Some much earlier accounts of apparent autogynephilia are in Hirschfeld's classic *Transvestites* (Hirschfeld 1910/1991); see also 'case 129' in another sexology classic (from the nineteenth century), Richard von Krafft-Ebing's *Psychopathia Sexualis* (Krafft-Ebing 1886/2011: 200–14).

27 Blanchard 1993c. More specifically, Blanchard 1993a found that the preferred fantasy of having a vulva was associated with greater gender dysphoria.

28 Blanchard 1991: 245–6.

29 Grosskurth 1980: 285–6.

30 Ellis 1937: pt 2, 1.

31 Kates 2001: 274.

32 '... fetichism ... self-admiration': Ellis 1937: pt 2, 1, 29; 'In ordinary life ...': Ellis 1938: 243–4. Was d'Eon an Eonist? In his biography, the historian Gary Kates writes, 'd'Eon was neither a transvestite nor a transsexual ... there is simply no indication that d'Eon hated his own body or that he wanted, or even imagined he would be better off with, the body of a woman' (Kates 2001: xxii). Jan Morris thought otherwise: 'what happened to him, happened to me' (Morris 1974/2002: 128–9; quoted by Kates at xxii).

33 Ellis 1938: 244, quoted in Blanchard 1991: 240; Blanchard 2005: 442. See also Ellis 1937: pt 2, 108.

34 Bártová et al. 2021.

35 'My rubber fetish ...': Anonymous 2018; paraphilias predominantly in men: Cantor 2012: 239, appealing to the fact that 'neither clinics, forensic institutions, nor social clubs for paraphilic enthusiasts report any substantial number

of female paraphilics.' The greater male sex drive may play a role in explaining sex differences in paraphilic interests (Dawson et al. 2016). With a qualification about the limitations of surveys, a survey of Québécois found high rates of paraphilic interests and lifetime behaviours among men and women (Joyal and Carpentier 2017). See also Madill and Zhao 2022 on male-male erotica ('Boys' Love') consumed by females.

Fedoroff (2020) argues that paraphilias are more mutable than usually thought; for scepticism (focusing on paedophilia), see Bailey 2015. Homosexuality has some of the features of classic paraphilias (including great prevalence among men (Cantor 2012). See also Hsu 2019: 19.

36 See note 40 to chapter 1. Sedda and Bottini 2014 is a review of recent work on apotemnophilia (understood broadly as the intense desire for amputation, whether accompanied by sexual arousal or not). See also Bailey and Hsu 2022a: 593–4.

37 Furry conventions: Soh and Cantor 2015; autoanthropomorphozoophilia: Bailey and Hsu 2022a: 596–7.

38 The inverted counterparts of externally directed sexual orientations are called *erotic target identity inversions* (Freund and Blanchard 1993: 559). See also Hsu 2019; Bailey and Hsu 2022a.

39 Blanchard and Hucker 1991. Autoerotic asphyxiation is much more common in males, with females comprising fewer than 2 per cent of cases (Gosink and Jumbelic 2000). Havelock Ellis noted a couple of similar examples, one from 1917 'of a robust married man found dead in his bedroom in a tightly laced corset and a weak electric battery with one pole to the base of abdomen, indicat[ing] an Eonist attempting to heighten voluptuous emotion' (Ellis 1937: pt 2, 29, fn. 1; see also 28–9).

40 Zavitzianos 1972: 474, cited in Freund and Blanchard 1993. See also Lawrence 2009; Bailey and Hsu 2022a: 599–600. It is controversial whether autoandrophilia occurs in females. See note 21 to chapter 5; female autoandrophilia, if it exists, does not seem to drive female-to-male transsexuality (see also note 51 to this chapter).

41 Blanchard 2005: 439.

42 See Mitchell et al. 2019. The explanation of the gap is complex and not entirely due to differences in gender norms.

43 Blanchard 2005: 445.

44 A point made by Anne Lawrence – see the main text below – in her first writings on autogynephilia (Lawrence 1998: 65).

45 Lawrence 2013: 67, 69, 70.

46 The cross-dresser Richard Novic (see note 26 to this chapter) went as far as taking estrogen (stopping it to get his wife pregnant), but didn't go all the way; it is clear that, if he had, autogynephilia would have been the motivation: 'I

loved being a woman when I went out and couldn't stop worrying that I might want to do it full time' (Novic 2008: 181).

47 'All gender dysphoric males …': Blanchard 1989a: 322–3. See also Blanchard 2008: 437.

48 James 2022.

49 Bailey 2003: 158.

50 Dreger 2008: 368, 417.

51 Ibid.: 412, 387. *Transgender Tapestry* was a magazine 'for and about crossdressers, transgendered, transsexual, intersexed, and other gender-variant persons, and those who support them', which started as *The TV-TS Tapestry Newsletter* in the 1970s and ceased publishing in 2008. Given the venue, it is remarkable that Lawrence got away with the title of her article, 'Men trapped in men's bodies' (Lawrence 1998). The next issue contained a letter praising Lawrence's piece as 'excellent' – 'while I don't find myself completely in the article there is enough of me there to at least say that I lean toward that corner of the universe of possibilities' (Stevens 1999: 6). Lawrence wrote a revised version which appeared in a subsequent issue of *Transgender Tapestry*, with the editorial introduction presciently saying, 'In broaching the subject of autogynephilia, Dr. Lawrence has courageously opened a virtual Pandora's box' (Lawrence 2000: 17). The next issue contained a variety of responses, some critical, some not. The first was by a trans man, Jamison Green, who doubted that autoandrophilia motivated FtM transsexuals. Green remarked, 'If we're going to talk about the combustible mixture of gender and desire, we have to recognize that it is not the exclusive province of transsexuals. This will help put it in perspective, and help to reduce the pathologizing we so logically dread' (Green 2001: 21).

52 James 2023.

53 '… anti-trans theory': Rider and Tebbe 2021: 41; '… defer to Julia Serano …': Lovell 2021; transvestic fetishism as a symptom: Blanchard 1989b: 621. Sharpe (2021) makes the same two mistakes mentioned in the main text below as Lovell, and also cites Serano.

54 A nearly exhaustive list of criticisms and citations is in Lawrence's review article, mentioned below in the main text. (See note 60 to this chapter.)

In her 2010 article Serano claims that Blanchard uses the word 'autogynephilia' in two ways. First, he uses it '*descriptively* to denote a type of erotic fantasy'. Second, Blanchard uses 'autogynephilia' '*theoretically* to describe a paraphilic model in which … such fantasies become the primary cause of any gender dysphoria' (Serano 2010: 176). Like the quotation above in the main text, this is doubly wrong. First, Blanchard never uses the word to label a theory or model. As we saw earlier in the chapter, he emphasizes the distinction between autogynephilia, on the one hand, and theoretical claims about it, on the other. Second, autogynephilia is not a type of erotic fantasy, any more than homosexuality is a type of erotic fantasy, although of course both are related to erotic fantasies. To repeat Blanchard's definition, autogynephilia is 'a male's propensity to be sexually aroused by the thought or image of himself as a female'. For reasons that will become clear later, this should be adjusted to conform more closely to the root meaning of the word, love of oneself as a woman, which is neutral as to who is doing the loving. 'A person's propensity to be sexually aroused by the thought or image of themself as a female' is better. Autogynephilia in women should not be ruled out by fiat.

Serano elects to 'use the term *autogynephilia* exclusively to denote the paraphilic model that Blanchard and others have forwarded', leaving herself no word to denote the love of oneself as a woman (Serano 2010: 177). So although Serano does not deny the existence of autogynephilia, it is effectively invisible in her writings.

55 'gender dysphoria ...' and '... most damaging ...': ibid.: 181, 183; cross-dressing: Hunt 1978: 50–1; 'His first specific recollection ...': Blanchard 1991: 238. See also Hayton 2022.

56 Lawrence 2007: 511.

57 Serano 2010: 183. Lawrence also pointed out that sexual feelings can sometimes develop in childhood. She cited a couple of case reports of penile erections in young cross-dressing boys, 'plausibly ... an early form of autogynephilic sexual arousal' (Lawrence 2007: 516). Serano objects that 'evok[ing] these highly atypical cases to account for the rather high percentage of nonandrophilic transsexual women who experience a desire to be female prior to puberty seems unreasonable' (2010: 183), but this is a misunderstanding. Lawrence was merely noting that there seem to be (rare) cases of childhood autogynephilic arousal, just as there are cases of childhood heterosexual arousal. (On the latter, see Friedrich et al. 1998.) She was *not* saying that all childhood cross-gender feelings in non-androphilic trans women are covertly erotic.

58 '... discursively ...' and '... constituted ...': Pearce et al. 2020: 679, 687; '... report FEFs': Serano 2020: 767.

59 Autogynephilia in females: Bailey and Hsu (2022b) gave Blanchard's 'Core Autogynephilia Scale' (sample question: 'Have you ever been sexually aroused by the thought of being a woman?') to large groups, including natal females. Females and non-autogynephilic males responded similarly, with very low scores. An exchange of letters ensued in the *Archives of Sexual Behavior*: Moser 2023; Serano and Veale 2023; Bailey 2023.

For a discussion of earlier studies that purport to show autogynephilia in women, see Lawrence 2017: 45–6. The basic problem is one of interpretation. For example, Moser (2009) recruited a convenience sample of women who worked at a hospital and gave them statements such as 'I have been erotically aroused by dressing in lingerie or sexy attire for a romantic evening or when hoping to meet a sex partner.' Eight of his twenty-nine participants responded 'Frequently' to that statement, with fourteen responding 'On occasion' (543). It is hardly clear that these respondents experienced sexual arousal at the thought of *being* a woman, as opposed to arousal at the thought of a romantic or sexual encounter.

'it seems both illogical ...': Serano 2020: 767.

60 Review article: Lawrence 2017. Here is another illustration of the exceptionally low level of quality in the 'TERF wars' issue, relevant to chapter 3. In her article, the sociologist Sally Hines claims that there is 'much evidence to counter binary readings of sex' (2020: 709). There is the inevitable appeal to Fausto-Sterling's 'The five sexes', which Hines apparently interprets as making the point that 'there are many human chromosomal combinations other than XX ... and XY' (709); in fact, Fausto-Sterling never mentions abnormal sex-chromosome combinations in that article. Hines also writes that 'neuroscientist Cordelia Fine challenges understandings of sex that are based on hormonal difference', citing Fine's book *Testosterone Rex* (708); Fine is not a 'neuroscientist' and her work has nothing to do with whether sex is binary. As is explicit in *Testosterone Rex*, Fine knows perfectly well what sex is (Fine 2017: 43).

61 'loathsome man', '... *the basic structure* ...', 'Did sissy porn ...': Chu 2019: 72, 74, 79; '... fucking therapist': quoted in Perry 2020, a penetrating review of *Females*.

62 'feminine counterpart': Ellis 1937: pt 2, 6; 'a perfect female': Du Preez and Dronfield 2016: 379. Barry may have had an affair with Lord Charles Somerset, the governor of the Cape Colony, South Africa (206). Easier employment or sexual inversion: Ellis 1937: pt 2, 32. On Barry's recent journey from feminist heroine (Du Preez and Dronfield 2016) to trans man, see Joyce 2021: 92–4. The trans activist Shon Faye, for example, takes Barry to be one of the 'historical trans men' on the slightest of evidence: that Barry did not want his body examined after death and (perhaps) also because Florence Nightingale thought Barry 'behaved like a brute' (202–3).

'Female husbands' are one interesting culture-bound group of women who lived as men and were married to women. The historian Jen Manion dates the first female husband to eighteenth-century England; they provided 'scandals' for the popular press. It is very plausible that the desire to have a romantic and sexual relationship with a woman was an important part of the motivation for most female husbands, since an overtly lesbian relationship was not possible (Manion 2020: 259–60). By the end of the nineteenth century, 'female husband' had fallen into disuse on both sides of the Atlantic.

Following the historian Emily Skidmore, one could use 'trans man' more liberally than in this book to refer to people who 'chose to live their lives as male even thought they had been assigned female at birth' (Skidmore 2019: 10). On this understanding, Barry was indisputably a trans man, no matter whether he suffered from gender dysphoria or behaved like a brute to Florence Nightingale. The problem with Skidmore's terminological choice is that it collapses very different motivations a female may have for living life as a male, creating an illusion of continuity from Barry's time to ours.

63 Ellis 1937: pt 2, 18–19.

64 'virtually does not exist …': Freund 1985: 262. Robert Stoller had earlier said the same. Describing 'female transsexuals', he wrote: 'From childhood on the patient is attracted to feminine females' (1975: 224); see also Stoller 1968: 196. Androphilic FtM transsexualism: Chivers and Bailey 2000. Some case reports: Coleman et al. 1993; Dickey and Stephens 1995. Stories of the more classic kind of FtM transsexualism are in Devor 2016.

65 Bailey and Hsu 2022a: 602.

66 The Jazz Age may soon be superseded by the Age of Autonomy, in which children (not just adults) are free to alter their bodies as they see fit with little or no medical gatekeeping, because people have 'an intimate understanding of their own gender subjectivity', where 'gender subjectivity' is 'the totality of one's phenomenological experiences of oneself as gendered, which includes gender embodiment' (Ashley 2023: 112, 111). On this view, there is no psychological problem to be dealt with or disorder to be ameliorated, only obstacles to self-realization.

67 Benvenuto 2012 and Thrace 2022 are compelling memoirs about a transitioning husband from the wife's perspective. Morys 2022 is a scathing account of Morris as a parent by one of her daughters.

Chapter 7 Is Biology Destiny?

1 Campbell 2013: 41. Campbell was a notable evolutionary psychologist (see note 28 to this chapter); she thinks twenty-first-century woman cannot be designed 'from scratch' because evolved sex differences are here to stay.

2 Goldberg 1973: 233.

3 The Married Women's Property Act of 1870 rectified some of the problems. Suffrage was not just a women's issue: many men could not vote in Mill's time, and full male suffrage had to wait until 1918.

4 Mill 1870/2006: 146, 223.

5 Du Preez and Dronfield 2016: 381.

6 Four out of ten male: Belkin 2021; 'is chock-full …': Cahill 2019; 'a leading voice …': Eliot 2019.

7 '… rational beings': Mill 1870/2006: 157; 'Physically …', 'usually superior to men …', and 'morally, …': Lecky 1895: 358, 358, 359; '… her sexuality': Nietzsche 1886/2007: 69. The Nietzsche quotation should be treated with

caution: according to the Nietzsche scholar Maude Marie Clark, his misogyny 'is not the simple and straightforward matter it appears to be' (Clark 2015: 142).

8 Rippon 2019: 5.

9 Moi 2001: 20, emphasis added.

10 Biological determinism need not be confined to the sexes: '... the lengthy tradition of biological determinism, in which biological differences among races, sexes, classes, and species in anatomy, hormones, and genes are studied to provide biological justifications for social, behavioral, and psychological inequalities' (Rosser 2003: 413).

11 Wilson 1910.

12 Brooks 1883: 263, emphasis added.

13 On feminist 'biophobia', see Campbell 2013: ch. 1, Vandermassen 2005: ch. 4. There are also ('biophilic') feminists who take biology seriously, for instance the anthropologist Barbara Smuts (1995), the cultural critic Camille Paglia (Paglia 1991b: ch. 1), the philosopher Janet Radcliffe Richards (2000) and the philosopher Christina Hoff Sommers (2013: ch. 3). A more recent example is the writer Louise Perry (2022a). Paglia, it is worth noting, has praised John Money for his research on 'the sexual territory between biology and psychology' and his 'many pioneering books on sex and gender identity' (Paglia 1991a: 180; Paglia's essay contains an excoriating takedown of Foucault, among others).

Even from a feminist perspective, biophobia makes little sense. As Richards puts it, 'feminists should not think that they have a vested interest in discovering the facts to be one way rather than another' (Richards 1980: 44). Suppression of female athletic talent: in 2022 a lecturer in the Department of Health at the University of Bath (UK) wrote a viral Twitter thread in which she claimed that 'Women's sport exists as a category because the dominance of men athletes was threatened by women competing' (Cramer 2022).

14 According to Judith Butler, 'the distinction between sex and gender has been crucial to the long-standing feminist effort to debunk the claim that anatomy is destiny' (Butler 1986: 35). 'Anatomy is destiny' is from Sigmund Freud (see Moi 2000); it is sometimes misquoted as 'Biology is destiny.' Butler is right that many feminists have taken the sex/gender distinction to be the silver bullet that killed off biological determinism, but the argument as standardly presented is flawed. Here's Butler's version:

> Sex is understood to be the invariant, anatomically distinct, and factic aspects of the female body, whereas gender is the cultural meaning and form that that body acquires, the variable modes of that body's acculturation. With the distinction [between sex and gender] intact, it is no longer possible to attribute the values

> or social functions of women to biological necessity, and neither can we refer meaningfully to natural or unnatural gendered behavior: all gender is, by definition, unnatural. (Butler 1986: 35)

When Butler says that 'all gender is, by definition, unnatural', she has essentially packed her conclusion in to her premise. If the premise is that gender as *social roles* and gender as *social role norms* (see chapter 2) all float free from biology, then it trivially follows that biology neither determines what sex-typed social roles *there are* or what sex-typed social roles *should be*. Presenting the premise merely as a 'distinction' creates the appearance of a powerful argument against biological determinism, moreover one that can be advanced from the comfort of the gender theorist's armchair, without empirical investigation. Who can object to a *distinction* between, say, sex and sex roles? But the empirical issue concerning the biological differences between the sexes has simply been concealed, not addressed. This is yet another reason why using 'gender' to mean anything other than *sex* only leads to confusion.

15 'No biological ...': Beauvoir 1949/2011: 283; Hubbard: Culpepper 2021.

16 'I am happy ...': Navratilova 2019; '... transphobic': Perraudin 2019; 'the fastest time ...': Joyce 2021: 180.

17 Young 1980: 143, 152.

18 Baseball pitches: Glenday 2022. There are occasional reports of women throwing around 80 mph. 'Women in sexist society ...': Young 1980: 152. Young noted that '[sex] differences in motor skills, movement, spatial perception ... increase with adolescence', which she took to support the conclusion that this was produced by 'the process of growing up as a girl' (153). But this is to ignore how puberty drives the sexes physically apart (Hooven 2021: ch. 5). Anatomical sex differences: 'The sex differences in the anatomy of the pectoral girdle are, with few exceptions, in the direction that would result in superior throwing performance by males' (Lombardo and Deaner 2018: 109–10).

19 '... real physical differences ...': Young 1980: 142; 'on average men ...' and 'there are very few ...': Fausto-Sterling 1985/1992: 214, 269.

Here is an interesting example of minimizing sexual dimorphism, partly due to imperfect citation practices and an academic game of telephone, and perhaps unconsciously influenced by the desirability of the conclusion. At one point in *Sex, Gender, and Society*, Ann Oakley (see chapter 2) writes that, on the Indonesian island of Bali,

> males and females lack the sort of differentiation of physique that is a visible sex difference in our culture. Geoffrey Gorer once described them as a 'hermaphroditic' people; they have little sex differential in height and both sexes have broad shoulders and narrow hips. They do not run to curves and muscles, to body hair or to breasts of

> any size. (Gorer remarked that you could not tell male and female apart, even from the front.) (Oakley 1972/2016: 31)

The citation is to Gorer's *Bali and Angkor: A 1930s Pleasure Trip Looking at Life and Death*, published in 1936, but no page reference is given. Gorer was an English anthropologist, and the book is the result of his three-month trip to Sumatra, Java, Bali and the surrounding region, travelling 'in considerable luxury' (Gorer 1936/1986: 11). *Bali and Angkor* is a travel book, not an ethnography.

The feminist philosopher Alison Jaggar, writing in 1983, paraphrases Oakley as follows: 'In some ethnic groups, there is little sexual differentiation between men and women. Women are as tall as men, have equally broad shoulders and narrow hips, and have breasts so small that it is often difficult to tell an individual's sex even when seen from the front' (Jaggar 1983: 110). Notice that Jaggar exaggerates Oakley in some respects ('*as tall* as men', '*equally* broad shoulders'), while toning Oakley down in another ('*often difficult* to tell'), perhaps because 'could not tell' sounded incredible. So what does Gorer himself say?

> The Balinese are a very hermaphroditic race; both sexes wear the same bright sarongs; in the outlying villages both sexes wear their hair long, and ornament it with the scarlet hibiscus; there is little difference in height between them; both have fairly broad shoulders and relatively narrow hips, so that from a back view it is very difficult to distinguish; the breast muscles of many of the men are so developed that even when they are seen from the front confusion is justifiable. Many of the older men have faces of great intellectual dignity. (Gorer 1936/1986: 61–2)

Clearly Gorer's characterization of the Balinese as 'hermaphroditic' is partly based on women and men's similar *clothing and hairstyles*, not just on their similar bodily features. Oakley correctly reports Gorer as saying that there is 'little' difference in height but incorrectly reports him as saying that the women 'do not run to breasts of any size'. His claim, rather, was that 'many' men have *large pectoral muscles* that can be mistaken for breasts. And, finally, Gorer's weak 'confusion is justifiable' becomes the very strong 'could not tell'. The original (1972) edition of *Sex, Gender, and Society*, incidentally, has a full-page photograph of a 'Balinese girl' opposite the quotation above; she does in fact have small breasts but is unmistakably a girl.

Gorer's claims themselves appear to be a little exaggerated. *The Last Paradise* is a 1930 book about Bali by the journalist Hickman Powell. To go by its many illustrations of Balinese men and topless Balinese women, the Balinese in the early twentieth century were far from hermaphroditic.

20 Sex difference in running: Cheuvront et al. 2005. Fausto-Sterling also speculated

that the difference in average height between the sexes would diminish 'by a few percentage points', 'given widespread changes leading to equal physical activity for boys and girls in an environment with adequate nutrition' (1985/1992: 216). In fact, increasing living standards and better health are associated with a *greater* difference in average height. Males are more vulnerable to nutritional stress than females and suffer a greater reduction in the growth of the 'long bones' in the arms and legs (Frayer and Wolpoff 1985: 431–2; German and Hochberg 2020).

21 Bossen and Gates 2017.

22 Berkhead 2020.

23 For the rape-prevention suggestion, see Thornhill and Palmer 2000: ch. 9. Richards 2000: ch. 9 has a careful discussion of an attempt to justify Victorian marriage laws by Sir James Fitzjames Stephen, a contemporary (and critic) of John Stuart Mill.

24 As Darwin put it, sexual selection 'depends on the advantage which certain individuals have over others of the same sex and species solely in respect of reproduction' (Darwin 1871/2004: 243, quoted in Gowaty 2004: 37).

25 One of the most important papers on sexual selection is Trivers 1972. For the significance of the ratio of sexually active males to females (the Operational Sex Ratio, or OSR) in explaining intrasexual competition, see Clutton-Brock and Parker 1992. On the oversimplified sketch in the text: 'the theory of sexual selection still provides a robust framework that explains much of the variation in the development of secondary sexual characters in males, although the mechanisms controlling the relative intensity of reproductive competition and the relative development of secondary sexual characters in the two sexes are more complex than was originally supposed' (Clutton-Brock 2007: 1185). A good introduction to sexual selection is Zuk and Simmons 2018.

26 Sexual selection in primates: Kappeler and Van Schaik 2004; evidence of selection for male–male competition: Puts et al. 2016; Geary 2021: ch. 5 (for upper body strength, see Puts et al. 2016: 390); deep voices: Puts et al. 2012.

27 '... staying alive': Campbell 1999: 204; fear: ibid.: 206; Benenson et al. 2022: 12–13.

28 For an accessible discussion of these and related points, see Stewart-Williams 2018: ch. 3. Stewart-Williams's book is about *evolutionary psychology*, the discipline that studies how evolution produces psychological traits. It is only fair to record that evolutionary psychology has attracted a lot of opprobrium. For example, one blisteringly critical book is by the philosopher of biology John Dupré – 'the evolutionary psychology of sex and gender offers us mainly simplifications and banalities' (Dupré 2001: 68). Dupré's and Stewart-Williams's books are a useful pairing for readers looking for both sides of the argument.

29 The 2021 *Oxford Handbook of Feminist Philosophy* offers, over its door-stopping

600 pages, 'a comprehensive overview of the contemporary state of the field' (quoting from the OUP blurb), aiming to 'showcase the rich diversity of subject matter, approach, and method among feminist philosophers' (Ásta and Hall 2021: 9). The number of pages devoted to evolution is zero. It is as if Darwin never existed. The gender-critical feminists take biology more seriously, although they might resist the conclusions of this chapter (see Lawford-Smith 2022a: 45).

30 See chapter 3, chapter 5. Babies also have a 'minipuberty': for boys, a testosterone surge in the first few months, the function of which is not well understood.

31 Arnold 2009; Hooven 2021: chs 6, 7.

32 Fausto-Sterling 1985/1992: 141.

33 Ibid.: 137.

34 Hines 2009: 1899–900.

35 Strong evidence for prenatal hormonal influences: Berenbaum and Beltz 2021; Spencer et al. 2021. See also Geary 2021: ch. 10. '... maybe, possibly?': Fausto-Sterling 2012: 39.

36 For a helpful exchange on whether 'ideological bias' is a factor in some feminist critiques of the science of sex differences, see Fine 2020 and von Hippel et al. 2020. For a defence of 'feminist science', see Fine 2018.

37 Goldberg 2003: 215.

38 Goldberg 1973: 30, 93; see also the second epigraph to this chapter, where Goldberg puts his conclusion more generally, in terms of 'biological differences'. Male dominance is male 'authority in familial and dyadic relationships' (31), sometimes called *domestic* patriarchy. As the quotation in the text suggests, Goldberg thought that male dominance or domestic patriarchy was universal; he was wrong about that (Wrangham forthcoming). Patriarchy at the level of societies – the kind relevant to this chapter – is sometimes called *societal* patriarchy.

39 Goldberg is not an unclear writer, yet he is occasionally misinterpreted as a biological determinist of the 'rightful' kind, like William Keith Brooks. The sociologist Catherine Hakim describes Goldberg's theory accurately and points out some of its advantages over rivals (Hakim 1996: 5–9).

40 Goldberg 1993: 64.

41 Kirkus Reviews 1973.

42 Leacock 1974: 363. More recent assessments from feminist scholars are equally dismissive: Goldberg's book is a 'misogynist pop science [screed]' (S. S. Richardson 2013: 10).

43 Mead 1935/1977: 253, 259, 279, 280. Mead's work in Samoa came under intense fire in the 1980s from the anthropologist Derek Freeman; the resulting controversy is judiciously examined in Shankman 2009.

44 Goldberg 1973: 43; see also Wrangham and Peterson 1996: 280–1; Brown 1991:

20–3. Textbooks in gender studies have perpetuated the myth of the sex-role-reversed society: 'Mead found … one culture [the Chambri] in which women and men were seen as extremely different from each other – but exactly the opposite of the model familiar to us' (Kimmel 2016: 61).

45 Mead 1973: 48; partly quoted in Goldberg 1993: 35.

46 Mead 1973: 48.

47 Ibid.: 52. Goldberg (1993: 158–9) later responded to Mead.

48 Harari 2015: 152. There are respects in which men are not valued more highly than women (at least in contemporary North America, although surely this holds more widely). For instance, participants in one experiment were given a hypothetical situation in which either a woman or a man can be sacrificed to save lives; the vast majority chose to sacrifice the man (FeldmanHall et al. 2016). See also Eagly and Mladinic 1994 on the 'women-are-wonderful effect', the finding that both sexes tend to view women more favourably than men. To take an example from the other side, there is the widespread phenomenon in developing nations of son preference and consequent female infanticide, with the female deficit in Asia since the 1950s getting close to 200 million (Hudson et al. 2020: 70–4, 514, n. 101).

Gerda Lerner, in *The Creation of Patriarchy*, gives another definition of patriarchy: 'the manifestation and institutionalization of male dominance over women and children in the family and the extension of male dominance over women in society in general. It implies that men hold power in all the important institutions of society and that women are deprived of access to such power' (1986: 239). Neither of the two parts of Lerner's definition capture patriarchy as Goldberg understands it. First, Goldbergian patriarchy has nothing to say about power relations in the family or 'male dominance over women'. Second, Goldbergian patriarchy is supposed to be compatible with women in public positions of authority, provided there are not too many of them. Margaret Thatcher and Golda Meir are not counterexamples to the claim that the UK and Israel were Goldbergian patriarchies throughout the twentieth century.

49 Ibid.: 29.

50 Representativeness of contemporary hunter gatherers: Harari 2015: 44–5; Agta: Von Rueden et al. 2018: 402 (but see Boehm 1999: 8); Aka: Moorhead 2005; Hewlett 1992: 27. See also Wrangham and Peterson 1996: 119–24; Boehm 1999: 5–9; Wrangham forthcoming.

51 Pre-agricultural societies: Whyte 1978: 90–1; Collier and Rosaldo 1981; '… the norm …': Harari 2015: 153. See also Pinker 2016: 437, 'males dominate public/political realm' is a 'human universal', citing Brown 1991.

52 Harari 2015: 153. Harari is talking about patriarchy in his sense (see the main text above), but the point is just as plausible for patriarchy in Goldberg's sense.

53 Time 1973: 34, partly quoted in Colapinto 2006: 69.

54 Goldberg 1973: 80.
55 Ibid. *The Inevitability of Patriarchy* used 'aggression' for what Goldberg later called 'dominance tendency', which he admitted was confusing. See Goldberg 1993: 65–6.
56 Money and Ehrhardt 1973/1996: 122.
57 Goldberg 1993: 69.
58 Mate preferences: Buss 2019: chs 4, 5; Walter et al. 2020; Geary 2021: ch. 7; status striving: Buss 2019: ch. 4; Geary 2021: ch. 8. The possibility that evolution might help explain patriarchy brings out the point that male hormonalization could be only (part of) the *proximal* explanation – the mechanism in the brain and body that inclines men to behave in ways that result in patriarchy. Once we have isolated the mechanism, the next (and deeper) question is, what explains why men are equipped with *that*? Goldberg's suggested explanation of patriarchy, even if correct, is thus rather superficial.
59 See note 35 above.
60 For an explanation of structural patriarchy as the product of powerful male alliances originally designed to control exceptionally violent men, see Wrangham forthcoming. (The importance of male alliances in explaining patriarchy had been stressed earlier in Smuts 1995: 13–15.) Wrangham's explanation ultimately appeals to a 'universal biological reason', so it is congenial to a revised version of Goldberg's argument.
61 Livingstone 1974: 367. Livingstone was another uncomplimentary reviewer: 'a pompous, turgid, onerously repetitive diatribe' (366).
62 Sex difference in sexual orientation: Hines 2004: 11; lethal violence: Daly and Wilson 1988; crime: Campbell 2013: ch. 7; psychological sex differences: Archer 2019; personality: Del Giudice et al. 2012; Geary 2021: 341–3; psychopathology: ibid.: 433–40; greater male variability: Stewart-Williams and Halsey 2021: 12–15; Geary 2021: 423–5; occupational interests: Stoet and Geary 2022; Tao et al. 2022; Browne 2023 (also Stewart-Williams and Halsey 2021). For an accessible review of sex differences, see Pinker 2016: ch. 18.
63 Sex differences in occupational interests increase with gender equality: Stoet and Geary 2022; sex and surgeons: Moberly 2018; Browne 2023: 7, fig. 4; Finnish CEOs: Minna 2020.

Chapter 8 True Selves and Identity Crises

1 Morris 1974/2002: 146. For those who discover identity 'to be only a mirage in the end', 'their latter quandary is hardly less terrible than their first.' For this reason, Morris hoped that medical transitioning was 'only a transient phenomenon', but suspected it was not.
2 Lawrence 2013: 218.
3 Singal 2020a.

4 Fukuyama 2020: 10.
5 'A recurring image of identity liberalism is that of a prism refracting a single beam of light into its constituent colors, producing a rainbow' (Lilla 2018: 9).
6 LGBTQIA+ = Lesbian/Gay/Bisexual/Transgender/Queer/Intersex/Asexual/+; LGBTQQIP2SAA+ = Lesbian/Gay/Bisexual/Questioning/Queer/Intersex/Pansexual/2-Spirit/Androgynous/Asexual/+.
7 Fukuyama 2020: 116–17.
8 Cf. the 'little theory' of identity in Appiah 2018: 8–12.
9 On stereotype accuracy, see Jussim et al. 2015.
10 McCloskey 1999: 176.
11 Benjamin 1966: 55. On the metaphor of transitioning as migration, see Brubaker 2016: ch. 3.
12 See also note 41 to chapter 5.
13 Snapes 2019.
14 Weiss 2022.
15 'I don't like …': Papisova 2018. See also Barker and Iantaffi 2019: ch. 2; Young 2019; Windust 2020; Weiss 2022. Some on the trans activist side accept that enbies are considerably more prevalent than is usually supposed: 'In one sense, the claim that everyone is non-binary isn't wrong' (Faye 2021: 258).
16 Weiss 2022.
17 The view that non-binary adults fall outside *woman* and *man* is not uncommon: 'To put it very simply, my nonbinary gender identity means that I am neither a man nor a woman' (Young 2019: 12). The feminist philosopher Kate Manne agrees: 'I regard the gender binary system – where people are divided into two mutually exclusive and exhaustive categories, of boys and men, on the one hand, and girls and women, on the other – as inaccurate and pernicious. Some people are intersex; some people are agender; and some people are genderqueer, moving back and forth between different gendered identities, among other non-binary possibilities' (Manne 2018: 26–7). Note that Manne implies not just that non-binary (genderqueer) adults are neither (exclusively) women nor (exclusively) men but that this also applies to 'intersex' adults.
18 Vasey and Bartlett 2007: 484. On the *muxe*, see Gómez Jiménez et al. 2020. On male third genders as cultural expressions of male androphilia, see Vasey and VanderLaan 2014; Hames et al. 2017. A useful collection on third sexes/genders (albeit with some assumptions and claims disputed in this book) is Herdt 1996; the introduction to that collection follows Robert Stoller in using the word 'sex' for *female/male* and 'gender' for *feminine/masculine* (22).
19 See, e.g., Benjamin 1966: 14–15, 159; Benjamin's foreword to Jorgensen 1967; Green and Money 1969: 39, 186–7, 250–1. In those early times, clinicians stated a patient's sex when necessary and before sex-reassignment used 'he' for males, etc.

20 Bollinger 2021.
21 Marcus 2021.
22 Sex-neutral pronoun proposals: Baron 1981; '… feelings of value': Herndon 2015.
23 Milton 2020.
24 So-called *singular* 'they', as in 'If a celebrity comes to the party, they will have a good time' and 'England expects everyone to do their duty', has been around since the fourteenth century. What *is* new is *non-binary* 'they', as in 'They are a singer' (pointing at Sam Smith), and 'If Sam comes to the party, they will have good time.' (See Pullum 2021; for an exhaustive study of singular 'they', see Lagunoff 1997.) Sam's mum: Parsons 2020.
25 Lilla 2018: 65.
26 Appiah 2018: 29.
27 For descriptions of some classic 1970s psychological experiments that divided people into arbitrary groups, and subsequent research, see Hornsey 2008.
28 Stock calls this the 'stick of rock' model of gender identity (2021: 112–19).
29 Ehrensaft 2014: 572; 2017b: 63.
30 Watchful waiting: de Vries and Cohen-Kettenis 2012; Zucker et al. 2012. Sometimes 'watchful waiting' is reserved for the approach developed by the Dutch, with the more interventional approach developed by Susan Bradley and Kenneth Zucker in Toronto called the 'live in your own skin' model (Ehrensaft 2017b: 61).
31 Ehrensaft 2014: 573, 578. The clinician Erica Anderson (note 32 to chapter 1) offers a contrary view: 'I get asked this time and time again: Is this kid *truly* trans? And I don't think that's a helpful question to ask' (Davis 2022).
32 Variations in prevalence and sex ratios: Zucker 2017; dysphoria and the *fa'afafine*: Vasey and Bartlett 2007.

According to *Histories of the Transgender Child* by the historian Jules Gill-Peterson, 'The bleached and medicalized image of the trans child circulating as unprecedented in the twenty first century is actually prefaced by an entire century of trans children' (Gill-Peterson 2018: 2–3). That gives the impression that Jazz Jennings is merely the most recent in a 100-year-long line of 'trans kids', but Gill-Peterson adopts a highly elastic account of childhood: 'Anyone under the medical age of consent during the twentieth century – typically twenty-one, but sometimes eighteen – is a child in the pages that [follow]' (9). In any case, the 'many trans children hiding in plain sight in the past' (3) fail to materialize in her book.

Gill-Peterson mentions Alan (Lucille) Hart (1890–1962), who was one of the first people to medically transition from female to male in the US, and who went on to conduct research into tuberculosis. (See also Manion 2020: 267–76.) Hart's psychiatrist, J. Allen Gilbert, reported that, as a child, Hart '[n]ever played house or at being the mother of dolls … and thought she would be a boy if only the family would cut her hair and let her wear trousers, which she earnestly besought them do to' (Katz 1976: 262). Whether Hart had any significant kind of gender dysphoria as a child is unclear, and there is no indication that puberty was a particularly difficult period. Hart went through medical school as Lucille (albeit passing as a man on many occasions); later Hart had a hysterectomy and, in Gilbert's words, 'made her exit as a female and started as a male with a new hold on life and ambitions worthy of her high degree of intellectuality' (276). Hart was clearly gynephilic; according to the historian Jonathan Ned Katz, Hart's story 'illustrates only too well one extreme to which an intelligent, aspiring Lesbian in early twentieth-century America might be driven by her own and her doctor's acceptance of society's condemnation of women-loving women' (279). However, Gill-Peterson writes that 'scholars now agree' that, in Hart's case, 'the term "homosexuality" … cannot be taken literally through its contemporary definition' (Gill-Peterson 2018: 60–1). Why scholars agree is not explained.

Gill-Peterson's other main example from the early twentieth century is 'Val', a trans woman who tried (apparently unsuccessfully) to obtain sex-reassignment surgery in the 1940s. Val recounted a gender dysphoric childhood, with her parents allowing her to dress as a girl from a very early age (61). That might well be true, but there is no independent confirmation. Apart from another trans woman, 'Karen', who did not report a dysphoric childhood (89–90), and much discussion of intersex patients, that's basically it. As Gill-Peterson says herself, 'evidence for trans childhood in the early twentieth century remains mostly implicit or retrospective' (91).

Moving on to the later part of the twentieth century, Gill-Peterson notes that, after the American George Jorgensen's transition to Christine in the 1950s was widely reported, Harry Benjamin, her doctor, 'received a huge number of letters from trans writers, among whom were children as young as thirteen' (150). The only younger letter writers Gill-Peterson mentions are natal males; whether they were dysphoric before puberty is not known. Probably some subsequently transitioned and some didn't. Nonetheless, Gill-Peterson calls them all 'trans girls'.

The point isn't that early onset gender dysphoria didn't occur a century ago; it would be surprising if it didn't, at least in some form. As to whether its prevalence was more than negligible, we can only speculate.

33 Crisp 1968/1997: 169.

34 'Everyone thought [Crisp] was "disgusting". I thought he was brave and stylish, I wanted to meet him' (George and Bright 1995: 54). Much later, Boy George got his wish (298–99).

35 Crisp 2017: 5, 9, 7.

36 'I think ...': ibid.: 6; sexual dysfunction: early treatment with puberty blockers seems to make males incapable of orgasm (Barnes 2023: 341–2).
37 Strohminger et al. 2017; Umscheid et al. 2023.
38 Cummins et al. 2019: 115.
39 Lawrence 2013: 218.

Coda

1 Beauvoir 1949/2011: 765. The 'certain differences' include woman's 'eroticism ... her relation to her body, to the male body, and to the child'. Although Beauvoir thought that socialization obscured the female potential, she was no biophobe (see note 13 to chapter 7).
2 'after the unification of man ...': Eriugena 866–7/1987: bk II, 533c. Eriugena (c.800–c.877) wrote his major works in France, then part of the Carolingian Empire. For more on Eriugena, see Moran and Guiu 2021; on sex and Christian theology more generally, see DeVun 2021: ch. 1.

The heyday of second-wave feminism was the 1960s and 1970s; the 'first wave' started in the nineteenth century and was focused on securing women's suffrage and legal equality more generally. One notable second-wave feminist, Shulamith Firestone, proposed the '*freeing of women from the tyranny of their biology by any means available*', which she thought would utterly transform human sexuality and society. Sounding somewhat like Eriugena, this 'revolt against the biological family' would 'create a paradise on earth anew' (Firestone 1971: 238, 242). The radicalism of the second wave is discussed in Lawford-Smith 2022a: ch. 2.

References

Abbruzzese, E., S. B. Levine, and J. W. Mason. 2023. The myth of 'reliable research' in pediatric gender medicine: a critical evaluation of the Dutch studies – and research that has followed. *Journal of Sex & Marital Therapy*: 1–27. doi: 10.1080/0092623X.2022.2150346.

Abell, C. et al. 2021. Open letter of solidarity with the University of Sussex from UK philosophers. October 11. https://bit.ly/3Y5ycf5.

Ablaza, C., J. Kabátek, and F. Perales. 2022. Are sibship characteristics predictive of same sex marriage? An examination of fraternal birth order and female fecundity effects in population-level administrative data from the Netherlands. *Journal of Sex Research* 59: 671–83.

Adams, R. 2021. Sussex professor resigns after transgender rights row. *The Guardian* October 28. www.theguardian.com/world/2021/oct/28/sussex-professor-kathleen-stock-resigns-after-transgender-rights-row.

Aitken, M., T. D. Steensma, R. Blanchard, D. P. VanderLaan, H. Wood, A. Fuentes, C. Spegg, L. Wasserman, M. Ames, and C. L. Fitzsimmons. 2015. Evidence for an altered sex ratio in clinic-referred adolescents with gender dysphoria. *Journal of Sexual Medicine* 12: 756–63.

Alcoff, L. M. 2006. *Visible Identities: Race, Gender, and the Self.* Oxford: Oxford University Press.

Alcoff, L., Ásta, S. Ayala-López, N. Bauer, T. M. Bettcher, S. Brennan, R. A. Briggs, S. Brison, S. Dea, E. Díaz-León, A. Garry, L. Gruen, K. Q. Hall, S. Haslanger, J. Holroyd, K. Jenkins, K. Jones, S. J. Khader, R. Kukla, K. Manne, J. McKitrick, M. Mikkola, A. J. Pitts, C. Russell, J. Saul, N. Scheman, N. Stoljar, A. Tanesini, Y. Thiem, C. Witt, A. Yap, R. Zambrana, and P. Zurn. 2019. On philosophical scholarship of gender: a response to '12 leading scholars'. Blog of the APA August 7. https://blog.apaonline.org/2019/08/07/on-philosophical-scholarship-of-gender-a-response-to-12-leading-scholars/.

Allen, S., E. Finneron-Burns, J. C. Jones, H. Lawford-Smith, M. Leng, R. Reilly-Cooper, and R. Simpson. 2018. Derogatory language in philosophy journal risks increased hostility and diminished discussion. *Daily Nous* August 27. https://dailynous.com/2018/08/27/derogatory-language-philosophy-journal-hostility-discussion/.

Allison, S., M. Warin, and T. Bastiampillai. 2014. Anorexia nervosa and social contagion: clinical implications. *Australian & New Zealand Journal of Psychiatry* 48: 116–20.

Alston et al., P. 2006. *The Yogyakarta Principles*. https://yogyakartaprinciples.org/principles-en/.

AMA. 2022. About the AMA. www.ama-assn.org/about.

AMA & AAMC. 2021. *Advancing Health Equity: Guide to Language, Narrative and Concepts*. Chicago, IL: American Medical Association. https://ama-assn.org/equity-guide.

Anderson, N. E., K. A. Harenski, C. L. Harenski, M. R. Koenigs, J. Decety, V. D. Calhoun, and K. A. Kiehl. 2019. Machine learning of brain gray matter differentiates sex in a large forensic sample. *Human Brain Mapping* 40: 1496–506.

Angier, N. 1998. Nothing becomes a man more than a woman's face. *New York Times* September 1. www.nytimes.com/1998/09/01/science/nothing-becomes-a-man-more-than-a-woman-s-face.html.

Anonymous. 2018. My life in sex: 'My rubber fetish has enriched my life'. *The Guardian* September 21. www.theguardian.com/lifeandstyle/2018/sep/21/my-rubber-fetish-has-enriched-my-life.

Anonymous. 2019. Philosophical discussion of trans identity: a guide for the perplexed. *Leiter Reports* June 17. https://leiterreports.typepad.com/blog/2019/06/philosophical-discussion-of-trans-identity-a-guide-for-the-perplexed.html.

Antony, L. 2020. Feminism without metaphysics or a deflationary account of gender. *Erkenntnis* 85: 529–49.

APA. 1980. *Diagnostic and Statistical Manual of Mental Disorders*. 3rd edn, Washington, DC: American Psychiatric Association.

———. 1994. *Diagnostic and Statistical Manual of Mental Disorders*. 4th edn, Washington, DC: American Psychiatric Association.

———. 2013. *Diagnostic and Statistical Manual of Mental Disorders*. 5th edn, Washington, DC: American Psychiatric Association.

———. 2022. *Diagnostic and Statistical Manual of Mental Disorders*. 5th edn, text revision, Washington, DC: American Psychiatric Association.

Appiah, K. A. 2018. *The Lies that Bind: Rethinking Identity*. New York: Liveright.

Archer, J. 2019. The reality and evolutionary significance of human psychological sex differences. *Biological Reviews* 94: 1381–415.

Archer, J., and B. Lloyd. 2002. *Sex and Gender*. Cambridge: Cambridge University Press.

Aristotle. 1995. *Generation of Animals. The Complete Works of Aristotle*, Vol. 2, ed. J. Barnes, trans. A. Platt. Princeton, NJ: Princeton University Press.

Arnold, A. P. 2009. The organizational–activational hypothesis as the foundation for a unified theory of sexual differentiation of all mammalian tissues. *Hormones and Behavior* 55: 570–8.

Arvan, M. Forthcoming. Trans women, cis women, alien women, and robot women are women: they are all (simply) adults gendered female. *Hypatia*.

Ashley, F. 2019. Shifts in assigned sex ratios at gender identity clinics likely reflect changes in referral patterns. *Journal of Sexual Medicine* 16: 948–9.

———. 2020. A critical commentary on 'rapid-onset gender dysphoria'. *Sociological Review* 68: 779–99.

———. 2023. Youth should decide: the principle of subsidiarity in paediatric transgender healthcare. *Journal of Medical Ethics* 49: 110–14.

Ásta. 2018. *Categories We Live By: The Construction of Sex, Gender, Race & Other Social Categories*. Oxford: Oxford University Press.

Ásta, and K. Q. Hall. (eds) 2021. *The Oxford Handbook of Feminist Philosophy*. Oxford: Oxford University Press.

Austin, J. L. 1975. *How to Do Things with Words*. Oxford: Oxford University Press.

Bachtrog, D., J. E. Mank, C. L. Peichel, M. Kirkpatrick, S. P. Otto, T.-L. Ashman, M. W. Hahn, J. Kitano, I. Mayrose, R. Ming, N. Perrin, L. Ross, N. Valenzuela, J. C. Vamosi, and the Tree of Sex Consortium. 2014. Sex determination: why so many ways of doing it? *PLOS Biology* 12: 1–13.

Bailey, J. M. 2003. *The Man Who Would Be Queen*. Washington, DC: Joseph Henry.

———. 2015. A failure to demonstrate changes in sexual interest in pedophilic men: comment on Müller et al. (2014). *Archives of Sexual Behavior* 44: 249–52.

———. 2023. Autogynephilia and science: a response to Moser (2022) and Serano and Veale (2022). *Archives of Sexual Behavior* 52: 479–81.

Bailey, J. M., and K. J. Hsu. 2022a. Erotic target identity inversions. *Gender and Sexuality Development*, ed. D. P. VanderLaan and W. I. Wong. Cham, Switzerland: Springer.

———. 2022b. How autogynephilic are natal females? *Archives of Sexual Behavior* 51: 3311–18.

Bailey, J. M., P. L. Vasey, L. M. Diamond, S. M. Breedlove, E. Vilain, and M. Epprecht. 2016. Sexual orientation, controversy, and science. *Psychological Science in the Public Interest* 17: 45–101.

Bannerman, L. 2018. Anger over women's business honour for cross-dressing banker. *The Times* September 22. www.thetimes.co.uk/article/anger-over-women-s-business-honour-for-cross-dressing-banker-hogv3l7nw.

Barker, M.-J., and A. Iantaffi. 2019. *Life Isn't Binary*. London: Jessica Kingsley.

Barnes, E. 2016. *The Minority Body: A Theory of Disability*. Oxford: Oxford University Press.

———. 2022. Gender without gender identity: the case of cognitive disability. *Mind* 131: 838–64.

Barnes, H. 2023. *Time to Think: The Inside Story of the Collapse of the Tavistock's Gender Service for Children*. Rugby, Warwicks.: Swift Press.

Baron, D. E. 1981. The epicene pronoun: the word that failed. *American Speech* 56: 83–97.

Barrett, S. C. H. 2002. The evolution of plant sexual diversity. *Nature Reviews Genetics* 3: 274–84.

Bártová, K., R. Androvičová, L. Krejčová, P. Weiss, and K. Klapilová. 2021. The prevalence of paraphilic interests in the Czech population: preference, arousal, the use of pornography, fantasy, and behavior. *Journal of Sex Research* 58: 86–96.

Bauer, J. E. 2004. Magnus Hirschfeld's doctrine of sexual intermediaries and the transgender politics of (no-)identity. *Past and Present of Radical Sexual Politics*, ed. G. Hekma. Amsterdam: Mosse Foundation.

BBC. 2019. RSPCA investigates after lawyer Jolyon Maugham kills fox with baseball bat. *BBC News* December 27. www.bbc.com/news/uk-50919327.

Beauvoir, S. de. 1949/1989. *The Second Sex*. Trans. H. M. Parshley. New York: Vintage.

———. 1949/2011. *The Second Sex*. Trans. C. Borde and S. Malovany-Chevallier. New York: Vintage.

———. 1980. From an interview. *New French Feminisms*, ed. E. Marks and I. de Courtivron. Amherst: University of Massachusetts Press.

Beauvoir, S. de, and J.-L. Servan-Schreiber. 1975. Questionnaire. TF1. https://youtu.be/g6eDMaDWquI.

Belkin, D. 2021. A generation of American men give up on college: 'I just feel lost'. *Wall Street Journal* September 6. www.wsj.com/articles/college-university-fall-higher-education-men-women-enrollment-admissions-back-to-school-11630948233.

Bell, K. 2021. Keira Bell: my story. *Persuasion* April 7. www.persuasion.community/p/keira-bell-my-story.

Bell, M. R. 2018. Comparing postnatal development of gonadal hormones and associated social behaviors in rats, mice, and humans. *Endocrinology* 159: 2596–613.

Belotti, E. G. 1976. *What Are Little Girls Made Of?* New York: Schocken Books.

Benenson, J. F. 2013. The development of human female competition: allies and adversaries. *Philosophical Transactions of the Royal Society B* 368: 1–11.

———. 2014. *Warriors and Worriers: The Survival of the Sexes.* Oxford: Oxford University Press.

Benenson, J. F., C. E. Webb, and R. W. Wrangham. 2022. Self-protection as an adaptive female strategy. *Behavioral and Brain Sciences* 45: 1–26.

Benjamin, H. 1963. 7 kinds of sex. *Transvestia* 22: 62–8.

———. 1966. *The Transsexual Phenomenon.* New York: Julian Press.

Bennett, A., H. L. Fraser, and H. Nater. 2019. Arbitral award: *Mokgadi Caster Semenya and Athletics South Africa* v. *International Association of Athletics Federations.* Court of Arbitration for Sport 30 April.

Benvenuto, C. 2012. *Sex Changes: A Memoir of Marriage, Gender, and Moving On.* New York: St Martin's Press.

Berenbaum, S. A., and A. M. Beltz. 2021. Evidence and implications from a natural experiment of prenatal androgen effects on gendered behavior. *Current Directions in Psychological Science* 30: 202–10.

Berenbaum, S. A., C. L. Martin, and D. N. Ruble. 2008. Gender development. *Child and Adolescent Development: An Advanced Course,* ed. W. Damon, R. M. Lerner and D. Kuhn. Hoboken, NJ: Wiley.

Berger, P. L., and T. Luckmann. 1966. *The Social Construction of Reality: A Treatise in the Sociology of Knowledge.* Garden City, NY: Doubleday.

Berglund, A., K. Stochholm, and C. H. Gravholt. 2020. The epidemiology of sex chromosome abnormalities. *American Journal of Medical Genetics* 184: 202–15.

Bering, J. 2013. *Perv: The Sexual Deviant in All of Us.* New York: Scientific American/Farrar, Straus & Giroux.

Berkhead, S. 2020. Russian women are ready to reclaim once-forbidden jobs. *Moscow Times* March 6. https://bit.ly/3YaqSPe.

Berkovitz, G., J. Rock, M. Urban, and C. Migeon. 1982. True hermaphroditism. *Johns Hopkins Medical Journal* 151: 290–7.

Bermúdez, J. L., C. Chambers, C. Fine, E. J. Hall, B. Hellie, T. Kelly, J. McMahan, F. Minerva, J. Schwenkler, P. Singer, N. A. Vincent, and J. Wilson. 2019. Philosophers should not be sanctioned over their positions on sex and gender. *Inside Higher Ed* July 22. www.insidehighered.com/views/2019/07/22/philosophers-should-not-be-sanctioned-their-positions-sex-and-gender-opinion.

Bettcher, T. M. 2009. Trans identities and first-person authority. *'You've Changed': Sex Reassignment and Personal Identity*, ed. L. Shrage. Oxford: Oxford University Press.

———. 2014. Trapped in the wrong theory: re-thinking trans oppression and resistance. *Signs* 39: 383–406.

Bettcher, T. M. et al. 2021. Open letter concerning transphobia in philosophy. January 8. https://bit.ly/3XNpoMH.

Beukeboom, L., and N. Perrin. 2014. *The Evolution of Sex Determination.* Oxford: Oxford University Press.

Bever, L. 2015. How a transgender teen became a nationally known activist. *Washington Post* March 19. www.washingtonpost.com/news/morning-mix/wp/2015/03/19/how-a-transgender-teen-became-a-nationally-known-activist/.

Biden, J. R. 2021. Executive order on preventing and combating discrimination on the basis of gender identity or sexual orientation. The White House January 20.

Biggs, M. 2020. Puberty blockers and suicidality in adolescents suffering from gender dysphoria. *Archives of Sexual Behavior* 49: 2227–9.

———. 2022a. The Dutch protocol for juvenile transsexuals: origins and evidence. *Journal of Sex & Marital Therapy.* doi: 10.1080/0092623X.2022.2121238.

———. 2022b. Suicide by clinic-referred transgender adolescents in the United Kingdom. *Archives of Sexual Behavior* 51: 685–90.

Billot, J. 2023. Publisher to retract paper on 'Rapid onset gender dysphoria'. *UnHerd* 24 May. https://unherd.com/thepost/publisher-to-retract-paper-on-rapid-onset-gender-dysphoria/.

Bissinger, B. 2015. Caitlyn Jenner: the full story. *Vanity Fair* June 25. www

.vanityfair.com/hollywood/2015/06/caitlyn-jenner-bruce-cover-annie-leibovitz.

Blackall, M. 2020. Twitter closes Graham Linehan account after trans comment. *The Guardian* June 27. www.theguardian.com/culture/2020/jun/27/twitter-closes-graham-linehan-account-after-trans-comment.

Blackless, M., A. Charuvastra, A. Derryck, A. Fausto-Sterling, K. Lauzanne, and E. Lee. 2000. How sexually dimorphic are we? Review and synthesis. *American Journal of Human Biology* 12: 151–66.

Blanchard, R. 1989a. The classification and labeling of nonhomosexual gender dysphorias. *Archives of Sexual Behavior* 18: 315–34.

———. 1989b. The concept of autogynephilia and the typology of male gender dysphoria. *Journal of Nervous and Mental Disease* 177: 616–23.

———. 1991. Clinical observations and systematic studies of autogynephilia. *Journal of Sex & Marital Therapy* 17: 235–51.

———. 1993a. Partial versus complete autogynephilia and gender dysphoria. *Journal of Sex & Marital Therapy* 19: 301–7.

———. 1993b. The she-male phenomenon and the concept of partial autogynephilia. *Journal of Sex & Marital Therapy* 19: 69–76.

———. 1993c. Varieties of autogynephilia and their relationship to gender dysphoria. *Archives of Sexual Behavior* 22: 241–51.

———. 2005. Early history of the concept of autogynephilia. *Archives of Sexual Behavior* 34: 439–46.

———. 2008. Deconstructing the feminine essence narrative. *Archives of Sexual Behavior* 37: 434–8.

———. 2018. Fraternal birth order, family size, and male homosexuality: meta-analysis of studies spanning 25 years. *Archives of Sexual Behavior* 47: 1–15.

Blanchard, R., and S. J. Hucker. 1991. Age, transvestism, bondage, and concurrent paraphilic activities in 117 fatal cases of autoerotic asphyxia. *British Journal of Psychiatry* 159: 371–7.

Blaxter, T. 2021. Letter to the editor. *The Times* October 17. www.thetimes.co.uk/article/we-will-not-bow-to-trans-activist-bullies-on-campus-5hb6sjxc6.

Bloom, A. 2002. *Normal: Transsexual CEOs, Crossdressing Cops, and Hermaphrodites with Attitude*. New York: Vintage.

Boehm, C. 1999. *Hierarchy in the Forest: The Evolution of Egalitarian Behavior*. Cambridge, MA: Harvard University Press.

Bogardus, T. 2020. Evaluating arguments for the sex/gender distinction. *Philosophia* 48: 873–92.

———. 2022. Why the trans inclusion problem cannot be solved. *Philosophia* 50: 1639–64.

Boleli, I. C., Z. L. Paulino-Simões, and M. M. Gentile Bitondi. 1999. Cell death in ovarioles causes permanent sterility in *Frieseomelitta varia* worker bees. *Journal of Morphology* 242: 271–82.

Bollinger, A. 2021. Judith Butler calls out transphobia as 'one of the dominant strains of fascism in our times'. *LGBTQ Nation* September 7. www.lgbtqnation.com/2021/09/judith-butler-calls-transphobia-one-dominant-strains-fascism-times/.

Bossen, L., and H. Gates. 2017. *Bound Feet, Young Hands: Tracking the Demise of Footbinding in Village China*. Stanford, CA: Stanford University Press.

Bouman, W. P., A. S. Schwend, J. Motmans, A. Smiley, J. D. Safer, M. B. Deutsch, N. J. Adams, and S. Winter. 2017. Language and trans health. *International Journal of Transgenderism* 18: 1–6.

Boylan, J. F. 2019. Coming out as trans isn't a teenage fad. *New York Times* January 8. www.nytimes.com/2019/01/08/opinion/trans-teen-transition.html.

———. 2021. Abortion rights and trans rights are two sides of the same coin. *New York Times* October 10. www.nytimes.com/2021/10/10/opinion/trans-abortion-rights.html.

Bradley, S. J., and K. J. Zucker. 2003. Reply to Pickstone-Taylor. *Journal of the American Academy of Child and Adolescent Psychiatry* 42: 266–8.

Bradley, S. J., G. D. Oliver, A. B. Chernick, and K. J. Zucker. 1998. Experiment of nurture: ablatio penis at 2 months, sex reassignment at 7 months, and a psychosexual follow-up in young adulthood. *Pediatrics* 102: 1–5.

Breslow, J. 2022. They would have transitioned me: third conditional TERF grammar of trans childhood. *Feminist Theory* 23: 575–93.

Brison, S. J. 2003. Beauvoir and feminism: interview and reflections. *The Cambridge Companion to Simone de Beauvoir*, ed. C. Card. Cambridge: Cambridge University Press.

Brooks, W. K. 1883. *The Law of Heredity: A Study of the Cause of Variation and the Origin of Living Organisms*. Baltimore: J. Murphy.

Brown, D. E. 1991. *Human Universals*. New York: McGraw Hill.

Brown University. 2018. Brown researcher first to describe rapid-onset gender dysphoria. *ScienMag* August 23. https://scienmag.com/brown-researcher-first-to-describe-rapid-onset-gender-dysphoria/.

Browne, K. R. 2023. The disjunction between evolutionary psychology and sex-discrimination law and policy. *Evolution and Human Behavior.* doi: 10.1016/j.evolhumbehav.2023.01.010.

Brubaker, R. 2016. *Trans: Gender and Race in an Age of Unsettled Identities.* Princeton, NJ: Princeton University Press.

Brunskell-Evans, H. 2021. Immaterial girls: a critical review of Kathleen Stock's *Material Girls. Savage Minds* July 2. https://savageminds.substack.com/p/immaterial-girls.

Buhrich, N., and N. McConaghy. 1978. Two clinically discrete syndromes of transsexualism. *British Journal of Psychiatry* 133: 73–6.

Bullough, V. L. 1991. Transvestism: a reexamination. *John Money: A Tribute*, ed. E. Coleman. New York: Haworth Press.

Bunce, P. 2017. Transformed: the Credit Suisse director known as Pippa and Philip. *Financial News* September 27. https://bit.ly/3kVtkLh.

Burns, C. 1997. Rich man, poor man, transsexual woman. *Press for Change* April.

———. (ed.) 2018. *Trans Britain: Our Journey from the Shadows.* London: Unbound.

Burr, V. 2015. *Social Constructionism.* New York: Routledge.

Buss, D. M. 2019. *Evolutionary Psychology: The New Science of the Mind.* London: Routledge.

Butler, J. 1986. Sex and gender in Simone de Beauvoir's *Second Sex. Yale French Studies* 72: 35–49.

———. 1988. Performative acts and gender constitution: an essay in phenomenology and feminist theory. *Theatre Journal* 40: 519–31.

———. 1990a. Gender trouble, feminist theory, and psychoanalytic discourse. *Feminism/Postmodernism*, ed. L. Nicholson. London: Routledge.

———. 1990b. *Gender Trouble: Feminism and the Subversion of Identity.* London: Routledge.

———. 1993. *Bodies That Matter: On the Discursive Limits of 'Sex'.* London: Routledge.

———. 1995. Contingent foundations. *Feminist Contentions: A Philosophical Exchange*, S. Benhabib, J. Butler, D. Cornell and N. Fraser. New York: Routledge.

———. 2004. *Undoing Gender.* London: Routledge.

———. 2019. Judith Butler: the backlash against 'gender ideology' must stop. *New Statesman* January 21.

———. 2021. Why is the idea of 'gender' provoking backlash the world over? *The Guardian* October 23. www.theguardian.com/us-news/commentisfree/2021/oct/23/judith-butler-gender-ideology-backlash.

Butler, J., and O. Jones. 2021. Feminist icon Judith Butler on JK Rowling, trans rights, feminism and intersectionality. YouTube January 1. https://youtu.be/tXJb2eLNJZE.

Butler, J., P. Osborne, and L. Segal. 1994. Gender as performance: an interview with Judith Butler. *Radical Philosophy* 67: 32–9.

Byers, E. S., K. M. Goldsmith, and A. Miller. 2016. If given the choice, would you choose to be a man or a woman? *Canadian Journal of Human Sexuality* 25: 148–57.

Byne, W. 2010. The sexed and gendered brain. *Principles of Gender-Specific Medicine*, ed. M. J. Legato. Amsterdam: Academic Press.

Byrne, A. 2020. Are women adult human females? *Philosophical Studies* 177: 3783–803.

———. 2021. Gender muddle: reply to Dembroff. *Journal of Controversial Ideas* 1: 1–24.

———. 2022a. The female of the species: reply to Heartsilver. *Journal of Controversial Ideas* 2: 1–22.

———. 2022b. Appendix to 'The female of the species: reply to Heartsilver'. https://bit.ly/35HeKjf.

Cadet, P. 2011. Androgen insensitivity syndrome with male sex-of-living. *Archives of Sexual Behavior* 40: 1101–2.

———. 2023. Characteristics of intersex pretenders. Manuscript.

Cadet, P., and M. D. Feldman. 2012. Pretense of a paradox: factitious intersex conditions on the internet. *International Journal of Sexual Health* 24: 91–6.

Cahill, L. 2019. Denying the neuroscience of sex differences. *Quillette* March 29. https://quillette.com/2019/03/29/denying-the-neuroscience-of-sex-differences/.

Callens, N., M. Van Kuyk, J. H. van Kuppenveld, S. L. Drop, P. T. Cohen-Kettenis, A. B. Dessens, and Dutch Study Group on DSD. 2016. Recalled and current gender role behavior, gender identity and sexual orientation in adults with disorders/differences of sex development. *Hormones and Behavior* 86: 8–20.

Campbell, A. 1999. Staying alive: evolution, culture, and women's intrasexual aggression. *Behavioral and Brain Sciences* 22: 203–14.

———. 2013. *A Mind of Her Own: The Evolutionary Psychology of Women.* Oxford: Oxford University Press.

Cantor, J. M. 2012. Is homosexuality a paraphilia? The evidence for and against. *Archives of Sexual Behavior* 41: 237–47.

Carmona, F. D., M. Motokawa, M. Tokita, K. Tsuchiya, R. Jiménez, and M. R. Sánchez-Villagra. 2008. The evolution of female mole ovotestes evidences high plasticity of mammalian gonad development. *Journal of Experimental Zoology Part B: Molecular and Developmental Evolution* 310: 259–66.

Caruso, J. P., and J. P. Sheehan. 2017. Psychosurgery, ethics, and media: a history of Walter Freeman and the lobotomy. *Neurosurgical Focus* 43: E6.

CBC. 2016. Genders, rights and freedom of speech. *The Agenda with Steve Paikin* October 26. https://youtu.be/kasiovoytEc.

Chambers, C. 2015. Judith Butler, *Gender Trouble. The Oxford Handbook of Classics in Contemporary Political Theory*, ed. J. T. Levy. Oxford: Oxford University Press.

Cheuvront, S. N., R. Carter, K. C. DeRuisseau, and R. J. Moffatt. 2005. Running performance differences between men and women. *Sports Medicine* 35: 1017–24.

Chivers, M. L., and J. M. Bailey. 2000. Sexual orientation of female-to-male transsexuals: a comparison of homosexual and nonhomosexual types. *Archives of Sexual Behavior* 29: 259–78.

Choudhury, A., C. Edwards, and M. V. McArthur. 2021. *Maya Forstater* v *CGD Europe, Centre for Global Development, Masood Ahmed.* Appeal Number: UKEAT/0105/20/JOJ. Employment Appeal Tribunal June 10.

Chu, A. L. 2019. *Females.* London: Verso.

Clark, B. A., A. Virani, D. Ehrensaft, and J. Olson-Kennedy. 2019. Resisting the post-truth era: maintaining a commitment to science and social justice in bioethics. *American Journal of Bioethics* 19: W1–W3.

Clark, M. 2015. *Nietzsche on Ethics and Politics.* Oxford: Oxford University Press.

Clutton-Brock, T. 2007. Sexual selection in males and females. *Science* 318: 1882–5.

Clutton-Brock, T. H., and G. A. Parker. 1992. Potential reproductive rates and the operation of sexual selection. *Quarterly Review of Biology* 67: 437–56.

Cohen-Kettenis, P. T. 2005. Gender change in 46,XY persons with 5α-reductase-2 deficiency and 17β-hydroxysteroid dehydrogenase-3 deficiency. *Archives of Sexual Behavior* 34: 399–410.

Cohen-Kettenis, P. T., and S. H. van Goozen. 1998. Pubertal delay as an aid in diagnosis and treatment of a transsexual adolescent. *European Child & Adolescent Psychiatry* 7: 246–8.

Cohen-Kettenis, P. T., S. E. E. Schagen, T. D. Steensma, A. L. C. de Vries, and H. A. Delemarre-van de Waal. 2011. Puberty suppression in a gender-dysphoric adolescent: a 22-year follow-up. *Archives of Sexual Behavior* 40: 843–7.

Colapinto, J. 2006. *As Nature Made Him: The Boy Who Was Raised as a Girl.* New York: Harper Perennial.

Colarossi, A. 1999. Nancy Hunt Bowman, ex-reporter. *Chicago Tribune* July 11. www.chicagotribune.com/news/ct-xpm-1999-07-11-9907110279-story.html.

Coldwell, W. 2015. Buck Angel: 'The man with a pussy'. *Dazed* December 30. https://bit.ly/3XOBoMq.

Coleman, E., W. O. Bockting, and L. Gooren. 1993. Homosexual and bisexual identity in sex-reassigned female-to-male transsexuals. *Archives of Sexual Behavior* 22: 37–50.

Coleman, E., A. E. Radix, W. P. Bouman, G. R. Brown, A. L. C. de Vries, M. B. Deutsch, R. Ettner, L. Fraser, M. Goodman, J. Green, A. B. Hancock, T. W. Johnson, D. H. Karasic, G. A. Knudson, S. F. Leibowitz, H. F. L. Meyer-Bahlburg, S. J. Monstrey, J. Motmans, L. Nahata, T. O. Nieder, S. L. Reisner, C. Richards, L. S. Schechter, V. Tangpricha, A. C. Tishelman, M. A. A. Van Trotsenburg, S. Winter, K. Ducheny, N. J. Adams, T. M. Adrián, L. R. Allen, D. Azul, H. Bagga, K. Başar, D. S. Bathory, J. J. Belinky, D. R. Berg, J. U. Berli, R. O. Bluebond-Langner, M. B. Bouman, M. L. Bowers, P. J. Brassard, J. Byrne, L. Capitán, C. J. Cargill, J. M. Carswell, S. C. Chang, G. Chelvakumar, T. Corneil, K. B. Dalke, G. De Cuypere, E. de Vries, M. Den Heijer, A. H. Devor, C. Dhejne, A. D'Marco, E. K. Edmiston, L. Edwards-Leeper, R. Ehrbar, D. Ehrensaft, J. Eisfeld, E. Elaut, L. Erickson-Schroth, J. L. Feldman, A. D. Fisher, M. M. Garcia, L. Gijs, S. E. Green, B. P. Hall, T. L. D. Hardy, M. S. Irwig, L. A. Jacobs, A. C. Janssen, K. Johnson, D. T. Klink, B. P. C. Kreukels, L. E. Kuper, E. J. Kvach, M. A. Malouf, R. Massey, T. Mazur, C. McLachlan, S. D. Morrison, S. W. Mosser, P. M. Neira, U. Nygren,

J. M. Oates, J. Obedin-Maliver, G. Pagkalos, J. Patton, N. Phanuphak, K. Rachlin, T. Reed, G. N. Rider, J. Ristori, S. Robbins-Cherry, S. A. Roberts, K. A. Rodriguez-Wallberg, S. M. Rosenthal, K. Sabir, J. D. Safer, A. I. Scheim, L. J. Seal, T. J. Sehoole, K. Spencer, C. St. Amand, T. D. Steensma, J. F. Strang, G. B. Taylor, K. Tilleman, G. G. T'Sjoen, L. N. Vala, N. M. Van Mello, J. F. Veale, J. A. Vencill, B. Vincent, L. M. Wesp, M. A. West, and J. Arcelus. 2022. Standards of care for the health of transgender and gender diverse people, version 8. *International Journal of Transgender Health* 23: S1–259.

Collier, J. F., and M. Z. Rosaldo. 1981. Politics and gender in simple societies. *Sexual Meanings: The Cultural Construction of Gender and Sexuality*, ed. S. B. Ortner and H. Whitehead. Cambridge: Cambridge University Press.

Congress.gov. 2021. H.R.5 – Equality Act. www.congress.gov/bill/117th-congress/house-bill/5/text.

Cook, J. 1893. *Captain Cook's Journal*, ed. W. J. L. Wharton. London: Elliot Stock.

The Core Writing Team, R. K. Pachauri, and L. Meyer. (eds) 2014. *Climate Change 2014: Synthesis Report*. Geneva, Switzerland: IPCC.

Costa, A. B. 2019. Formal comment on: parent reports of adolescents and young adults perceived to show signs of a rapid onset of gender dysphoria. *PLOS One* 14: 1–3.

Coyne, J. A. 2004. Charm schools. *Times Literary Supplement* July 30: 5.

Cramer, M. 2022. How women's sports teams got their start. *New York Times* April 28. www.nytimes.com/2022/04/28/sports/title-ix-anniversary-womens-sports.html.

Crisp, Q. 1968/1997. *The Naked Civil Servant*. London: Penguin.

———. 2017. *The Last Word: An Autobiography*. San Diego: MB Books.

Cudd, A. E. 2012. Resistance is (not) futile: analytical feminism's relation to political philosophy. *Out from the Shadows: Analytical Feminist Contributions to Traditional Philosophy*, ed. S. L. Crasnow and A. M. Superson. Oxford: Oxford University Press.

Culpepper, C. 2021. New Zealand weightlifter Laurel Hubbard makes Olympic history as a transgender athlete. *Washington Post* August 2. www.washingtonpost.com/sports/olympics/2021/08/02/laurel-hubbard-transgender-olympics-weightlifter/.

Cummins, I., M. Foley, and M. King. 2019. *Serial Killers and the Media: The Moors Murders Legacy*. Cham, Switzerland: Palgrave Macmillan.

Daly, M., and M. Wilson. 1988. *Homicide*. London: Routledge.

Darwin, C. 1871/2004. *The Descent of Man, and Selection in Relation to Sex*. London: Penguin.

Davis, G. 2015. *Contesting Intersex*. New York: New York University Press.

Davis, L. S. 2020. *Tomboy: The Surprising History and Future of Girls Who Dare to Be Different*. New York: Hachette.

———. 2022. A trans pioneer explains her resignation from the US Professional Association for Transgender Health. *Quillette* January 6. https://quillette.com/2022/01/06/a-transgender-pioneer-explains-why-she-stepped-down-from-uspath-and-wpath/.

Dawkins, R. 1976/2016. *The Selfish Gene*. Oxford: Oxford University Press.

———. 2022. Race is a spectrum. Sex is pretty damn binary. *Areo* May 1. https://areomagazine.com/2022/01/05/race-is-a-spectrum-sex-is-pretty-damn-binary/.

Dawson, S. J., B. A. Bannerman, and M. L. Lalumière. 2016. Paraphilic interests: an examination of sex differences in a nonclinical sample. *Sexual Abuse* 28: 20–45.

de Vries, A. L. C., and P. T. Cohen-Kettenis. 2012. Clinical management of gender dysphoria in children and adolescents: the Dutch approach. *Journal of Homosexuality* 59: 301–20.

de Vries, A. L. C., T. F. Beek, K. Dhondt, H. C. W. de Vet, P. T. Cohen-Kettenis, T. D. Steensma, and B. P. C. Kreukels. 2021. Reliability and clinical utility of gender identity-related diagnoses: comparisons between the ICD-11, ICD-10, DSM-IV, and DSM-5. *LGBT Health* 8: 133–42.

Dea, S. 2016. *Beyond the Binary: Thinking about Sex and Gender*. Peterborough, Ontario: Broadview Press.

Deeb, A., C. Mason, Y. Lee, and I. Hughes. 2005. Correlation between genotype, phenotype and sex of rearing in 111 patients with partial androgen insensitivity syndrome. *Clinical Endocrinology* 63: 56–62.

Del Giudice, M. 2023. Ideological bias in the psychology of sex and gender. *Ideological and Political Bias in Psychology: Nature, Scope, and Solutions*, ed. C. L. Frisby, R. E. Redding, W. T. O'Donohue, and S. O. Lilienfeld. Cham, Switzerland: Springer.

Del Giudice, M., T. Booth, and P. Irwing. 2012. The distance between Mars and Venus: measuring global sex differences in personality. *PLOS One* 7: 1–8.

Del Giudice, M., R. A. Lippa, D. A. Puts, D. H. Bailey, J. M. Bailey, and

D. P. Schmitt. 2016. Joel et al.'s method systematically fails to detect large, consistent sex differences. *Proceedings of the National Academy of Sciences* 113: E1965.

Dembroff, R. 2019. Moving beyond mismatch. *American Journal of Bioethics* 19: 60–3.

———. 2021. Escaping the natural attitude about gender. *Philosophical Studies* 178: 983–1003.

Dembroff, R., R. Kukla, and S. Stryker. 2019. Retraction statement by Robin Dembroff, Rebecca Kukla and Susan Stryker. *IAI News* August 26. https://iai.tv/articles/retraction-statement-by-robin-dembroff-rebecca-kukla-and-susan-stryker-auid-1256.

Descartes, R. 1642/1984. Meditations on first philosophy. *The Philosophical Writings of Descartes*, ed. J. Cottingham, R. Stoorthoff, and D. Murdoch. Cambridge: Cambridge University Press.

Devor, A. 2016. *FTM: Female-to-Male Transsexuals in Society*. Bloomington: Indiana University Press.

DeVun, L. 2021. *The Shape of Sex: Nonbinary Gender from Genesis to the Renaissance*. New York: Columbia University Press.

Dhejne, C., P. Lichtenstein, M. Boman, A. L. Johansson, N. Långström, and M. Landén. 2011. Long-term follow-up of transsexual persons undergoing sex reassignment surgery: cohort study in Sweden. *PLOS One* 6: 1–8.

Diamond, M. 2002. Sex and gender are different: sexual identity and gender identity are different. *Clinical Child Psychology and Psychiatry* 7: 320–34.

Diaz, S., and J. M. Bailey. 2023. Rapid onset gender dysphoria: parent reports on 1655 possible cases. *Archives of Sexual Behavior*. doi: 10.1007/s10508-023-02576-9 [This paper was subsequently considered for retraction by the publisher for reasons unrelated to its scientific validity; see Billot 2023].

Dickey, R., and J. Stephens. 1995. Female-to-male transsexualism, heterosexual type: two cases. *Archives of Sexual Behavior* 24: 439–45.

Doležal, R., and S. Reback. 2017. *In Full Color: Finding My Place in a Black and White World*. Dallas, TX: BenBella Books.

Dorr, C. 2016. To be F is to be G. *Philosophical Perspectives* 30: 39–134.

Downing, L., I. Morland, and N. Sullivan. 2015. *Fuckology: Critical Essays on John Money's Diagnostic Concepts*. Chicago: University of Chicago Press.

Dreger, A. D. 1998. *Hermaphrodites and the Medical Invention of Sex*. Cambridge, MA: Harvard University Press.

———. 2008. The controversy surrounding *The Man Who Would Be Queen*:

a case history of the politics of science, identity, and sex in the internet age. *Archives of Sexual Behavior* 37: 366–421.

———. 2015. *Galileo's Middle Finger: Heretics, Activists, and One Scholar's Search for Justice*. New York: Penguin.

Du Preez, M., and J. Dronfield. 2016. *Dr James Barry: A Woman ahead of Her Time*. London: OneWorld.

Dua, A. 2010. Apotemnophilia: ethical considerations of amputating a healthy limb. *Journal of Medical Ethics* 36: 75–8.

Duffy, N. 2018. 'Trans women are women, get over it!' Stonewall takes on anti-trans rhetoric. *Pink News* September 20. www.pinknews.co.uk/2018/09/20/stonewall-tshirts-trans-women-are-women-get-over-it/.

Dupré, J. 1986. Sex, gender, and essence. *Midwest Studies in Philosophy* 11: 441–57.

———. 2001. *Human Nature and the Limits of Science*. Oxford: Oxford University Press.

Dworkin, A. 1974. *Woman Hating*. New York: Plume.

Eagly, A. H., and A. Mladinic. 1994. Are people prejudiced against women? Some answers from research on attitudes, gender stereotypes, and judgments of competence. *European Review of Social Psychology* 5: 1–35.

Ebert, J. 2005. Cuttlefish win mates with transvestite antics. *Nature* January 19.

Eckert, A. J. 2021. Irreversible damage to the trans community: a critical review of Abigail Shrier's *Irreversible Damage* (part one). *Science-Based Medicine* July 4. https://sciencebasedmedicine.org/irreversible-damage-to-the-trans-community-a-critical-review-of-abigail-shriers-book-irreversible-damage-part-one/.

The Economist. 2018. Why are so many teenage girls appearing in gender clinics? *The Economist* September 1.

———. 2020. Cold comforts – our books of the year. *The Economist* December 3.

Edgerton, R. B. 1964. Pokot intersexuality: an East African example of the resolution of sexual incongruity. *American Anthropologist* 66: 1288–99.

Editors of Lingua Franca. (ed.) 2000. *The Sokal Hoax: The Sham That Shook the Academy*. Lincoln: University of Nebraska Press.

Edwards-Leeper, L., and E. Anderson. 2021. The mental health establishment is failing trans kids. *Washington Post* November 24. www.washingtonpost.com/outlook/2021/11/24/trans-kids-therapy-psychologist/.

Ehrensaft, D. 2011. *Gender Born, Gender Made: Raising Healthy Gender-Nonconforming Children*. New York: The Experiment.

———. 2014. Found in transition: our littlest transgender people. *Contemporary Psychoanalysis* 50: 571–92.

———. 2016. *The Gender Creative Child: Pathways for Nurturing and Supporting Children Who Live Outside Gender Boxes*. New York: The Experiment.

———. 2017a. Declaration of Diane Ehrensaft, Ph.D. United States District Court for the Middle District of Florida, Jacksonville Division No. 3:17-cv-00739-TJC-JBT.

———. 2017b. Gender nonconforming youth: current perspectives. *Adolescent Health, Medicine and Therapeutics* 8: 57–67.

Eliot, L. 2019. Neurosexism: the myth that men and women have different brains. *Nature* 566: 453–4.

Elliott, C. 2000. A new way to be mad. *The Atlantic* September. www.theatlantic.com/magazine/archive/2000/12/a-new-way-to-be-mad/304671/.

Ellis, H. 1937. *Studies in the Psychology of Sex*. Vol. 2. New York: Random House.

———. 1938. *Psychology of Sex*. New York: Emerson Books.

Epstein, J. 1990. Either/or – neither/both: sexual ambiguity and the ideology of gender. *Genders* 7: 99–142.

Erickson-Schroth, L., and B. Davis. 2021. *Gender: What Everyone Needs to Know*. New York: Oxford University Press.

Eriugena, J. S. 866–7/1987. *Periphyseon*. Trans. I. P. Sheldon-Williams and J. J. O'Meara. Montreal: Bellarmin.

EWHC. 2020. *Bell* v. *Tavistock*. 3274 (Admin) Case No: CO/60/2020.

Fang, B., F. Cho, and W. Lam. 2013. Prostate gland development and adrenal tumor in a female with congenital adrenal hyperplasia: a case report and review from radiology perspective. *Journal of Radiology Case Reports* 7: 21–34.

Fast, A. A., and K. R. Olson. 2018. Gender development in transgender preschool children. *Child Development* 89: 620–37.

Fausto-Sterling, A. 1985/1992. *Myths of Gender: Biological Theories about Women and Men*. New York: Basic Books.

———. 1993a. The five sexes: why male and female are not enough. *The Sciences* March/April: 20–4.

———. 1993b. How many sexes are there? *New York Times* March 12. www.nytimes.com/1993/03/12/opinion/how-many-sexes-are-there.html.

———. 1993c. Replies. *The Sciences* July/August: 4.

———. 2000a. The five sexes, revisited. *The Sciences* July/August: 19–23.

———. 2000b. *Sexing the Body: Gender Politics and the Construction of Sexuality*. New York: Basic Books.

———. 2012. *Sex/Gender: Biology in a Social World*. London: Routledge.

———. 2018. Why sex is not binary. *New York Times* October 25. www.nytimes.com/2018/10/25/opinion/sex-biology-binary.html.

———. 2020a. Science won't settle trans rights. *Boston Review* February 10. https://bostonreview.net/science-nature-gender-sexuality/anne-fausto-sterling-science-wont-settle-trans-rights.

———. 2020b. *Sexing the Body: Gender Politics and the Construction of Sexuality*. 2nd edn, New York: Basic Books.

Faye, S. 2021. *The Transgender Issue: An Argument for Justice*. London: Allen Lane.

Fedoroff, J. P. 2020. *The Paraphilias: Changing Suits in the Evolution of Sexual Interest Paradigms*. New York: Oxford University Press.

Feinbloom, D. H. 1976. *Transvestites and Transsexuals*. New York: Delacorte Press.

FeldmanHall, O., T. Dalgleish, D. Evans, L. Navrady, E. Tedeschi, and D. Mobbs. 2016. Moral chivalry: gender and harm sensitivity predict costly altruism. *Social Psychological and Personality Science* 7: 542–51.

Fénichel, P., F. Paris, P. Philibert, S. Hiéronimus, L. Gaspari, J.-Y. Kurzenne, P. Chevallier, S. Bermon, N. Chevalier, and C. Sultan. 2013. Molecular diagnosis of 5α-reductase deficiency in 4 elite young female athletes through hormonal screening for hyperandrogenism. *Journal of Clinical Endocrinology & Metabolism* 98: E1055–9.

Ferber, A. 2020. Judith Butler on the culture wars, JK Rowling and living in 'anti-intellectual times'. *New Statesman* September 22. www.newstatesman.com/uncategorized/2020/09/judith-butler-culture-wars-jk-rowling-and-living-anti-intellectual-times.

Fine, C. 2017. *Testosterone Rex: Myths of Sex, Science, and Society*. New York: Norton.

———. 2018. Feminist science: who needs it? *The Lancet* 392: 1302–3.

———. 2020. Constructing unnecessary barriers to constructive scientific debate: a response to Buss and von Hippel (2018). *Archives of Scientific Psychology* 8: 5–10.

Firestone, S. 1971. *The Dialectic of Sex: The Case for Feminist Revolution*. New York: Bantam. Original edn, 1970.

Flanagan, N., G. Mufti, and V. Sen. 2021. Dr Adrian Harrop. *Medical Practioners Tribunal Service* November 30.

Flier, J. S. 2018. As a former dean of Harvard Medical School, I question Brown's failure to defend Lisa Littman. *Quillette* August 31. https://quillette.com/2018/08/31/as-a-former-dean-of-harvard-medical-school-i-question-browns-failure-to-defend-lisa-littman/.

Fodor, J. 1998. *Concepts: Where Cognitive Science Went Wrong*. Oxford: Oxford University Press.

Folk, J. 2022. *What is a Woman?* www.imdb.com/title/tt20256528/.

Fonseca, S. 2021. The constitutional conflationists: on Abigail Shrier's 'Irreversible Damage' and the dangerous absurdity of anti-trans trolls. *Los Angeles Review of Books* January 17. https://lareviewofbooks.org/article/the-constitutional-conflationists-on-abigail-shriers-irreversible-damage-and-the-dangerous-absurdity-of-anti-trans-trolls/.

Forcier, M., G. V. Schalkwyk, and J. L. Turban. 2020. *Pediatric Gender Identity: Gender-Affirming Care for Transgender & Gender Diverse Youth*. Cham, Switzerland: Springer.

Foucault, M. 1978/1990. *The History of Sexuality*, Vol. 1: *An Introduction*. New York: Vintage.

———. 2010. *Herculine Barbin: Being the Recently Discovered Memoirs of a Nineteenth-Century French Hermaphrodite*. New York: Vintage.

Fox, T. 2019. A butch eradication, served with a progressive smile. *AfterEllen* April 26. https://bit.ly/3x5aJk4.

Frayer, D. W., and M. H. Wolpoff. 1985. Sexual dimorphism. *Annual Review of Anthropology* 14: 429–73.

Freund, K. 1985. Cross-gender identity in a broader context. *Gender Dysphoria*, ed. B. W. Steiner. New York: Plenum Press.

Freund, K., and R. Blanchard. 1993. Erotic target location errors in male gender dysphorics, paedophiles, and fetishists. *British Journal of Psychiatry* 162: 558–63.

Friedman, M. 1991. Reclaiming the sex/gender distinction. *Noûs* 25: 200–1.

———. 1996. The unholy alliance of sex and gender. *Metaphilosophy* 27: 78–91.

Friedrich, W. N., J. Fisher, D. Broughton, M. Houston, and C. R. Shafran.

1998. Normative sexual behavior in children: a contemporary sample. *Pediatrics* 101: 1–8.

Frieze, I. H., and J. C. Chrisler. 2011. Editorial policy on the use of the terms 'sex' and 'gender'. *Sex Roles* 64: 789–90.

Fukuyama, F. 2020. *Identity: The Demand for Dignity and the Politics of Resentment*. New York: Farrar, Straus & Giroux.

Geary, D. C. 2021. *Male, Female: The Evolution of Human Sex Differences*. Washington, DC: American Psychological Association.

George, B., and S. Bright. 1995. *Take it Like a Man*. New York: HarperCollins.

George, B. R., and S. Goguen. 2021. Hermeneutical backlash: trans youth panics as epistemic injustice. *Feminist Philosophy Quarterly* 7: 1–34.

George, B. R., and D. M. Wenner. 2019. Puberty-blocking treatment and the rights of bad candidates. *American Journal of Bioethics* 19: 80–2.

German, A., and Z. Hochberg. 2020. Sexual dimorphism of size ontogeny and life history. *Frontiers in Pediatrics* 8: 387.

Gheaus, A. 2023. Feminism without 'gender identity'. *Politics, Philosophy & Economics* 22: 31–54.

Gibb, L. 2014. *The Extraordinary Life of Rebecca West*. Berkeley, CA: Counterpoint.

Gill-Peterson, J. 2018. *Histories of the Transgender Child*. Minneapolis: University of Minnesota Press.

GLAAD. 2020. *Covering LGBTQ Athletes at the 2020 Olympics and Paralympics*. www.glaad.org/sites/default/files/GLAADOlympicsMediaGuide.pdf.

Glander, K. E., P. C. Wright, D. S. Seigler, V. Randrianasolo, and B. Randrianasolo. 1989. Consumption of cyanogenic bamboo by a newly discovered species of bamboo lemur. *American Journal of Primatology* 19: 119–24.

Glenday, C. (ed.) 2022. *Guinness World Records*. www.guinnessworldrecords.com.

Goddard, C., and A. Wierzbicka. 2013. *Words and Meanings: Lexical Semantics across Domains, Languages, and Cultures*. Oxford: Oxford University Press.

Goldberg, S. 1973. *The Inevitability of Patriarchy*. New York: William Morrow.

———. 1993. *Why Men Rule: A Theory of Male Dominance*. Chicago: Open Court.

———. 2003. *Fads and Fallacies in the Social Sciences*. New York: Humanity Books.

Goldie, T. 2014. *The Man Who Invented Gender: Engaging the Ideas of John Money*. Vancouver: UBC Press.

Gómez Jiménez, F. R., L. Court, and P. L. Vasey. 2020. A retrospective study of childhood sex-typed behavior in Istmo Zapotec men, women, and *muxes*. *Archives of Sexual Behavior* 49: 467–77.

Gooren, L., and H. Delemarre-van de Waal. 1996. The feasibility of endocrine interventions in juvenile transsexuals. *Journal of Psychology & Human Sexuality* 8: 69–74.

Gorer, G. 1936/1986. *Bali and Angkor: A 1930s Pleasure Trip Looking at Life and Death*. Oxford: Oxford University Press.

Gosink, P. D., and M. I. Jumbelic. 2000. Autoerotic asphyxiation in a female. *American Journal of Forensic Medicine and Pathology* 21: 114–18.

Gowaty, P. A. 2004. Sex roles, contests for the control of reproduction, and sexual selection. *Sexual Selection in Primates: New and Comparative Perspectives*, ed. P. M. Kappeler and C. P. Van Schaik. Cambridge: Cambridge University Press.

Graves, J. A. M. 2002. Sex chromosomes and sex determination in weird mammals. *Cytogenetic and Genome Research* 96: 161–8.

Green, J. 2001. Autoandrophilia? *Transgender Tapestry* 93: 20–1.

Green, R. 1974. *Sexual Identity Conflict in Children and Adults*. New York: Basic Books.

———. 1987. *The 'Sissy Boy Syndrome' and the Development of Homosexuality*. New Haven, CT: Yale University Press.

———. 2009. The three kings: Harry Benjamin, John Money, Robert Stoller. *Archives of Sexual Behavior* 38: 610–13.

Green, R., and J. Money. (eds) 1969. *Transsexualism and Sex Reassignment*. Baltimore: Johns Hopkins University Press.

Greenberg, J. A. 1999. Defining male and female: intersexuality and the collision between law and biology. *Arizona Law Review* 41: 265–328.

Greenson, R. R. 1964. On homosexuality and gender identity. *International Journal of Psycho-Analysis* 45: 217–19.

Griffiths, S. 2021a. Autistic girls seeking answers 'are seizing on sex change'. *Sunday Times* January 9. www.thetimes.co.uk/article/autistic-girls-seeking-answers-are-seizing-on-sex-change-3r8285ogw.

———. 2021b. Kathleen Stock, the Sussex University professor in trans row, urged to get bodyguards. *The Times* October 10. www.thetimes.co.uk/article/kathleen-stock-the-sussex-university-professor-in-trans-row-urged-to-get-bodyguards-2khmgzk98.

Grosskurth, P. 1980. *Havelock Ellis: A Biography*. New York: Knopf.

Grove, J. 2020. Kathleen Stock: life on the front line of transgender rights debate. *THE* January 7. www.timeshighereducation.com/news/kathleen-stock-life-front-line-transgender-rights-debate.

GuessImAfab. 2019. Genderflux: how one young woman fell down the rapid-onset rabbit hole. *4thWaveNow* May 16. https://4thwavenow.com/2019/05/16/genderflux-how-one-young-woman-fell-down-the-rapid-onset-rabbit-hole/.

Haig, D. 2004. The inexorable rise of gender and the decline of sex: social change in academic titles, 1945–2001. *Archives of Sexual Behavior* 33: 87–96.

———. 2020. *From Darwin to Derrida: Selfish Genes, Social Selves, and the Meanings of Life*. Cambridge, MA: MIT Press.

Hakim, C. 1996. *Key Issues in Women's Work: Female Heterogeneity and the Polarisation of Women's Employment*. London: Athlone Press.

Hall, H. A. 2013. Sex, gender, and sexuality: it's complicated. *Science-Based Medicine* February 19. https://sciencebasedmedicine.org/sex-gender-and-sexuality-its-complicated/.

———. 2021a. Trans science: a review of Abigail Shrier's *Irreversible Damage: The Transgender Craze Seducing Our Daughters*. *Skeptic* June 19. www.skeptic.com/reading room/trans-science-review-of-abigail-shier-irreversible-damage-transgender-craze-seducing-our-daughters/.

———. 2021b. Gender dsyphoria in adolescents. *SkepDoc* July 13. https://bit.ly/40cA5sj.

Hamerton, J. L. 1971. *Human Cytogenetics*, Vol. II. New York: Academic Press.

Hames, R., Z. Garfield, and M. Garfield. 2017. Is male androphilia a context-dependent cross-cultural universal? *Archives of Sexual Behavior* 46: 63–71.

Harari, Y. N. 2015. *Sapiens: A Brief History of Humankind*. New York: Harper Perennial.

Harper, C. 2007. *Intersex*. New York: Berg.

Harris, J. R. 2009. *The Nurture Assumption: Why Children Turn Out the Way They Do*. New York: Free Press.

Harrop, A., and K.-J. Keen-Minshull. 2018. Woman billboard was 'transphobic' and 'dangerous'. Sky News. https://youtu.be/y8nViKYmEhU.

Haslanger, S. 2012. *Resisting Reality: Social Construction and Social Critique*. Oxford: Oxford University Press.

———. 2020. Going on, not in the same way. *Conceptual Engineering and*

Conceptual Ethics, ed. A. Burgess, H. Cappelen and D. Plunkett. Oxford: Oxford University Press.

Hausman, B. L. 1995. *Changing Sex*. Durham, NC: Duke University Press.

Hay, C. 2019. Who counts as a woman? *New York Times* April 1. www.nytimes.com/2019/04/01/opinion/trans-women-feminism.html.

———. 2020. *Think Like a Feminist: The Philosophy behind the Revolution*. New York: Norton.

Hayton, D. 2022. My autogynephilia story. *UnHerd* May 9. https://unherd.com/2022/05/the-truth-about-autogynephilia/.

Heartsilver, M. 2021. Deflating Byrne's 'Are women adult human females?'. *Journal of Controversial Ideas* 1: 1–16.

Heber, J. 2019. Correcting the scientific record on gender incongruence – and an apology. *PLOS One* March 19. https://everyone.plos.org/2019/03/19/correcting-the-scientific-record-and-an-apology/.

Hellen, N. 2019. Trans woman Debbie Hayton faces ban for transphobia. *The Times* December 22. www.thetimes.co.uk/article/trans-woman-debbie-hayton-faces-ban-for-transphobia-96tfkl5gc.

Helms, M. F. 2019. *More Than Just a Flag*. San Diego: MB Books.

Hendricks, M. 1993. Is it a boy or a girl? *Johns Hopkins Magazine* November: 10–16.

Herdt, G. (ed.) 1996. *Third Sex, Third Gender: Beyond Sexual Dimorphism in Culture and History*. New York: Zone Books.

Herlin, M. K., M. B. Petersen, and M. Brännström. 2020. Mayer-Rokitansky-Küster-Hauser (MRKH) syndrome: a comprehensive update. *Orphanet Journal of Rare Diseases* 15: 214.

Herndon, A. W. 2015. Harvard allows students to pick new gender pronouns. *Boston Globe* September 2. https://bit.ly/3WQ6faa.

Hewlett, B. S. 1992. *Intimate Fathers: The Nature and Context of Aka Pygmy Paternal Infant Care*. Ann Arbor: University of Michigan Press.

Hidalgo, M. A., D. Ehrensaft, A. C. Tishelman, L. F. Clark, R. Garofalo, S. M. Rosenthal, N. P. Spack, and J. Olson. 2013. The gender affirmative model: what we know and what we aim to learn. *Human Development* 56: 285–90.

Hines, M. 2004. *Brain Gender*. Oxford: Oxford University Press.

———. 2009. Gonadal hormones and sexual differentiation of human behavior. *Hormones, Brain and Behavior*, ed. D. W. Pfaff, A. P. Arnold, A. M. Etgen, S. E. Fahrbach and R. T. Rubin. Oxford: Academic Press.

Hines, S. 2018. *Is Gender Fluid?* London: Thames & Hudson.

———. 2020. Sex wars and (trans) gender panics: identity and body politics in contemporary UK feminism. *Sociological Review* 68: 699–717.

Hirschfeld, M. 1910/1991. *Transvestites: The Erotic Drive to Cross-Dress*. Trans. M. A. Lombardi-Nash. New York: Prometheus Books.

Holden, D. 1974. James and Jan. *New York Times* March 17.

Holter, H. 1970. *Sex Roles and Social Structure*. Oslo: Universitetsforlaget.

Hooven, C. 2021. *T: The Story of Testosterone, the Hormone That Dominates and Divides Us*. New York: Henry Holt.

Hornsey, M. J. 2008. Social identity theory and self-categorization theory: a historical review. *Social and Personality Psychology Compass* 2: 204–22.

Hrdy, S. B. 1999. *The Woman That Never Evolved*. Cambridge, MA: Harvard University Press.

Hsu, K. J. 2019. *Erotic Target Identity Inversions in Male Furries, Adult Baby/Diaper Lovers, and Eunuchs*. PhD thesis, Department of Psychology, Northwestern University.

Hsu, K. J., A. Rosenthal, D. Miller, and J. Bailey. 2016. Who are gynandromorphophilic men? Characterizing men with sexual interest in transgender women. *Psychological Medicine* 46: 819–27.

Hudson, V. M., D. L. Bowen, and P. L. Nielsen. 2020. *The First Political Order: How Sex Shapes Governance and National Security Worldwide*. New York: Columbia University Press.

Hull, C. 2003. Letter to the editor. *American Journal of Human Biology* 15: 112–16.

———. 2006. *The Ontology of Sex*. New York: Routledge.

Human Rights Campaign. 2021. 5 things to know to make your feminism trans-inclusive. https://bit.ly/3HHKGnJ.

Hunt, N. 1978. *Mirror Image*. New York: Holt, Rinehart & Winston.

Hyde, J. S. 2005. The gender similarities hypothesis. *American Psychologist* 60: 581–92.

Hyde, J. S., R. S. Bigler, D. Joel, C. C. Tate, and S. M. van Anders. 2019. The future of sex and gender in psychology: five challenges to the gender binary. *American Psychologist* 74: 171–93.

Iantaffi, A., and M.-J. Barker. 2018. *How To Understand Your Gender: A Practical Guide for Exploring Who You Are*. London: Jessica Kingsley.

Imperato-McGinley, J., L. Guerrero, T. Gautier, and R. E. Peterson. 1974. Steroid 5α-reductase deficiency in man: an inherited form of male pseudohermaphroditism. *Science* 186: 1213–15.

Jacobson, D. et al. 2021. Open letter concerning academic freedom. January 13. https://bit.ly/3jopgVU.

Jaggar, A. M. 1983. *Feminist Politics and Human Nature*. Totowa, NJ: Rowman & Allanheld.

James, A. 2022. J. Michael Bailey vs. transgender people. Transgender Map November 2. https://bit.ly/3j77DaF.

———. 2023. 'Autogynephilia': a disputed diagnosis. Transgender Map January 16. https://bit.ly/3JnXUHG.

Jarvis, E. 2022. 'Men' and 'Women' in everyday English. *Journal of Controversial Ideas* 2: 1–7.

Jaschik, S. 2017. Journal apologizes for article on 'transracialism'. *Inside Higher Ed* May 2. www.insidehighered.com/quicktakes/2017/05/02/journal-apologizes-article-transracialism.

Jeffreys, S. 2014. *Gender Hurts: A Feminist Analysis of the Politics of Transgenderism*. London: Routledge.

Jenkins, K. 2016. Amelioration and inclusion: gender identity and the concept of woman. *Ethics* 126: 394–421.

———. 2018. Toward an account of gender identity. *Ergo* 5: 713–44.

Jenner, C. 2017. *The Secrets of My Life*. New York: Grand Central.

Jennings, J. 2016. *Being Jazz: My Life as a (Transgender) Teen*. New York: Crown.

Joel, D., A. Persico, J. Hänggi, J. Pool, and Z. Berman. 2016. Reply to Del Giudice et al., Chekroud et al., and Rosenblatt: do brains of females and males belong to two distinct populations? *Proceedings of the National Academy of Sciences* 113: E1969–70.

Johnson, T. W., M. A. Brett, L. F. Roberts, and R. J. Wassersug. 2007. Eunuchs in contemporary society: characterizing men who are voluntarily castrated (part I). *Journal of Sexual Medicine* 4: 930–45.

Jorgensen, C. 1967. *Christine Jorgensen: A Personal Autobiography*. New York: Paul S. Eriksson.

Joshi, H. 2021. *Why it's OK to Speak Your Mind*. London: Routledge.

Joyal, C. C., and J. Carpentier. 2017. The prevalence of paraphilic interests and behaviors in the general population: a provincial survey. *Journal of Sex Research* 54: 161–71.

Joyce, H. 2021. *Trans: When Ideology Meets Reality*. London: OneWorld.

Jussim, L., J. T. Crawford, and R. S. Rubinstein. 2015. Stereotype (in) accuracy in perceptions of groups and individuals. *Current Directions in Psychological Science* 24: 490–7.

Kabátek, J., F. Perales, and C. Ablaza. 2021. Evidence of a fraternal birth order effect on male and female same-sex marriage in the Dutch population: a reply to Blanchard and Semenyna, Gómez Jiménez & Vasey. *Journal of Sex Research*: 1–7.

Kaltiala-Heino, R., H. Bergman, M. Työläjärvi, and L. Frisén. 2018. Gender dysphoria in adolescence: current perspectives. *Adolescent Health, Medicine and Therapeutics* 9: 31–41.

Kappeler, P. M., and C. P. Van Schaik. 2004. *Sexual Selection in Primates: New and Comparative Perspectives*. Cambridge: Cambridge University Press.

Karkazis, K. 2008. *Fixing Sex: Intersex, Medical Authority, and Lived Experience*. Durham, NC: Duke University Press.

Kates, G. 2001. *Monsieur d'Eon Is a Woman: A Tale of Political Intrigue and Sexual Masquerade*. Baltimore: Johns Hopkins University Press.

Katz, J. 1976. *Gay American History*. New York: Thomas Y. Crowell.

Katz, P. A. 1975. Sex Roles: a journal of research. *Sex Roles* 1: 1–2.

Kennedy, A. 2018. *Masterpiece Cakeshop, Ltd., et al. v. Colorado Civil Rights Commission et al.* Supreme Court of the United States 16–111.

Kennedy, P. 2007. *The First Man-Made Man: The Story of Two Sex Changes, One Love Affair, and a Twentieth-Century Medical Revolution*. New York: Bloomsbury.

Kessler, S. J. 1990. The medical construction of gender: case management of intersexed infants. *Signs* 16: 3–26.

———. 1998. *Lessons from the Intersexed*. New Brunswick, NJ: Rutgers University Press.

Kessler, S. J., and W. McKenna. 1978. *Gender: An Ethnomethodological Approach*. Chicago: University of Chicago Press.

Khorashad, B. S., Z. Aghili, B. P. C. Kreukels, M. Hiradfar, G. M. Roshan, M. Afkhamizadeh, M. R. Abbaszadegan, N. Ghaemi, B. Khazai, and P. T. Cohen-Kettenis. 2016. Psychosexual outcome among Iranian individuals with 5α-reductase deficiency type 2 and its relationship with parental sexism. *Journal of Sexual Medicine* 13: 1629–41.

Kimmel, M. (ed.) 2016. *The Gendered Society*. Oxford: Oxford University Press.

Kirby, V. 2006. *Judith Butler: Live Theory*. London: Continuum.

Kirkpatrick, K. 2019. *Becoming Beauvoir: A Life*. London: Bloomsbury Academic.

Kirkup, J. 2020. How women won the war against gender 'self-ID'. *The Spectator* September 22. www.spectator.co.uk/article/how-women-won-the-war-against-gender-self-id-.

Kirkus Reviews. 1973. Review of *The Inevitability of Patriarchy*. *Kirkus Reviews* August 1.

Krafft-Ebing, R. von 1886/2011. *Psychopathia Sexualis*. New York: Arcade.

Kripke, S. A. 1980. *Naming and Necessity*. Oxford: Blackwell.

Krob, G., A. Braun, and U. Kuhnle. 1994. True hermaphroditism: geographical distribution, clinical findings, chromosomes and gonadal histology. *European Journal of Pediatrics* 153: 2–10.

Lagunoff, R. 1997. *Singular* they. PhD thesis, Department of Linguistics, UCLA.

Lampen, C. 2020. J. K. Rowling triples down on transphobia. *The Cut* July 5. www.thecut.com/2020/07/j-k-rowling-writes-essay-defending-her-transphobic-remarks.html.

Lavery, G. 2020a. Egg theory's early style. *TSQ: Transgender Studies Quarterly* 7: 383–98.

———. 2020b. A high court decision in Britain puts trans people everywhere at risk. *Foreign Policy* December 15. https://foreignpolicy.com/2020/12/15/uk-transphobia-transgender-court-ruling-puberty-blockers/.

Lawford-Smith, H. 2019a. How the trans-rights movement is turning philosophers into activists. *Quillette* September 20. https://quillette.com/2019/09/20/how-the-trans-rights-movement-is-turning-academic-philosophers-into-sloganeering-activists/.

———. 2019b. Thinking about climate change, global justice, and trans. *3AM Magazine* March 18. Repr. at www.3-16am.co.uk/articles/thinking-about-climate-change-global-justice-and-trans.

———. 2022a. *Gender-Critical Feminism*. Oxford: Oxford University Press.

———. 2022b. Trashing & tribalism in the gender wars. *The Moral Psychology of Hate*, ed. N. Birondo. Lanham, MD: Rowman & Littlefield.

Lawrence, A. A. 1998. Men trapped in men's bodies: an introduction to the concept of autogynephilia. *Transgender Tapestry* 85: 65–8.

———. 2000. Sexuality and transsexuality: a new introduction to autogynephilia. *Transgender Tapestry* 92: 17–29.

———. 2007. Becoming what we love: autogynephilic transsexualism conceptualized as an expression of romantic love. *Perspectives in Biology and Medicine* 50: 506.

———. 2009. Anatomic autoandrophilia in an adult male. *Archives of Sexual Behavior* 38: 1050–6.

———. 2013. *Men Trapped in Men's Bodies: Narratives of Autogynephilic Transsexualism*. New York: Springer.

———. 2017. Autogynephilia and the typology of male-to-female transsexualism. *European Psychologist* 22: 39–54.

Lawrie, E. 2021. University of Sussex backs professor in free speech row. *BBC News* October 8. www.bbc.com/news/education-58841887.

Leacock, E. 1974. Review of *The Inevitability of Patriarchy*. *American Anthropologist* 76: 363–5.

Lecky, W. E. H. 1895. *History of European Morals from Augustus to Charlemagne*, Vol. II. New York: D. Appleton.

Lehmiller, J. J. 2018. *Tell Me What You Want: The Science of Sexual Desire and How it Can Help You Improve Your Sex Life*. New York: Hachette.

Lehtonen, J., and G. A. Parker. 2014. Gamete competition, gamete limitation, and the evolution of the two sexes. *Molecular Human Reproduction* 20: 1161–8.

Leiter, B. 2004. Introduction. *The Future for Philosophy*, ed. B. Leiter. Oxford: Oxford University Press.

———. 2019. Zealots working overtime now to shut down gender critical feminists. *Leiter Reports* September 19. https://leiterreports.typepad.com/blog/2019/09/zealots-working-overtime-now-to-shut-down-gender-critical-feminists.html.

Lerner, G. 1986. *The Creation of Patriarchy*. Oxford: Oxford University Press.

LeVay, S. 2017. *Gay, Straight, and the Reason Why: The Science of Sexual Orientation*. Oxford: Oxford University Press.

Li, G., K. T. F. Kung, and M. Hines. 2017. Childhood gender-typed behavior and adolescent sexual orientation: a longitudinal population-based study. *Developmental Psychology* 53: 764–77.

Liao, L.-M., P. Hegarty, S. Creighton, T. Lundberg, and K. Roen. 2019. Clitoral surgery on minors: an interview study with clinical experts of differences of sex development. *BMJ Open* 9: 1–7.

Lilla, M. 2018. *The Once and Future Liberal: After Identity Politics*. London: Hurst.

Lippa, R. A. 2005. *Gender, Nature, and Nurture*. London: Lawrence Erlbaum.

Lips, H. 2013. *Gender: The Basics*. London: Routledge.

Liptak, A. 2020. Civil rights law protects gay and transgender workers,

Supreme Court rules. *New York Times* June 15. www.nytimes.com/2020/06/15/us/gay-transgender-workers-supreme-court.html.

Littman, L. 2017. Rapid onset gender dysphoria in adolescents and young adults: a descriptive study. *Journal of Adolescent Health* 60: S95–6.

———. 2018a. Rapid-onset gender dysphoria in adolescents and young adults: a study of parental reports. *PLOS One* 13: 1–41.

———. 2018b. Parent reports of adolescents and young adults perceived to show signs of a rapid onset of gender dysphoria. *PLOS One* 13: 1–44 [revised version of 2018a].

———. 2019. Correction: parent reports of adolescents and young adults perceived to show signs of a rapid onset of gender dysphoria. *PLOS One* 14: 1–7.

———. 2020. The use of methodologies in Littman (2018) is consistent with the use of methodologies in other studies contributing to the field of gender dysphoria research: response to Restar (2019). *Archives of Sexual Behavior* 49: 67–77.

Livingstone, F. B. 1974. Review of *The Inevitability of Patriarchy. American Anthropologist* 76: 365–7.

Lloyd, M. 2007. *Judith Butler: From Norms to Politics*. Cambridge: Polity.

Lombardo, M. P., and R. O. Deaner. 2018. On the evolution of the sex differences in throwing: throwing is a male adaptation in humans. *Quarterly Review of Biology* 93: 91–119.

Lopez, G. 2017. 9 questions about gender identity and being transgender you were too embarrassed to ask. *Vox* February 22. www.vox.com/2015/4/24/8483561/transgender-gender-identity-expression.

Lovell, R. 2021. Abigail Shrier's *Irreversible Damage*: a wealth of irreversible misinformation. *Science-Based Medicine* July 2. https://sciencebasedmedicine.org/abigail-shriers-irreversible-damage-a-wealth-of-irreversible-misinformation/.

Lugones, M. 2007. Heterosexualism and the colonial/modern gender system. *Hypatia* 22: 186–219.

Lundberg, T., P. Hegarty, and K. Roen. 2018. Making sense of 'intersex' and 'DSD': how laypeople understand and use terminology. *Psychology & Sexuality* 9: 161–73.

Lüpold, S., M. K. Manier, N. Puniamoorthy, C. Schoff, W. T. Starmer, S. H. B. Luepold, J. M. Belote, and S. Pitnick. 2016. How sexual selection can drive the evolution of costly sperm ornamentation. *Nature* 533: 535–8.

McCloskey, D. N. 1999. *Crossing: A Memoir*. Chicago: University of Chicago Press.

MacKenzie, K. R. 1978. Gender dysphoria syndrome: towards standardized diagnostic criteria. *Archives of Sexual Behavior* 7: 251–62.

McKie, A. 2021. Kathleen Stock: UCU statement 'ends my career' at Sussex. *THE* October 12. www.timeshighereducation.com/news/kathleen-stock-ucu-statement-ends-my-career-sussex.

McKinnon, R. 2018. The epistemology of propaganda. *Philosophy and Phenomenological Research* 96: 483–9.

McKitrick, J. 2015. A dispositional account of gender. *Philosophical Studies* 172: 2575–89.

McNamara, B. 2017. Miley Cyrus opens up about gender identity and smoking marijuana. *Teen Vogue* May 4. www.teenvogue.com/story/miley-cyrus-gender-identity-smoking-weed.

Madill, A., and Y. Zhao. 2022. Are female paraphilias hiding in plain sight? Risqué male–male erotica for women in Sinophone and Anglophone regions. *Archives of Sexual Behavior* 51: 897–910.

Maimoun, L., P. Philibert, B. Cammas, F. Audran, P. Bouchard, P. Fenichel, M. Cartigny, C. Pienkowski, M. Polak, N. Skordis, I. Mazen, G. Ocal, M. Berberoglu, R. Reynaud, C. Baumann, S. Cabrol, D. Simon, K. Kayemba-Kay's, M. De Kerdanet, F. Kurtz, B. Leheup, C. Heinrichs, S. Tenoutasse, G. Van Vliet, A. Grüters, M. Eunice, A. C. Ammini, M. Hafez, Z. Hochberg, S. Einaudi, H. Al Mawlawi, C. J. del Valle Nuñez, N. Servant, S. Lumbroso, F. Paris, and C. Sultan. 2011. Phenotypical, biological, and molecular heterogeneity of 5α-reductase deficiency: an extensive international experience of 55 patients. *Journal of Clinical Endocrinology & Metabolism* 96: 296–307.

Maitra, N. 2016. Feminism. *The Oxford Handbook of Philosophical Methodology*, ed. H. Cappelen, T. Gendler and J. Hawthorne. Oxford: Oxford University Press.

Mallon, R. 2016. *The Construction of Human Kinds*. Oxford: Oxford University Press.

Manion, J. 2020. *Female Husbands: A Trans History*. Cambridge: Cambridge University Press.

Manne, K. 2018. *Down Girl: The Logic of Misogyny*. Oxford: Oxford University Press.

Marcus, E. 2021. A guide to neopronouns. *New York Times* April 8.

www.nytimes.com/2021/04/08/style/neopronouns-nonbinary-explainer.html.

Mason, M. 1994. *The Making of Victorian Sexuality*. Oxford: Oxford University Press.

Mason, R. 2022. Women are not adult human females. *Australasian Journal of Philosophy*. doi: 10.1080/00048402.2022.2149824.

Mason-Schrock, D. 1996. Transsexuals' narrative construction of the 'true self'. *Social Psychology Quarterly* 59: 176–92.

Massie, A. 2021. Death threats don't sit on the right side of history. *The Times* July 25. www.thetimes.co.uk/article/alex-massie-death-threats-dont-sit-on-the-right-side-of-history-932582lw3.

Mayhew, R. 2010. *The Female in Aristotle's Biology: Reason or Rationalization*. Chicago: University of Chicago Press.

Mazur, T. 2005. Gender dysphoria and gender change in androgen insensitivity or micropenis. *Archives of Sexual Behavior* 34: 411–21.

Mead, M. 1935/1977. *Sex and Temperament in Three Primitive Societies*. London: Routledge & Kegan Paul.

———. 1973. Does the world belong to men – or to women? *Redbook* October: 46–52.

Medley, S., and G. Sherwin. 2019. Banning trans girls from school sports is neither feminist nor legal. *ACLU* March 12. www.aclu.org/blog/lgbtq-rights/transgender-rights/banning-trans-girls-school-sports-neither-feminist-nor-legal.

Merke, D. P., and S. R. Bornstein. 2005. Congenital adrenal hyperplasia. *The Lancet* 365: 2125–36.

Merriam-Webster. 2022. *Merriam-Webster Dictionary*. www.merriam-webster.com.

Meyerowitz, J. J. 2004. *How Sex Changed: A History of Transsexuality in the United States*. Cambridge, MA: Harvard University Press.

Meyers-Wallen, V. N. 2012. Gonadal and sex differentiation abnormalities of dogs and cats. *Sexual Development* 6: 46–60.

Mikkola, M. 2016. *The Wrong of Injustice: Dehumanization and its Role in Feminist Philosophy*. Oxford: Oxford University Press.

———. 2022. Feminist perspectives on sex and gender. *Stanford Encyclopedia of Philosophy* Spring. https://plato.stanford.edu/archives/spr2022/entries/feminism-gender/.

Mill, J. S. 1869/2006. On liberty. *On Liberty and The Subjection of Women*. London: Penguin.

———. 1870/2006. The subjection of women. *On Liberty and The Subjection of Women*. London: Penguin.

Milton, J. 2020. Boy George slammed as 'transphobic' after mocking pronouns as a 'modern form of attention seeking'. *Pink News* January 8. www.pinknews.co.uk/2020/01/08/boy-george-pronouns-transphobic-attention-seeking-twitter-backlash-lgb-alliance/.

Minna. 2020. A look at corporate leadership in Finland: who are they? *Finnwards* September 17. https://bit.ly/3wFDAtH.

Missé, M. 2022. *The Myth of the Wrong Body*. Cambridge: Polity.

Mitchell, K. R., C. H. Mercer, P. Prah, S. Clifton, C. Tanton, K. Wellings, and A. Copas. 2019. Why do men report more opposite-sex sexual partners than women? Analysis of the gender discrepancy in a British national probability survey. *Journal of Sex Research* 56: 1–8.

Mittleman, J. 2022. Intersecting the academic gender gap: the education of lesbian, gay and bisexual America. *American Sociological Review* 87: 303–35.

Moberly, T. 2018. A fifth of surgeons in England are female. *BMJ* 363: k4530.

Moi, T. 2000. Is anatomy destiny? Freud and biological determinism. *Whose Freud? The Place of Psychoanalysis in Contemporary Culture*, ed. P. Brooks and A. Woloch. New Haven, CT: Yale University Press.

———. 2001. *What is a Woman? and Other Essays*. Oxford: Oxford University Press.

Money, J. 1955. Hermaphroditism, gender and precocity in hyperadrenocorticism: psychologic findings. *Bulletin of the Johns Hopkins Hospital* 96: 253–64.

———. 1968. *Sex Errors of the Body: Dilemmas, Education, Counseling*. Baltimore: Johns Hopkins University Press.

———. 1985. The conceptual neutering of gender and the criminalization of sex. *Archives of Sexual Behavior* 14: 279–90.

———. 1993. Letter. *The Sciences* July/August: 4.

———. 1995. *Gendermaps: Social Constructionism, Feminism, and Sexosophical History*. New York: Continuum.

———. 2002. *A First Person History of Pediatric Psychoendocrinology*. New York: Kluwer.

Money, J., and A. A. Ehrhardt. 1973/1996. *Man & Woman, Boy & Girl: Gender Identity from Conception to Maturity*. Northvale, NJ: Jason Aronson. Original edn, 1972.

Money, J., and R. J. Gaskin. 1970. Sex reassignment. *International Journal of Psychiatry* 9: 249–69.

Money, J., J. G. Hampson, and J. L. Hampson. 1955. An examination of some basic sexual concepts: the evidence of human hermaphroditism. *Bulletin of the Johns Hopkins Hospital* 97: 301–19.

———. 1957. Imprinting and the establishment of gender role. *AMA Archives of Neurology & Psychiatry* 77: 333–6.

Moore, M. 2016. Crossing over: the complex, tortured world of Ridgely Hunt. *Green Valley News* May 10. https://bit.ly/3Y3Xfil.

Moorhead, J. 2005. Are the men of the African Aka tribe the best fathers in the world? *The Guardian* June 15. www.theguardian.com/society/2005/jun/15/childrensservices.familyandrelationships.

Moran, D., and A. Guiu. 2021. John Scottus Eriugena. *Stanford Encyclopedia of Philosophy* Winter. https://plato.stanford.edu/archives/win2021/entries/scottus-eriugena/.

Morris, J. 1974/2002. *Conundrum*. London: Faber & Faber.

Morys, S. 2022. Jan Morris was a trans pioneer – and a cruel parent. *The Times* December 10. www.thetimes.co.uk/article/jan-morris-was-a-trans-pioneer-and-a-cruel-parent-9x82s5cg9.

Moser, C. 2009. Autogynephilia in women. *Journal of Homosexuality* 56: 539–47.

———. 2023. A response to Bailey and Hsu (2022): it helps if you stop confusing gender dysphoria and transvestism. *Archives of Sexual Behavior* 52: 469–71.

Moyer, J. W. 2015. The surprising ways Caitlyn Jenner and Rachel Dolezal are now linked. *Washington Post* June 15. www.washingtonpost.com/news/morning-mix/wp/2015/06/15/the-surprising-ways-caitlyn-jenner-and-rachel-dolezal-are-now-linked/.

Muller, M. N., and R. Wrangham. 2002. Sexual mimicry in hyenas. *Quarterly Review of Biology* 77: 3–16.

Murray, D. 2019. *The Madness of Crowds: Gender, Race and Identity*. London: Bloomsbury Continuum.

Murray, S. O. 2000. *Homosexualities*. Chicago: University of Chicago Press.

Navratilova, M. 2019. The rules on trans athletes reward cheats and punish the innocent. *Sunday Times* February 17. www.thetimes.co.uk/article/the-rules-on-trans-athletes-reward-cheats-and-punish-the-innocent-klsrq6h3x.

Nelson, L. H., and J. Nelson. 2003. *Feminist Interpretations of W. V. Quine*. University Park: Pennsylvania State University Press.

New, M. I., and L. S. Levine. 1984. *Congenital Adrenal Hyperplasia*. Berlin: Springer.

Newton, E. 1972. *Mother Camp: Female Impersonators in America*. Chicago: University of Chicago Press.

Nicholson, G. H. 2020. On being a transamorous man. *TSQ: Transgender Studies Quarterly* 7: 268–71.

Nietzsche, F. 1886/2007. *Beyond Good and Evil: Prelude to a Philosophy of the Future*. Trans. J. Norman, ed. R.-P. Horstmann and J. Norman. Cambridge: Cambridge University Press.

Norton, R. 1997. *The Myth of the Modern Homosexual: Queer History and the Search for Cultural Unity*. London: Cassell.

Novic, R. J. 2008. *Alice in Genderland: A Crossdresser Comes of Age*. New York: iUniverse.

Nussbaum, M. C. 1999. The professor of parody. *New Republic* February 22. https://newrepublic.com/article/150687/professor-parody.

Oakley, A. 1972/2016. *Sex, Gender, and Society*. London: Routledge.

———. 1984. *Taking it Like a Woman*. New York: Random House.

———. 1997. A brief history of gender. *Who's Afraid of Feminism?*, ed. A. Oakley and J. Mitchell. New York: New Press.

OED. 2022. *Oxford English Dictionary*. www.oed.com.

Ofshe, R., and E. Watters. 1996. *Making Monsters: False Memories, Psychotherapy, and Sexual Hysteria*. Berkeley: University of California Press.

Olson, K. 2017. *Masculinity and Dress in Roman Antiquity*. London: Routledge.

Orwell, G. 1949/1961. *1984*. New York: Signet Classics.

———. 2000. *Essays*. London: Penguin.

Overzier, C. (ed.) 1963. *Intersexuality*. London: Academic Press.

Ovesey, L., and E. Person. 1974a. The transsexual syndrome in males: part I. Primary transsexualism. *American Journal of Psychotherapy* 28: 4–20 [page reference to the reprint in Person 1999].

Ovesey, L., and E. Person. 1974b. The transsexual syndrome in males: part II. Secondary transsexualism. *American Journal of Psychotherapy* 28: 174–93 [page reference to the reprint in Person 1999].

Padva, G. 2018. Joseph/Josephine's angst: sensational hermaphroditism in Tod Browning's freaks. *Social Semiotics* 28: 108–24.

Paglia, C. 1991a. Junk bonds and corporate raiders: academe in the hour of the wolf. *Arion* 1: 139–212 [page reference to the reprint in Paglia 1992].

Paglia, C. 1991b. *Sexual Personae: Art and Decadence from Nerfertiti to Emily Dickinson*. New York: Vintage.

Paglia, C. 1992. *Sex, Art, and American Culture: Essays*. New York: Vintage.

Papisova, V. 2018. Here's what it means when you don't identify as a girl or a boy. *Teen Vogue* February 12. www.teenvogue.com/story/what-is-non-binary-gender.

Parker, G. A. 2011. The origin and maintenance of two sexes (anisogamy), and their gamete sizes by gamete competition. *The Evolution of Anisogamy: A Fundamental Phenomenon Underlying Sexual Selection*, ed. T. Togashi and P. A. Cox. Cambridge: Cambridge University Press.

Parker, J. D. 2004. A major evolutionary transition to more than two sexes? *Trends in Ecology & Evolution* 19: 83–6.

Parsons, V. 2020. Even Sam Smith's mum sometimes struggles to remember to use their pronouns. *Pink News* March 5. www.pinknews.co.uk/2020/03/05/sam-smith-mum-they-them-pronouns-non-binary-the-project-australia/.

Pauly, I. B. 1965. Male psychosexual inversion: transsexualism: a review of 100 cases. *Archives of General Psychiatry* 13: 172–81.

Pearce, R., S. Erikainen, and B. Vincent. 2020. TERF wars: an introduction. *Sociological Review* 68: 677–98.

Pedersen, S. 2020. *The Politicization of Mumsnet*. Bingley, West Yorks: Emerald.

———. 2022. They've got an absolute army of women behind them: the formation of a women's cooperative constellation in contemporary Scotland. *Scottish Affairs* 31: 1–20.

Penny, L. 2015. How to be a genderqueer feminist. *BuzzFeed News* October 31. www.buzzfeednews.com/article/lauriepenny/how-to-be-a-genderqueer-feminist.

Pepper, R. (ed.) 2012. *Transitions of the Heart: Stories of Love, Struggle and Acceptance by Mothers of Transgender and Gender Variant Children*. Berkeley, CA: Cleis Press.

Perraudin, F. 2019. Martina Navratilova criticised over 'cheating' trans women comments. *The Guardian* February 17. https://www.theguardian.com/sport/2019/feb/17/martina-navratilova-criticised-over-cheating-trans-women-comments.

Perry, L. 2020. Sissy porn and trans dirty laundry. *The Critic* January. https://thecritic.co.uk/issues/january-2020/sissy-porn-and-trans-dirty-laundry/.

———. 2022a. *The Case Against the Sexual Revolution*. Cambridge: Polity.

———. 2022b. Why the next wave of feminism is conservative. *The Spectator* October 29. www.spectator.co.uk/article/why-the-next-wave-of-feminism-is-conservative/.

Person, E. 1999. *The Sexual Century*. New Haven, CT: Yale University Press.

Pike, J. 2020. Safety, fairness, and inclusion: transgender athletes and the essence of rugby. *Journal of the Philosophy of Sport* 48: 155–68.

Pinker, S. 2016. *The Blank Slate: The Modern Denial of Human Nature*. New York: Penguin.

Plato. 2004. *Republic*. Trans. C. D. C. Reeve. Indianapolis: Hackett.

Powell, H. 1930. *The Last Paradise*. New York: Jonathan Cape & Harrison Smith.

Prete, F. R. 1991. Can females rule the hive? The controversy over honey bee gender roles in British beekeeping texts of the sixteenth–eighteenth centuries. *Journal of the History of Biology* 24: 113–44.

Priest, M. 2019. Transgender children and the right to transition: medical ethics when parents mean well but cause harm. *American Journal of Bioethics* 19: 45–59.

Prince, V. 1960. The intent and purpose of this magazine. *Transvestia* 6.

———. 1967. *The Transvestite and His Wife*. Los Angeles: Argyle Books.

———. 1971. *How to Be a Woman Though Male*. Los Angeles: Chevalier.

———. 1997. Seventy years in the trenches of the gender wars. *Gender Blending*, ed. B. Bullough, V. L. Bullough and J. Elias. New York: Prometheus Books.

Pullum, G. K. 2021. The use and abuse of 'they'. *National Review* March 8. www.nationalreview.com/magazine/2021/03/08/the-use-and-abuse-of-they/.

Puts, D. A., C. L. Apicella, and R. A. Cárdenas. 2012. Masculine voices signal men's threat potential in forager and industrial societies. *Proceedings of the Royal Society B: Biological Sciences* 279: 601–9.

Puts, D. A., D. H. Bailey, and P. L. Reno. 2016. Contest competition in men. *The Handbook of Evolutionary Psychology*, Vol. 1, ed. D. M. Buss. Hoboken, NJ: Wiley.

Quine, W. V. 1987. *Quiddities*. Cambridge, MA: Harvard University Press.

Quinn, E. 2019. The way we think about biological sex is wrong. TED.

www.ted.com/talks/emily_quinn_the_way_we_think_about_biological_sex_is_wrong.

Raymond, J. 1979/1994. *The Transsexual Empire: The Making of the She-Male.* New York: Teachers College Press.

Reilly-Cooper, R. 2016. Gender is not a spectrum. *Aeon* June 28. https://aeon.co/essays/the-idea-that-gender-is-a-spectrum-is-a-new-gender-prison.

Reis, E. 2021. *Bodies in Doubt: An American History of Intersex.* 2nd edn, Baltimore: Johns Hopkins University Press.

Reischel, J. 2006. See Tom be Jane. *Village Voice* May 30. www.villagevoice.com/2006/05/30/see-tom-be-jane/.

Remnant, R. 1637. *A Discourse or Historie of Bees.* London: Thomas Slater.

Restar, A. J. 2020. Methodological critique of Littman's (2018) parental-respondents accounts of 'rapid-onset gender dysphoria'. *Archives of Sexual Behavior* 49: 61–6.

Richards, J. R. 1980. *The Sceptical Feminist: A Philosophical Enquiry.* London: Routledge & Kegan Paul.

———. 2000. *Human Nature after Darwin: A Philosophical Introduction.* London: Routledge.

Richardson, K. 2022. The metaphysics of gender is (relatively) substantial. *Philosophy and Phenomenological Research.* doi: 10.1111/phpr.12916.

Richardson, M. 2013. Good and messy: lesbian and transgender identities. *Feminist Studies* 39: 371–4.

Richardson, S. S. 2013. *Sex Itself.* Chicago: University of Chicago Press.

Rider, G. N., and E. A. Tebbe. 2021. Anti-trans theories. *Sage Encyclopedia of Trans Studies*, ed. A. E. Goldberg and G. Beemyn. Thousand Oaks, CA: Sage.

Riley, D. 1988. *'Am I That Name?': Feminism and the Category of 'Women' in History.* Minneapolis: University of Minnesota Press.

Rippon, G. 2019. *The Gendered Brain: The New Neuroscience that Shatters the Myth of the Female Brain.* London: Bodley Head.

Ristori, J., and T. D. Steensma. 2016. Gender dysphoria in childhood. *International Review of Psychiatry* 28: 13–20.

Rizza, A. 2018. CAMH to pay more than half a million settlement to head of gender identity clinic after releasing fallacious report. *National Post* October 8. https://nationalpost.com/news/camh-reaches-settlement-with-former-head-of-gender-identity-clinic.

Robinson, N. J. 2021. The arguments against trans athletes are bigoted and irrational. *Current Affairs* May 31. www.currentaffairs.org/2021/05/the-arguments-against-trans-athletes-are-bigoted-and-irrational/.

Robitaille, J., and V. S. Langlois. 2020. Consequences of steroid-5α-reductase deficiency and inhibition in vertebrates. *General and Comparative Endocrinology* 290: 1–17.

Romano, A. 2019. J. K. Rowling's latest tweet seems like transphobic BS. Her fans are heartbroken. *Vox* December 19. www.vox.com/culture/2019/12/19/21029852/jk-rowling-terf-transphobia-history-timeline.

Rosser, S. V. 2003. Coming full circle: refuting biological determinism. *Evolution, Gender, and Rape*, ed. C. B. Travis. Cambridge, MA: MIT Press.

Rothblatt, M. 2011. *From Transgender to Transhuman: A Manifesto on the Freedom of Form.* Martine Rothblatt.

Roughgarden, J. 2004. *Evolution's Rainbow: Diversity, Gender, and Sexuality in Nature and People.* Los Angeles: University of California Press.

Rowling, J. K. 2020. J. K. Rowling writes about her reasons for speaking out on sex and gender issues. June 20. www.jkrowling.com/opinions/j-k-rowling-writes-about-her-reasons-for-speaking-out-on-sex-and-gender-issues/.

Rubin, A. J. 2014. French film goes viral, but not in France. *New York Times* April 6. www.nytimes.com/2014/04/07/movies/oppressed-majority-provokes-debate-on-internet.html.

Rudacille, D. 2004. *The Riddle of Gender: Science, Activism and Transgender Rights.* New York: Pantheon Books.

Russell, B., and J. Freeman. 1959. Face to face. BBC. https://youtu.be/a1oA5PneXlo.

Ryle, R. 2021. *Questioning Gender: A Sociological Exploration.* 4th edn, Thousand Oaks, CA: Sage.

Sadjadi, S. 2020. The Vulnerable Child Protection Act and transgender children's health. *TSQ: Transgender Studies Quarterly* 7: 508–16.

Salih, S. 2002. *Judith Butler.* London: Routledge.

Saul, J. 2003. *Feminism: Issues & Arguments.* Oxford: Oxford University Press.

———. 2012. Politically significant terms and philosophy of language. *Out from the Shadows: Analytical Feminist Contributions to Traditional Philosophy*, ed. S. L. Crasnow and A. M. Superson. Oxford: Oxford University Press.

Sax, L. 2002. How common is intersex? A response to Anne Fausto-Sterling. *Journal of Sex Research* 39: 174–8.

Scalia, A. 1994. Dissent in *J.E.B. v. Alabama.* 511 U.S. 127.

Scharping, N. 2017. Why this fungus has over 20,000 sexes. *Discover* November 6. www.discovermagazine.com/planet-earth/why-this-fungus-has-over-20-000-sexes.

Schiappa, E. 2022. *The Transgender Exigency: Defining Sex and Gender in the 21st Century.* London: Routledge.

Schneider, M. S., W. O. Bockting, R. D. Ehrbar, A. A. Lawrence, K. Rachlin, and K. J. Zucker. 2009. *Report of the Task Force on Gender Identity and Gender Variance.* Washington, DC: American Psychological Association.

Schudson, Z., W. Beischel, and S. Anders. 2019. Individual variation in gender/sex category definitions. *Psychology of Sexual Orientation and Gender Diversity* 6: 448–60.

Schuessler, J., and E. A. Harris. 2020. Artists and writers warn of an 'intolerant climate'. Reaction is swift. *New York Times* July 7. www.nytimes.com/2020/07/07/arts/harpers-letter.html.

Schuller, K. 2021. *The Trouble with White Women: A Counterhistory of Feminism.* New York: Bold Type Books.

Science Vs. 2018. The science of being transgender. *Gimlet* December 13. https://gimletmedia.com/shows/science-vs/j4hl23/the-science-of-being-transgender.

Scruton, R. 2018. The art of taking offence. *The Spectator* August 9. www.spectator.co.uk/article/the-art-of-taking-offence-.

Sedda, A., and G. Bottini. 2014. Apotemnophilia, body integrity identity disorder or xenomelia? Psychiatric and neurologic etiologies face each other. *Neuropsychiatric Disease and Treatment* 10: 1255–65.

Serano, J. 2007. *Whipping Girl: A Transsexual Woman on Sexism and the Scapegoating of Femininity.* Berkeley, CA: Seal Press.

———. 2010. The case against autogynephilia. *International Journal of Transgenderism* 12: 176–87.

———. 2020. Autogynephilia: a scientific review, feminist analysis, and alternative 'embodiment fantasies' model. *Sociological Review* 68: 763–78.

Serano, J. M., and J. F. Veale. 2023. Autogynephilia is a flawed framework for understanding female embodiment fantasies: a response to Bailey and Hsu (2022). *Archives of Sexual Behavior* 52: 473–77.

Shankman, P. 2009. *The Trashing of Margaret Mead.* Madison: University of Wisconsin Press.

Shannon, R., and N. Nicolaides. 1973. True hermaphroditism with oogenesis and spermatogenesis. *Australian and New Zealand Journal of Obstetrics and Gynaecology* 13: 184–7.

Shapiro, J. 1981. Anthropology and the study of gender. *Soundings: An Interdisciplinary Journal* 64: 446–65.

Sharpe, A. 2021. Review of Helen Joyce's *Trans: When Ideology Meets Reality*; and Kathleen Stock's *Material Girls: Why Reality Matters for Feminism. Critical Legal Thinking* October 8. https://bit.ly/3kVO2dM.

Shrier, A. 2020a. Does the ACLU want to ban my book? *Wall Street Journal* November 15. www.wsj.com/articles/does-the-aclu-want-to-ban-my-book-11605475898.

———. 2020b. *Irreversible Damage: The Transgender Craze Seducing Our Daughters.* Washington, DC: Regnery.

Simpson, M. 2002. Meet the metrosexual. *Salon* July 22. www.salon.com/2002/07/22/metrosexual/.

Singal, J. 2016. How the fight over transgender kids got a leading sex researcher fired. *The Cut* February 7. www.thecut.com/2016/02/fight-over-trans-kids-got-a-researcher-fired.html.

———. 2017. This is what a modern-day witch hunt looks like. *New York Magazine* May 2. https://nymag.com/intelligencer/2017/05/transracialism-article-controversy.html.

———. 2020a. The deeply depressing unpublishing of 'I sexually identify as an attack helicopter'. *Singal-Minded* January 17. https://jessesingal.substack.com/p/the-deeply-depressing-unpublishing.

———. 2020b. The reaction to the *Harper's* letter on cancel culture proves why it was necessary. *Reason* July 8. https://reason.com/2020/07/08/the-reaction-to-the-harpers-letter-on-cancel-culture-proves-why-it-was-necessary/.

———. 2020c. A response to *Foreign Policy*'s deeply misleading article, 'A High Court decision in Britain puts trans people everywhere at risk' (updated). *Singal-Minded* December 17. https://jessesingal.substack.com/p/a-response-to-foreign-policys-deeply.

Singh, D., S. J. Bradley, and K. J. Zucker. 2021. A follow-up study of boys with gender identity disorder. *Frontiers in Psychiatry* 12: 1–18.

Skidmore, E. 2019. *True Sex: The Lives of Trans Men at the Turn of the Twentieth Century.* New York: New York University Press.

Slothouber, V. 2020. (De)trans visibility: moral panic in mainstream media reports on de/retransition. *European Journal of English Studies* 24: 89–99.

Smuts, B. 1995. The evolutionary origins of patriarchy. *Human Nature* 6: 1–32.

Snapes, L. 2019. Sam Smith on being non-binary: 'I'm changing my pronouns to they/them'. *The Guardian* September 13. www.theguardian.com/music/2019/sep/13/sam-smith-on-being-non-binary-im-changing-my-pronouns-to-theythem.

Soh, D. 2020. *The End of Gender: Debunking the Myths about Sex and Identity in Our Society*. New York: Threshold.

Soh, D. W., and J. M. Cantor. 2015. A peek inside a furry convention. *Archives of Sexual Behavior* 44: 1–2.

Solovitch, S. 2018. When kids come in saying they are transgender (or no gender), these doctors try to help. *Washington Post* January 21. https://bit.ly/3yhZns2.

Sommers, C. H. 2010. Not lost in translation. *Clairmont Review of Books* X. https://claremontreviewofbooks.com/not-lost-in-translation/.

———. 2013. *The War Against Boys: How Misguided Policies Are Harming Our Young Men*. New York: Simon & Schuster.

Speiser, P. W., W. Arlt, R. J. Auchus, L. S. Baskin, G. S. Conway, D. P. Merke, H. F. L. Meyer-Bahlburg, W. L. Miller, M. H. Murad, S. E. Oberfield, and P. C. White. 2018. Congenital adrenal hyperplasia due to steroid 21-hydroxylase deficiency: an Endocrine Society clinical practice guideline. *Journal of Clinical Endocrinology & Metabolism* 103: 4043–88.

Spencer, D., V. Pasterski, S. A. S. Neufeld, V. Glover, T. G. O'Connor, P. C. Hindmarsh, I. A. Hughes, C. L. Acerini, and M. Hines. 2021. Prenatal androgen exposure and children's gender-typed behavior and toy and playmate preferences. *Hormones and Behavior* 127: 1–9.

Srinivasan, A. 2021. *The Right to Sex*. London: Bloomsbury.

Stanley, J. 2018. Replies. *Philosophy and Phenomenological Research* 96: 497–511.

Statutes of Canada. 2017. Bill C-16. Parliament of Canada June 19.

Steensma, T. D., J. Van der Ende, F. C. Verhulst, and P. T. Cohen-Kettenis. 2013. Gender variance in childhood and sexual orientation in adulthood: a prospective study. *Journal of Sexual Medicine* 10: 2723–33.

Steinmetz, K. 2014. The transgender tipping point. *Time* May 29. https://time.com/135480/transgender-tipping-point/.

Stevens, K. 1999. Letter. *Transgender Tapestry* 86: 6–7.

Stevenson, A. (ed.) 2010. *Oxford Dictionary of English*. Oxford: Oxford University Press.

Stewart-Williams, S. 2018. *The Ape that Understood the Universe: How the Mind and Culture Evolve*. Cambridge: Cambridge University Press.

Stewart-Williams, S., and L. G. Halsey. 2021. Men, women and STEM: why the differences and what should be done? *European Journal of Personality* 35: 3–39.

Stock, K. 2018. Academic philosophy and the UK Gender Recognition Act. *Medium* May 7. https://bit.ly/3RpK3m3.

———. 2021. *Material Girls: Why Reality Matters for Feminism*. London: Fleet.

———. 2022. The importance of referring to human sex in language. *Law and Contemporary Problems* 85: 25–43.

Stoet, G., and D. C. Geary. 2022. Sex differences in adolescents' occupational aspirations: variations across time and place. *PLOS One* 17: 1–18.

Stoljar, N. 1995. Essence, identity, and the concept of woman. *Philosophical Topics* 23: 261–93.

Stoller, R. J. 1964a. A contribution to the study of gender identity. *International Journal of Psycho-Analysis* 45: 220–6.

———. 1964b. The hermaphroditic identity of hermaphrodites. *Journal of Nervous and Mental Disease* 139: 453–7.

———. 1968. *Sex and Gender: On the Development of Masculinity and Femininity*. New York: Science House.

———. 1975. *The Transsexual Experiment*. London: Hogarth Press.

———. 1982. Near miss: 'sex-change' treatment and its evaluation. *Eating, Sleeping and Sexuality: Treatment of Disorders in Basic Life Functions*, ed. M. R. Zales. New York: Brunner/Mazel.

———. 1992. Gender identity development and prognosis: a summary. *New Approaches to Mental Health from Birth to Adolescence*, ed. C. Chiland and J. G. Young. New Haven, CT: Yale University Press. Originally pubd 1990 as 'Identité de genre: developpement et pronostic: une vue d'ensemble'.

Stölting, K. N., and A. B. Wilson. 2007. Male pregnancy in seahorses and pipefish: beyond the mammalian model. *BioEssays* 29: 884–96.

Stone, A. 2007. *An Introduction to Feminist Philosophy*. Cambridge: Polity.

Strohminger, N., J. Knobe, and G. Newman. 2017. The true self: a psychological concept distinct from the self. *Perspectives on Psychological Science* 12: 551–60.

Strum, P. 1999. *When the Nazis came to Skokie: Freedom for Speech We Hate.* Lawrence: University Press of Kansas.

Stryker, S. 1994. My words to Victor Frankenstein above the village of Chamounix – performing transgender rage. *GLQ* 1: 227–54 [page reference to the reprint in Stryker and Whittle 2006].

———. 2008. *Transgender History*. Berkeley, CA: Seal Press.

Stryker, S., and S. Whittle. 2006. *The Transgender Studies Reader*, Vol. 1. London: Taylor & Francis.

Tannehill, B. 2019. *Everything You Ever Wanted to Know about Trans (but Were Afraid to Ask)*. Philadelphia: Jessica Kingsley.

Tao, C., A. Glosenberg, T. J. G. Tracey, D. L. Blustein, and L. L. Foster. 2022. Are gender differences in vocational interests universal? Moderating effects of cultural dimensions. *Sex Roles* 87: 327–49.

Tayler, J. 2019. *Maya Forstater* v *CGD Europe, Centre for Global Development, Masood Ahmed*. Case Number: 2200909/2019. The Employment Tribunals December 18.

Telegraph Reporters. 2021. 'I don't think JK Rowling is transphobic,' says gender-fluid comedian Eddie Izzard. *The Telegraph* January 1. www.telegraph.co.uk/comedy/what-to-see/dont-think-jk-rowling-transphobic-says-gender-fluid-comedian/.

Telò, M. 2022. A tribute to Judith Butler. *UC Press Blog* June 6. www.ucpress.edu/blog/59673/a-tribute-to-judith-butler/.

Temple Newhook, J., J. Pyne, K. Winters, S. Feder, C. Holmes, J. Tosh, M.-L. Sinnott, A. Jamieson, and S. Pickett. 2018. A critical commentary on follow-up studies and 'desistance' theories about transgender and gender-nonconforming children. *International Journal of Transgenderism* 19: 212–24.

Terrier, L.-M., M. Lévêque, and A. Amelot. 2019. Brain lobotomy: a historical and moral dilemma with no alternative? *World Neurosurgery* 132: 211–18.

Thomsen, C., and L. Essig. 2022. Lesbian, feminist, TERF: a queer attack on feminist studies. *Journal of Lesbian Studies* 26: 27–44.

Thornhill, R., and C. T. Palmer. 2000. *A Natural History of Rape: Biological Bases of Sexual Coercion*. Cambridge, MA: MIT Press.

Thrace, S. 2022. *18 Months: A Memoir of a Marriage Lost to Gender Identity*. Indianapolis: Firebush Books.

Time. 1973. The sexes: biological imperatives. *Time* January 8: 34.

Trivers, R. L. 1972. Parental investment and sexual selection. *Sexual Selection and the Descent of Man 1871–1971*, ed. B. Campbell. Chicago: Aldine Press.

Tuerk, C. 2011. Considerations for affirming gender nonconforming boys and their families: new approaches, new challenges. *Child and Adolescent Psychiatric Clinics* 20: 767–77.

Turner, C. 2021. Pro-transgender activists try to 'bully' university into sacking professor who questioned their views. *The Telegraph* October 7. www.telegraph.co.uk/news/2021/10/07/pro-transgender-activists-try-bully-university-sacking-professor/.

Turner, J. 2019. Can't we all have a view on spaces for women? *The Times* May 30. www.thetimes.co.uk/article/can-t-we-all-have-a-view-on-spaces-for-women-983089gxz.

Tuvel, R. 2017a. In defense of transracialism. *Hypatia* 32: 263–78.

———. 2017b. Statement. *Daily Nous* May 2. https://dailynous.com/2017/05/01/philosophers-article-transracialism-sparks-controversy/.

UN 2013. *World Fertility Report 2012*. New York: United Nations.

———. 2017. Fact sheet: intersex. United Nations Human Rights Office of the High Commissioner, May. www.unfe.org/wp-content/uploads/2017/05/UNFE-Intersex.pdf.

Umscheid, V. A., C. E. Smith, F. Warneken, S. A. Gelman, and H. M. Wellman. 2023. What makes Voldemort tick? Children's and adults' reasoning about the nature of villains. *Cognition* 233: 105357.

Vagrancy Act. 1824. (5 Geo. 4. c. 83).

van Anders, S. M. 2013. Beyond masculinity: testosterone, gender/sex, and human social behavior in a comparative context. *Frontiers in Neuroendocrinology* 34: 198–210.

van der Loos, M. A. T. C., D. T. Klink, S. E. Hannema, S. Bruinsma, T. D. Steensma, B. P. C. Kreukels, P. T. Cohen-Kettenis, A. L. C. de Vries, M. den Heijer, and C. M. Wiepjes. 2023. Children and adolescents in the Amsterdam cohort of gender dysphoria: trends in diagnostic and treatment trajectories during the first 20 years of the Dutch Protocol. *Journal of Sexual Medicine* 20: 398–409.

Vandermassen, G. 2005. *Who's Afraid of Charles Darwin? Debating Feminism and Evolutionary Theory*. Oxford: Rowman & Littlefield.

Vasey, P. L., and N. H. Bartlett. 2007. What can the Samoan 'fa'afafine' teach us about the Western concept of gender identity disorder in childhood? *Perspectives in Biology and Medicine* 50: 481–90.

Vasey, P. L., and D. P. VanderLaan. 2014. Evolving research on the evolution of male androphilia. *Canadian Journal of Human Sexuality* 23: 137–47.

Vega-Frutis, R., R. Macías-Ordóñez, R. Guevara, and L. Fromhage. 2014. Sex change in plants and animals: a unified perspective. *Journal of Evolutionary Biology* 27: 667–75.

Verite, M. 2018. Controversy intensifies over Littman ROGD study. *4thWaveNow* September 4. https://4thwavenow.com/2018/09/04/controversy-intensifies-over-littman-rogd-study-petition-now-signed-by-3700-no-word-from-brown-university-or-plos-one/.

Vincent, N. 2006. *Self-Made Man*. New York: Viking.

Vollrath, F. 1998. Dwarf males. *Trends in Ecology & Evolution* 13: 159–63.

von Fintel, K., and L. Matthewson. 2008. Universals in semantics. *Linguistic Review* 25: 139–201.

von Hippel, W., D. M. Buss, and G. B. Richardson. 2020. Science progresses through open disagreement: rejoinder to Fine (2020). *Archives of Scientific Psychology* 8: 11–14.

Von Rueden, C., S. Alami, H. Kaplan, and M. Gurven. 2018. Sex differences in political leadership in an egalitarian society. *Evolution and Human Behavior* 39: 402–11.

Walter, K. V., D. Conroy-Beam, D. M. Buss, K. Asao, A. Sorokowska, P. Sorokowski, T. Aavik, G. Akello, M. M. Alhabahba, and C. Alm. 2020. Sex differences in mate preferences across 45 countries: a large-scale replication. *Psychological Science* 31: 408–23.

Wamsley, L. 2021. A guide to gender identity terms. *NPR* June 2. www.npr.org/2021/06/02/996319297/gender-identity-pronouns-expression-guide-lgbtq.

Ward, V. 2018. Gender equality campaigner defends Freemason membership. *The Telegraph* July 30. www.telegraph.co.uk/news/2018/07/30/gender-equality-campaigner-defends-freemason-membership/.

Warrier, V., D. M. Greenberg, E. Weir, C. Buckingham, P. Smith, M.-C. Lai, C. Allison, and S. Baron-Cohen. 2020. Elevated rates of autism, other neurodevelopmental and psychiatric diagnoses, and autistic traits in transgender and gender-diverse individuals. *Nature Communications* 11: 1–12.

Webster, N. 1828. *An American Dictionary of the English Language*. New York: S. Converse.

Weiss, S. 2022. 12 things people get wrong about being non-binary. *Teen Vogue* May 20. www.teenvogue.com/story/9-things-people-get-wrong-about-being-non-binary.

West, R. 1974. Male and female He made them. *New York Times* April 14. www.nytimes.com/1974/04/14/archives/conundrum-by-jan-morris-a-helen-and-kurt-wolff-book-174-pp-new-york.html.

Whitam, F. L. 1987. A cross-cultural perspective on homosexuality, transvestism and trans-sexualism. *Variant Sexuality: Research and Theory*, ed. G. D. Wilson. London: Croom Helm.

Whittaker, K. 2022. The limits of identity: running Tuvel's argument the other way. *Journal of Controversial Ideas* 2: 1–21.

Whyte, M. K. 1978. *The Status of Women in Preindustrial Societies*. Princeton, NJ: Princeton University Press.

Wiepjes, C. M., M. den Heijer, M. A. Bremmer, N. M. Nota, C. J. M. de Blok, B. J. G. Coumou, and T. D. Steensma. 2020. Trends in suicide death risk in transgender people: results from the Amsterdam Cohort of Gender Dysphoria study (1972–2017). *Acta Psychiatrica Scandinavica* 141: 486–91.

Williams, C. 2020. The ontological woman: a history of deauthentication, dehumanization, and violence. *Sociological Review* 68: 718–34.

Wilson, H. V. 1910. William Keith Brooks: a sketch of his life by some of his former pupils and associates. *Journal of Experimental Zoology* 9: 1–52.

Wilson, J. D. 1999. The role of androgens in male gender role behavior. *Endocrine Reviews* 20: 726–37.

Wilson, T. D., and D. T. Gilbert. 2005. Affective forecasting: knowing what to want. *Current Directions in Psychological Science* 14: 131–4.

Windust, J. 2020. *In Their Shoes: Navigating Non-Binary Life*. London: Jessica Kingsley.

Witt, C. 2011. *The Metaphysics of Gender*. Oxford: Oxford University Press.

Wittig, M. 1993. One is not born a woman. *The Lesbian and Gay Studies Reader*, ed. H. Abelove, M. A. Barale and D. M. Halperin. New York: Routledge.

World Health Organization. 2021. Gender and health. *WHO*. www.who.int/health-topics/gender#tab=tab 1.

Worthen, M. G. F. 2022. This is my TERF! Lesbian feminists and the stigmatization of trans women. *Sexuality & Culture* 26: 1782–803.

WPATH. 2012. *Standards of Care*, 7th Version. East Dundee, IL: World Professional Association for Transgender Health.

Wrangham, R. Forthcoming. The evolution of institutional patriarchy. *Tanner Lectures on Human Values* 39, ed. M. Matheson. Salt Lake City: University of Utah Press.

Wrangham, R., and D. Peterson. 1996. *Demonic Males: Apes and the Origins of Human Violence*. New York: Houghton Mifflin.

Wright, C. M., and E. N. Hilton. 2020. The dangerous denial of sex. *Wall Street Journal* February 13. www.wsj.com/articles/the-dangerous-denial-of-sex-11581638089.

WSJ Editorial Board. 2021. Booksellers for censoring books. *Wall Street Journal* July 15. www.wsj.com/articles/booksellers-for-censoring-books-11626389778.

Wyndham, J. 1960/2022. *Trouble with Lichen*. New York: Modern Library.

Yaeger, L. 2017. Model Hanne Gaby Odiele on what it means to be intersex – and why she's going public. *Vogue* January 23. www.vogue.com/article/hanne-gaby-odiele-model-intersex-interview.

Yang, M. 2021. 'I'm team Terf': Dave Chappelle under fire over pro-JK Rowling trans stance. *The Guardian* October 7. www.theguardian.com/stage/2021/oct/07/dave-chappelle-transgender-netflix-special-backlash.

Yoshizawa, K., R. L. Ferreira, I. Yao, C. Lienhard, and Y. Kamimura. 2018. Independent origins of female penis and its coevolution with male vagina in cave insects (Psocodea: Prionoglarididae). *Biology Letters* 14: 20180533.

Young, E. 2019. *They/Them/Their: A Guide to Nonbinary and Genderqueer Identities*. London: Jessica Kingsley.

Young, I. M. 1980. Throwing like a girl: a phenomenology of feminine body comportment motility and spatiality. *Human Studies* 3: 137–56.

Zavitzianos, G. 1972. Homeovestism: perverse form of behaviour involving wearing clothes of the same sex. *International Journal of Psycho-Analysis* 53: 471–7.

Zucker, K. J. 1999. Intersexuality and gender identity differentiation. *Annual Review of Sex Research* 10: 1–69.

———. 2010. The DSM diagnostic criteria for gender identity disorder in children. *Archives of Sexual Behavior* 39: 477–98.

———. 2017. Epidemiology of gender dysphoria and transgender identity. *Sexual Health* 14: 404–11.

———. 2018. The myth of persistence: response to 'A critical commentary on follow-up studies and "desistance" theories about transgender and gender non-conforming children' by Temple Newhook et al. (2018). *International Journal of Transgenderism* 19: 231–45.

———. 2019. Adolescents with gender dysphoria: reflections on some contemporary clinical and research issues. *Archives of Sexual Behavior* 48: 1983–92.

Zucker, K. J., and M. Aitken. 2019. Sex ratio of transgender adolescents: a meta-analysis. Paper presented at the meeting of the European Association for Transgender Health, Rome, Italy.

Zucker, K. J., and S. J. Bradley. 1995. *Gender Identity Disorder and Psychosexual Problems in Children and Adults*. New York: Guilford Press.

Zucker, K. J., R. Green, S. J. Bradley, K. Williams, H. M. Rebach, and J. E. Hood. 1998. Gender identity disorder of childhood: diagnostic issues. *DSM-IV Sourcebook* 4: 503–12.

Zucker, K. J., A. A. Lawrence, and B. P. C. Kreukels. 2016. Gender dysphoria in adults. *Annual Review of Clinical Psychology* 12: 217–47.

Zucker, K. J., D. P. VanderLaan, and M. Aitken. 2019. The contemporary sex ratio of transgender youth that favors assigned females at birth is a robust phenomenon: a response to the letter to the editor re: 'Shifts in assigned sex ratios at gender identity clinics likely reflect change in referral patterns'. *Journal of Sexual Medicine* 16: 949–50.

Zucker, K. J., H. Wood, D. Singh, and S. J. Bradley. 2012. A developmental, biopsychosocial model for the treatment of children with gender identity disorder. *Journal of Homosexuality* 59: 369–97.

Zuk, M., and L. W. Simmons. 2018. *Sexual Selection: A Very Short Introduction*. Oxford: Oxford University Press.

Index